BUSINESS COMMUNICATION

BUSINESS COMMUNICATION

DR. K SUNDAR
Associate Professor, Commerce Wing
Directorate of Distance Education
Annamalai University, Chidambaram
Tamil Nadu

DR. A KUMARA RAJ
Principal (Retired)
Tamil Nadu Goverment Collegiate
Teaching Service, Tamil Nadu

Vijay Nicole Imprints Private Limited
CHENNAI

Published by

Vijay Nicole Imprints Private Limited

No. 4, Velachery-Madipakkam Main Road
Ram Nagar South, Chennai – 600 091
Phone: 91 44 4281 1452 , 4281 1349
Email: vni@vijaynicole.co.in Website: www.vijaynicole.co.in

BUSINESS COMMUNICATION

ISBN-13: 978-81-8209-319-5
ISBN-10: 81-8209-319-8

Laser typeset at: Maven Learning Private Limited, Chennai - 600 091.

Printed at: **Karis Offset Printers,** Chennai - 600 029.

CONTENTS

PART THREE
SPECIAL BUSINESS CORRESPONDENCE

PART SIX
SPOKEN COMMUNICATION

PART SEVEN
TECHNOLOGY - AIDED BUSINESS COMMUNICATION

PART EIGHT
INTERNAL COMMUNICATION

PART NINE
CORPORATE COMMUNICATION

PART TEN
EMPOLOYMENT COMMUNICATION

PREFACE

"Employers see communication skills as critical to customer service and workplace harmony, effective operations and productivity."

- *www.dest.govt.au* (A Study of Employability Skills)

We start communicating from birth and continue to communicate in different ways through various stages of our lives. In addition to listening, speaking, reading and writing, some researchers have included counseling, facilitating, interviewing, networking, neuro-linguistic programming, media management, assertiveness, appearance, negotiating and transactional analysis as essential communication skills.

Communication skills are vital for anyone from any sphere of life. They are critical skills that help in getting, keeping, progressing and excelling in any given profession.

Communication is both verbal and non-verbal. In today's world, business communication happens in myriad ways by using multiple channels. The emphasis is on clarity, speed and effectiveness.

This book, Business Communication is designed as a textbook for commerce and management students. The book is in 10 parts and has 36 chapters. The first part on communication foundations covers nature and scope , process and means, flow of communication, non-verbal communication and listening. A significant portion of this book is on business writing. Parts 2 and 3 covering 14 chapters are on different types of letter writing. Part 4 is on Reports and Proposals.

Group communication, Internal communication and Corporate communication—important aspects of organizational working are covered in parts 5,8 and 9. Topics on Public Speaking and Conversational Ability are covered in part 6 'Spoken communication'. Technology plays an important role in all business activities and the importance of e-mail, internet and web based communication and the latest IT trends are highlighted in Part 7. Employment communication covers topics on resumes, employment documentation and interviews.

The key features of this book are as follows:

1. Comprehensive coverage: Covers a wide variety of topics including process of communication, business letters, reports and proposals, memos, e-mails, corporate, group, spoken, technology and employment communication.

2. Emphasis on written communication: Includes 14 chapters on various types of business letters, 3 chapters on report writing and proposals, 2 chapters on memos, circular, notes and minutes.

3. Tips/formats: The book provides a clear structure and process for all types of business writing. It helps readers by giving appropriate tips and methods to handle varying situations.

4. Real world examples: Presents numerous real world examples of letters, e-mails, memos, minutes, notes, reports, proposals, and resumes.

5. Pedagogical features: Summaries, formats, examples, end of chapter review questions, objective type questions, glossary and index.

I have been greatly inspired by my father Dr. A. Kumara Raj, a pioneering author and teacher. His book on Business Communication was a resounding success some 40 years ago. I am grateful to my mother Mrs K Punitham, my brothers K Maran and K Paari for their moral support at all times. My special thanks to my wife Dr Radha and my daughter Aruvi for their encouragement and and patience.

I would like to place on record the professionalism shown by my publishers Vijay Nicole Imprints Pvt Ltd and thank Mr PK Madhavan, the publisher and his team for their cooperation, expertise and encouragement.

I request readers to share their thoughts, opinion, and suggestions on improving the book.

K Sundar

PART 1

COMMUNICATION FOUNDATIONS

1

CHAPTER

NATURE AND SCOPE OF BUSINESS COMMUNICATION

INTRODUCTION

Communication is an integral part of human existence. The success or failure of any human activity is based on how we communicate. All living things communicate. For example, a baby conveys his or her feelings like hunger, wants, satisfaction, sleep etc., a dog barks to alert the master on noticing a stranger and withering crops cry for want of water. Corporate entities convey information through management information systems, decision support systems, strategic information systems etc., to run their business. Communication enables a person to maintain contact with others and also make himself understood. Man being a social animal, he communicates to express his feelings and emotions and also to exchange information. An organization is considered to be a group of people constituted to achieve certain specific objectives. It is communication that increases co-ordination and integration of people, which in turn leads to attainment of certain predetermined objectives. The expression *business* stands for any economic activity undertaken to earn profit and the communication undertaken in the process of attaining the goal is termed as *business communication*. It is the lifeblood of any organization. It includes oral, written, gestural, upward, downward, horizontal, inward, outward and diagonal communication.

DEFINITIONS OF COMMUNICATION

Communication can be defined in many ways. A few well known definitions are reproduced below which explain the nature of communication.

Communication is the sum of all the things, a person does when he wants to create an understanding in the mind of another. It involves a systematic and continuous process of telling, listening and understanding.

Allen Louis

It is the transfer of information from one person to another, irrespective of whether or not it elicits confidence.

Koontz and O' Donell

Communication is an exchange of facts, ideas, opininons or emotions, by two or more persons.

George Terry

The process of passing information and understanding from one person to another. It builds bridges of meaning between people, enabling them to safely cross the rivers of misunderstanding.

George Vardman

Purposive interchange, resulting in workable understanding and agreement between the sender and receiver of a message.

Keith Davis

Communication is an interchange of thoughts, opinions or information through speech, writing or signs.

Robert Anderson

Communication is the process by which information is passed between individuals or organizations by means of previously agreed symbols.

Peter Little

Communication is any behaviour that results in an exchange of meaning.

The American Management Association

Communication may be broadly defined as the process of meaningful interaction among human beings. More specifically, it is the process by which meanings are perceived and understandings are reached among human beings.

D E McFarland

CHARACTERISTICS OF COMMUNICATION

Communication animates and activates life. The following are the characteristics of communication:

- It is a two-way process. The sender has to transmit the information and the receiver has to give his response or reaction to the message sent. In other words, feedback is an essential part of communication.
- Communication is an ongoing process. As long as human activities continue, communication would continue to exist.

- It is all pervasive and universal. It exists across various levels of management and across different cadres of human assets working therein.
- Communication nurtures four specific skills namely reading, listening, writing and speaking.
- Communication is as important as any other essentials of human life. An individual who is provided with all physical comforts and basic necessities but is deprived of the right to speak, write, read or listen, would become mentally deficient. In other words, communication is a social process which helps him to interact and socialize with others.
- Communication happens with reference to context. The same word conveys different meanings in different contexts. Hence its meaning is situation-dependent.
- It dispels misunderstanding among people thereby building comaraderie.
- The main purpose of every communication is to promote proper understanding of the message in the minds of the parties to communication. Both receiver and the sender should understand the message in the manner that the sender intends.
- Communication consists of facts, ideas and emotions. It is much more than words. The tone, facial expressions, signs, symbols and gestures all carry meaning.
- It is a goal-oriented process. It can be effective if both sender and receiver are aware of the goal of communication and there is goal congruence.
- It is a dynamic process. It involves the participants and environment dynamics. Changes in the mood and thinking of sender and receiver influence its effectiveness. Therefore, the way a message is received by a receiver depends on how the message is received by his sense organs.

NEED FOR COMMUNICATION

Communication has become indispensable due to the following reasons:

Size of Enterprise

When an organization grows in terms of size with a network of branches with several thousand people working in different parts, efficient communication is required among the different branches, the head office and the branches and among people across different managerial hierarchies.

Increasing Specialization

Growing specialization tends to regiment its operation to a given domain. In the absence of communication among domains, no organization can function. For example, orders booked by the sales department cannot be executed by the production department in the absence of inter-departmental communication between the production and sales department.

Technological Advancement

Advancement in science and technology forces an organization to keep its employees posted of recent trends. In other words, communication is needed to persuade the employee to accept change in technology and impress upon them the need to upgrade their skills and competency.

Smooth Industrial Relations

The more transparently an organization functions, smoother would be the industrial relations. Periodical intra-department meetings, a mechanism by which the progress of the organization on various development indices are informed to the employees, stock-taking meetings etc., proclaim the transparent functioning of an organization. This will lead to less industrial conflicts in the organizations. Thus, free flow of information between management and employees strengthens the relation between the two.

Better Human Relations

Involving employees in decision making through various participative forums, Kaisen management, quality circles, suggestion schemes, Employee Stock Ownership Plan (ESOP) etc., promote harmonious workplace relations among the employees across hierarchies.

Cut-throat Competition

Embracing capitalist economic model entails severe and acute competition in market place. Companies need to advertise through different media to be heard by all in the market. They employ different communication channels like a Public Relation Officer (PRO), press meet, newsletters, event sponsoring, community service etc., to build a favourable image among their different stakeholders of the society. Besides it is through best employee-oriented welfare measures that they create a employer brand in the job market. Further, adherence to various laws and the observance of corporate ethics by the company goes a long way towards promoting a good image. All these serve as competitive advantage in the market.

Public Relations

Companies across different sectors are engaged in discharging their social obligations to various stakeholders like the Government, suppliers, investors, local community, distributors etc. PROs are employed to act as an interface between the company and the external stakeholders. Free flow of communication facilitated by the interface helps to heighten the image of the company.

Personal Asset

Improving communication skills is essential for the success of every human. Non-administrative employees at the lower level need to develop their drafting and reporting skills, secretaries for the various officers need to hone their note-making skills, managers across hierarchies need to improve the way they deliver speeches, write documents and conduct interviews. Teachers, lawyers, journalists, receptionists etc., need to constantly improve their verbal communication skills to perform their job effectively.

IMPORTANCE OF EFFECTIVE BUSINESS COMMUNICATION

Effective business communication is important for the following reasons:

Co-ordination within the Organization

Employees working in large organizations are spread over different parts of a country and sometimes across countries. Sending instructions to them, collecting their feedback and generating a performance report would be possible only by opening various channels of communication.

Harmonious Industrial Relations

Effective communication promotes a harmonious and smooth industrial relation between the management and the trade unions.

Promoting Relations with Stakeholders

Organizations can promote good relations with the different stakeholders of society through effective communication.

Updating Employees

Ever-changing technology makes the existing skill-sets of employees obsolete. Hence, regular training is needed to update their skills.

Convincing Employees of the Need for Change

Effective communication is needed to convince the employees across organizational hierarchies to embrace changes to different duties.

Motivating Employees

Employees are not mere cogs in the machinery. They are sensitive human beings. They need constant motivation and inspiration to develop a positive attitude. Management has to communicate with its employees through various interventions to turn them into productive and long-lasting assets.

Developing a Corporate Image

Communication is essential for every organization to develop and sustain favourable corporate image in the society. Through various forms of communication, it can improve its relationship with the different stakeholders of the society.

SUMMARY

Communication is defined as the process of passing information and understanding from one person to another.

Communication has become indispensible due to the size of business enterprise, increasing specialization, technological advancement, smooth industrial relations, better human relations, cut-throat competition and public relations.

The points stressing the importance of business communication are co-ordination within the business, harmonious industrial relations, promoting relations with stakeholders, ever- changing technology, need to update skills, vehicle to motivate employees and need to develop corporate image.

REVIEW QUESTIONS

Part A: Short Questions

1. Define communication.
2. Define business communication.
3. Why do we need communication? Give a few reasons.
4. List five points on the importance of business communication.

Part B: Paragraph Questions

1. Point out the characteristics of communication.

Part C: Essay Questions

1. Emphasize the need for communication in an organization.
2. Bring out the significance of effective buisiness communication.

Prt D: Objective Type Questions

Choose the correct answer

1. Which helps in ensuring the receipt of communication in right from and in right sense

    a. Feed back b. Timely reach

    c. Prompt response d. Delayed response

    (Ans: a)

2. Communication is a

    a. Static process b. Dynamic process

    c. Neither static nor dynamic d. Either static or dynamic

    (Ans: b)

Fill in the blanks

1. Communication is a ________________ process. (Two way)
2. Communication promotes ____________ ____________ ____________ and ____________ skills.(Reading, writing, listening, speaking)
3. Communication is process of ________________. (Passing information)

2

CHAPTER

PROCESS, PRINCIPLES AND MEANS OF COMMUNICATION

PROCESS OF COMMUNICATION

Process means a systematic series of actions or operations of a series of changes directed to some end. Communication is a two way process wherein there is an exchange and progression of ideas towards a mutually acceptable goal. The process of communication involves two parties – the *sender* and the *receiver*. The former conveys a message through a medium to the latter who acknowledges receipt of the delivered message.

Components of the Communication Process

The process of communication involves the following major components:

Sender / Encoder / Speaker

Sender is the person who starts the process of communication. He communicates opinions, ideas, facts, thoughts or information, instructions, directions, advice etc. He is the transmitter of the message.

Receiver / Decoder / Listener

The process of converting thoughts into suitable words, charts, symbols or any other form understandable to the receiver is called decoding.This is the person who receives the message and decodes, understands or attaches some meaning to it. Thus the receiver has to perform three functions at the receiving point. The first function is to receive the message. But the original message may not reach the receiver or may reach the intended receiver in a different shape due to many reasons like interception of message conveyed by a third person, receipt of the message by a third person, etc. Suggestions sent through the message may be misconstrued as an order. The second function of the receiver is to attach meaning to it. The third one is to understand the message in the same sense which it is conveyed by the sender.

Message

This refers to information, written or spoken, which is sent from one person to another. It can be verbal and non-verbal. Since the message has to trigger response, it needs to be simple, precise, complete, unambiguous and courteous. The sender has to gauge the requirements of the receiver in advance and accordingly design the message to be transmitted. He chooses a right medium to get the maximum impact from the message conveyed.

Channel

The medium through which communication is sent is called a *channel*. It can be a letter, e-mail, fax, telegram, telegraph, telephone, report, bulletin, poster or person. The sender has to select an appropriate channel, given the nature of message to be transmitted either orally or written. Each medium has its own rules and regulations. For instance, one can afford to be a little informal in oral communication but has to be very formal in a written communication which has its own rules.

Feedback

The receiver's reaction or response to the message delivered is feedback. Feedback may be oral or written. A smile nod, sight etc., are oral feedbacks while sending replies through letters, documents etc., are written feedbacks. The feedback in oral communication is quicker than written communication. It minimizes or eliminates the chance of errors. In written feedback sometimes, a receiver may not give feedback to the message delivered. This leads to a lot of wrong assumptions, erroneous conclusions and fallacious statements. It reduces the effectiveness of communication. In other words, the success or failure of communication is determined by the feedback. Feedback completes the cycle of communication.

Working of the Communication Process

The Working of Process can be either one-way or two-way.

One-way process

- Sender selects the message according to his ideas and intention
- Encodes the message
- Transmits it to the receiver through a channel
- Receiver decodes it and gives internal response to the perceived message. The response is not in relation to the content of message but to the perception.

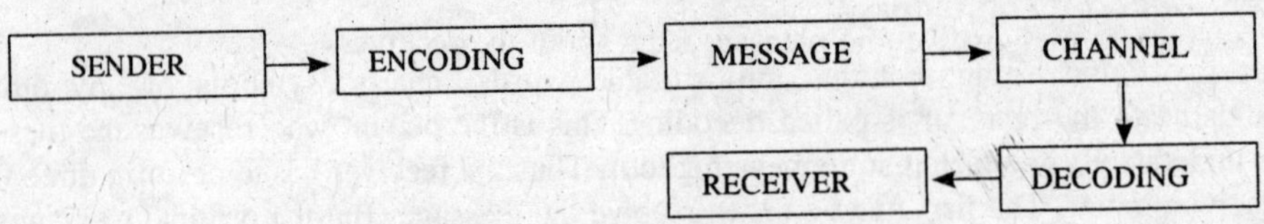

Fig. 2.1 One-way Process

Two-way process

After receiving the sender's message, the receiver formulates his response, encodes it and transmits it to the original sender who now becomes the receiver. This stage is called *feedback*. If the feedback is in sync with the intent of the original sender, communication flows without any hitch. However, there could be times when the receiver does not agree with the message of the original sender and does not give any feedback immediately. This should not be misconstrued as communication breakdown but it should be held as *temporary suspension or hold up* of communication.

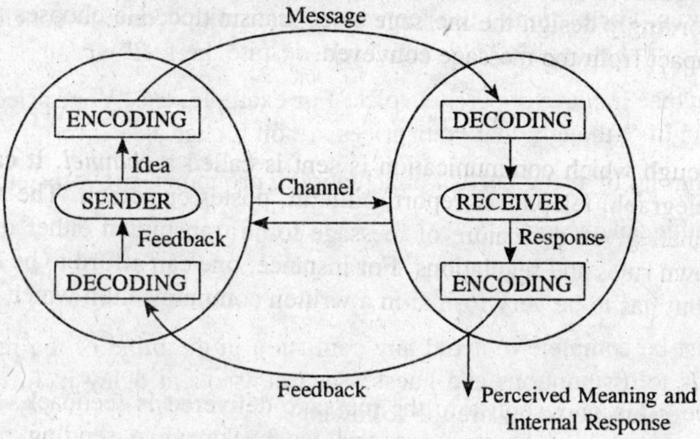

Fig. 2.2 Two-way Process

PRINCIPLES OF COMMUNICATION

Communication is perceived to be effective only if the receiver receives the message in the same form and context as it is sent by the sender. When there is no error in interpretation and the sender gets a correct feedback, then communication is said to be effective. There are certain principles observed in ensuring communication effectiveness. These, listed below, are the seven C's of effective communication.

Courtesy / Consideration

It means preparing every message from the viewpoint of the receiver. The sender has to emphasize the needs, aspirations, emotions, desires etc., of the receiver. In the business world, everything starts and ends with courtesy and consideration. Much can be achieved if courtesy and consideration is interwoven into the messages. The following points highlight courtesy:

- Focus on the *you* attitude instead of an *I* attitude.
- Show interest in the receiver and highlight the accruing benefits.
- Stress the positive and pleasant facts about the receiver.
- Be thoughtful and appreciative.
- Use expressions that convey respect.
- Choose non-discriminatory expressions.

Clarity

Clarity of ideas gives meaning to the message. The message of the sender should be understood in the same sense and context in which it is transmitted. Clarity can be achieved through the following ways:

- Avoid technical jargons used in their profession.
- Split running matter into paragraphs or highlighting key points.
- Choose simple language and use simple words in place of high sounding words.
- Avoid phrases. For example, use 'conclude' instead of 'come to conclusion', 'please' for "will you be kind enough", "although" for 'despite the fact' etc.
- Use active voice in place of passive voice. For example, use 'Your prices are on the higher side' instead of 'I thought that your prices are on higher side'.
- Avoid ambiguity by using correct punctuations, pronouns, proverbs etc.
- Avoid lengthy sentences.

Completeness

Communication must be complete to avoid any confusion in the mind of the receiver. Incomplete communication leads to assumptions and guesses and consequent delay in further action plan. In this connection, the sender has to ensure the following:

Provide all the necessary information: The sender has to answer all the five 'w's – who, what, when, where and why. These five questions help in preparing a request, announcement etc. For example, while ordering for goods, one needs to make it clear what is wanted, when it is needed, to whom it is addressed to, where it is to be sent and how the payment would be made.

Answer all questions asked while replying to an enquiry: The sender has to note all the points and answer all of them. Incomplete reply leads to further communication and wastage of time. Even unfavourable responses need to be given tactfully.

Provide additional information: It would help the receiver to make a better decision. For example, a hotel manager gets questions about the different types of rooms. He should be able to furnish details like rental per day, facilities provided, seasonal change in the rent, nearness to transport facilities etc.

Conciseness

The message to be communicated should be brief. The volume of information should be just right, neither too much nor too little. Lengthy letters may not result in desired actions. High sounding phrases may reflect sender's knowledge but may not ensure desired actions. Therefore, brevity is the soul of communication. A concise message saves time and energy of both the sender and the receiver. The following suggestions help in shortening communication:

Eliminate wordy expressions: Use one word substitutes instead of pharases. For example,

Wordy : In most of the cases it has been seen that the date of policy lapses.
Concise : Usually, the date of policy lapses.
Wordy : Allow me to say how helpful your last response was.
Concise : Your latest response was very helpful.

Include only relevant information: Omission of wordy expressions and irrelevant information helps in shortening the communication. Following advice is useful in this regard.

Stick to the purpose of the message: Delete irrelevant words and rambling sentences, omit information obvious to the receiver; avoid lengthy messages, unnecessary explanations and excessive adjectives. Get to the point sensibily.

Avoid repetition: Though repetition is necessary for emphasis, unnecessary repetition leads to boredom. The following suggestions can be followed in this regard:

- Use a shorter name after you have mentioned the longer one.
- Use pronouns or initials rather than using long names.
- Combine two or more sentences by using subordinate clauses or pharases.

Correctness

The term correctness in communication means using correct format, grammar, punctuation, spelling etc., besides giving correct facts.

Concreteness

Concreteness means specific, definite and vivid communication. We should use denotative words rather than connotative words. The principle of concreteness ensures supply of specific facts to the reader or listener. It increases the likelihood of the message being interpreted in the way it is originally intended. In other words, there is no room for misinterpretation.

For example, use specific facts. Instead of saying 'there is a substantial increase in sales', say 'sales have risen by 70%.' Instead of saying, 'it would be delivered some time in the next week,' say 'it would be delivered by 19th January 2011.'

Credibility

This means the receiver accepts the statement of the sender without any doubt. But this does not happen immediately. It is a long-drawn process wherein the receiver, through constant interaction with the sender, understands the latter and accepts his statement to be true and honest.

MEANS OF COMMUNICATION

Different occasions require different types of communication. All communication cannot be of the same type and it cannot flow through the same means. It depends on who sends the message, to whom and for what purpose. The following chart illustrates the means or types of communication:

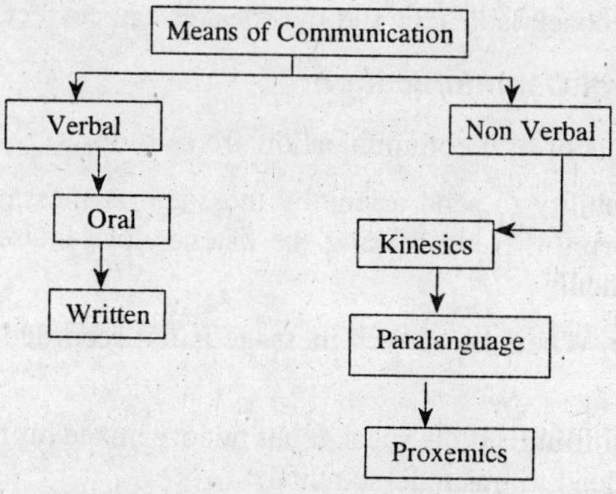

Fig. 2.3 Means of Communication

Verbal Communication

The term verbal communication means *use of words*. Human beings are the only gifted species who can use words that make up languages.

Words are the most accurate and powerful set of symbols. Thus, a common set of symbols is used between the sender and the receiver in the process of verbal communication. The words may be spoken or written. Spoken communication is called *oral communication*. Communication conveyed through written words is called *written communication*.

Oral Communication

Speech normally precedes writing. People speak on what they agree before committing themselves in writing. Oral communication plays an important role in families and organizations, among friends, relatives, acquaintances, neighbours, etc. It can be in the form of speeches, discussions, debates, face-to-face talk, telephonic conversation, video conferencing, interview and chat. It may be formal or informal. Oral communication would be effective if the principle of brevity and conciseness is observed. Miscommunication or ineffective oral communication can trouble the relationship and growth. Mechanical devices used for oral communication include telephone, intercom, dictating machines, internal addressing system, internet, etc.

Positive Aspects of Oral Communication

Some of the positive aspects of oral communication are as follows:

Saves paper work: As the message is delivered face-to-face, necessary clarifications can be given on the spot for the doubts expressed. This saves paper work.

Reduces message preparation time: The time of composing message and sending it to the receiver is reduced, thus saving time.

Saves money: Money spent on stationary is cut down considerably.

Powerful and persuasive: Oral message is powerful and persuasive.

Personal touch: Since it is done in person, it builds better relationships.

Communication clarity: Voice modulation, tone, pitch, loudness, etc. give clarity to the communication.

Instant feedback: Feedback is instant and the speaker can correct the miscommunication.

Negative Aspects of Oral Communication

Some of the negative aspects of oral communication are as follows:

Lengthy message: Inability to send a lengthy message. A message that is exceptionally long may turn out to be boring thereby making the listener lose interest. Besides, remembering a lengthy message is difficult.

Loss of legal validity: When the spoken message is not recorded using a recording device, it has no legal validity.

Scope for misunderstanding: If the speaker has not organized his thoughts and words carefully, the oral message may lead to misunderstanding.

Limited retention: The oral message cannot be fully retained by the listener. The speaker himself may not recall what he said. Inconclusive meetings only consume more time thereby defeating the concept of time-saving.

Written Communication

Messages put in black and white constitute written communication. Written communication is binding on the organization and it constitutes as a documentary evidence. It can be in the form of notices, telex messages, circulars, reports, e-mails or manuals. The components involved in written communication include the writer, the content, the language, purpose of communication, style adopted and the receiver.

Positive Aspects of Written Communication

The following are some of the positive aspects of written communication:

Preciseness: Written communication ought to be precise. The writer of the written message has to be choosy with the words. Since written communication is amenable to verification, insertion of irrelevant or false matter may invite unnecessary problems.

Scope for alteration: There is no scope for altering the original letter to receiver's advantage. It serves as a documentary evidence as well as a good reference material for future course of action.

Responsibility fixation possible: Responsibility can be fixed on both the sender or the receiver. The person committing an error can be found in written communication.

Legal validation: Written communication is accepted as a legal document. Hence it has legal validity.

Suitable for lengthy communication: It is more suitable for sending lengthy communication. There is less chance of message being misunderstood and misinterpreted in written communication.

Negative Aspects of Written Communication

The negative aspects of written communication are as follows:

Time consuming: Written communication is time consuming. First the sender prepares the message which might take a few hours or days. The receiver then receives the message only after a few hours or days.

Paper work: It leads to too much paper work.

Clarification is time consuming: If the receiver needs any clarification, he is forced to wait for a reply. There is bound to be a time gap thereby consuming more time.

Higher cost: Written communication entails cost. Several persons are involved in sending outward mails in an organization. Their time costs the company money.

Suitable only for literates: Written communication serves its purpose only when the sender and the receiver are comfortable in the written language. When the receiver is not conversant with the language in which the message is delivered, then the message conveyed is not understood properly.

No correction possible after dispatch: Once a written message is mailed, no correction is possible thereafter. In such cases, a further written communication is needed to nullify or alter an earlier written message.

Non-verbal communication is dealt with in Chapter 4.

SUMMARY

The components of the process of communication are sender, message, decoding, channel, receiver and feedback.

A one-way process involves sending an encoded message through a channel which is received by the receiver after decoding.

In a two-way process, the receiver, after receiving the message sends a feedback to the sender who receives it after decoding.

Principles of communication include courtesy, clarity, completeness, conciseness, correctness, concreteness and credibility.

Means of communication are of two types: Verbal and Non-verbal. The former includes oral and written methods of communication and the latter includes kinesics, paralanguage and proxemics.

Oral communication has merits like saving preparation time and stationary, powerfulness and persuasiveness, personal touch, communication clarity and instant feedback.

Demerits include inability to transmit lengthy messages, loss of legal validity, scope for misunderstanding and limited capacity for retention.

The merits of written communication are preciseness, scope for alteration, responsibility fixation, legal validation and suitability for lengthy communication.

The demerits include time consumption, too much paper work, higher cost, suitable only for literates and no scope for correction after dispatch.

REVIEW QUESTIONS

Part A: Short Questions

1. What is meant by feedback?
2. Give the meaning of encoding and decoding.
3. What do you mean by channels of communication?
4. What is verbal communication?
5. Give examples of written communication in an organization.

Part B: Paragraph Questions

1. What are the components of the communication process?
2. Explain the working of communication.

Part C: Essay Questions

1. Elaborate on the principles of communication or the seven C's of communication.

Part D: Objective Type Questions

State whether the following statements are true or false.

1. The process of the receiver sending back a message is feedback. Ans:True
2. Memo, notice, telegraph etc., are written communication. Ans: True
3. The process of translating symbols into words is called decoding. Ans: True
4. Written communication is formal communication. Ans: True
5. Oral communication needs the presence of a speaker and a listener. Ans: False

Choose the correct answer

1. Which of the following principles stipulate that the message should be understood in the same sense in which it is sent

   a. Principle of credibility b. Principle of brevity

   c. Principle of clarity d. Principle of specificity

   (Ans: c)

2. Spoken communication is called

   a. Verbal communication b. Non-verbal communication

   c. Gestual communication d.Lateral communication

   (Ans: a)

3. Team member is discussion of target along with team member in a periodical meeting is

   a. Written communication b. Oral communication

   c. Gestural communication d. Non-verbal communication

   (Ans: b)

4. Which type of communication serves more as a documentary evidence

   a. Verbal communication b. Written communication

   c. Gestural communication d. Non-verbal communication

   (Ans: b)

5. Telephonic conversation is

   a. Verbal communication b. Non-verbal

   c. Body language d. straight communication

   (Ans: a)

Fill in the Blanks

1. The process of receiver sending back a message is ________. (Feed back)
2. Written communication is __________ communication. (Formal)
3. Memo, notice, telegraph, etc., are ____________ type of communication. (Written)
4. Communication falls into two types, namely __________ and __________ .(Verbal, Non-verbal)
5. The process of converting communication received into understandable to the receiver is __________ .(Decoding)
6. ____________ starts the communion. (Sender)
7. Medium through which communication is sent is __________ .(Channel)
8. Information i.e. Written or spoken, sent from one person to another is ___________. (Message)

3

CHAPTER

FLOW OF COMMUNICATION

INTRODUCTION

Communication flows in all directions in any organization. Depending upon the direction, it can be classified as follows:

- Downward
- Upward
- Horizontal
- Diagonal

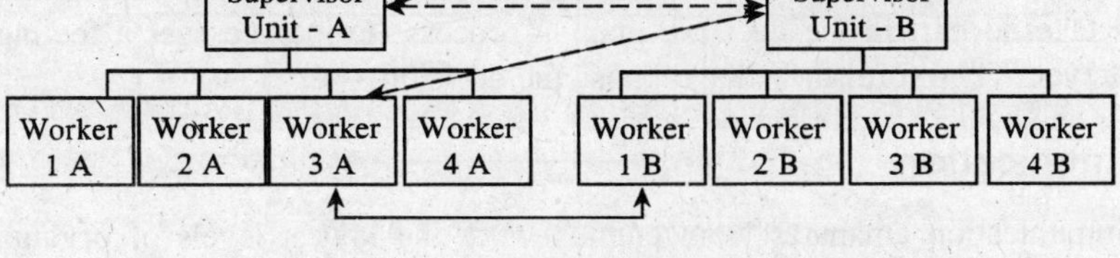

Fig. 4.1 Flow of Communication

Downward Communication

Communication that is cascading from top echelons of the management to the lower levels is downward communication. In other words, it comes from superiors to subordinates in a vertical fashion. It takes the form of an order, circular, policy statement, memos and procedural documents.

Objectives of Downward Communication

1. Giving instructions about a job.
2. Illustrating procedures.
3. Apprising subordinates of a procedure, highlighting the significance of the job assigned to subordinates.

Advantages of Downward Communication

1. This channel is used for giving necessary instructions to the subordinates.
2. This channel helps in performance evaluation of Staff.
3. It facilitates orientation of subordinates to the vision and mission of organisation.
4. This channel is useful in explaining the process of work perfomance to subordinates.

Disadvantages of Downward Communication

The disadvantages of downward communication are:

Possible distortion: The message communicated in downward communication could be distorted or misunderstood. Suppose a supervisory officer misunderstands the message passed on by his immediate superior, the subsequent people may also get the wrong message. By the time it reaches the bottom layer of the organization, the crux of the communication may be lost.

Loss in transmission: When a message has to pass through several officers across an organizational hierarchy, there may be a loss of original content of the information. Written communication can address this loss of information to a certain extent.

Delayed communication: Since the communication has to pass through various levels of an organization to reach the intended people, there may be a delay in communication.

Possibility of over or under communication: When superiors speak too much or too little, it results in over communication or under communication. Both mar the efficacy of communication.

Reflective of bureaucratic structure: It reflects an authoritarian set up. It signifies that the subordinates take no part in the decision making process. Employees get a feeling of being instructed forever. Therefore, they may oppose the decision.

Upward Communication

This type of communication emanates from employees at the lowest levels of organization and reaches the top. This takes the form of suggestions, complaints, grievances and performance reporting. Increasing democratization of workplace paves way for upward communication.

Advantages of Upward Communication

The following are the advantages of upward communication:

Feedback: Managers at different layers of organizational hierarchy can get a feedback of whether subordinates have understood the message or the instructions passed through formal channels.

Outlet for pent up emotions: This types of communication can serve as an outlet to give vent to the pent up emotions and grievances of the affected employee.

Opportunity to provide ideas/suggestions: This channel provides on opportunity to suggest sound ideas or advice on various matters. When right suggestions are implemented and the concerned employee is rewarded, his ego-needs get fulfilled. This welds him with the organization. Other employees may also be inspired by him.

Creating smooth relationship: Upward communication develops harmony and understanding between management and employees. This results in cordial industrial relationships.

Tool to introduce change: This channel may be used by the management to introduce necessary changes in the organization. Consulting with the employees and convincing them of the inevitability of changes in the organization creates a conducive environment for change absorption.

Disadvatages of Upward Communication

The disadvantages of upward communication includes:

Bureaucratic apathy: Some bureaucratic managers do not like the idea of seeking consultation from workers in the process of decision making.

Lack of receptive mindset: Most superiors do not have a mindset to accept negative opinions against their decision.

Fear of victimization: Subordinates themselves may not like to complain to their superiors for fear of being victimized.

Possibility of bypassing authority: Some lower level functionaries may pass their complaint with higher level officers. Thus, work relations between the immediate superior and the subordinate may come under strain.

Possible misuse by sycophants: Sycophants may misuse upward communication for their personal gains. They may want to endear themselves to superior officers, passing selective information and suppressing the material information.

Horizontal Communication

This type of communication takes place among equal cadres in an organizational hierarchy. Communication among domain/functional heads is one example. Similarly, when any person in a particular cadre interacts with his counterparts working in other departments, horizontal communication takes place. This communication is meant to maintain co-ordination and keep every department informed of its needs and activities of other departments. For example, the production and marketing departments must work hand in hand with each other, so that production planning and marketing strategies prove to be effective.

Advantages of Horizontal Communication

The advantages of horizontal communication include:

1. Promotes understanding and trust among various departments.
2. Facilitates co-operation and co-ordination among functional departments.
3. Irons out inter-departmental and intra-departmental conflicts.

Disadvantages of Horizontal Communication

The disadvantages of horizontal communication are:

1. It may give rise to gossip. It can be used for spreading rumours and spreading fictitious information.
2. It can work effectively only when there is proper co-ordination.
3. Ego clashes among departmental heads block free flow of horizontal communication.

Diagonal Communication

It takes place when people working at the same level interact with those working at a higher or lower level in an organizational hierarchy and also across the boundary of their reporting relationship.

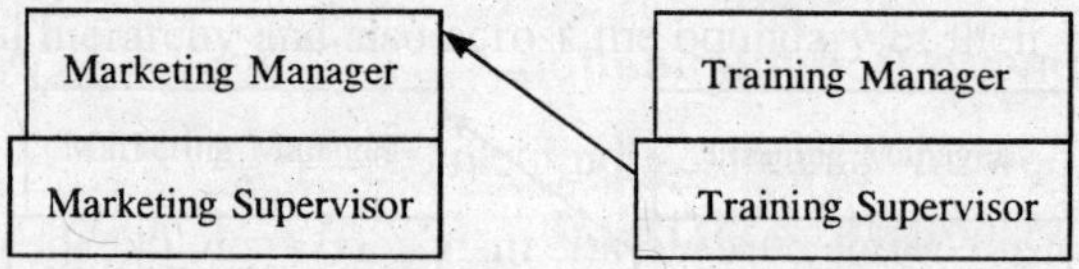

Fig. 4.2 Diagonal Communication

In other words, communication flows across the levels among employees in an organization who may not have direct reporting relationship. Informal meetings, lunch-hour meetings, formal conferences, project-organization meetings, interactions with advisory authorities, bulletins, company newsletters, in-house journals, etc., are examples of diagonal or multidimensional communication.

Advantages of Diagonal Communication

The advantagesof diagonal communication are:

1. It helps to improve co-ordination among employees.
2. It enhances their mutual understanding.
3. Interactions across the levels boost the morale of the employees.

Limitations of Diagonal Communication

The disadvantages of diagonal communication are:

1. Superiors may fear of being bypassed in the official hierarchy as the subordinates may have an upperhand in this type of communication.
2. This communication can lead to a complex network. Absence of accepted procedures may lead to internal chaos. As a result, there may be displeasure among employees.
3. Suggestions resulting from diagonal communication may not be accepted by superiors as they feel uninvolved in the process.

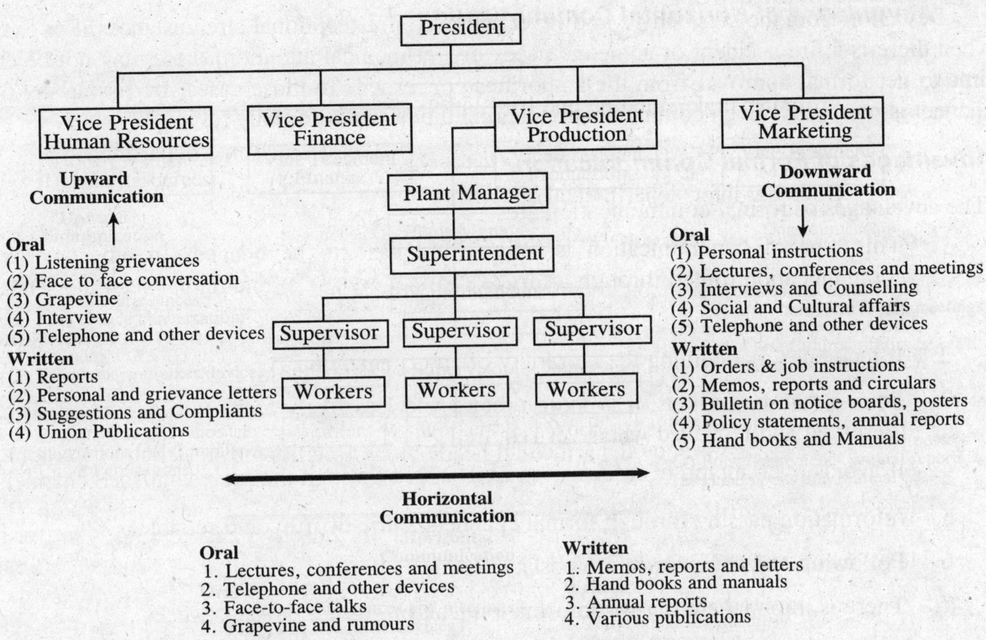

Fig. 4.3 Flow of Communication in an Organization

TYPES OF COMMUNICATION

Formal Communication

It is the communication that flows through official channels or formal organizational hierarchy. Organizational objectives, vision, mission, policies, procedures, programmes, budgets, schedules, strategics, goals, instructions, targets etc., are communicated from the superiors to the subordinates through this mode of communication. Similarly, grievances, complaints, performance, reporting etc., are made through upward communication in an organizational hierarchy.

Source: Internet

Fig 4.4: Formal Communication

Deviation from the hierarchy is, however, allowed in exceptional circumstances. For example, when there is a fire accident or someone needs urgent medical attention, there may not be enough time to get formal approval from the authorities concerned. In those cases, bypassing the official channel is permitted. Even communication among the heads is formal.

Advantages of Formal Communication

The advantages of formal communication are:

1. This type of communication is official and has to be obeyed. In other words, any communication routed through a formal channel creates a binding between the sender and the receiver.
2. It facilitates maintaining the hierarchy of an organization.
3. Since it can be written, it is more precise and less likely to be misunderstood. It can be preserved and retrieved whenever required.
4. It avoids overlapping of information as it passes through the pre-established channels.
5. Information passing through formal channels is trustworthy and reliable.
6. Follow up and compliance are possible easily.
7. There is minimal chance for information leak or gossip.
8. Better co-operation and co-ordination are achieved through formal communication.

Limitations of Formal Communication

The limitations of formal communication are:

1. It is time-consuming, since every piece of information has to pass through many layers of organizational hierarchy.
2. It may delay decision making—some emergency decisions which do not allow sufficient time to route it through formal channels may not be taken because authority has to be bypassed.
3. It inhibits the free flow of communication among the various levels of the organization.
4. It does not allow social and emotional bonds to be developed. Therefore, the organizational climate becomes more rigid.

Informal or Grapevine Communication

One cannot always communicate only through formal channels. Informal channels are required to go alongside formal channels for effective functioning.

Source: Internet

Fig 4.5 Informal Communication During a Coffee Break

Informal communication is not an officially sanctioned channel. Since this communication happens in all directions, just like grapes in a bunch growing in all possible directions, it is also called grapevine communication. It is very common in the following situations:

- When an organization is passing through crisis, insecure feelings may give rise to it.
- Personal problems experienced by employees.
- Unusual happenings in an organization.
- Managers favouring a specific group which spreads a feeling of insecurity among others.
- Feeling of inadequacy or lack of self-confidence of an employee may end up in formation of an informal group.

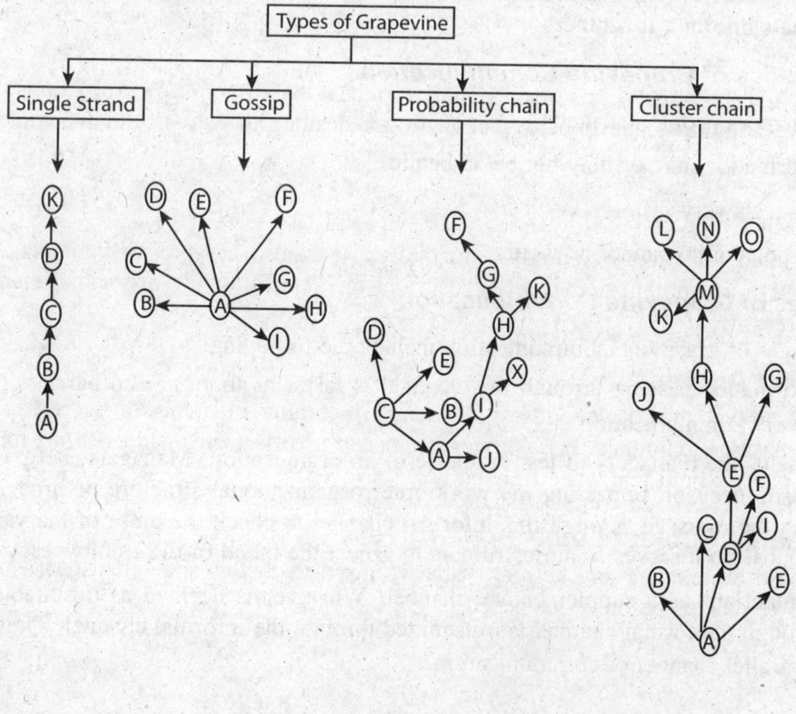

Fig. 4.6 Types of Grapevine

Figure 4.7 shows how the grapevine communication network happens in an organization and beyond.

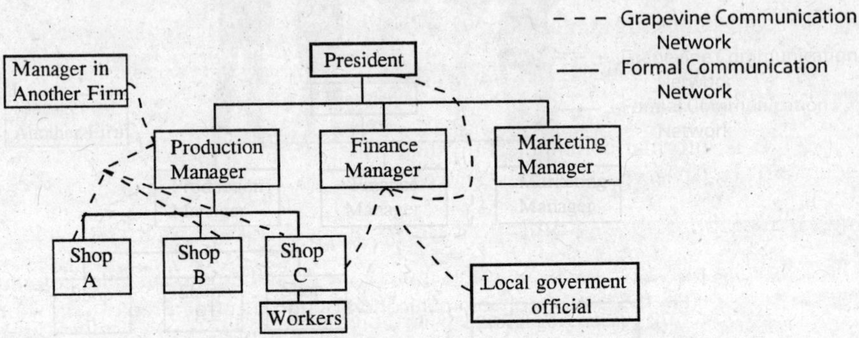

Fig. 4.7 Grapevine in an Organizational Setup

There are different types of grapevine communication. They are:

Single strand chain: A person communicates the message to another. For example, A tells something to B, who in turn passes it on to C and so on.

Group chain: A single individual communicates a message to all employees in the group.

Probability chain: Each person randomly tells a number of people, who in turn tell others at random.

Cluster chain: A tells something to a few selected individuals and then some of these individuals inform a few others.

Characteristics of Grapevine Communication

1. It is more people-oriented.
2. Information may or may not be authentic.
3. It travels very fast.
4. Responsibility cannot be fixed.

Advantages of Grapevine Communication

The advantages of grapevine communication include the following:

1. Information passing through this channel is faster as there are no barriers hindering the flow of communication.
2. It helps the managers to test the pulse of an organization. Managers, before taking some drastic decision impacting the workforce, organizational structure or process, purposely float the message through this informal channel to check the pulse of the various interest groups. So it serves as an instrument to reflect the mood of the employees.
3. It functions as a supplementary channel. Whatever is deemed as unsuitable for routing through the formal channel is transmitted through the informal channel. Thus, it serves as a parallel channel of communication.

4. It yields enormous psychological satisfaction. Formal channel distances the people while informal channel brings them closer to each other. Thus, it keeps the organization intact as a social entity.
5. It may generate more ideas and multiple views which might help in effecting good policies and wise decisions.
6. Informal channel promotes personal relationship, which in turn leads to good public relations.
7. It is informal communication that brings people together in matters of common interest. Thus, it serves as a binding force among the employees.

Streamlining Informal Communication

The following proactive measures can regulate the functioning of parallel communication system:

- Conducting regular meetings with the employees through various forum.
- Providing a mechanism to update the knowledge of employees.
- Managers not to practice favoritism and nepotism.
- Spotting role-model employees and making them serve as leaders.
- Managers are not to indulge in loose talks.
- Being a good listener helps to reduce miscommunication.
- Involving employees in decision making processes.
- Getting feedback about a person's style of behaviour.

Outward Communication

An organization is a social entity. It has to interact with government and non-government agencies. It may have to correspond with the local and district administration offices, tax authorities, regulatory agencies, banks, insurance companies, justice department and law enforcement agencies.

It needs to have a communication with the media, advertisement agencies, outsourcers, investment companies, private funding agencies, suppliers, customers, competitors, funding agencies, shareholders, environment associations, local groups, etc. Communication may take the form of tele-conference, correspondence, e-mail, face-to-face meetings, press conference, panel discussion, exhibition or events, advertisement, telephonic conversation, tender, notices, negotiations etc.

Inward or Internal Communication

When communication happens within an organization, its departments or sections and among the branches of an organization, it is called Internal or Inward Communication. Notices, circulars, programmes, agenda, objectives, targets, feedback, performance reporting, grievance redressal, brainstorming, suggestion scheme, get-togethers, progress report, review meetings, board meetings, conference, committee meetings etc., are the channels of internal communication.

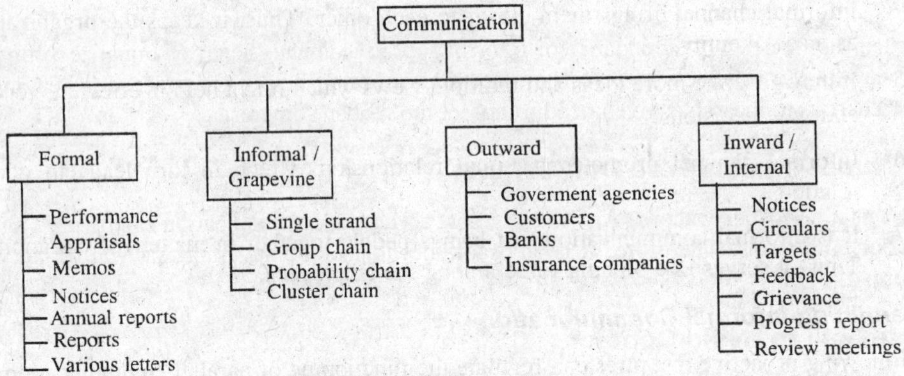

Fig. 4.8 Types of Communication

SUMMARY

Flow of communication involves downward, upward, horizontal and diagonal patterns.

Objectives of downward communication are giving direction, illustrating procedure, apprising employees of procedure and highlighting significance of job.

Limitations of downward communication are possibility of distortion, message lost in transmission, delayed communication, possibility of over or under communication and reflective of bureaucratic structure.

Advantages of upward communication are feedback, outlet for pent up emotions, opportunity for giving suggestions, building relations, and acting as a tool to introduce change.

Limitations of upward communication are bureaucratic apathy, lack of receptive mind set, fear of victimization, possibility of authority bypass, and possible misuse by sycophants.

Advantages of horizontal communication are promoting understanding, facilitating co–operation and co-ordination and removing conflict.

Limitation of horizontal communication include scope for rumour, works only with co-ordination and scope for ego clash.

Advantages of diagonal communication are facilitating co-ordination, improving understanding and acting as a morale booster.

Limitations of diagonal communication are fear of being bypassed, complex network and lack of support from superiors.

Advantages of formal communication are the need to obey, maintaining hierarchy, documentation advantage, no overlap of information reliability, easy follow-up and minimum scope for information blockage.

Limitations of formal communication are time consuming, delay in decision making, inhibiting flow of communication and less scope for emotional bonding.

Types of informal (grapevine) communication are single stand chain, group chain, probability chain and cluster chain.

Characteristics of grapevine communication are people oriented lack of authenticity, faster spread and responsibility fixation not possible.

Advantages of grapevine communication are faster transmission, tool to test the pulse of the public, tool to gauge the mood of staff, supplementary channel, provides psychological satisfaction, more idea generation and nurturing public relation unifying force.

Measures to streamline informal communication are conducting meetings, instituting a mechanism for not practicing favoritism or loose talks, promote listening, involving employees in decision making and getting feedback.

REVIEW QUESTIONS

Part A: Short Questions

1. What is upward communication?
2. What is diagonal communication?
3. What is meant by downward communication?
4. What is gesture?
5. What is formal communication?
6. What is informal communication?
7. What is inward communication?
8. What is outward communication?
9. What is single strand chain in grapevine communication?
10. What is cluster chain in grapevine?

Part B: Paragraph Questions

1. Briefly mention the objectives of downward communication.
2. Point out the types of grapevine.
3. Mention the merits of grapevine communication.
4. Suggest measures to streamline informal communication.

Part C: Essay Questions

1. What do you mean by downward communication and elaborate on its merits and demerits.
2. Discuss the merits and demerits of formal communication.

Part D: Objective Type Questions

State whether the following statements are true or false

1. Communication with superiors is external communication. Ans: False
2. Communication with suppliers is internal communication. Ans: False
3. Circular from managing dirctor to all heads is downward communication. Ans: True
4. Employees transmitting grievance is not upward communication. Ans: True
5. Conversation among the heads of department is horizontal communication. Ans: True
6. Communication by movement of organs of body is gestural communication. Ans: True
7. Silence is not one of modes of communication. Ans: False
8. Sending performance report is external communication. Ans: False
9. Advertisement is one of the modes of mass communication. Ans: True
10. Informal communication in an organization is called grapevine communication. Ans: True
11. External communication may be inward or outward. Ans: False
12. Communication within an organization is internal communication. Ans: False

Choose the correct answer

1. Employee transmitting his complaint is
   a. Downward communication b. Upward communication
   c. Diagonal communication d. Grapevine communication.
   (Ans: b)

2. Interview is an example of
   a. Verbal communication b. Grapevine communication
   c. Non-verbal communication d. Outward communication
   (Ans: a)

3. Body language comes under
   a. Verbal communication b. Non–verbal communication
   c. Both verbal and non verbal communication d. Grapevine communication.
   (Ans: a)

4. Study of body movement is
   a. Kinesics b. Paralanguage
   c. Proxemics d. Semantic barrier
   (Ans: a)

5. Doing a function of a language without being a part of language is
   a. Paralanguage b. Supplementary language
   c. Kinesics d. Proxemics
   (Ans: a)

6. Production manager telephonically directing the lift operator to attend lift repair of production department is an example of

a. Downward communication b. Upward communication

c. Horizontal communication d. Diagonal communication

(Ans: d)

7. Marketing manager is informed of a fact during his chat with the production manager in a cafeteria is

a. Grapevine communication b. Horizontal communication

c. Upward communication d. Diagonal communication

(Ans: a)

Fill in the blanks

1. Communication through words is called ____________. (Verbal communication)
2. Communication without words spoken or written is called ____________. (Non-Verbal communication).
3. Informal communication in an organization is known as ____________. (Grapevine communication)
4. Written communication is ____________communication. (Formal)
5. The process of ensuring that the receiver has understood the message is ____________. (Feedback)
6. Communication from Government suppliers, customers, competitors' share holders and meetings are ____________communication (External) but ____________in nature. (Inward)
7. Communication by an organization with outsiders by advertisement, media, tender, notice, telephone, mails, publication are ____________ communication but ____________ in nature. (External, Outward).
8. Scope of communication encompasses both ____________(Internal) and ____________ communication. (External)
9. Flow of communication among persons at different levels who have no direct reporting relationship is ____________. (diagonal communication)
10. Letters, notices, complaints, contracts, manuals, policy, procedure, programme are ____________ communication. (Written)
11. Verbal communication may be ____________ (Oral) or ____________. (Written)
12. Communication can be ____________ (Verbal) or ____________. (Non-verbal)
13. Communication through body language is ____________. (Kinesics).

4

CHAPTER

NON-VERBAL COMMUNICATION

INTRODUCTION

Communication takes place even without words spoken or written. Many research studies have established the efficacy of non-verbal communication. Gestures, postures, body movement and physical apperance are some examples of non-verbal communication through which messages are expressed. The classification of non-verbal communication is illustrated in Figure 3.2.

KINESICS

The study of body movement is known as *kinesics*. Our body conveys several messages consciously or unconsciously. For example, raised eyebrows indicates surprise; creased forehead suggests worries, pursed lips shows reservation to comment, yawning points to boredom, smile expresses happiness while frown conveys discomfiture or confusion.

Components of Kinesics

The following are the components of kinesics:

Facial expression

Face is the index of the mind. It can convey a person's anger, displeasure, grief, sincerity, cheerfulness and other positive or negative emotions. Researchers estimate that a human face can display 2,50,000 expressions. The face serves as a window to express a person's emotions. It can be used to supplement verbal communication.

Source: Internet

Fig. 3.1 Facial Expressions

Facial expressions need to be read in context. A smile may be a sign of happiness, amusement or pleasure. When you on see a beaming smile on the face of the interviewer, it can either mean that the interviewer is happy with your performance or that he is sarcastic about it. When you observe a frown on your boss's face, you understand that he is not in a good mood. There are some people who deliberately exhibit a different expression on their face. If an employee is upbraided, it is natural for him to show his anger, but he holds back his emotions because he knows that exhibiting anger would cost him his job or privilege. Overall, facial expressions are important to a receiver's perception of credibility. Therefore, a speaker should radiate dynamism, interest and enthusiasm for a high credibility rating.

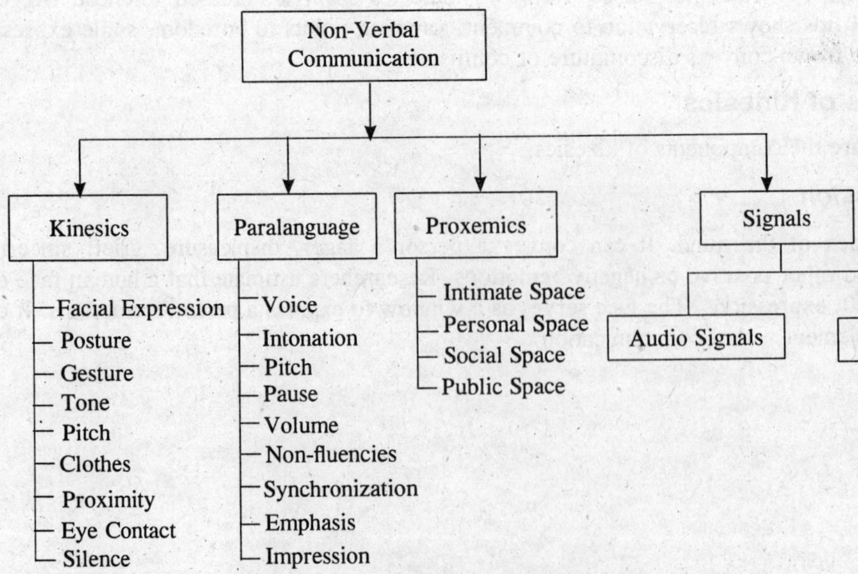

Fig. 3.2 Classification of Non-verbal Communication

Posture

It is the position adopted by the body. For example, a raised head indicates openness while a tilted head marks curiosity. However, none of these postures have a definite meaning but they acquire meaning in the context of communication.

TORSO	ARMS	HANDS AND FINGERS	FEET AND LEGS
Leaning away from some one: Means we dislike or disagree with them  Leaning towards someone: Means we like or agree with them	Fingertips spread apart on a surface:  A display of confidence and authority	Thumbs up:  A good indication of positive thoughts	Wriggling/Kicking foot:  Indicates discomfort
Spreading out:  A sign of comfort becomes a display of dominance when there are serious issues being discussed	Arms on the hips:  Establishes dominance and communicates there are 'issues'	Steepling: (Fingertip to Fingertip) 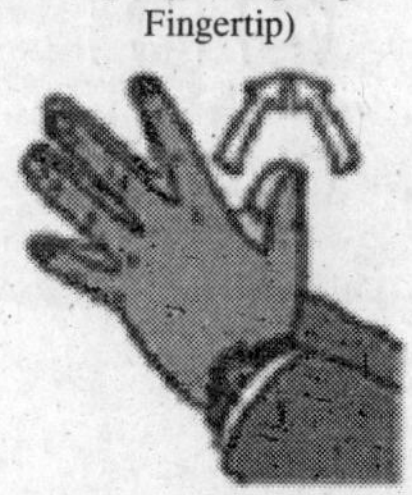 A powerful display of confidence	Crossing legs:  Indicates we are comfortable
Crossed arms:  Suddenly crossing arms tightly is a sign of discomfort	Arms behind the back:  Means 'Don't come near – Keeps people at bay	Neck touching:  Indicates emotional discomfort, doubt or insecurity	Toe points upward:  Signals a good mood

Source: Internet

Fig: 3.3 Postures

Gesture

Gestures refer to body movements that transmit messages. Some gestures are made consciously while some are involuntary. The way you move your arms, legs, eyes, hands, head and shoulders convey different messages. Even the style of sitting communicates your emotion.

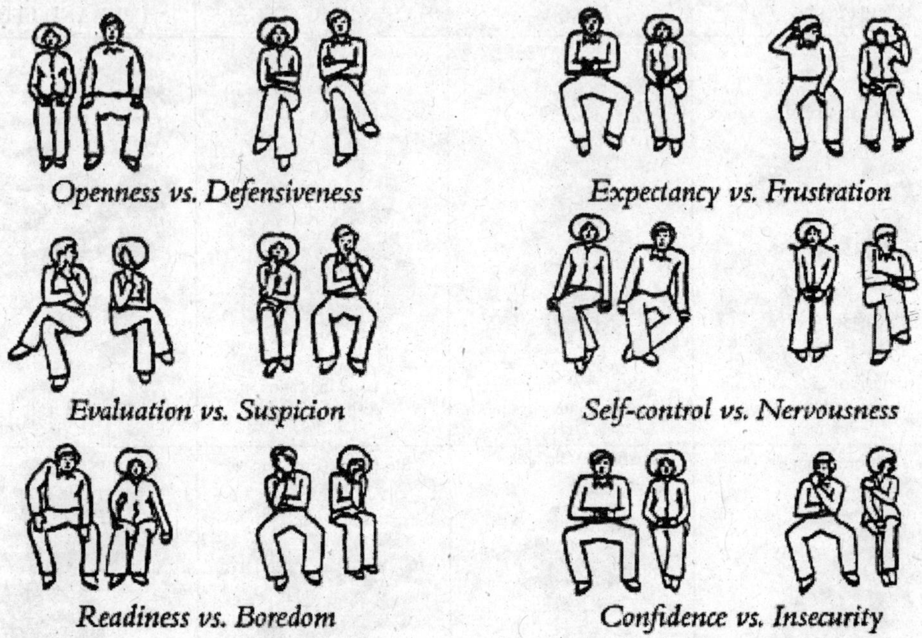

Source: Internet

Fig.3.4 Body Language

Tone

Tone is one of the important aspects of communication. Tone means the manner of speaking. Tone expresses a person's appreciation, sarcasm, admiration or anger. Tone can be gentle or aggressive. For example, a person exclaims what a painting it is. The speaker may express his surprise or sarcasm through this phrase. Thus, the tone conveys a person's attitude.

Pitch

It means variation in volume and tone. A constant pitch is monotonous. The speaker has to vary his pitch to ensure effective listening. Pitch of the voice reflects a person's emotions like anger, excitement, happiness etc. Even the confidence level of a person can be gauged from the pitch of his voice. Voice also varies with a person's emotional state. Loudness of voice occurs when a person experiences anger, cheerfulness, joy, strength, fearlessness, high status etc., whereas softness of voice happens with affection, boredom, sadness, intimacy, empathy, fear, low status, passivity etc.

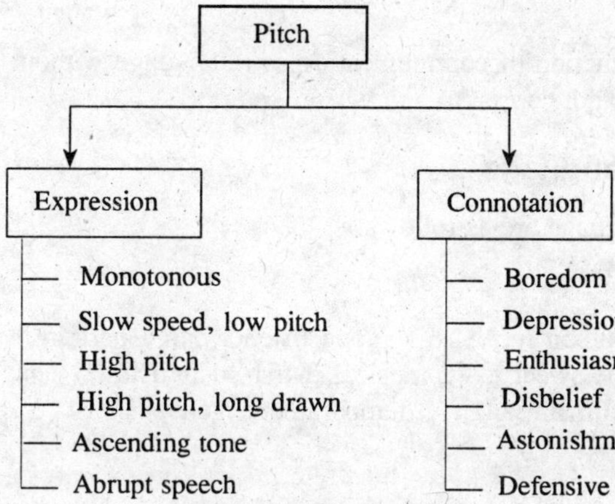

Fig. 3.5 Components of Pitch

Clothes

Man is judged by his appearance though it may be deceptive at times. A shabbily dressed person creates an impression of being unenthusiastic, dull, depressed, cheerless and sad. Whereas a professional look conveys that he is serious, sincere, committed, happy and excited. In short, dress-care reflects a person emotional state.

Proximity

The space and distance between the speaker and the listener conveys a certain message. The extent of space between them may point to the degree of formalness or informalness of behaviour. One may not sit close to a stranger but might sit close to a friend. There are norms or social expectations regarding the distance to be maintained. Thus, the distance a person maintains conveys a subtle message to an outsider.

Eye contact

Eyes are the windows to the soul. Movement of the eyes communicate a person's frame of mind. A brief eye contact indicates that the speaker is nervous and excited. A long and fixed gaze shows interest. Eye movements are connected with emotions like anger, pain, nervousness, cheerfulness, etc.

Silence

Silence is one method of non–verbal communication. A person may be quiet either due to acceptance of the message or non–acceptance. The message conveyed through silence can be understood with respect to context. For example,

- If the boss keeps silent when an employee asks for casual leave during a busy season, the silence means refusal.
- When employees become silent on the boss entering the office, it indicates respect or fear towards the boss.

  When employees ask for a pay hike, if the boss remains silent, the silence refers to denial.
- When audience applaud the speaker's remark, it means that they appreciate the point made.

PARALANGUAGE

Anything performing the function of communication as a language without being a part of one is called paralanguage. It does not consist of any word.

Components of Paralanguage

The components of paralanguage are as follows:

Voice

Voice is the first signal a person receives. A good listener can ascertain the mood of the speaker from his voice. Voice can be sweet, soft, musical, harsh or indistinct. Thus, the voice reveals the speaker's mental frame, optimism, anxiety, temperament, gender etc.

Intonation

Voice modulation is used to stress or under-stress a point. It makes the communication effective. A louder voice is needed to highlight a point and a serious message needs to be conveyed in a sober tone.

Pause

Just like a comma is required for prose, pause is required for speech. A pause at the wrong moment leads to miscommunication. For example, the difference between fruit trees and fruits, trees is vast. A pause can indicate an upcoming subject. At the same time, too frequent pauses have potential to spoil the speech.

Volume

The speaker has to vary the volume of his voice depending on the size of the audience. A higher volume is needed for a larger audience. However, if the speaker switches from high to low volume and vice-versa, it would turn out to be an effective speech.

Non-fluencies

Utterances like *oh, ah, um, you know, you see, ok, well, fine, right* are known as *non-fluencies*. They give speaker breathing time and the audience time to think over what has been said. Too frequent non-fluencies irk the listeners.

Synchronization

Tone, pitch and facial expressions of the speaker should function in harmony with the speech. The non-synchronization among the three conveys a different message to the listener. For example, if a speaker congratulates a listener in a harsh tone and with a stern face, the listener may think that the speaker is not happy with his achievement. Similarly, praise or commendation delivered in a sarcastic tone conveys mockery. Hence the synchronization of speech with the expressions is very important.

Emphasis

Stressing key words lend more effect to the quality of communication.

Advantages of Paralanguage

The advantages of paralanguage are:

Supplementary communication: Paralanguage supplements oral communication. Without the latter, the former is ineffective.

Indicative of the speaker's position: It indicates the speaker's position in the formal organizational hierarchy.

Indicative of educational status: Paralanguage points to a person's educational background.

Indicative of the speaker's mood: It is indicative of the speaker's mood. A discerning listener can derive the right conclusion from the pitch, tone and speed of the message.

Disadvantages of Paralanguage

The disadvantages of paralanguage are:

Lacks the advantages of a language: Though paralanguage is like a language, all the advantages associated with a language are lacking.

Lack of uniformity: There can not be any uniformity in paralanguage as speakers come from different communities.

Prejudice possible: The voice quality, speed, pitch etc. may prejudice the receiver while receiving the message.

PROXEMICS

The word proxemics is derived from the word proximity which means *closeness*. It is used with reference to space or territory. A lot of communication takes place non-verbally in the space one shares with an other.

Classification of Proxemics

The space or distance one keeps is classified as follows:

Intimate Space

The lesser the space between two people while communicating, the more intimate is their nature of communication. For example, a pat on the back, pinching, handshake, whisper, touching, hugging etc., indicate the intimacy between the two. The space between them is within eighteen inches.

Personal Space

Personal space extends from eighteen inches to four feet. Our normal conversation with friends, neighbors, colleagues and associates take place in this space.

Social Space

It is anywhere between four feet and twelve feet. The relationship between the speaker and the listener is more formal. Communication in this space is dominated by reason and planning. Interview, review meeting, committee meeting etc., come under this category.

Public Space

This starts from a distance of twelve feet. The speaker has to amplify his voice to be heard by the audience. The communication is more formal in this area than the social space.

SIGNALS

Signals can be of two types. They are:

Audio Signals

The message is conveyed by audio signals.

Examples

- Curfew is communicated by the ringing of bells or sirens to signal that night is approaching.
- Blaring of sirens directed people to go under the bunker during the war.
- Ringing of the telephone means someone is calling.
- Ringing of the calling bell indicates someone is outside the door.
- Ringing of bells at temples and churches indicate prayer time.
- Buzzers call the visitors inside VIP's cabin.

Visual Signals

Pictures, posters, cartoons, drawings, symbols, signs etc., are visual signals.

Examples

- Coloured lights in traffic signals.
- Picture of gender in public conveniences and public transport.
- Lights in the railway traffic signal.
- Stripes in highways and zebra crossings on roads.
- A lit cigarette with a red-cross.

SUMMARY

The types of Non-verbal communication are Kinesics, Paralanguage and Proxemics.

Kinesics includes posture, gesture, tone, clothes, proximity, eye contact and silence.

Paralanguage includes voice intonating, pitch, pause, volume, mixed signal, emphasis and impression.

Advantage of paralanguage include supplementary communication, indicative of speaker's position in the hierarchy, indicative of speaker's educational status and mood.

Limitations of paralanguage are lack the advantages of a language, lack of uniformity, and possiblity of prejudice.

The clasification of Proxemics include intimate space, personal space, social space and public space.

REVIEW QUESTIONS

Part A: Short Questions

1. What is non-verbal communication?
2. What are kinesics?
3. What do you mean by paralanguage?
4. What do you mean by proxemics?
5. What is meant by body language?

Part B: Essay Questions

1. Discuss the advantages and disadvantages of paralanguage.

Part D: objective Type Questions

Choose the correct Answer

1. Study of body movement is
   a. Paralanguage b. Kinesics c. Posture
   (Ans: a)
2. Kinesics is
   a. Verbal communication b. Non-verbel communication
   c. Indirect communication d. Gestural communicatsion
   (Ans: b)
3. Modulation of voice comes under
   a. Kinesics b. proxemics
   c. paralanguage d. incantation
   (Ans: c)
4. Clothes one wear is
   a. Signals b. proxemics
   c. Kinesics type of communication d. Verbal type
   (Ans: c)
5. The space one shares conveys information to other it is called
   a. proxemics b. Kinesics
   c. Signals d. Visuals
   (Ans: a)

Fill in the Blanks

1. Study of movement of body is ____________ (Kinesics)
2. Manner of speaking is called _________ (Tone)
3. Variation of volume of tone is ____________ (Pitch)
4. Silence is a method of ____________ communication (Non-verbal)
5. Signals are of ___________ and __________ types (Audio, visual)
6. The word proxemics in English means ___________ (Proximits)
7. Voice modulation is called ____________ (Intonation)
8. Anything performing the function of communication as a language without being a part of one is ____________ (Paralanguage)

5

CHAPTER

LISTENING

IMPORTANCE OF LISTENING

Listening plays a significant role in the interactive process of business transactions. And yet, any suggestion to improve listening skills through conscious efforts is sometimes viewed with surprise or even amusement.

The amount of time spent on listening to others in person or on the phone or to recorded and broadcast material is substantial. In fact, listening is an important every day means of gathering information and acquiring knowledge. As a student, one has to listen to lectures, seminar presentations, instructions and views expressed in discussions and conversations. As a professional, one has to to listen to the boss, colleagues and subordinates within the organisation and also to outside contacts. Whatever be the circumstances, if one does not listen effectively, they are likely to land themselves in trouble or in an embarrassing situation. We have to remember that all successful executives and managers are usually good listeners. Cultivation of listening skills deserves as much attention as the other three ways of communication, namely, speaking, writing and reading. A number of benefits would accrue by cultivating this skill:

- Improves the intellectual ability to understand and evaluate the views and opinions expressed by others.
- Enables a person to gather proper and accurate information, facilitating appropriate decision making.
- Assists in establishing rapport with co-workers quickly.
- Helps the speaker give his best both in one-to-one, dyadic and group communication.

Communication takes place only when the receiver listens to the information conveyed. Listening is distinct from hearing. Hearing is just a physical process of sound waves hitting the ear drums. But listening is intimately connected with the brain. It draws attention to the subject matter and tries to make sense of what the speaker is talking about. Hence, hearing is through the ears and listening is through the mind. Listening is dynamic rather than passive. Good listening is essential for success. A good listener is more liked and appreciated than a one-way speaker.

THE LISTENING PROCESS

It involves the five stages of sensing, interpreting, evaluating, remembering and responding.

Sensing: Out of the multiple stimuli, the listener selects one stimulus that appeals to him and converts it into a message.

Interpreting: The listener seeks to draw the meaning from the message.

Evaluating: The listener reviews the meaning, draws the inference, seeks accuracy of information and evidence.

Remembering: Listening serves the purpose only when it is recorded. A person may take notes or create a mental picture for effective remembrance.

Responding: The listener has to act on the message received. He has to ensure to the speaker that he has received the message. He does this by verbal means such as using expressions like *I see, I understand, Is it so?, yes, correct, okay, right,* etc., and non-verbal means like nodding one's head in approval, showing one's thumb, raising one's hand, etc.

TYPES OF LISTENING

Listening can be of different types. They are as follows:

Informative listening

It refers to a situation where one listens to understand the message. Much of the learning happens through informative listening. Students listening to lectures, workers listening to understand the work practice or procedures and listening to instructions, briefings and speeches are all examples of informative listening. Vocabulary, concentration and memory are the three components that influence informative listening. The words one uses, the degree of attention one pays to what is being said and the extent of one's memory all play a supportive role to informative listening.

Fake listening or Passive listening

Fake or passive listening is only hearing the message delivered by the speaker without taking the message in to the mind for memory. For example watching television or listening to the radio represent passive listening.

Selective listening

The listener chooses to listen to what needs to be stored in memory and ignores the rest of what is heard.

Attentive listening

When people listen attentively, their goal is to understand and remember what they are hearing. In this case, the listener himself contributes his inputs to the speaker so that he can create an impact.

Emphatic listening

The listener takes in the message delivered in writing and spirit. He moves from his preconceived notion and allows himself to be influenced.

Relationship listening

Listeners like counsellors, mentors and medical doctors listen to the other person to understand them completely. Similarly, one can listen to a friend or acquaintance and allow him to talk about his troubled emotions. Here listening fosters the relationship between the listener and the speaker.

Appreciative listening

Listening to music for enjoyment, listening to speakers because one likes the speakers' style, listening to a favorite show on the radio, television or a film are examples of appreciative listening.

Intuitive listening

It is the power above reasoning. It leads one to have a direct insight into the truth. A mere hint, an undertone or silence is enough to read the other person's mind. Deep listeners have the power to develop a hunch above what is said. A classic example is that of a good mother knowing the child's mood and responding appropriately.

Discriminative listening

The listener makes keen note of every aspect of the speaker's speech like volume, pitch, tone, emphasis and force. Usually, informative listening involves discriminative listening. In other words, the listener listens to every aspect of what is delivered in a speech.

BARRIERS TO EFFECTIVE LISTENING

Effective listening can be hampered due to various reasons. The barriers to effective listening are:

Impaired faculty: When the faculty of hearing is faulty, a person cannot be an effective listener. Unless he seeks medical assistance, he cannot improve his listening skills.

Jargons: Use of jargons or too much simplification of ideas may come in the way of effective listening.

Mental preoccupation: When a person's mind is preoccupied with something, his listening efficiency is reduced.

Egoistic listener: When the listener is less knowledgeable, he may listen to information within his understanding.

Speaker's invisibility: When the speaker is not visible to the listener or when there is no face-to-face interaction, listening effectiveness suffers.

External stimuli: External stimuli like sound, odour, light, voice, moving objects, etc., can distract listeners and reduce their listening effectiveness.

Listener's mood: Listeners' mood, attitude, emotional well-being, all influence listening ability.

Speed of speech: The speed of speech has an impact on listening. The average speaking rate is 125-150 words per minute and the average listening rate is 500 words per minute. Both speedy delivery and slow delivery leaves the listener with idle time which causes his mind to wander.

Inappropriate feedback: Inappropriate feedback like premature comments, biting comments from audience, restless crowd, etc., may demoralise the speaker, who in turn confuses the listener.

Physical surrounding: Physical conditions like poor acoustics, uncomfortable seating, physical discomfort, distracting noise, etc., reduce the listening effectiveness.

Listener's prejudice: The absence of seriousness on the part of the listener because of his prejudice forms a listening barrier.

Narrow review: Some people tend to evaluate what is being said from their own point of view and are unable to carry out post-speech analysis which shows in their response to the speaker.

Speaker's status: The listener's impression of a speaker's status determines the success or failure of communication.

STEPS FOR BETTER LISTENING

The following are some tips for effective listening:

Encourage the speaker: Encourage the speaker by using phrases like *Please go ahead*, *Tell me about it*, etc.

Donot interrupt the speaker: Never interrupt the speaker! Even if you already know the subject that the speaker is speaking on, you have to listen to it. A show of knowledge by the listener reduces the speaker's interest.

Avoid external disturbance: Avoid external disturbances to ensure effective listening.

Maintain silence during speech: When someone else is speaking, one should only listen in silence.

Exhibit your interest: Demonstrate your interest in the speaker's speech through facial expressions or active questions.

Defer any judgement: Suspend your judgement to avoid premature evaluation.

Give no place for prejudice: Listen to the speech without any preconceived notion or prejudice.

Make the speaker feel comfortable: Make the speaker feel at ease by smiling and saying soothing words so that the speaker delivers his speech to his full potential.

Provide time to the speaker: Give the speaker sufficient time to clarify his point.

Total listening: Let your listening be total and not selective.

Donot allow negative emotion: The listener should not have any negative emotion that mars the listening effectiveness.

SUMMARY

Listening process involves sensing, interpreting, evaluating, remembering and responding.

Types of listening include informative listening, fake listening, selective listening, attentive listening, emphatic listening, relationship listening, appreciative listening, intuitive listening and discriminative listening.

The steps to improve listening are encouraging the speaker, not interrupting the speaker, avoiding external disturbance, maintaining silence during speeches, exhibition of interest in the speaker's speech, deferment of judgment, not having prejudice, making speakers feel comfortable, providing time to the speaker, total listening and not having negative emotions.

REVIEW QUESTIONS

Part A: Short Questions

1. Distinguish between hearing and listening.

Part B: Paragraph Questions

1. State the stages in the listening process.

Part C: Essay Questions

1. What are the types of listening?
2. Suggest measures to improve listening.
3. Discuss the barriers to effective listening.

Part D: Objective Type Questions

Choose the correct answer

1. Casually watching TV or listening to music radio is

   a. Active listening b. Passive listening

   c. Attending d. Intuitive listening

   (Ans: b)

2. Trainees listening to instructions given at a training seminar is an example of

   a. Appreciative listening b. Active listening

   c. Fake listening d. Relationship listening

   (Ans: b)

Fill in the blanks

1. Listener paying attention to other person on three different levels through mind, body and emotion is ______________. (Active listening)
2. Listening with empathy is ________________. (Relationship listening)
3. Listening to a selective aspect of a speech is _____________________. (Selective listening)

6

CHAPTER

BARRIERS IN COMMUNICATION

INTRODUCTION

Communication is said to be successful only when the message is received by the receiver in time and the latter understands the sense of the message in the way it is intended by the sender. But there are several hindrances or barriers that may disrupt communication. Misunderstanding, irrelevant response and undesirable reactions are the consequences of a failed communication. Besides, communication failure results in loss of valuable time, resources, material and even life. The following chart explains the barriers in communication.

MECHANICAL BARRIERS

In case of a failure in the mechanism through which communication passes, the message may not Teach the intended person in the intended form and volume. Possible mechanical failures include poor sound quality, faulty telephone lines, computer system breakdown, poor printing quality and signal problems in radio or television during adverse weather conditions.

PHYSICAL BARRIERS

Time, place, space, climate and noise may hinder the flow of communication.

Time

Messages not delivered in time become useless. An organization that wants quick results may not give instructions to the concerned employees to get the task done in time. Time differences among the countries also delay timely communication. The control rooms monitoring the movement of vehicles may not provide timely information to the crew, thereby causing accidents and traffic chaos. All these emphasize the importance of the time element in the communication process.

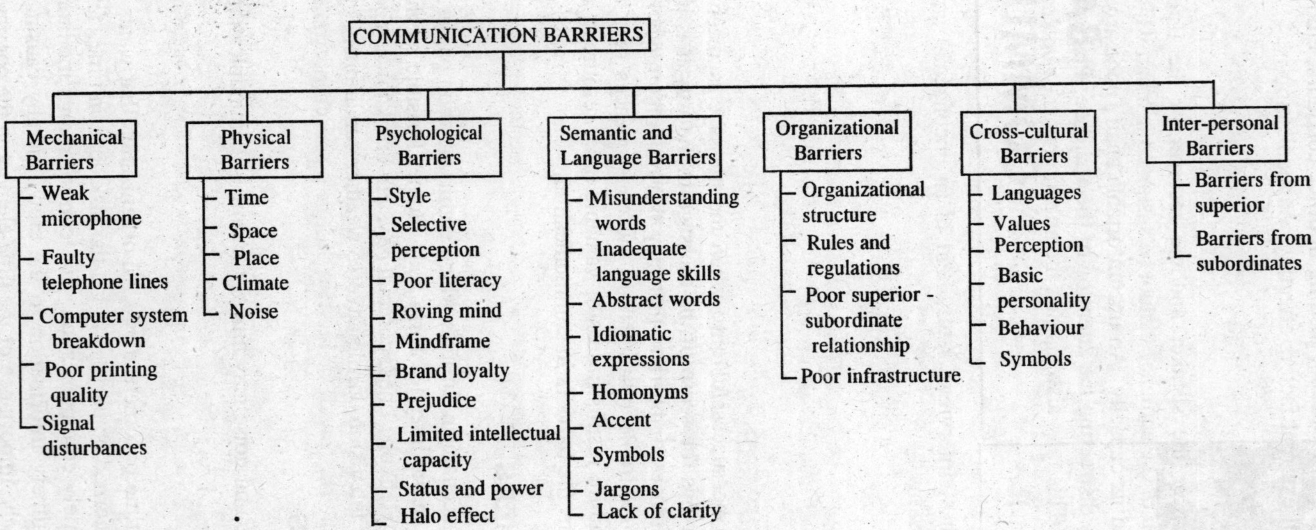

Fig. 6.1 Communication Barriers

Space

It represents the distance between the sender and the receiver. It may be one of the barriers to communication. Overcrowding in elevators, jostling in office corridors, elbowing others in public transport system, etc., are all external factors affecting communication.

Place

The place where the sender or the speaker and the receiver or the listener exist influences communication. The attention of the audience cannot be sustained in a hall which is poorly lit, badly ventilated and packed beyond its capacity. An uncomfortable chair, poor acoustics, poor lighting, etc., are some of the reasons distracting the attention of the audience. Places near vehicular traffic are prone to noise pollution. This may also distract the attention of the audience.

Climate

Talks, conversations, speeches, interviews, etc., held in an uncongenial ambience may lead to misperception or wrong decisions.

Noise

Noise distorts the message and thus acts as a barrier.

PSYCHOLOGICAL BARRIERS

Individual or psycho-sociological barriers are the major bottlenecks in inter-personal communication. The meaning assigned to the message depends upon the emotional and psychological status of both the sender and the receiver in the process of communication.

Style

It is the manner in which a person communicates. Lack of proper style can cause barriers in communication.

Accent variation: Differences in accent affects the clarity in comprehension.

Avoiding idiomatic expressions: Usage of idioms and phrases may not go down well with the audience. So, a limited use of such expressions is advisable.

Over-dosage of humour: Too much of humour in one's speech prevents the main message from reaching the audience.

Brevity: Choice of brevity where full detail is required has the potential to suppress the material information.

Selective perception

Some people who live in their self-created world take in only those pieces of information that they feel relevant. This attitude leaves them with incomplete and inappropriate information.

Poor literacy

Poor literacy undermines one's understanding of certain messages.

Roving mind

A person with a wandering or roving mind cannot fully gather the inputs given to him. This results in less attention or limited attention span. Sometimes visual or audio distractions too inhibit attentiveness of the listeners.

Frame of mind

The emotional state of a person can act as a barrier. When a person is influenced by emotions like anger, shock, fear, depression, cheerlessness, etc., he may not be able to listen alertly.

Brand loyalty

When a person is loyal to a particular brand, he may not be receptive to another brand. He may not even relish the praises or compliments heaped on the rival product.

Prejudice

Racial, communal and religious prejudices blind a person from reasoning out the facts.

Limited intellectual capacity

Limited intellectual exposure, limited reading and parochial interest cause a person to be narrow-minded. People with closed minds do not appreciate the suggestions given for their betterment.

Status and power

Status and power may hinder the communication process and affect the communication effectiveness. For example, seniors may not listen to smart juniors.

Halo effect

Good impressions formed due to earlier occasions (halo effect) causes a person to lend a deaf ear to the negative information about the other person.

SEMANTIC AND LANGUAGE BARRIERS

This occurs when the speaker (writer) means one thing and the listener (reader) understands it as something else. For example, a person gives an advertisement for selling a fierce dog which actually refers to the attacking power of a dog to guard the house. But the reader may misunderstand it.

Some common reasons for misunderstanding are listed below:

1. The meaning of words differ according to the context in which they are used.
2. Idiomatic words should not be taken in their literal sense. For example, *go to dogs* means *to be ruined*. It does not mean that we have to go near dogs.
3. A person's own opinions may be given as facts.
4. Using abstract words can send a wrong message. For example, instead of saying students of a certain *college are bad*, generalising it as *students are bad* conveys a different meaning.

5. Inadequate language skills lead to wrong choice of words or words with associative values. For example, people say that *My boss's behaviour towards juniors is good,* while the proper usage would be *My boss's treatment of juniors* is good.
6. Homonyms distort the meaning. For example, there and their; once and ones.
7. Differences in accent hinder effective speech delivery and understanding of listeners.
8. Inadequate vocabulary is a handicap in communication. The speaker may insert a word from another language when he does not know the equivalent word in the language he is supposed to be using.
9. Symbols cause communication problems. For example, the swastika is worshipped by the Hindus while the reverse swastika is a Nazi symbol.
10. Poor composition of speech, harsh voice, lengthy paragraphs, verbosity, etc., spoil communication effectiveness.
11. Use of technical the jargon creates confusion between the sender and the receiver.
12. A sender sending confusing messages may lead the receiver to make his own assumptions.
13. Lack of clarity, precision and coherence leads to the creation of a bad message.

INTERPERSONAL BARRIERS

Communication effectiveness depends on the relationship between two people, the sender and the receiver. There are superior and subordinate barriers that affect the free flow of communication between them.

Barriers originating from superiors

Superiors may not spend enough time with subordinates for discussion and clarification.

Suppression of information: Superiors may deliberately suppress necessary information from subordinates.

Reluctance to listen to subordinates: A superiors' unwillingness to listen to subordinates acts as a barrier to effective communication.

Inadequate information: In some cases, superiors share inadequate information or give incomplete and inaccurate information. Moreover, the instruction issued may be confusing. But, out of fear, subordinates may not seek clarification and this acts as a barrier to effective communication.

Misguidance: Superiors may misguide subordinates, which results in them doing the job wrongly.

Barriers originating from subordinates

Fear Psychosis: Subordinates may not seek adequate clarification wherever necessary from superiors due to fear.

Filtered information: Subordinates send only selective information to the superiors for fear of being penalised.

Over/under reporting: Subordinates over/under report their performance.

Difficulty to express: Subordinates do not disclose their practical difficulties in completing a task for fear of being mistaken.

Withholding suggestions: Subordinates may not suggest workable solutions to a problem due to lack of incentives for their effort.

Personal inadequacies of subordinates: Poor educational background, insufficient communication skills, inferiority complex and lack of confidence of subordinates debilitate the communication process.

CROSS-CULTURAL BARRIERS

Culture is a shared set of values and attributes of a group. It is the way of living built by a group which is transmitted from generation to generation. Culture differs in terms of language, values, norms of behaviour, concept of time and space, perception, basic personality, national character etc. Words, colours and symbols can have different meanings with different cultures. Here are the examples to illustrate this point:

- Wearing a white colour dress is inauspicious in some countries while it is the wedding dress in others.
- When a Japanese says *yes*, he means *he is listening;* however, *yes* in American means *I agree.*
- Punctuality is the norm in some countries while it is a matter of convenience in other nations.

Thus communication can acquire different connotations and meanings due to cross-cultural barriers.

ORGANIZATIONAL BARRIERS

Organization culture

The climate and culture of an organization influences freedom, trust and interaction patterns among its people. It may take time for employees in any organization to get used to the climatic variables. In this context, communication bottlenecks are inevitable.

Rigid Rules: Information flow in an organization is dependent upon rules and regulations that are in effect. Rigid and strict rules block free flow of communication.

Poor communication infrastructure: Communication infrastructure for different forums like meetings, seminars, conferences, etc., influence communication effectiveness.

Organizational structure: Organization structure like *flat organization, vertical organization* etc., impacts the communication network. While a flat structure eases flow of communication, a vertical structure slows it down.

Poor working relationship: Communication flow depends upon the relationship between the superior and the subordinates. Strained relations and lack of co-operation hinders communication flow.

MEASURES TO IMPROVE COMMUNICATION BARRIERS

The following measures address the barriers to communication:

Procedure simplification: Simplification of procedures, authority delegation and decentralization would address the barriers to communication.

Encouraging two way communication: Encouraging two-way communication coupled with good feedback avoids distortions.

Clarity and completeness: The message sent should be clear, complete, concise, concrete and correct. It should be of interest to the listener.

Patient listening: Patient listening is one of the most important and most neglected skills in communication. Listening with emphatic understanding clears misunderstanding and makes communication effective.

Speedier method of communication: Choosing speedier means of communication avoids delayed communication.

Pictorial presentation: Presentation of information in a pictorial narrative and graphical form adds to the appeal value.

Informal communication: Use of informal communication in addition to formal communication makes the communication effective.

Simple language: The language used should be simple, straightforward and easy to understand.

Seating comfort: Provisions for comfortable seating, good acoustics, use of noise proof materials etc., create a conducive atmosphere for communication.

Use of right word: Usage of the words such as *we* in place of *I, me, and myself* creates a bond between the speaker and the listeners.

Cross-cultural meet: Arranging cross-cultural get-togethers, address communication barriers on the cultural dimension.

Audience analysis: Audience analysis should precede the speaker's address for effective presentation of speeches.

Verbal communication: The speaker must supplement his verbal communication with gestures and postures.

More communication channels: Providing more communication channels like meetings, get-togethers, conferences, seminars, celebration of events and milestones achieved by the company, releasing newsletters, counselling, brainstorming, mentoring sessions etc., brings the employees close to the management and clears up the air of misunderstanding, thereby avoiding the spread of rumours and gossips.

SUMMARY

Barriers to communication encompasses mechanical barriers, physical barriers, psychological barriers, semantic and language barriers, interpersonal barriers, cross-cultural barriers and organizational barriers.

Measures to tone up the communication procedure include simplification, encouraging two- way communication, clarity, completeness and conciseness of the message, patient listening to be cultivated, choice of speedier methods of communication, pictorial representation, use of informal communication as a supplement to formal communication, simple language, augmenting seating comfort, arranging cross-cultural meet, audience analysis, provision of more communication channels.

REVIEW QUESTIONS

Part A: Short Questions

1. What is meant by barrier in communication?
2. What do you understand by physical barrier?
3. What is meant by mechanical barrier?
4. What is psychological barrier?
5. What is semantic barrier?
6. What is interpersonal barrier?
7. What is cross-cultural barrier?
8. What is organizational barrier?

Part B: Paragraph Questions

1. Write a note on mechanical barrier.
2. What are the physical barriers in communication?
3. What are the interpersonal barriers in communication?
4. Write an explanatory note on cross-cultural communication barriers.
5. What are organizational barriers in communication?

Part C: Essay Questions

1. What are the psychological barriers in communication?
2. What are the semantic barriers in communication?
3. Elaborate on the various types of communication barriers.
4. Write down the measures to address communication barriers.

Part D: Objective Type Questions

State whether the following statement are true or false.

1. Barriers arising from different meanings of a word form semantic barrier. Ans: True
2. In attention or poor attention is psycho-sociological barrier. Ans: False

Choose the Correct Answer

1. A message sent from Bombay to Chennai very belatedly is an example of

   a. Physical barrier
   b. Mechanical barrier
   c. Psychological barrier
   d. Organizational barrier

   (Ans: a)

2. Using idiomatic expression, technical jargon and poorly organised speeches are barrier.

   a. Semantic barrier
   b. Psychological
   c. Organization barrier
   d. Encoding

   (Ans: a)

3. The process of ensuring that the receiver has understood the message is

   a. Decoding
   b. Sending
   c. Feedback
   d. Encoding

   (Ans: c)

4. Barriers springing form inattention, poor memory, prejudice, mental block are

   a. Language barrier
   b. Sociological barrier
   c. Psychological barrier
   d. Mechanistic barrier

   (Ans: c)

Fill in the blanks

1. Barriers arising out of different meanings assigned to a word are called ____________. (Semantic barriers)
2. Barriers springing from organizational climate, culture, policies etc., are ____________. (Organizational barriers)
3. Barriers resulting from difference in cultural values, beliefs of the sender and receiver are ____________. (Cultural barriers)
4. Barriers of distance, defect in medium environment and noise are ____________. (Physical barriers)

PART 2

BUSINESS CORRESPONDENCE

7

CHAPTER

INTRODUCTION TO BUSINESS WRITING

The term *correspondence* means communication by exchange of letters, telegrams, written messages etc. Written communication passes between individuals, firms or companies who have business contacts.

IMPORTANCE OF BUSINESS CORRESPONDENCE

The importance of business correspondence can never be over-emphasized. A large part of the world's business is done through mails, written or through a computer. Given below are some points stressing the need for proper business correspondence.

To cope up with increased volume of business

The need for business correspondence was not so keenly felt in olden days as it is today because the area of business operations was confined mostly to local limits. With the advancement of science and technology, the volume of business has increased multifold. Business letters are required to keep close and uninterrupted business relations with customers spread world wide. In the competitive business world of today, commercial communication occupies a unique position.

Business correspondence expands markets

With the advent of industrial revolution and the consequent expansion of world trade, contact with people in distant countries can be maintained only through correspondence. Correspondence opens up new markets and creates valued customers even in distant lands. Through correspondence, the businessman gets vital information on the habits and tastes of his customers and on the financial standing of his dealers.

A weapon to combat competition

To face the stiff competition, an effective business letter is a strong weapon. Correspondence helps a businessman in knowing the changing tastes of people, finding reasons for the popularity of his competitor's goods and in arresting the sagging demand of his own products. Thus, it enable the business to face even cut–throat competition.

Lifeblood of modern business

A variety of business letters like enquiries, circulars, collection letters, complaints and adjustment letters, correspondence with banking and financial institutions, raising claims with transport and insurance companies have all become such essential business activities that business correspondence is viewed as the *lifeblood of modern commerce*.

Easy access to all

Letters reach even those people who cannot be approached easily because of their busy schedule. Letters have the advantage of waiting until the reader is in a position to devote time to them.

Evidence of business transactions

Its greatest value lies in providing written evidence of the communication that has passed between the parties concerned. In case of disputes, they can be furnished as effective proof of contracts which have been agreed upon earlier.

Prevents unpleasant misunderstanding

Agreements reached over a telephonic conversation must be confirmed by means of a letter. If they are not confirmed in writing, misunderstandings may develop in the future, leading to unnecessary disputes. Ultimately they embitter business relations too. A confirmation by means of a letter avoids such an unhappy situation.

Avoids unpleasantness of miscommunication

The use of certain epithets at some unguarded moments during business conversations harm business relations. But business letters are written with care and after enough thought. Angry outbursts have no place in business letters.

Avoids annoyance

A stiff refusal at a personal interview is unpleasant and sometimes irritating. But a politely worded letter explaining reasons for such a refusal will make the person understand and appreciate. Thus, business correspondence guards against unpleasantness and annoyances.

Dispenses with personal interviews

Personal interviews with parties for concluding contracts can be easily and profitably eliminated. In a personal interview, there is usually not enough time to consider the pros and cons of a transaction. But settlement by means of correspondence leaves sufficient time for a thorough and deep analysis and avoids hasty decisions.

Low cost of sales promotion

Effective sales letters and attractively designed circulars can even replace travelling salesmen. As a result, payment of salaries, commission, travelling allowances, etc., can be, to a large extent, saved. Business correspondence thus becomes an economical and convenient instrument of sales promotion.

FUNCTIONS OF BUSINESS CORRESPONDENCE

It is indeed true that commercial correspondence goes a long way in opening up trade relations, maintaining them and in promoting business growth. The functions performed by commercial correspondence are discussed below:

Reference function

When incoming letters and copies of outgoing letters are carefully and systematically filed, they serve as a ready reference. The attention of the addressee can be drawn to the company's earlier letters or to addressee's letters to enforce compliance with performance.

Evidence function

Correspondence can be produced as evidence for supporting or opposing a business contention. Business letters are also accepted as evidence in courts of law.

To clear misunderstanding

Whenever a dispute arises, earlier business letters can be produced to eliminate misunderstanding and to establish the correct position of the company.

Sales promotion

Effective sales letters couched in an attractive language promotes sales. They even replace travelling salesmen there by reducing cost of sales promotion. While face-to-face conversations may not last long in memory, effective commercial correspondence creates a favourable image.

Promotion of goodwill

Business letters are very effective in fortifying the reputation of the company, thus strengthening its goodwill. While new customers are created, the existing ones are retained. Good business letters can soften the angry customers and pacify the disappointed ones, thereby promoting business.

CHARACTERISTICS OF A BUSINESS LETTER

A business letter, to be effective, must satisfy the following essentials:

Know what to say

The writer should first know what exactly is to be communicated. He should grasp all the necessary facts and then arrange them systematically.

Clarity

The words and phrases should be carefully arranged so that they convey the exact meaning. Flowery expressions and unnecessary words tire the reader and obscure the meaning. In short, a good letter is one that contains simple, clear-cut and unambiguous sentences.

Conciseness or Brevity

The business letter should be brief and to the point. Brevity does not mean omitting essential facts; it only requires that all irrelevant facts and figures be avoided.

Accuracy

The statements in a business letter should be accurate. False and misleading statements will have a damaging effect on the reputation of the business house and will result in the loss of profitable customers.

Completeness

A reply letter must furnish full and complete information that are requested. Otherwise, unnecessary further correspondence may become essential.

Courtesy

Courtesy is an essential attribute of a good business letter. Politeness costs nothing but it wins friends and pacifies even an offended person. A courteously worded letter wins the loyalty and co-operation of the subordinates too.

Even when a request is to be rejected, the letter should be worded so as to not annoy or irritate the other party.

Pleasant

Every business letter should be a pleasure to read. Even a refusal loses much of its sting if it is carefully worded.

Avoid commercial english

The correspondence should avoid commercial expressions that were fashionable in the part. For example, in the expression, '*with reference to your esteemed favour of the 5th inst*' instead of 'esteemed favour', 'letter' can be used. Some examples of commercial english which should be avoided are *we beg to acknowledge receipt, we would be greatly obliged, if you would be so kind as to....*

Forceful and convincing

This characteristic is essential in letters relating to a prolonged negotitation. A stereotyped letter will have no effect. Arranging the facts in the best possible order and using forceful expressions will make the letter convincing.

PHYSICAL ASPECTS OF BUSINESS LETTERS

Since people are often influenced by appearance, the appearance of a letter is as importants as its contents. The design of the letter head, the neatness with which it is typed, the quality of the paper used etc., can create a favourable impression in the mind of the recipient about the firm. A sales letter, the physical appearance of which is attractive, is sure to win the favourable attention and hence secure orders. The important physical aspects are:

Paper

Quality: Cheap paper lowers the image of the firm. Paper of a superior quality creates a lasting memory.

Colour: White is the popular colour widely used for business letters. If tinted paper is used, it should be of a light shade.

Size: The commonly used paper sizes are 8 inches x 10 inches as followed in UK or 8.5 inches x 11 inches as followed in the USA. Foolscap paper (34.5 cm x 21.5 cm) is used for letters or applications addressed to Government departments.

Typing

A letter generated using a computer creates a more pleasing impression and more legible than a hand written letter.

Margin

There should be margins of a reasonable width on all sides of the typed matter. Very small margins affect the beauty of a letter.

Folding

A letter should have a minimum number of folds. Careless folding and consequent refolding creates an unfavourable impression.

Envelope

The envelope should be corresponding to the paper not only in colour but also in size. Long envelopes should not be used for letters of small size.

KINDS OF BUSINESS LETTERS

With the widening of the area of business operations along with the stupendous increase in the volume of business done by each business unit, business letters take different forms and are of diverse varieties. The various kinds of business letters are briefly discussed below:

Enquiries and replies

These are meant for knowing the availability of goods, price lists, terms of trade, request for lowest quotations, etc., and replies from business units.

Offers and quotations

These are letters in the form of a circular announcing offers of goods, cautioning the probability of poor supply in the future and emphasising the benefits of buying while the goods are still in stock. Letters containing quotations sent in response to an offer therefore state the rates at which the goods will be offered on sale.

Orders and their execution

Letters placing orders with firms for the supply of specified quantities of goods, letters intimating execution of orders or requesting condoning of delays also come under this category.

Status enquiries

Letters written to business houses to ascertain the advisability of granting credit to specified parties when fresh applicants approach them for credit are called *letters of status enquiries*. The persons addressed are the firms furnished as references by such applicants.

Replies furnishing opinion on the credit-standing of parties referred also come under this type.

Complaints, claims and adjustments

Letters of complaints are many. They may be with regard to poor quality of goods supplied, short supply, delay in the execution of orders etc. Replies assuaging the wounded feelings require to be drafted with tact and courtesy.These are called *adjusment letters*.

Circular letters

These letters convey a message to number of clients who may be customers, business friends, dealers etc. For example, shifting of business to a new premises, obtaining an new agency, clearance sales, retirement of a partner etc.

Letters relating to an agency

Applications requesting the grant of an agency, letters granting an agency, letters seeking reasons for poor sales performance, etc., come under this type.

Collection or Dunning letters

These are letters demanding settlement of dues, granting extension of time for payment, threatening legal action against continued default etc.

Application for a post

These refer to applications put in for appointment to advertised posts or vacanices in a company. Appointment letters and letters verifying references will also come under this category.

Recommendation letters

They may be testimonials or letters introducing business friends to other business houses.

Letters relating to export and import

These comprise letters seeking price quotations, placing orders with foreign suppliers, advice of shipment, advice of sales, etc.

Bank correspondence

Correspondence of the business house with their bankers is very frequent. Some of them include standing instructions to bankers, letters regarding dishonoured cheques and requesting loan facilities. Correspondence between the bankers and business houses includes asking the business house to produce more securities. Letters from banks to their head offices and vice versa, letters from one bank to another bank also come under this type.

Insurance correspondence

Requests for cover against damages by fire or water, notice of damage by fire along with the claim, and replies of insurance companies accepting liability or rejecting claims, all come under insurance correspondence.

Secretarial correspondence

The correspondence of the company secretary with the directors, shareholders, office staff, registrar of joint stock companies, with various government bodies, banks, stock exchanges etc., come under secretarial correspondence.

Correspondence with government departments

No business unit can function without having to do deals with the various government departments. Obtaining licences, submission of various statistical data, seeking clarifications on various government orders, all come under this category.

SUMMARY

Importance of business correspondence includes coping with the increased volume of business, expansion of markets, acts as a weapon to combat competition, lifeblood of modern business, easy access, evidence of business transactions, avoids misunderstanding, miscommunication and annoyance, dispenses with personal interviews, low cost sales promotion.

Functions of business correspondence are reference functions, evidence function, clearing up misunderstanding, sales and goodwill promotion.

Characteristics of a business letter are knowing what to say, clarity, conciseness, accuracy, completeness, courtesy, pleasant, avoiding commercial english, forceful and convincing.

Physical aspects of a business letter are the quality, colour and size of the paper, typing, margin, folding and the envelope

The kinds of business letters are letters of enquiries and replies, offers and quotations, orders and their execution, status enquiries, complaints, claims and adjustments, circular letters, letters relating to agency, collection letters, applications, letters of recommendations, letters relating to export and import, bank correspondence, insurance correspondence, secretatial correspondence and correspondence with government departments.

REVIEW QUESTIONS

Part A: Short Questions

1. What is business correspondence?
2. What is status enquiry?
3. What are dunning letters?

4. What are circular letters?

Part B: Paragraph Questions

1. What are the functions of business correspondence?
2. State the physical aspects of a business letter.

Part C: Essay Questions

1. Write about the importance of business correspondence.
2. What are the characteristics of a business letter?
3. What are the different kinds of business letters?

Part D: Objective Type Questions

Choose the correct answer

1. Letter written to number of people conveying message

   a. Collection letter   b.Circular letter   c.Status enquiry letter

   (Ans:a)

2. Letters intended for collection from debtors comes under

   a. Circular letter   b.Dunning letter   c.Adjustent letter

   (Ans:b)

3. Collection letters are also called

   a.Status enquiry letter   b.Adjustent letter   c.Dunning letter

   (Ans:c)

4. Letters assuaging the wounded feelings of complaintents is

   a. Adjustent letter   b.Dunning letter   c. Circular letter

   (Ans:a)

5. Letters seeking advisibility of granting credit to a party is

   a. Circular letter   b.Dunning letter d.   c.Status enquiry letter

   (Ans:c)

Fill in the blanks

1. Letter written to business houses to ascertain the advisability of granting credit are __________. (Status enquiry)
2. Reply to a complain letter assuaging the wounded feelings are called __________. (Adjustment letter)
3. Letters conveying a message to a number of people is called __________. (Circular letters)
4. Letters demanding settlement of dues are called __________. (Collection letters)
5. Collection letters are also called __________. (Dunning letters)

8

CHAPTER

STRUCTURE LAYOUT OF A BUSINESS LETTER

COMPONENTS OF A BUSINESS LETTER

The different parts of a business letter are :

- Heading
- Date
- Inside Address
- Salutation
- Body
- Complimentary Close
- Signature
- Enclosure and Post Scripts, if any

Heading

The name of the firm, its postal address and the nature of its business are all given at the top. The heading printed at the top of the letter is called the *letter head*. Though the name and address are usually centered at the top, the address is sometimes given in the right–hand corner too, a little below the name. Since the letter head itself has publicity value, the layout of the heading is usually designed by a commercial artist.

* EF7 PVR: rrn.
* OF4 Encl: Illustrated catalogue
OF5 CC
OF6: Mr. K. Paari – General Manager.

* Essential Feature
* Optional Feature

India Handlooms

Telephone: 87165288

Cable: Entireness
63, Wilcokson Road
Chennai – 7

(or)

Modern Furnishing House Limited

Post Box No.172
171, Anna Salai,
Chennai – 600 022

Date

This is written on the right hand side of the letter, below the heading. This gives the date, month and the year. Since date facilitates quick reference, this should never be omitted.

It is better to avoid abbreviations for months. Do cut short the year as '85. Date can be written in any one of the following ways:

22nd February, 2011

(or)

February 22, 2011

The practice of writing the date as 3-8-11 or 3/8/11 should be discouraged.

Inside Address

This inside address consists of the name and address of the firm or the individual to whom the letter is addressed and is written at the left margin and few spaces below the date line.

It can be written in a indented form as shown below or in the blocked form.

Vijai Nicole Publishers
14/66, Rodier Mil Street
Pondicherry – 605 004

Addressing individuals

If a letter is addressed to an individual, the name should be preceded by *Mr. or Shri*. While *Miss or Kumari* is used for an unmarried lady, *Mrs.* (abbreviation of Mistress) *is used for married ladies.*

In all official correspondence of the Government of Tamil Nadu, India, *Selvi* is used for an unmarried lady, Thirumathi for a married lady and *Thiru* for men.

In the case of women, if they have any special title such as Dr. Prof. etc., their marital status may be indicated within brackets after the special title. Example: Prof. (Mrs) Sasikala Ashok.

The word *Messrs* is used before the name of a firm trading under a personal name, while the article *The* is used before the name of a firm with an impersonal name.

Salutation

Sir and *Madam* are used in official correspondence while *Dear Sir*, *Dear Madam*, *Dear Mesdames*, *Gentlemen* are commonly used in commercial correspondence. The word *Sirs* or *Gentleman*, is not used.

In circular or sales letters, saluation such as *Dear customer*, *Dear member* are also used. The first and the last words of the saluation should begin with capitals.

Body of the letter

This part of the letter contains the message to be communicated and hence is the most important part.

Opening paragraph: This may commence with an expression of thanks or pleasure, or with a reference to the letter that is being replied.

Main paragraph: This should be brief and to the point. It should be written in simple but effective words. Each aspect of the subject should be written in a new paragraph. Short paragraphs are preferable. It should always be borne in mind that a business letter should deal with only one subject.

Closing paragraph: This should consist of a few sentences which must motivate theaction. In sales letters, this part of the letter must be so effectively worded that it should register in the reader's memory. It must be noted that the final paragraph should not end with participle phrases such as *Trusting to be favoured with your order* or *Thankingyou in anticipation for your order*.

Complimentary close

This must correspond with the saluation used. The most commonly used forms are *Yours faithfully*, *yours truly* or *yours very truly*. The first letter of the closure must be in capital letter and a comma should always follow a complimentary close. The complimentary close should never be abbreviated.

Signature

This is placed below the complimentary close. The signature of the concerned authority is made here. The name of the firm can be written first followed by the signature and closed by the designation. For example,

Yours faithfully,
for Vijai Nicole,
R. Madhavan

(or)

The Southern Sales Corporation Limited,
K. Fredman
Secretary

When an employee signs a letter as a legal authority (when he is given a power of attorney), he is said to sign per procurationem (per pro or P.P.). For example,

Per Pro Queens Limited,
Sharma
(or)
P.P. ABC Limited,
Sharma

In the case of ladies signing the letters, they should indicate their marital status within brackets along with their signatures such as (Miss) Radha (Signature) or (Mrs.) K. Punitham (Signature).

Enclosures and Postscripts

In case the letter is accompanied by any enclosure, this fact must be indicated by the nature of the enclosure such as draft, price list, Railway Receipt (RR) etc.

Postscript (P.S) means *Written afterwards*. Since this is written after the letter is closed, it points to the carelessness of the letter-writer, and hence should be avoided. Sometimes it may not be unavoidable. For example, some information may be received after the letter is signed. In such a case, it can be incorporated in the letter under postscript. This should be signed or initialed by the writer.

Indication of the dictator and the typist

The initials of the person typing it are indicated in the left hand margin like PSK/AS. The initials before the oblique dash point to the initials of the dictator and the latter to those of the typist.

GENERAL LAYOUT

(i) Heading ____________________

(ii) Date ____________________

(iii) Your Reference ____________________

Our Reference ____________________

(iv) Inside address ____________________

____

(v) Attention ____________________

____

(vi) Salutation ____________________

____

(vii) Subject ____________________

(viii) Body ____________________

____

____

____

(ix) Complimentary close ____________________

(x) Signature ____________________

(xi) Identification Marks ____________________

(xii) Enclosure ____________________

TYPES OF LAYOUT

A business letter is to be prepared in a particular manner, arranging each part in a particular place on the letterhead. Arrangement of these parts while typing as per a plan is called a *Layout*. The purpose is to ensure that each part is visible clearly to the reader, so that he need not waste time in locating every part containing an information.

There are three types of layout by which a letter can be written:

- Full Block Mathod (Block Method)
- Full Indant/Indent Method(Hanging Style)
- Semi-Block Method (Mixed Style)

Full Block Method (Block method)

When a line of any part is written blocking the space next to the margin, it is called *block method*. Each line (except the reference number and date which are printed on the letterhead with space for typing them) of every part is typed touching the main left hand side margin blocking space leaving three-line space between each part. It is a time saving method originated in America. Hence it is also known as *American Style*. But the letter written in this method is not very beautiful to look at.

Sketch showing Full Block Method of Layout of a Business Letter

Telephone: ____________

Mobile No: ____________

1. Name of Sender

(Details of Business)

Address

____
____
____
____

2. Ref No: 3. Date ____________

4. Inside Address

____
____
____
____

5. Sub: ____________

6. Salutation ____________

7. Introductory Para ____________
____
____

Main Body ____________
____

____

Closing Para ____________________
____
____

8. Complimentary close

Sd/-

(Name)

9. Designation

For: __________

10. Encl: 1. __________
2. __________

11. Copy to: 1. __________
2. __________
3. __________

Full Indent / Indent Method (Hanging style)

In this type of layout, each of the lines following the first line of *Inside Address*, *Subject*, *Enclosures* etc., are typed in different margins. This is also known as *Hanging Style*. This method consumes a lot of time for preparing a letter, and is also shabby to look at. Hence this method has been out of practice for a long time.

Sketch showing Indent Method of Layout of a Business Letter

Telephone: __________ Telegram: __________

Post Box No: __________ Telex: __________

1. Name of Sender

(Details of Business)

Address

____
____
____

2. Ref: __________ 3. Date: __________

4. Inside Address

____
____
____
____

Ref: __________ (Receiver's reference) __________

5. Sub: __________

6. Salutation ________________

7. Introductory Para ____
____
____

Main Body ____
____
____

Closing Para ____
____
____

8. Complimentary close

Sd/-

(Name)

9. Designation

For: ________________

10. Encl: 1. ________________
2. ________________

11. Initials of Dictator and Typist

12. Copy to: 1. ________________
2. ________________
3. ________________

Semi-Block Method (Mixed style)

In this style of layout, some parts are typed in block method and other parts are in indent method. This is the most widely followed method in our country especially in Government offices. Since the letterhead is evenly spaced with the matter both on the left and right hand side, it is more beautiful to look at.

It should be noted that every part should be typed normally in single line space only. The main purpose of arranging the various parts of a letter, whatever type of layout in which it is prepared, is for the receiver to identify each and every part clearly. This is done by giving more space between every two parts.

Sketch showing Semi-Block Method of Layout of a Business Letter

Telephone: ________ Telegram: ________

Post Box No: ________ Telex: ________

1. Name of Sender

(Details of Business)

Address

____

____

____

2. Ref: ________ 3. Date: ________

4. Inside Address ________

____

____

____

Ref: ________ (Receiver's Reference) ________

5. Sub: ________

6. Salutation ________

7. Introductory Para ________

____

____

Main Body ________

____

____

Closing Para ________

____

____

8. Complimentary close

Sd/-

(Name)

9. Designation

For:

10. Encl: 1. ________

2. ________

11. Initials of Dictator and Typist

12. Copy to: 1. ________

2. ________

3. ________

USAGE OF CERTAIN WORDS AND TERMS

Certain words and terms are commonly used in business correspondence. The usage of some of these are explained as follows:

Messrs

The word Messrs is the abbreviation of the French word Messieurs.

It should be used before the names of firms trading under a personal title. For example,

Messrs Chatterji & Sons,
35, Chittaranjan Avenue,
Calcutta.

However, in the following cases the word 'Messrs' should not be used:

- If the company has an impersonal name, only the article *The* must be put before the name and not Messrs. For example,

  Correct: The New Century Book House (P) Limited

  Wrong : Messrs New Century Book House (P) Limited

- Even when a firm has a personal name but a title forms part of the name, the word Messrs should not be used. For example,

  Sir A Ramaswamy Mudaliar & Co

  Sir Isaac Pitman & Sons Limited

When a personal name forms a part of the name of a firm but is not the important part, Messrs should not be used. For example,

Sundaram Motors Limited (Here the word *Motors* is the principal word.)

Esquire

The word *Esquire* or its abbreviation *Esq.* is used after the names of professionals like doctors, advocates etc.

In Great Britain, the word Esquire was used in the past to address the graduates of Universities, members of the House of Commons and members of certain professions. The name of the trader was written with only *Mr.* Now a days, *Esq.* is used for all men other than manual workers.

Usage:

M.Bava Mohideen,Esq.,
21, Main Road
Coimbatore

- Whenever Esq. is used after the name, Mr should not precede it.

  Correct: M. David, Esq.

  Wrong: Mr.M.David, Esq.

- If the first name or the initials does not precede a name, Esq. should not be used.

Correct: C.Richard,Esq.

Wrong: Richard,Esq.

- Letters denoting academic degrees should follow Esq.

Correct: M.S.Paul, Esq.,M.A.,M.S.

Wrong: M.S.Paul, M.A., M.S., Esq.

- When a person already has a title and uses it before his name such as Dr., Prof., Rev., Capt, Lieut, Major, Col etc., Esq. should not be used.

Wrong: Prof.S.Kasim, Esq.

Correct: Prof.S. Kasim.

Per Pro

The word Per Pro or merely P.P. is the abbreviation of *per procurationem* meaning representative of another. An employee may be authorised to sign letters, cheques etc., on behalf of the firm. This authority may be granted by executing a legal instrument known as *Power of Attorney*. When he signs under such a legal authority, he is said to be signing *per procurationem*. For example,

If Mr.V. Spring is authorised to sign letters for Metal Trading Corporation, he will sign as:

Per Pro The Metal Trading Corporation

V. Spring.

(or)

P.P. The Metal Trading Corporation

V. Spring.

Attention Line

When it is desired that the letter should be attended by a particular person in the addressed firm, a direction to that effect should be given in the letter, below the inside address but above the salutation.

This is usually mentioned in the middle of the line and underlined. For example,

Messrs.A.Roosevelt & Co.,

171, Anna Salai,

Chennai 600 002

Attention: Mr.A.Paterson

(or)

For the attention of Mr.A. Paterson

Dear Sirs, ...

Subject Matter

If the subject matter is indicated briefly, it would be convenient to the recipient of the letter. This brief, one line mention of the major theme, adds to the clarity. Hence, this is usually given below the saluation. This is typed in the centre of the letter head. The last line should be underlined.

Sometimes the word *Re* (Regarding) is also used in the place of subject.

Dear Sir,

Re: Payment of Bills-Extension of time.

Reference Number

Reference number in a letter is of immense help, both to the firm sending out the letter and the firm receiving it, for back reference or for sending replies. This is given just below the subject but before commencement of the body of the letter.

The reference number usually indicates the previous letter to which this forms the reply. For example,

Dear Sir,

Sub: Payment of Bills—Extension of time.

Ref: Your letter dated 2nd January 1985.

(or)

Your letter No. 17/c/85 dated 2nd January 1985.

Enclosures

Whenever any price list, catalogue, cheque, railway receipt, way bill, invoice etc., is sent with a letter, it should be indicated in the letter after the signature at the left margin.

Methods of indicating enclosures:

- It may be mentioned as follows:

  Encl 1 or Encls 3. (*Encl* is the abbreviation of the word *Enclosure* and the number indicates the number of items enclosed).

- The nature of the enclosure itself may be noted such as

  Encl: Draft for ₹ 5,000.

  This helps the dispatch section in seeing whether any enclosure has to accompany the letter. The recipient of the letter can also verify whether all the stated enclosures have been received.

Illustration of address, salutation and complimentary close

Example	Form of Addresss	Salutation	Complimentary Close
A firm of ladies with personal names *Thamizh* and *Ezhil*	Mesdames Thamizh and Ezhil	Mesdames	Yours faithfully
ABC Limited	Messrs ABC Ltd.	Dear Sirs,	Yours faithfully
Novelty Ltd.	The Manager, The Novelty Ltd.	Dear Sir,	Yours faithfully

Example	Form of Addresss	Salutation	Complimentary Close
Dr. K. Sundar	K. Sundar, Esq.M.B.B.S.	Dear Sir,	Yours faithfully
Rev. A. Mariadoss	The Rev. A. Mariadoss	Rev. Sir,	Yours faithfully
Mayor of Chennai	The Worshipful Mayor of Chennai	Sir,	Yours Worship's Obedient
Director of Collegiate Education	The Director of Collegiate Education	Sir,	Yours faithfully,
V. Keishna Iyer (Judge of High Court)	The Honourable Mr. Justice	Sir,	Yours respectfully
Post Master General	The Postmaster General	Sir,	Yours faithfully
Dr. K. K. Vincent Member of Parliament	Shri K. Vincent, M P	Dear Sir,	Yours faithfully

In the case of the clergyman, the title Rev.(abbreviation of Reverend) must be used with the surname or as Rev.A.Mariadoss. However, if the initials are not known *Mr* should be used along with Rev. For example, The Re. Mr. Mariadoss.

COMMON ERRORS IN LETTER WRITING

Commercial English which was in vogue during the Victorian period has lost much of its charm these days. They have become meaningless jargons, lacking sincerity. The use of simple, natural English is preferred in commercial correspondence. For example,

No	Commercial English	Simple Usage
1.	Yours of the 18th instant to hand and the same shall receive prompt attention	We thank you for your letter of the 18th January 1985. It shall receive our prompt attention.
2.	We beg to acknowledge receipt of your favour	We have received your letter
3.	We enclose herewith or Enclosed please find	We enclose, We have enclosed
4.	I am to point out that the prices quoted are subject to a trade discount of 25%	The prices quoted are subject to a trade discount of 25% (The words *I am to point out*, are redundant)
5.	With a view to a discussion of the matter	To discuss the matter
6.	It will be appreciated that owing to fluctuation in price, it is impossible for us to quote	Owing to frequent price change, we are unable to quote
7.	Adverting to your favour	Referring to your letter
8.	We beg to thank you	Thank you for your letter, We thank you
9.	The favour of your early reply will oblige	I shall be glad to hear from you soon

No	Commercial English	Simple Usage
10.	Assuring you of our best attention at all times/Thanking you in anticipation/We beg to remain/A waiting the favour of your early reply	Meaningless endings. Hence better to avoid them altogether.
11.	As per	According to
12.	At you earliest convenience	As soon as possible
13.	Only too pleased to	Very glad to
14.	Please be good enough to advise us	Please tell us
15.	Contents noted	Unnecessary expressions and can be omitted
16.	2nd inst., Proximo, ultimo	Better to mention the name of the month.
17.	Our Mr. Antony	Mr. Antony, our Sales Officer
18.	Commence	Begin
19.	In the course of his speech, he talked on the question of security	During his speech, he talked about security
20.	Rules have been made for avoiding and settlement of disputes	Rules have been made for avoiding and settling disputes
21.	Achievement of this goal is not possible without the Co-operation of the staff	This goal cannot be achieved without the Co-operation of the staff
22.	We shall advise you as soon as goods are ready	We shall inform you as soon as the goods are ready
23.	We do not anticipate any difficulty in meeting your requirements	We do not expect any difficulty in meeting your requirements

SUMMARY

Structure of a business letter includes the heading, the date, the inside address, the salutation, the body, the complementary close, the signature, enclosure and postscript if any.

The types of layout are full block method, indent method and semi-block method.

REVIEW QUESTIONS

Part A: Short Questions

1. What is a business letter?
2. What is the inside address?
3. What is an indented form of a business letter?
4. What is meant by salutation?
5. What is complementary close?
6. What is per pro signature?

7. What is esquire?
8. What is postscript?
9. What is reference number?
10. What is semi-block method of letter layout?

Part B: Paragraph Questions

1. Where should Messrs be used and where should it not be used?
2. State the different methods of indicating enclosures.
3. Write a note on indented and blocked forms of writing the inside address.
4. Specify the functions of business correspondence.
5. State when the word *esquire* should be used.
6. What is the purpose served by subject matter in a business letter?
7. What is the significance of writing reference in a business letter?

Part C: Essay Questions

1. Explain the different types of layout or structure of a business letter.
2. Name the different kinds of business letters.
3. Bring out the significance of the physical appearance of a business letter.
4. Highlight the features of a good business letter.
5. State the need for a business letter.

Part D: Objective Type Questions

Choose the correct answer

1. What word given below means representatives

   a. Esquire b. Per pro c. Salutation d. Post script

   (Ans: b)

2. The word that is inviting the attention of the reader to the previous correspondence

   a. Enclosure b. Reference c. Esquire d. Salutation

   (Ans: b)

3. Abbreviation pointing to the status of professionals

   a. Reference b. Esquire c. Subject matter d. Salutation

   (Ans: b)

4. The appropriate word used to add message after a letter is closed is

   a. Per pro b. Postscript c. Esquire d. Enclosure

   (Ans: b)

5. When a company has an impersonal name, for example, The New Century Book House Pvt. Ltd., the correct usage before the name is

a. Messrs The New Century Book House Ltd.
b. The New Century Book House Pvt. Ltd.
c. Both are correct
d. Mr. New Century Book Ltd.

(Ans: b)

6. Which one of the following per pro usage is correct?
   a. Per pro The Metal Trading Company Vijaykumar
   b. P.P. The Metal Trading Company Vijaykumar
   c. Both are correct
   d. Both are wrong

(Ans: c)

7. When the writer of a letter is attaching something with the mail, what word is used?
   a. Post Script b. Attachment c. Enclosure d. Annexure

(Ans: c)

Fill in the Blanks

1. Name of the firm as postal address is given in ________ (letter head)
2. Addressing the receipient of the letter in an appropriate manner is ________ (Salutation)
3. The first letter of the complimentary close should be in ________ letter (capital)
4. Yours faithfully, yours truly and yours sincearly refer to ________ (Complimentary close)
5. Signature is placed below ________ (Complimentary close)
6. Arrangement of letters in a proper format as per plan is ________ (layout)

Rewrite the following sentences in straight-forward English:

1. With reference to your order of 10th instant, we have sent the goods by passenger train.
2. We have great pleasure in advising you that on the 1st prox, our Mr. Mohamed Ismail, will call on you.
3. In reply to yours of yester date, we very much regret the delay in executing the balance of your esteemed order.
4. Your esteemed enquiry of the 29th instant is duly to hand. We now beg to quote you for the supply of 20 tonnes of zinc ashes as requested.

Answers

1. The goods which you ordered on 10th January have been sent to you by passenger train.
2. We are pleased to inform you that Mr.Mohammed Ismail, our Sales Manager will call on you on 1st February, 1985.
3. We thank you for your letter of 11th January. We are sorry for the delay in carrying out the remaining orders.

4. We thank you for your enquiry dated 29th January 1985. As required by you, we quote our rates for the supply of 20 tonnes of zinc ashes.

Correct the following

1. 9 persons (Ans: Nine persons)
2. Twelve days (Ans: 12 days)

   (Rule: Figures must be used for numbers 10 and above; they must be spelt out below ten.)
3. Thirty five members attended (Ans: Thirty-five)

   (Rule: A hyphen must be used to join the compound numbers from 21 to 99.)

   4. 0.45 (Ans: 00.45)

   (Rule: Two zeroes must be placed before the decimal point in case there is no integer in a figure.)
5. Twenty-fifth December 1989 (Ans: 25 December 1989)

   (Rule: Date must be written in figures.)
6. (Rule: If O'clock is used to indicate time, the numeral must be spelt out.)
7. Please acknowledge receipt of this letter.

   (Ans: Please acknowledge receipt of this letter.)
8. The Sales Manager and not his assistant were responsible for this omission.

   (Ans: The Sales Manager and not his assistants, was responsible for this omission.)
9. One of the directors have resigned. (Ans: One of the directors has resigned.)
10. The committee is unable to agree on the proposal

    (Ans: The Committee are unable to agree on the proposal)
11. The committee have submitted (Ans: The committee has submitted)

    Rule: Here the committee is referred to as a single unit).
12. None have turned up for the meeting. (Ans: None has turned up for the meeting.)
13. Everybody are entitled the to vote at the meeting.

    (Ans: Everybody is entitled to vote at the meeting.)
14. Neither the chairman nor the the members has turned up.

    (Ans: Neither the chairman nor the members have turned up.)
15. Two-thirds of this pole are rotten. (Ans: Tow-thirds of this pole is rotten.)

    (Rule: The complete subject determines the number of the verb.)
16. Some of the files has been stolen. (Ans: Some of the files have been stolen.)
17. One thousand rupees are a lot of money for the poor.

    (Ans: One thousand rupees is a lot of money for the poor.)
18. The number of files missing are very small.

    (Ans: The number of files missing is very small.)
19. Mr. K.is more successful than me. (Ans: Mr. K is more successful than I am.)
20. We have received your order of Ist June 2011 and the same order is receiving attention.

    (Ans: We thank you for your order dated 1, June 2011 and will fill order early.)

9 CHAPTER ENQUIRIES, OFFERS, QUOTATIONS AND TENDERS

ENQUIRIES

Enquiry letter is a letter written by a potential customer who desires to buy goods and services offered by another organization, seeking information on various matters such as availability of goods, prices of certain goods, quality, trade terms, delivery mode, etc.

Occasions warranting enquiry

Traders write enquiry letters when:

- they want to buy new goods.
- they want to renew a contract under fresh terms.
- they discover new sources of supply.
- they want to have better terms.

A Letter of Enquiry

A letter of enquiry seeks information on varied matters, such as availability of goods, prices of certain products, quality, terms of trade, mode of despatch, etc. These types of letters are received most frequently in any business. There are two types of enquiry letters. They are Solicited letter enquiry and Unsolicted letter of enquiry.

Solicited letter of enquiry

When a letter of enquiry is sent in response to an advertisement inviting the reader to correspond with more particulars, it is called a solicited letter of enquiry.

Unsolicited letter of enquiry

Where a buyer takes the initiative to ask for information, it is called an unsolicited letter of enquiry.

Purpose of an enquiry letter

Some of the purposes for which letters of enquiry are sent are as follows:

1. To know the availability of certain goods of specified quality.
2. To know the current price of goods.
3. To ensure purchase of goods from the cheapest source of supply as letters of enquiry are addressed to a number of dealers.
4. To tap new sources of supply.
5. To know the details of allowed financing-credit.
6. To ask for samples.

Important aspects of an enquiry letter

As the required information is to be obtained without loss of time, the following points must be considered while drafting a letter of enquiry:

1. The purpose of enquiry must be clearly stated.
2. Details of requirement including the quality as well as quantity must be unambiguously described.
3. Order size may also be indicated. The supplier is likely to quote a lower rate in case of bulk buying.
4. If any special form of packing or mode of delivery is desired, it must be clearly mentioned.
5. The probable time required for delivery, terms of payment, discount allowable etc., must be ascertained.
6. If samples or patterns are desired before ordering for supplies, it must be indicated.
7. If the seller is approached for the first time, it should be indicated whether the purchase would be for cash or on credit. In case a credit purchase is planned, trade references must be invariably given.
8. It must be indicated that if favourable prices are quoted, frequent orders will be placed and there will be a large volume of business in the future.
9. Letters of enquiry should be brief, specific and clear. Sentences should not be long, but should be simple.

Reply Letter

Some hints for drafting replies to letters of enquiry

Giving prompt attention to an enquiry is done through a reply letter. One can use a reply letter as a sales promotion vehicle. The seller has to present facts about the goods/services to persuade the potential buyer to be his customer.

It must be realised that a letter of enquiry represents a real opportunity for turning a request for information into an order. Hence a reply to an enquiry must be carefully worded and it must be a goodwill-builder. The following are some of the points to be considered:

1. All enquiries must be answered promptly.
2. There should be a reference to the date and number of the enquiry. The reply to an enquiry must express appreciation of interest shown by the inquirer and must also express thanks. A brief sales message on the quality of service to be rendered should also be included.
3. Answers to all the questions must be furnished.
4. Terms of trade—if credit will be granted and if so, the period of credit allowed, discount on bulk buying, cash discount for prompt payment, time required to execute the order, place and mode of delivery—all these details must be furnished in clear terms.
5. The time for which the order is open must be clearly indicated (Firm Offer). The seller undertakes not to sell the goods before the expiry of the period for which the offer remains open.
6. Whether the price list or the catalogue is enclosed or has been sent separately should be stated.
7. In case sample or patterns have been sent, a mention should be made about it in the reply.
8. The reply should contain an assurance to furnish any further information needed by the buyer.

Sample Letters

Sample 1: Solicited Enquiry Letter

Paari Cycle Mart

(Direct Importer and Cycle dealer)

51, Prakasam Street,
Tambaram, Chennai - 45

12th June 2011

M/S Maria Doss Cycle Traders,
167, Ponnappan Road,
Pondicherry – 605 007

Dear Sir,

We are happy to inform you that we have just received a large supply of super bikes of superior quality from Japan. We can offer you a bike at the rate of ₹ 1,500 on FOR terms subject to a cash discount of 5% against cash paid within 7 days. We have booked nine orders from all over India for 75 per cent of our total consignment. We can offer you 400 bikes. This offer, however, will remain open only up to July 2011. We hope that you would avail yourself of this great opportunity.

Yours faithfully,
For Paari Cycle Mart,
K. Pallavan
Sales Executive

Sample 2: Solicited Enquiry Letter

Southern Sales Corporation

172, Tailors Road,
Royapettah
Chennai –600 004

17th February 2011

Messrs Janakiram Paper Stores,
14, Mada Street,
Cuddalore

Dear Sir,

You would be happy to know that we have been given dealership for fountain pens, ball pens, roller pens, gel pens and jotter pens produced by Reynolds Ltd. All these pens been have been made to match international standards. These pens last longer and refills with gel are also available. The company has been promoting the brand name through print and electronic media. They have announced a special offer which will remain valid till June 15th, 2011 as a part of their sales promotional measure. Their offers is as follows:

Discounts are 20 per cent for 10 dozens; 25 per cent for 50 dozens and 30 per cent for orders above 100 dozens.

As we are keen to increase our sales, we are passing on all these discounts to our retailers. We assure you that your orders will be executed promptly and would bear delivery charges at your godown.

An order form has been enclosed to enable you to send orders immediately in view of the ongoing examination season and the consequent demand for these pens.

Yours sincerely,
Ravanan. H
Sales Manager

Encl: order form/colour poster.

Sample 3: Solicited Enquiry Letter

Tamil Nadu Electrical (Pvt) Ltd.

(Leading retailers of all electrical goods)

25, Church Road,
Ernakulam,
Kerala – 682 011

15th March 2011

Ref: NEP/253/11

All India Electrical Pvt. Ltd.,
Brown House,
123, Milton Road,
Calcutta – 5

Dear Sir,

Sub: Ceiling fans Agency

Ref: Your advertisement in Newspapers.

We have read your advertisement in The Hindu, dated 10-03-11 for stockist of your Fast Tracker brand of fans.

We are an old and established firm in the city of Kerala. We deal in a wide range of electrical goods among other things. We are willing to take up dealership for your ceiling fans and would appreciate it if you would kindly send us your terms and conditions of awarding dealership. We can furnish you with satisfactory bank and other references.

Thanking you,

Yours faithfully,
R. Radha
Manager
For Tamil Nadu Electrical (Pvt) Ltd.

Sample 4: Unsolicited Enquiry Letter

A dealer in sunglasses drafts a letter asking for a catalogue.

Raj Opticals

1, Junction Road,
Tirunelveli – 627 756

30th July 2010

M/S Ansar Ali & Sons,
Chakla Street,
Mumbai – 400 056

Dear Sir,

As we intend to purchase large stocks of your sunglasses, please send us your latest catalogue and price list.

Should your prices and terms suit us, we will soon place an order on cash basis.

Yours faithfully,

P. Jayapandian

Proprietor

Sample 5: Rao & Sons require a large quantity of handloom shirts and lungis to execute a foreign contract. They write to National Handloom House Ltd., Chennai for quotation. Draft the letter of enquiry and the reply.

Rao & Sons

17, Veer Nariman Road,
Church Gate,
Mumbai – 400 020

22nd February 1991

The National Handloom House Ltd.,
234, Ramasamy Street,
Mannadi,
Chennai – 600 001

Dear Sir,

We are shortly going to export a large consignment of handloom shirts and lungis. We require 30,000 handloom shirts in three different sizes —85 cm, 90 cm, 95 cm in checks, stripes and plains of different shades and 30,000 pieces of lungis.

We will be glad if you kindly send us samples and pattern s of cloth in different shades with quotations for large quantities, at the earliest. Also please mention the time you would require to effect delivery.

Please note that we are looking for quality as goods are meant for export. If your prices and terms prove favourable, we hope to place large orders and that business will result to our mutual advantage.

Yours faithfully,

A.K.Rao

Manager

Sample 6: Drafting a suitable reply to an unsolicited letter of enquiry

The National Handloom House Ltd.

234, Ramaswamy Street,
Mannadi,
Chennai – 600001

25th February 2011

Messrs Rao & Sons,
245, Abdul Rahman Street,
Mumbai – 400 003

Dear Sir,

We are delighted to learn from your enquiry of February 22, 1991 that you are arranging for export of handloom shirts and lungis.

As requested in your letter, we have sent today under a separate cover, patterns of shirts and lungis in different shades.

	Medium ₹	Fine ₹
Shirts – 85 cms	75	90
90 cms	85	100
95 cms	95	110
Lungis – 100 x 80 counts	95	120
80 x 60 counts	40	50

Trade Discount at 20% is normally allowed for an order above ₹ 1,00,000. In view of the bulkness of order, we are pleased to allow T.D at 25%.

We require a period of 3 months from the date of receipt of order to complete execution.

You are aware how fast our 'Handmade' shirts and lungis sell. We are receiving many enquires from different parts of the country proving beyond doubt the superior quality and the unfading colour quality of our handloom products.

We believe you will find our terms quite competitive. We enclose an order form for your convenience.

Yours faithfully,
S. Selvanathan
Sales Manager

Sample 7: As a dealer in footwear having 50 branches in the State of Tamil Nadu and Karnataka, make an enquiry for a large number of pairs of chappals of different sizes.

BSC Sales Corporation

120, Nungambakkam High Road,
Chennai – 600 034

11th October 2011

M/S Lethochap Ltd.,
15, Gandhi Road,
Kanpur – 208 005

Dear Sir,

We are pleased to introduce ourselves as a dealer in footwear having 50 branches in the states of Tamil Nadu and Karnataka.

We like to place an order with you for 30,000 pairs of shoes and chappals of different sizes and qualities for the ensuing Christmas season.

We will be pleased to have your illustrated catalogues and also know your other terms of trade and the period of credit allowed.

Please note that this is only our initial requirement. In view of the large network of branches, we hope to place frequent repeat orders with you if we find your price and other terms favourable and most competitive.

We give below the names of two firms as references. We hope you offer us the most favourable terms.

Yours faithfully,
Mohamed Ibrahim
Partner

References:

1. Footwear Co,
77, Shivaji Road,
Mumbai – 400088

2. The Shoe Co Ltd.,
35, Dr. B.C. Ray Avenue,
Kolkotta - 700 053

Sample 8: Messrs Varma Brothers of Mumbai on receipt of catalogue from Sunshine Paints Ltd., are willing to place orders if higher rate of discount is allowed and carriage is borne by the supplier.

Varma Brothers

78, Ginjee Road,
Tindivanam – 604 001

30th July 2011

Messrs.Sunshine Paints Ltd.,
49, Victoria Crescent Road,
Chennai – 600 105

Dear Sir,

We thank you for your letter dated 27th July 2011 enclosing your catalogue. We are sorry to observe that your terms are not competitive, as another firm is prepared to allow a trade discount of 10% as against what has been allowed by you and to despatch goods freight paid.

In case you agree to bear the freight charges and allow us the higher TD, we would very much like to place orders with you for large quantities.

We like to hear from you soon.

Yours faithfully,
R. Nambiar
Partner

Sample 9: **Drafting a reply to the above letter of enquiry on behalf of Sunshine Paints Ltd.**

Sunshine Paints Ltd

49, Victoria Crescent Road,
Chennai – 600 105

4th August 2011

Mr. R. Nambiar,
Messrs Varma Brothers,
78, Ginjee Road,
Tindivanam - 604 002

Dear Mr. R. Nambiar,

We thank you for your letter of 30th July 2011.0

We carefully considered your request for a further discount of 3 percent but we regret our inability to concede it.

We would like you to know that our 'Sunshine Paints' is a well known name not only in this country but also in some of the Middle Eastern and African countries, through a 10 year sustained advertising campaign. It is no exaggeration to say that because of the superior quality of our paints, which does not peel off easily, they constitute the fast selling line of business.

In view of these factors, the discount of 7 percent offered by us is the maximum we can allow.

However, if each order is for ₹ 30,000 and above, we agree to bear freight charges.

We hope that you will take advantage of our special concession shown to you and look forward to the beginning of a pleasant business relationship.

Yours sincerely,
Superking
Manager

Status Enquiry

A letter seeking information from a businessman, credit information agencies or banks as regards to the financial standing, credit worthiness and the paying habits of new customers is called *status enquiry*. Since credit sales entail the risk of delayed payment or non-payment, status enquiry is made before establishing business relations with new customers.

Trade Reference

Whenever an unknown person orders supply of goods on credit terms or applies for an agency or distributorship, he will furnish *trade references*. In other words, trade references are names and addresses of firms or individuals who can be contacted for getting information about the credit standing of these applicants.

Contents of letters seeking status enquiry

The credit applicant who has given their name as reference.

The letters should seek information with regard to

- the advisability of granting credit upto a specified amount.
- the paying habits of the credit applicant
- his credit worthiness.

The letter should contain a promise to keep the information in confidence and a promise to help the party addressed on similar occasions.

Contents of letters giving status enquiry

- Though a reply to status enquiries should be mentioned non-committal, it should point to the general financial conduct and character of the party about whose credit standing, opinion is sought. If the reply is too vague, no definite opinion can be formed and status enquiries become useless.
- They should be brief as far as possible but should be clear.
- Opinion should be expressed based on personal experience and not on hearsay.
- The amount upto which credit can be granted safely need not be unless opinion on this point is specifically sought. If required, their experience can be stated like *we granted them credit upto ₹ 10,000/-*. This is better than giving a definite opinion.

- The period taken by the credit applicant for clearing the bill can also be stated.
- In case any unfavourable opinion is to be given, the better alternative is to emphasize one's inability to express an opinion to the person. It is also wiser not to mention the name of the firm.
- The letter should make it clear that the firm expressing opinion is in no way responsible for the information and that it should not be quoted.
- Such a letter should contain a direction that the information given should be treated in utmost confidence.
- All such letters should be marked *Private and Confidential*.

Sample 10: You have received an order for the supply of white printing paper for ₹ 10,000 on credit. Draft a letter requiring him to suggest two references.

Cuddalore Paper Mills Ltd.

1, Bodi Chetty Street,
Cuddalore – 607 101

4th May 2011

The Southern Sales Corporation,
33/7/E, T.T.E. ROAD,
Chennai – 600 014

Dear Sir,

We thank you for your order of 29th April. We greatly appreciate the opportunity you have given us to do business with your firm.

Since this is our first transaction with you, we must ask you for a couple of trade references. This is part of our regular routine in handling all new accounts.

Your account will be opened and your order carried out once this information reaches us.

It is our hope that this is the beginning of a long standing business relationship. We shall do our best to make it a pleasant and profitable one for you.

Yours faithfully,
K. Pallavan
Sales Manager

Sample 11: Seeking credit information (verifying status enquiry)

Draft a letter to a business house whom a fresh credit customer has referred seeking their opinion as to the advisability of granting credit.

Cuddalore Papers Ltd.

1, Bodi Chetty Street,
Cuddalore – 607 101

10th May 2010

The Chennai Paper Mart,
208, Bunder Street,
Chennai – 600 001

Dear Sirs,

We have received an order for the supply of white printing paper from the firm mentioned in the slip. They have given us your name as a reference.

We would be grateful if you could give us information regarding their financial status and your experience with this firm as a credit customer. In particular, we shall be pleased to have your advice as to whether it would be safe on our part to grant credit upto ₹.20,000/-.

Your estimate of their financial responsibility and their credit reputation will be very helpful to us.

Any information you may like to pass on will be kept confidential.

We would be glad for an opportunity to return this courtesy, should an occasion arise.

We enclose a stamped, addressed envelope for your convenience.

Yours faithfully,
K.Sundar
Sales Manger

Slip:
Southern Sales Corporation,
337/E, T.T.K. ROAD,
Chennai – 600 014

Sample 12: Giving status information (First model)

You have received an enquiry whether a credit to the tune of ₹ 20,000 can be granted to a business firm in your locality. Draft a favourable reply stating that the party enjoys good reputation in the market and you allow him credit for greater amounts.

Chennai Paper Mart

208, Bunder Street,
Chennai – 607 001

17th May 2011

The Sales Manager,
Cuddalore Paper Mills Ltd.,

Cuddalore – 607 101

Dear Sir,

M/s. Southern Sales Corporation, 52 Anderson Street, Chennai, about whom you have asked us on 10th May, has always had a good credit relation with us.

The firm has been our customer for five years and it has usually paid its bills in the first week of the month following purchase. Their dealings with us have usually exceeded the amount you have mentioned.

Further, their business contacts are widely respectable. Please note that this is our personal opinion of the firm given without any obligation on our part. Please treat this letter as strictly confidential.

Yours faithfully,
Taqi Mohammed Saied
Partner

Sample 13: Reply to status enquiry (Second model)

You have received an enquiry whether a credit for ₹ 20,000 be granted to a firm in your locality. Draft a favourable reply.

Karur Hardwares Co.

123, Pandiyan Nagar
Karur – 639003

8th December 2011

Messrs Paari and Sozhan & Co.,
123, West Boulevard Road,
Trichirapalli – 6200 115

Dear Sirs,

We have your enquiry dated 4th December and have the pleasure to inform you that the firm you have mentioned (name on the enclosed slip) has been our valued customer since 1980.

We have always found them straightforward and prompt in clearing the bills. They are known in the market for their integrity.

It is understood that one of the partners who has recently joined the firm is a man of vast resources and business acumen and the firm is expected to expand considerably.

We ourselves would not have any hesitation in granting credit for an amount beyond the sum mentioned by you.

Please note that this is our personal opinion for which we accept no responsibility and treat this information with discretion.

Yours faithfully,
Parithi
Managing Partner

Sample 14: Unfavourable reply due to lesser quantity of transaction (First model)

You have received an enquiry whether a credit to the extent of ₹ 50,000 may be allowed to a business firm in your locality

The Indian Porcelain Works

111, D.N. Road,
Mumbai 400078.

9th September 2011

M/S Shah Brothers,
C.R. Das Road,
Pune – 411026

Dear Sirs,

In reply to your enquiry of 6th September 2011, regarding the party whose name was on the enclosed slip, we can only say that our dealings with the firm have been too small to justify expressing any opinion on their credit standing.

Please treat this information as very confidential.

Yours faithfully,
(Mrs) Sasikala Ashok
Partner

Sample 15: Unfavourable reply on the ground of delayed payments and poor resources (Second model)

The Indian Porcelain Works

111, D.N.Road,
Mumbai – 400078

9th September 2011

M/S Shah Brothers,
C.R.Das Road,
Pune – 411026

Dear Sirs,

We have your enquiry dated 5th September 2011.

The individual you have mentioned and whose name is on the enclosed slip, has been our customer for less than a year and has a poor credit record with us. We are already having difficulty in collecting dues from him.

His credit limit with us was ₹ 20,000 but presently we are dispatching goods to him on a strictly cash basis.

Yours faithfully,
Nunnun
Partner

Sample 16: Unfavorable reply with a suggestion to reduce the credit limit (Third model)

The Indian Porcelain Works

111, D.N. Road,
Mumbai – 400078

9th September 2011

M/S Shah Brothers,
C.R.Das Road,
Pune – 411 026

Dear Sirs,

We have your letter dated 5th September 2011 enquiring about the credit standing of the party whose name is on the enclosed slip.

From the enquiries made about the party, it would be observed that his scale of business is modest and his contacts limited.

The credit he asked for appears a little ambitious and should be reduce considerably.

We hope we have been of assistance to you and that you will keep the information strictly confidential.

Yours faithfully,
V. Kalathar
Partner

Sample 17: Status enquiry

Sunshine Automobiles

30, Jawahar Street,
Manali,
Chennai 600 002

July 15, 2011

Our Ref: ww2 11/5/

(Confidential)

The Manager,
Karur Vysya Bank,
Gandhi Road,
Virugambakkam

Sir,

I have to state that the managing director of Southern Sales Corporation has asked for dealership in automobile. They have mentioned that they have been holding an account with your bank for the past 20 years. I request you to kindly enlighten us on the financial status of the Southern Sales Corporation. The information provided by you will be treated as confidential matter and it would help us to consider offering dealership to them.

Yours faithfully,
K. Maran
General Manager

Sample 18: Status enquiry from one bank to another

Syndicate Bank

34, Simson Street,
Mylapore – 600 011

The Branch Manager,
State Bank of India,Tambaram,
Chennai – 600 045

25th August 2011

(Confidential)

Dear Sir:

Sub: Status enquiry about Annamalai Eletronics, Tambaram.

We understand that Annamalai Electronics, Tambaram is one of your clients for more than a decade. Our client Sakthi Corporation has been approached by Annamalai Corporation for credit supplies of ₹ 6,00,000. I request you to kindly advise us whether you consider the grant of credit of such volume to Annamalai Electronics a safe business deal.

May I solicit an early reply from you so that our client may process your clients' order.

Thanking you

Yours faithfully,
G. Udayam,
Branch Manager,
Syndicate Bank.

Sample 19: Banker's reply to status enquiry from another banker

State Bank of India

24, Gandhi Road,
Tambaram,
Chennai – 600 045

29th August 2011

The Branch Manager
Syndicate Bank,
22, Bharathi Street,
Mylapore – 600 011

Dear Sir:

We received your letter dated 25th August,2011 enquiring about Annamalai Electronics, Tambaram. We enclose details about their constitution and credit worthiness for your perusal. This is expressed in strictest confidence and without any responsibility on our part.

Yours faithfully,
Vaigarai
Branch Manager,
SBI, Tambaram.

Enclosure

Status enquiry about: Annamalai Electronics & Co.

Constitution: Started in 1998 as a partnership firm of

Mr. K. Paari 5 years

Mr. P. Parithi 20 years

Estimated network: ₹ 30 Lakhs.
Reputation: Good.
Remarks: The firm enjoys a credit with us and their account is healthy.
Their term loans are regular for the past 5 years.

Sample 20: Banker's reply to enquiring bank about the client having unsatisfactory credit record.

State Bank of India

22, Shanmuga Road,
Tambaram,
Chennai – 600 045.

20th September 2011

To

The Branch Manager
Syndicate Bank,
40, SouthCar Street,.

Mylapore,
Chennai – 600 004

(Confidential)

Dear Sir,

We refer to your letter dated 16th September 2011 enquiring the status of Brutus & Co. We have received a reply from ICICI Bank Ltd., Chrompet and Karur Vysya Bank, Pallavaram. We must say that both the bankers have reported that Brutus & Co has slipped into non-performing category for the past two years and both the banks are about to file a recovery suit. As such, it is considered inadvisable to extend credit limit to them. This information is provided to you without any responsibility on our part.

Yours faithfully,
Sulai Mann
Branch Manager

Sample 21: Sellers reply to potential buyer refusing credit on the basis of unfavourable reply from bank

Good Luck Emporium

20, Nehru street,
Pondicherry – 605 010

August 15th 2011

To

Pondicherry Emporium,
24, Kosa Kadai Street,
Lawspet,
Pondicherry – 605 001

Dear Sir,

We refer to your letter dated 9th July 2011 and wish to state that we have given the matter our consideration. In the current context, we regret to extend credit facility to you. At the same time welcome you to have a trade relationship on C.O.D. basis and take the benefit of the good reputation our products enjoy in the market.

We hope to be of service to you.

Yours faithfully,
K.Ram
Sales Manager

OFFERS

An offer is a proposal made by a person to do or to abstain from doing something for another party. If the other person accepts the proposal, it becomes a valid contract.

The proponent makes an offer voluntarily. The trader sends the offer letter to select customers. The offer quotes a price and remains open for a given period for acceptance.

Difference between an offer and a quotation

Though the terms *offer* and *quotation* are frequently used as synonyms, there is a slight difference.

While a quotation is always furnished in response to an enquiry, an offer may or may not follow an enquiry. For instance, when a manufacturer or a wholesaler announces an offer of goods to a large number of customers, no enquiry precedes it. The offer, in such a case, assumes the form of a printed circular letter. Such letters are also known as *Sales Letters*.

Only when an offer is made to the inquirer, it is equivalent to a quotation. The objectives of making an offer are:

- to open up new markets.
- to strengthen the weak business relations and stimulate action.

Points to be remembered while writing an offer letter

1. An offer should not exaggerate facts.
2. It should point out the likelihood of poor harvest or impending shortage of goods.
3. It may also state that if there is a delay in receiving the order, the stock in hand is likely to be sold out.
4. It may also draw the attention of the customers to the probability of a hike in price as a result of increased levy of customs or excise duty.
5. If any special discount or allowance is granted to old customers, that should be stated. The period for which this concession would apply must also be specified.
6. The nature and quality of goods offered needs to be stated.
7. The mode and place of delivery i.e. FOB, FOR, ex-warehouse, etc., should be clearly indicated.
8. Terms of payment like for cash, on credit or against acceptance must be stated. Packing charges, if any, must be mentioned.

Types of Offers

An offer letter can be of different types depending on certain factors. They are discussed below:

Firm Offer

A firm offer is one where the seller undertakes to accept an order at the specified price and conditions within the specified time only.

When prices are expected to rise, it is difficult to quote a price. In such a situation, the seller keeps the offer of goods at the specified price open until the expiry of the period mentioned by him. Even if prices shoot up in between, he will charge only at the quoted rate. He keeps the goods unsold despite the heavy demand.

A firm offer is thus made when stock falls short of demand. The seller, by forgoing the benefits of rising price and passing on the benefit to the customer, builds up goodwill. A firm offer is usually given for a period of 3 to 15 days. It has no legal force.

Offer without engagement

When the seller does not make himself obligated to accept an order at the stipulated price without further negotiation, it is called *Offer without engagement*.

An offer only contains the price. It is not a quotation. The following chart compares the two:

Offer	Quotation
An offer quotes the price	It too quotes the price
It is made voluntarily	It is sent only in response to a specific enquiry
An offer is sent to all	Sent only to specific persons or parties
It is followed by an acceptance or rejection	It is followed by selection
Offer, when accepted, become a contract	It is an invitation to make a proposal, thereby entering into a contract

Revival Letter

When a customer drops out and ceases to buy from a supplier, the letter written to him by the supplier with a view to re-establishing his old contact, is called a *revival letter*.

Points to be stressed in a revival letter

1. An expression of regret over non-receipt of any order from the customer for the past few months.
2. A reference to the prevalence of cordial relations in the past.
3. No apparent cause for dissatisfaction which could have prevented him from placing repeat orders and a request to come out with any cause of dissatisfaction.
4. A reference to the recent expansion of business and to the stocking of a variety of better products.
5. Offer of more attractive terms.

Sample 22: A letter to your customers offering to supply 5 quintals of 1 kg tins of milk powder at 3 percent, 10 days, stating that this order will remain open only for seven days.

Miltin Products Distributors

178, Broadway,
Ahmedabad – 380 008

10th June 2011

Vasudevan & Co,
18 Junction Road,
Virdhachalam – 606 001

Dear Sir,

I am sure you would have had difficulties on account of non-availability of our Miltin products. .

Despite the heavy pressure of demand from local dealers, we offer you, our valued customer, five quintals of one Kg tin at ₹ 100 per tin of milk powder, FOR subject to 3% discount against cash in ten days.

Please note that this order is firm only till 5 p.m. on 17th June, 2011. We are sure you will take advantage of this offer.

Yours faithfully,
Miltin products Distributors,
M. Rathinam
Sales Manage

Sample 23: A sample letter informing your customers that you have been compelled to raise your prices owing to an increase in government duty. Add that you have resorted to raising prices rather than lowering standard of quality.

Erode Stainless Steels Ltd.

22, Kutchery Road,
Erode – 638 013.

2nd June 2011

M/S Jaffer Stores,
27 TH Road,
Kumbakonam – 612001

Dear Sir,

We know well that price-rise hits the consumers hard and causes dissatisfaction among customers whose satisfaction we always strive hard to sustain.

The recent catalogue which we have enclosed, points clearly to the upward revision of prices of all our items. We have not resorted to this to maximize our earnings, for we always operate on the principle of lower prices, higher turnover and fairer profits.

You must be aware of the steep recent hikes in excise duty and other taxes on stainless steel by the Government. The direct consequence of this is the raise in the prices of the various grades of stainless steel which is the main material for our products.

In the context of increased steel prices, we had only two alternatives.One was to lower the quality of our products to keep the price unchanged or to raise the prices so that quality is kept intact. This is to inform you that we prefer the second alternative and have decided not to compromise on quality. It is the quality of our products that has won esteemed consumers and enhanced their goodwill.

We hope that your quality-conscious customers would not mind paying the extra amount. Please note the compelling circumstances which have forced us to raise the prices proportionately.

We have every hope that you would continue your patronage as before.

Yours faithfully,
Kharim Bhoy
Secrsetary

Sample 24: Raj & Co., who used to buy large quantities, ceases to do business with you. Write a revival letter to ascertain the reasons offering him to induce to regain their custom.

Kitchen Comforts Ltd.

217, Al-Karim Trade Centre,
Ranigunj,
Secunderabad – 500 003

4th June 2011

Messrs Raj & Co.,
13, G.A.Canal Road,
Thanjavur – 613 005

Dear Mr.Raj,

We are sorry to find from the scrutiny of our records, that we have not received any orders from you for quite some time now.

We have not heard of any complaint from you against the goods supplied. It is possible that we might have unwittingly given you a cause for dissatisfaction.

If so, please feel free to write to us so as to enable us to make necessary adjustments. We would like to point out that we have set customer satisfaction as our primary goal.

We are indeed pleased to inform you that we have added many new products to our business. In keeping with our policy of offering old patrons our new products first, we have enclosed samples of a variety of kitchen appliances that we have recently started manufacturing.

Our revised price-list will indicate that our prices and terms are more favourable now. We also offer 'carriage paid' terms to our long-standing customers.

A blank order is enclosed for your convenience.We hope you would give us an other opportunity to serve you.

Yours sincerely,
For Kitchen Comforts, Ltd.,
Basheer
Sales Manager

Sample 25: Replies to letters asking for favours

Write a suitable letter for Chennai Cements Ltd., Ariyalur regretting inability to send goods carriage paid owing to narrow margin of profit. Stress the special features of your cement with a view to obtain the business.

The Chennai Cements Ltd.

Ariyalur – 605 801

9th September 2011

Villupuram Constructions,
138, Thiru V.K.Road,
Villupuram – 605602

Dear Sir,

We thank you for your letter dated 6th September 2011 for the supply of 500 bags of cement. But we regret our inability to accept your request that we should bear the carriage charges.

Please note that while quoting the price, we have offered the lowest rate, keeping a low margin of profit, since we consider you to be our valued and long-standing customer.

It is needless to mention the special features of our brand. They are known for their strength and high grade. The fact that demand for our product far exceeds its supply is a pointer to its unfailing quality.

We are sure that you now understand our difficulty in carrying out the order carriage paid and hope that you place an order on the originally offered terms.

Yours faithfully,
V. Sulai Mann

QUOTATIONS

Besides the price of the goods, the seller has to charge in his invoice various items of expenses incurred by him such as cost of packing, carriage to railway station or port, shipment charges, insurance premium, etc. A question arises as to who should bear these expenses and whether the price quoted by the exporter or the local seller should include them too. With a view to clearly indicate the expenses that the price quotation should include and the expenses to be charged separately, various price quotations are used. Some of them are as follows:

LOCO: This indicate the cost of goods at the place of purchase. The buyer will be responsible for all the expenses of moving the goods to the final destination. This quotation is also known as *Ex-warehouse* or *Ex-factory price*.

FOR (Free on Rail): This quotation is inclusive of all the loading charges of the goods into wagons. In short, this is the at-station price plus loading expenses.

At Station: This quotation includes expenses incurred upto the point of carrying the goods to the railway station.

Carriage Forward (Carr Fwd): Freight for the transport of goods to the destination of the buyer must be borne by the buyer.

Carriage Paid (Carr Pd): The seller is to deliver the goods at his cost to the buyer's destination.

C.O.D. (Cash on Delivery): This means that payment must be made on delivery of the goods to the buyer.

C.W.O. (Cash with Order): Cash must be sent along with the order; otherwise order will not be considered.

Franco or Rendu: When goods are quoted on these terms, the price includes all charges up to the delivery at the buyer's address.

Prompt Cash: This quotation requires payment of cash as soon as goods are delivered. Two to three days are allowed for payment so as to examine the goods.

2 per cent, 10 days: This indicates that if payment is made within 10 days of the date of invoice, 2 per cent discount will be allowed on the price quoted.

Sample 26: Arvind Garments, 5, Deshpriya Park East, Kolkotta, submits a quotation to City Cloth Centre, Chidambaram. Draft the letter offering a quotation.

Arvind Garments

5, Deshpriya Park East,
Kolkatta – 700 045

19th June 2011

M/S. City Cloth Centre,
2, V.O.C. Street,

Chidambaram – 608 001

Dear Sir:

We thank you for your enquiry of 12th June and we are pleased to quote as follows;

	Perdozen ₹.
Linen Handkerchiefs No.98.	96.00
Export Quality Handloom Handkerchief	240.00
Wollen socks (First Quality)	360.00
Woollen socks (Second Quality)	240.00
Woollen Pullovers 96 cms.	2400.00
Cost Wool Shirts 96 cms. (Full sleeves)	3600.00

The rates are ex-Railway station.

We allow 15 per cent discount with 30 days credit.

We believe you will find the quotation favourable and we enclose an order form for your conveniance.

Your faithfully,
Per Pro Arvind Garments,
C. Raghavan

Sample 27: Punitham Hardwares submit their quotation to Sarawathi and Brothers. Draft a suitable quotation letter.

Punitham Hardwares Ltd.

123, Nelson Maincam Road,
Kanpur – 208 007

25th July, 2011

Your Ref: Saq/MAS/12 dated July 10th, 2011.

Our Ref: 3x/756.
Saraswathi and Brothers,
1200 Rasak Street,
Pondicherry – 605 008

Dear Sir,

We thank you for your enquiry cited above. We are pleased to submit the quotation for the motors we sell. This quotation is subject to general and specific conditions printed below.

Model	Horse power	Price per piece ₹.
Suguna 100 X	10 H.P	25,000
Suguna 200 X	15. H.P	30,000
Maxmuller XXX	20 H.P	40,000

Yours faithfully,
A. Kumara Raj,
Manager
Proprietor

Specification: The price given above is based on the current price. It may raise subject to rise in production cost.

Payment Terms: Net 50 days.

When ordering please quote the number of this quotation.

Sample 28: Anna Nithi & Co gives a quotation to the Orient Trading Co. Draft a quotation letter.

Anna Nithi & Co. Ltd.

Manufacturers and Exporters of Woollen Textiles

5, Robertson Street,
Orissa – 751 005

5 th August 2011

Ref: 1/ap/sd/100/11.

The Orient Trading Co,
60, Samuvel Street,
Delhi – 110012
Sub: Sale of Woollen Textiles – quotation.
Ref: Your enquiry letter OTC/Pur/15 July
19/11/ 2011.

Dear Sir,

We thank you for your enquiry cited above. We place the following quotation for the items demanded.

1. Pattern A: 100 Raymond suiting @ ₹ 100 per meter - 10 Rolls
2. Pattern B: 200 Raymond suiting @ ₹ 210 Per meter - 15 Rolls
3. Pattern C: 140 quantifier suiting @ ₹ 140 per meter - 20 Rolls
4. Pattern D: 133 Digjam suiting @ ₹ 160 per meter - 10 Rolls

You will notice that these prices are exceptionally low. Yet we are allowing you a quantity discount of 20% for the purchases above ₹ 1,00,000. Besides this, we also give a cash discount of 3% if payment is made within a month's time. Other terms and conditions are

1. Packing charges extra @ 1%
2. Payment should be made by draft within 3 months after satisfactory dispatch of goods.
3. All disputes will be settled at high court.
4. All charges will be borne by the consignee.

We hope that you will find our terms competitive and will be kind enough to place an order soon.

Always assuring you of our best attention.

Yours faithfully,
For Annanithi & Co, Ltd.,
Sd/Paar
Manager

Sample 29: PVS Coal Suppliers gives a quotation to Om Steel Industries. Draft a quotation letter on behalf of PVS Coal Suppliers.

PVS Coal Suppliers

Regd. Office: 33, Central Avenue, Nagpur – 440002

Tel:0712- XXX XXXX email: pvs@satyam.netin

Ref: CSI777

April 15th, 2011
OM Steel Industries,
C-5, Royal Industrial Area,

Nagpur – 440016
Kind attn: Mr Mate, Works Manager.

Dear Sir,

Sub: Your query about supply of A and B grade coal.

We are pleased to receive your enquiry dated 5th April on the above subject and a quote with our rates for the supply of coal are as under:

Coal grade A

Price: ₹ 1700 PMT

Transportation: ₹ 900 per truck

Coal grade B

Price: ₹ 1600 PMT

Transportation: ₹ 900 per truck

Terms and conditions:

1. Advance payment @ ₹ 20,000 per truck is required, which will be adjusted in the bill.
2. The freight charges should be paid to the driver against the delivered material. The cost of any shortage exceeding 150 kg per truck, may be deducted from the freight and the balance amount paid to us in the name of Nagpur Roadways.
3. You will allow a shortage of 150 kg per truck.
4. We look forward to your order and thank you for your interest.

Yours faithfully,
For PVS Coal Suppliers Ltd.,
Sales Manager

TENDERS

It is a published advertisement issued by companies and government department inviting vendors or service providers to make their offer for supply of goods and services.

Agencies give tender notices. The willing suppliers respond to the tender notice. If the agencies approve the tender, it becomes a binding contract.

Guidelines for preparing tender

- The advertiser has to give his name and address at the top. Below, the advertiser's name, date and tender notice number should be printed.
- The authors giving tender should be stated. E.g. Martin Luther, M.D., ABC Ltd.
- The content of the tender includes:
    - i. Date and time of issue of the tender document
    - ii. Date and time of receipt of the tenders
    - iii. Date and time of opening tender
    - iv. Cost of tender document
    - v. Earnest money to be deposited.
    - vi. Eligibility criteria prescribed.
    - vii. The issuing authority of the tender reserves the right to accept or reject the tender without assigning any reason.
    - viii. Signature of the issuing authority.

Sample 30: Tender Notice

KSR Enterprises Ltd.

Gandhi Marg, Surat
Notice inviting Tenders

No.5/CE/2006 1st May 2011

The Purchase Manager, PVS Enterprises Ltd., Gandhi Marg, Surat, invites sealed tenders from Indian vendors for the supply of goods stated below. Further details are available in the tender documents available on our website www.pvs.org from where they may be downloaded.

1. Tender reference no. : NIT/121/2011
2. Items : Handicams, digital cameras worth ₹10 lacs (estimated)
3. Tender fee : ₹ 500
4. Earnest money deposit : ₹ 50,000

Note:

Date of issue of tender documents : 05-05-2011 to 20-05-2011
Last date for receipt of tenders : 23-05-2011 (upto 3.00 p.m.)
Date of opening of tenders : 24-05-2011 at 11.00 a.m.

The company reserves the right to reject any or all tenders without assigning any reason.

Sd/-
Purchase Manager

Sample31:Tender Notice

PRS Ltd Invites

15th May 2011

Professional Marketing Agencies

Khadi & Village Industries Commission (Ministry of ARI, Govt. of India) is an apex Central Government agency for rural industrialization, effecting annual sales of ₹ 10,193.34 crores of PRS products through 7000 sales outlets. In order to build and promote marketing of PRS products, it has intended to engage on product basis, panel of professional agencies. Offers are invited from professional agencies with a proven track record at National and Zonal Levels in marketing of basic consumer products particularly in the field of supply chain and distribution management, brand promotion, packing and design development, quality control and market research. Interested professional agencies may collect the brief along with the application form within 7 days and submit their offers at either of the following addresses:-

Tender Reference no:ABC/123/2011

Director (Marketing)	The Manager
PRS Ltd,	PRS Ltd
3,lrla Road, Vile Parle(w),	24, Regal Building,
Mumbai-400056.	Connaught Place,
Tel:022 – 2671 6670	New Delhi – 110056.
Fax: 022 – 26716680	Tel.: 011-23411651
	Fax: 011-23418126

E-Mail:karnaiisingh@kvlc.gov.in website: www.prs.org.in

Sample 32: Tender Notice

Chennai Corporation

Rippon Buildings, Park Town,

Chennai.

Tender Notice

Ref:TN/101/2011 30th June 2011

Sealed tenders in the prescribed form are invited for the following work from CMC's registered contractors of appropriate class who have done similar work in Government/semi-government or local self-government institutions of amounts mentioned against the work.

Sr.No	Name of work	Estimated cost (₹)	Cost of tender from (₹)	Eligible contractor
1	Maintenace of Central Garden for a period of One year	11,92,890	12,000	Work experience of 5 lakhs

2	Maintenance of Gandhi Garden for one year	4,41,440	4,500	Work experience of ₹ 2 lakhs

Note:

- Blank tender forms can be obtained from the office of the Garden Superintendent, Chennai Municipal Corporation, Civil Lines, Chennai after producing documents pertaining to eligibility of the contractor.
- Earnest money deposit to be paid in the form of DD/pay order from any local branch of a nationalized bank in favour of Garden Superintendent, Chennai.
- Recent income tax clearance certificate, sales tax clearance certificate and a document pertaining to eligibility for the contract will have to be submitted in a separate envelope (envelope no. I) along with the tender.
- Competent authority reserves the right to reject or accept any tender without assigning any reason.

Garden Superintendent
RMK, Chennai

Schedule of dates is as given below:

1. Sale of blank tender forms : From 01-07-2011 to 08.07.2011 (upto 2.00 p.m)
2. Submission of filled-in tender forms : 09-07-2011(upto 2.00 p.m)
3. Opening of tender forms : 9-7-2011 at 4.00 p.m.

SUMMARY

Status enquiry is a letter seeking information from a businessman, credit information agency or banks regarding financial standing, credit worthiness and paying habit of a new customer.

Reference is a list of names and addresses of people who can be contacted for getting information about the credit-standing of an applicant.

The content of status enquiry letter includes the name of credit applicant, advisability for granting credit paying habit of the credit-applicant his credit worthiness and a promise to keep the information confidential.

Points to be remembered while writing status information letters include non-commital reply, being brief, specifying the amount of credit period taken by the credit applicant for clearing the bill, disclaimer clause and instruction to treat the information as confidential.

Purpose of an enquiry letter is to know the availability of goods, the current price, tapping new sources of supply and to ensure purchase from cheap sources.

Points to be noted while writing an enquiry letter are mentioning the details of requirement, indication of order size, specifying mode of package, mode of delivery, time of delivery, asking for samples, giving trade references, promising large volume of orders in future if credit is allowed.

Points to be noted while writing a reply to an enquiry letter are answering promptly, mentioning of reference number, mention of terms of credit, indication of enclosure of catalogue and samples sent and assurances to supply further information if needed.

Quotation letter is written by the seller to the prospective buyer.

Offer is a proposal made by one potential party to another for sale or services. There are two kinds of offers—*firm offer* and *offer without engagement.*

Points to be noted while drafting an offer letter are the letter has to arouse interest, make a distinct promise, highlight positive features, persuade the reader to grab the opportunity, make a request for an action and tell the terms and conditions.

REVIEW QUESTIONS

Part A: Short Questions

1. What is an enquiry letter?
2. What is solicited enquiry?
3. What is an unsolicited enquiry?
4. What is status enquiry letter?
5. What is trade reference?
6. What is a firm offer?
7. What is a quotation?
8. What is a tender?
9. What is a review letter?
10. What is meant by Loco or Ex-factory price?
11. What is FOR?
12. What is COD?
13. Explain franco or Rendu.

Part B: Paragraph Questions

1. What points should be borne in mind while drafting a status enquiry letter?
2. What is the purpose of sending a letter of enquiry?
3. What are the points to be remembered while writing replies to letters of enquiry?
4. State the types of enquiry letters.
5. Distinguish between offer and quotation.

6. State the guidelines for preparing a tender notice.
7. Highlight the points to be noted while writing a letter of offer.
8. State the points to be borne in mind while writing a revival letter?
9. Distinguish between carriage paid and carriage forward.

Part C: Essay Questions

1. Write a letter of enquiry to a sunglasses dealer asking for a catalogue.
2. Write a letter to National Textiles asking for quotation for knitwears.
3. As a dealer of footwear, draft a letter of enquiry for larger number of pairs of chappals of different sizes.
4. Messrs Verma brothers of Trivandram, on receipt of a catalogue from Sunshine Paint Ltd, are willing to place an order if a higher discount is allowed and carriage is borne by the supplier. Draft a letter to this effect.
5. Write a letter to Canara Bank Manager from State Bank of India (SBI), Tambaram asking for details of Mohan Kumar, a current account holder.
6. Syndicate Bank has received a letter of enquiry from one of its customers seeking details of credit-worthiness of another person holding an account in Canara Bank. Write a letter of enquiry as a branch manager of Syndicate Bank to the branch manager of Canara Bank.
7. You have received an enquiry regarding whether credit for ₹ 2,00,000 can be granted to a firm in your locality. Draft a favourable reply.
8. Draft an unfavourable reply on the ground of delayed payment and poor resources on behalf of Indian Porcelain Works to M/S Shah Brothers of Pune.
9. Draft an unfavourable reply with a suggestion to reduce credit limit for the Indian porcelain Works to M/S Shah Brothers of Pune.
10. Write a letter for Aravind Mills, Ahmedabad to Aruvi City Centers, Chidambaram. Giving Quotation for 100 sets of kids ware, 110 sets of women's ware
11. Draft a letter to your customer offering to supply 5 quintals of 1 kg tins of milk powder at 3% and 10 days. State that the order will be open only for seven days.
12. Draft a letter informing one of your customers that you are forced to raise the price due to increase in government duty without reducing the quality of your product.
13. Write a revival letter to Saravana Brothers, who ceased to do business with you, ascertaining the reasons for stopping trade relations and offering him concessions to regain their patronage.

Part D: Objective Type Questions

State whether the following statement are true or false

1. Reply to a status enquiry should be non-commital. Ans: True
2. Reply to a status enquiry should be a lengthy letter. Ans: False

3. The question of furnishing trade reference arises in the case of unknown persons ordering supply of goods. Ans True
4. When a buyer takes initiative in asking for information, it is an unsolicited letter. Ans:True
5. A quotation is a specific offer sent by the seller offering sale/service in response to enquiry. Ans: True
6. Ex-warehouse means price quoted for goods at buyers warehouse. Ans:False
7. Revival letter is sent to new customer. Ans:False
8. Tender when it is accepted does not become contract. Ans:False
9. Quotation is sent to specific persons. Ans:True
10. Quotation is a contract. Ans:False

Choose the correct answer

1. To tap new source of supply, we write a

   a. Letter of enquiry b. Letter of quotation c. Letter of complaint

   (Ans: a)

2. To order goods, ____________ is written.

   a. Solicited letter b. Unsolicited letter c. Collection letter

   (Ans: a)

3. Letter clarifying the details sought by is

   a. Enquiry letter b. Reply letter c. Status enquiry letter

   (Ans: b)

4. Revival letter is sent to

   a. Old customer b. New customer c. Potential customer

   (Ans:a)

5. Quotation is a

   a. Specific offer b. General offer c. Anonymous offer

   (Ans: a)

6. Tender when accepted becomes

   a. Contract b. Agreement c. Contract for agreement

7. Loco price means

   a. Price at the place of purchase b. Price at the place of sale

   c. Price in transit.

(Ans: a)

8. Franco price means

   a. Up to delivery to buyers addressb. Up to delivery to seller's warehouse

   c. Up to delivery to buyer's port

(Ans: b)

Fill in the blank

1. Letter seeking information from businessmen regarding financial standing, credit worthiness and paying habit of a new customer is ____________. (Status enquiry)
2. Name and addresses of persons who can be contacted for getting necessary information about credit standing of applicant are known as

   ____________. (Reference)
3. Where a buyer himself takes initiative in asking for information, it is an ____________ letter of enquiry. (Unsolicited)
4. Where a letter of enquiry is written in response to an advertisement inviting the reader to write in for further details. It is a ____________.

   (Solicited letter of enquiry)
5. Revival letter is drafted to an ____________customer only. (Old)
6. Loco price represents price at the place of ____________. (Purchase)
7. Quotation is ____________ offer. (Specific)
8. Tender when accepted becomes____________. (Contract)
9. FOB means goods loaded free of cost on board and any expenses thereafter should be borne by the____________. (Buyer)
10. ____________pays delivery charges in a carriage forward price. (Buyer)
11. In ex-factory price ____________ has to bear the cost of movement of goods from the point of factory. (Buyer)
12. An offer without the guarantee of sale is____________. (offer without engagement)
13. An offer stipulating a time frame within which the buyer has to accept the offer is ____________. (Firm offer)

10

CHAPTER

ORDERS, THEIR EXECUTION AND CANCELLATION

ORDERS

Introduction

Business correspondence starts with an enquiry and follows with getting a quotation and execution of the order. Once the quotation is accepted, the next logical step for the buyer is to place an order and for the seller to fulfill the order. The order represents a commitment on the part of the buyer to pay for the product once it is executed. An order should be prepared with caution and meticulous care.

Main contents of an order letter

Since an order letter requesting goods constitutes a contract of purchase, proper care should be exercised in drafting it to eliminate subsequent doubts or misunderstanding. An order letter should contain the following points:

Description of goods: The letter should contain correct and complete particulars about the goods ordered, the quality, brand, grade, colour, size, etc. If orders are placed on the basis of a dealer's catalogue, the number or other distinguishing marks indicated in the catalogue must be specified.

Quantity: The quantity ordered must be stated precisely.

Packing: The type of special packing, if required, must be specifically stated.

Mode of Carriage: The buyer should state how the ordered goods should be delivered like goods train, passenger train, parcel post, steamer, etc. If delivery is to be made carriage paid, the seller normally selects the mode of transport.

Time and place of delivery: In cases where time is the essence of the contract, the order letter should clearly state the time before which delivery should be effected.

The price of the goods: The order letter should also mention the price at which goods are ordered. Even when the price and terms have already been settled, it is advisable to state the terms in the order letter as this will avoid any misunderstanding.

Mode of payment: The order letter should also clearly state whether goods are ordered on credit cash or against acceptance.

If a cheque or draft is enclosed, it should be mentioned in the letter.

Special Instructions: Special instructions regarding insurance of goods, etc., should be given at the end of the letter.

Model Letters

Sample 1: Ramanan & Co., Ram Nagar, Dindugal places an order with National Nutriments Co., Mumbai for the following items to be sent by passenger train, where the amount of the invoice is to be collected by negotiating the RR through Indian Bank.

Ramanan and Co.

28, Ram Nagar,
Dindugal – 624003

11th October 2011

The National Nutriments Co.,
Second Floor,
Nariman Point,
Mumbai – 400 021

Dear Sir,

Please send us by passenger train, Carriage forward the following items listed in your latest catalogue.

500 x 500 tins of condensed milk	@ ₹ 50.00
500 x 1kg tins of condensed milk	@ ₹ 90.00
500 x 1kg tins of Vitbon	@ ₹ 100.00
500 x 1kg tins of Nucafe	@ ₹ 90.00

Goods may be packed as usual and the R/R sent through Indian Bank, Dindugal.

Please see that goods reach us not later than 25th October, 2011.

Yours faithfully,
For the National Nutriments Co.,
S. Charles
Proprietor

Sample 2: The Managing Partner of Pondicherry Emporium places an order for 3 cases of velvet soap, each case containing 144 cakes by passenger train. Draft a model letter reserving the right to reject if delivered more than 10 days after the date of order.

Pondicherry Emporium

150, Mahatma Gandhi Road,
Panruti – 607 106

10th April, 2011

Narumalar Soap Ltd.,
17, Residency Road,
Bangalore – 560 025

Dear Sir,

We thank you for your quotation of 6th April, 2011 and the samples of Velvet Toilet Soap.

The reports of our customers to whom we have distributed the samples have found it quite satisfactory.

We request you to send us three cases of Velvet Toilet Soap as per the enclosed order form by Passenger Train and send the RR directly to us. As agreed upon, the order is on the terms of 2 percent 20 days.

As the goods are urgently required and the time factor is very important, we reserve the right to reject the goods, if they are delivered later than 20th April, 2011.

You may rely on us for giving repeat orders.

Yours faithfully,
R.Annamalai
Managing Partner

Sample 3: Confirmation of Order by Telegram

Draft a letter for Pondicherry Textiles, 14/66, Mudaliarpet, Pondicherry addressed to Radha Silk Emporium, Kanchipuram confirming the telegram for the supply of 30 silk sarees of pattern No. 15 and 10 silk sarees of pattern No. 20.

Pondicherry Textiles

14/66 Rodier Mill Street,
Mudaliarpet,
Pondicherry – 605 004

10th June 2011

Radha Silk Emporium,
11, Mamallan Street,
Kancheepuram 631 501

Dear Sir,

We thank you for your quotation dated 6th June 2011 and confirm our order sent today by telegram which reads as follows:

Send 30 silk sarees of pattern No. 15 @ ₹ 1000 each and 10 silk sarees of pattern No. 20 @ ₹ 2000 each. Despatch by ABT Lorry Services.

As the patterns are urgently required, please send them by ABT Lorry Service, Carriage forward to Pondicherry.

You may cover yourself by drawing upon us a bill payable by us at one month from the date of your invoice.

Please treat this order as most urgent.

Yours faithfully,
For Malar Textiles
A. Kumar
Sole Proprietor

Confirmation of Orders

An order represents the direction given by the buyer to the seller to dispatch or deliver goods as per the agreed terms and conditions. The person placing an order acts upon the information collected from catalogues, advertisements, etc. However, orders may be booked through voluntary offers, personal approach, agents and sales representatives. Order letter is a legally binding one. Therefore it needs to be drafted cautiously. Even if an order is placed over the phone, it is confirmed by a written letter or by electronic mail.

Contents of the order confirmation letter

An acknowledgement letter is a mark of courtesy. If there is a time gap between the time of receipt of order and the time of its execution or when the order has been received by telegram, it is customary to write such letters. Such a letter should contain the following points:

- In the case of a new customer, the acknowledgment letter should be personal in nature welcoming him to the list of other satisfied patrons.
- In the case of a regular customer, if the order placed is large-sized, it can contain an expression of thanks for the business.
- It should refer to the number and date of the order letter.
- It can contain essential points such as the description and quantity of goods, terms and conditions.
- In case the order letter is lacking in certain essential information, the acknowledgement letter, after thanking the customer for the order, should ask for the missing information.
- Where delay is anticipated because of low stock, the acknowledgement letter should thank the customer for the order and then express inability to supply goods immediately specifying the reason. If suitable substitutes are available, it can also contain a suggestion about it.

Sample 4: Reply to an order letter

Grand Bakers

12, Lawrence Road,
Cuddalore – 607 005

2nd June 2011

To
Kumara Raj & Sons,
14, Thomas Street,
Lawspet.
Pondicherry – 605 011

Dear Sir,

Thank you for your order dated 29th May, 2011 for 10,000 cartons with corrugated partitions for packing biscuits.

We shall deliver it to you by 20th June, 2011 as requested. The bill will be dispatched along with the goods. Payment within 10 days entitles you to a discount of 2 per cent.

You will find that our goods and services are of high standard. We look forward to a long-lasting business relation for a regular supply of packing materials for your biscuits and confectionery.

Yours faithfully,
Sethu
Manager

EXECUTION OF ORDERS

As soon as an order is received, the seller has to take steps to despatch the goods. Timely execution of an order enhances the image of the seller in the mind of the buyer and it leads to strengthening business ties.

The execution letter should encompass the following points:

- A reference to the date and number of the order.
- An expression of thanks for the order.
- An intimation about its execution.
- Information about date of despatch and mode of transport.
- A statement of the total amount of invoice and the mode of recovery.
- A solicitation for future orders.

Delay in the Execution of Order

At times, the seller may not be able to execute the order due to a variety of factors beyond his control. Under such circumstances, he may have to lose his valuable customers. In such cases, the seller can sustain the business relationship with his customers by convincing the buyers of the inevitability of circumstances forcing delay. Drafting of such letters call for greater care, caution and extraordinary skill. The following points are worth mentioning in the letter:

- Illustration of circumstances forcing delay of execution.
- Indication of probable time within which the order can be executed.
- Request the customer to condone the delay.
- An assurance that his order will receive prompt attention once situation turns normal.
- Acknowledgement of the incidental cause of delay to the buyer and expression of hope that the buyer would not mind it in view of their earlier record of good service.

Inability to Execute Order

Sometimes, the seller may not be able to execute the orders placed with him. In such circumstances, the acknowledgement letter can be classified into two broad categories:

Refusal of an offer

- Seller may not have sufficient inventory to execute the order.
- When the terms stipulated or prices quoted by the buyer are not agreeable to him, the seller may not execute the order.
- When the sale is only through authorized agents, order may not be executed.

Substitutes and counter offer

Sometimes goods ordered may be out of stock. In such cases, the seller may offer to give substitutes to the buyer. The seller has to act tactfully and offer cogent reasons for not stocking the goods ordered. He should emphasise that substitutes are not inferior to the original goods. When the goods ordered have gone out of fashion, he should explain the present trends and also offer substitutes on equally liberal terms.

Sample 5: Letter of Execution

Draft a letter to M/s. Sen & Sons intimating despatch of certain kitchen appliances and advising them that you have drawn from them for the value of goods through Canara Bank, Pondicherry.

Moonshine Kitchen Appliances Ltd.

326, Armenian Street,
Chennai – 600 001

22nd July 2011

M/s Sen & Sons,
32, Mahatma Gandhi Road,
Pondicherry – 605 001

Dear Sir,

We thank you for your order worth ₹ 25,00,000 of kitchen appliances (Details noted in the invoice) and have the pleasure to inform you that we have dispatched all your requirements by passenger train today.

As desired, we have sent the relative Railway Receipt No.P 12345 dated 22nd July through Canara Bank, Pondicherry and we are enclosing our Invoice No. 112 thereof.

We welcome you to our list of satisfied patrons and we hope that our appliances will prove to be of high standard.

We trust that this trial order will pave way for an ensuing business relation with you.

Yours faithfully,
S. Choudhury
Sale Manager.

Sample 6: You have received a big order for steel furniture, cupboards and book-shelves but you are unable to execute it within the time requested owing to certain difficulties. Write to the customer asking for extension of time.

The Great Western Steel Products Ltd.

75, Bhagat Sing Road,
New Delhi – 110008

13th September 1991

M/s. Fernandes Furniture Co.,
95, Periyar Ramasamy Road,
Erode – 638010

Dear Sir,

We thank you for your valuable order dated 14th April, 2011 for the supply of large quantities of steel cupboards, folding chairs and book shelves of various sizes and types.

Unfortunately, we are unable to book your order since our present stock is not adequate even for meeting the order on hand. Our supplies of galvanised sheets are delayed on account of acute shortage in the market and this has compelled us to limit our production. We believe that the situation will ease in another two weeks and normal production will resume thereafter.

All orders are being executed strictly on 'first come first serve' basis and since we already have a large number of orders to be filled, it will not be possible for us to book your order earlier than 3 weeks from today.

If you can agree to extend the date of delivery to 15th October, we will be able to accept your order. Please let us have your advice as early as possible.

We apologise for the inconvenience caused by this delay and look forward to receiving your instructions.

Yours faithfully,
Simon
Secretary

Sample 7: The customer's reply to this letter. The customer is willing to grant extension of time upto a certain date.

Fernandes Furniture Co.

95, Periyar Ramasamy Road,
Erode – 638 010

17th September 2011

The Great Western Steel Products Ltd.,
74, Bharat Singh Road,
New Delhi – 110 008

Dear Sir,

We have your letter of 13th September 2011.

Since we have committed ourselves to supply to our customers (dealers) in the first week of October in view of the ensuing Deepavali season, any delayed supply will prove fatal to our business.

We fully realise that nothing can be done about the non-availability of steel sheets but we feel that you can relax your order of priority and move up our order. The large orders and our long established business relations will justify this step.

The order stands before 5th October, if you can see your way to supplying our requirements.

We shall be waiting to hear from you.

Yours faithfully,
G. Fernandas
Proprietor

Sample 8: You have received an enquiry for the supply of 50 steel cupboards made by Widerage Ltd. Draft a letter that you do not stock Widerage products but you deal in Tansteel Products which are superior in quality.

Rosario Furniture Mart

1, Church Street,
Tirupapuliyur – 607 002.

22nd July 2011

Joseph Furniture Mart,
20, Arcot Road,
Padi – 607106

Dear Sir,

We have your enquiry dated 19th July, 2011 for the supply of 50 steel cupboards made by Widerage Ltd. We are, however, sorry to tell you that we do not stock Widerage steel cupboards but deal in Tansteel Products and have enclosed our catalogue of steel cupboards and furniture.

Pages 25 – 27 of our illustrative catalogue describes the various types of steel cupboards and they also disclose the special features of the brand handled by us. Our cupboards are superior to any other in the market with respect to colour, design, durability and fire-resisting quality. We may add that they satisfy even the most discriminating and fastidious buyers. Our terms of business are given on page 5 of our catalogue.

However illustrative our catalogues are, only a personal inspection will convince you of the variety and beauty of the furniture we have in our showroom. We, therefore, request you to pay us a visit.

Yours faithfully,
For Rosario Furniture Mart,
Lazer
Proprietor

Sample 9: You are a wholesaler in fountain pens and have received an order for 10 gross of Pioneer pens and ball pens. You do not have them in stock but can supply another variety of pens, Pointer pens, which are equally good.

Write a letter regretting your inability to supply the pens your customer wants and encouraging him to buy the ones you can supply.

Pen Corner

121, Gandhi Margh,
Mumbai – 400 002

10th June 2011

M/s. Punitham Stationery Stores,
Kamaraj Road,
Virudhunagar – 626 002
Sir,

We thank you for your order No.876 dated 5th June, 2011 for 10 gross of Pioneer pens and ball pens of various qualities and patterns.

The pens you want are, unfortunately, out of stock. We have just learnt from the manufacturer that in view of the labour trouble in their factory, they can resume normal supplies only after a month.

If your demand is not pressing for Pioneer pens only, we suggest to you that the Pointer pens brought out in the Mumbai market by a company from Kolkatta are becoming quite popular. They are trouble-free, smooth-writing and of exquisite workmanship. The repeat orders we receive indicate that it is well on the way to capturing the market here.

We are confident that you will find them a good substitute for Pioneer pens. We enclose a catalogue for Pointer pens. We look forward to your reply.

Yours faithfully,
for Pen Corner,
P.S. Lakshmanan
Proprietor

Sample 10: You have received an order for goods which you no longer stock. Write a tactful reply trying to get the customer interested in a substitute.

Chatterjee Bros

11, Dalhousie Square,
Kolkatta – 700 038

2nd June 2011

M.Bava Mohideen & Co.,
11, Factory Road,
Cuddalore – 607 105

Dear Sir,

We thank you for your order for the supply of 40 dozen bottles of Jai Hair Cream.

We regret to inform you that we no longer stock Jai Hair Cream as the total absense of enquiries from our customers suggest that this product is going out of fashion.

But we have a new variety **Sunshine Hair Darkener** which is in great demand these days. This is based on a new formula derived after a long and laborious research. Its mild smell is an additional welcome feature. It is available in a wide range of sizes with attractive packing.

We are confident that this will prove to be very popular with your customers too, as it has been hailed in other cities.

Two dozen bottles of Sunshine Hair Darkner have been despatched to your address. If it does not suit your customers, please return them at our cost.

Yours faithfully,
Roy Choudhri
Manager

Sample 11: As the Sales Manager of Modern Biscuit Factory, Chennai write a tactful letter to your customer expressing inability to supply on account of heavy orders on hand.

Modern Biscuit Factory

111, T.H.Road,
Chennai – 600 019

2nd July 2011

Messrs Royal Stores,
1, Raja Street,
Pudukottai – 622 001

Dear Sir,

We thank you for your order of 25th June 2011 for 500 tins of varied types of biscuits.

We very much appreciate your interest in our milk cream biscuits and wish we were in a position to accept your order. But huge unfilled orders on hand will keep our machines and workmen engaged for a few more months and we are, therefore, unable to book your order even if you are kind enough to extend the date of delivery.

To cope with the mounting demand for our biscuits, we are making all efforts to install a new plant but it will be months before the actual production starts.

We regret our inability to serve you at present but we look forward to the day when we can accept your order.

Yours faithfully,
For The Modern Biscuit Factory,
Maran
Sales Manager

Sample 12: Radha Textiles, Madurai express their regret at their inability to supply Jubilee Voile Sarees ordered by Krishna Dressland, Karaikudi. They add that the offer was firm for 7 days only and that goods were sold immediately after the expiration of the offer. Draft the letter and offer substitutes.

Radha Textiles

72, North Veli Street,
Madurai – 625003

2nd May 2011

Krishna Dress Land,
78, Bazzar Street,
Karaikudi-623 001

Dear Sir,

We thank you for your order dated 28th April for the supply of 100 printed Jubilee Voile Sarees (Pattern No.25) which we received today.

While we greatly appreciate your interest in our Jubilee Voile Sarees, may we remind you that our quotation dated 21st April was firm only for 7 days.

The response to our offer was so overwhelming that the whole lot was sold off on 28th itself.

We can, however, offer you our Diamond Printed Voile sarees known for their attractive designs, fast colour and durability, yet priced moderately. They are a good substitute for the Jubilee Voile Sarees. Stock is readily available and we shall despatch them on hearing from you.

Yours faithfully,
Joycee
Proprietor

Sample 13: You have received an order for the supply of 3 cases of Narumanam Soaps from Novelty Stores, Namakkal. Draft a letter refusing to entertain the direct order from the dealers but stating that order has been forwarded to their Sole Selling Agents.

Fragrant Soaps Ltd.

320, Avenue Road,
Bangalore-560 002

19th November 2011

The Novelty Stores,
77, Salem Road,
Namakkal-637 001

Dear Sir,

We thank you for your order No.75 dated 14th November, 2011 for the supply of 3 cases of Narumanam soaps but we regret that we are unable to accept any order direct from dealers, as we have given exclusive agency for your State to Messrs. Amarchand Bros.,75, Pycrofts Road, Chennai.

We have, however, forwarded your order to Messrs. Amarchand Bros, for consideration. You will doubtlessly hear from them soon. We thank you for the interest you have shown in our products and we hope that it will work out to our mutual advantage.

Yours faithfully,
B.S.Hegde
Secretary

Defective Order

When an order letter is defective in some respects, it is called a defective order. For instance, correct and complete information concerning the goods might not have been furnished, instructions regarding time and place of delivery or certain others information might have been withheld. In such cases, the order should not be confirmed.

Given below are some points to be looked into while drafting a letter pointing out the defects:

- The letter should contain an expression of thanks for the interest shown in the goods.
- Request for the missing information.
- To stress that if the information sought is furnished, order will be executed strictly as per the requirements of the buyer.
- The letter should in no way offend the customer.

Sample 14: The East End Clock Company, Mumbai, have received an order from a customer for 100 electronic clocks. The order does not specify colour or design. Draft a letter on behalf of the company acknowledging the order.

The East End Clock Company

25, Fort Road,
Mumbai – 400 016
2nd June 2011

Zaviour,
73, Nehru Street,
Pondichrrry - 605 001

Dear Sir,

We thank you for your order of 30th May, 2011 for 100 electronic clocks. You have not specified the design and the colour. Since we do not have any intention of forcing the design and colour of our choice on you, we will be glad if you indicate your preference. We enclose an illustrated folder so that you can quote the respective number of the model which appeals to you the most.

We will be pleased to fill the order promptly if you let us have your instructions as early as possible.

Yours faithfully,
Martin
Manager

CANCELLATION OF ORDERS

Due to certain unforeseen circumstances as mentioned below, an order placed already may have to be cancelled:

- Insolvency of the customer or closure of business by the customer for whom the order was meant.
- Fall in the market price.
- Undue delay in the execution of the order.
- The reseller's counter-offer of a substitute on account of non-availability, anticipated delay in its procurement, etc.
- The subsequent raising of prices by the seller.

The following points must be borne in mind while drafting a letter of cancellation:

- It must point out clearly the reason for cancellation.
- It should contain an expression of regret.
- It should contain an assurance to place future orders with the supplier to make good the loss of the order cancelled.

Note: The letter of cancellation should reach the supplier sufficiently early, i.e. before action is initiated for producing the goods. It is therefore desirable to send intimation of cancellation by telegram or telephone and follow it up with a letter.

Sample 15 : Ooty Grament Traders who placed an order with Kashmir Wools Company, Kolkatta for the supply of Woollen graments cancel their order on account of undue delay in its execution.

Ooty Garment Traders

11, Lakeview Road,
Othagamandalam,
Nilgris – 634 001

15th November 2011

M/s Kashmir Wools Company,
7, Dalhouie Square,
Kolkatta – 700 035

Dear Sirs,

We confirm our telegram which reads as follows:

"Order 215 Cancelled - Letter Follows"

Please note that we have placed an order No. 215 dated 11th October, for the supply of woollen garments valued at ₹.50,000. We have also requested therein that goods should reach us before 25th October, 2011.

We are sorry that we have received neither the goods ordered even three weeks after the expiry of the specified date of delivery nor any letter stating the delay in the execution of order.

As the winter season is coming to a close shortly, we are compelled to cancel the order. Since the time of delivery has expired long ago, we will refuse to take delivery of the goods in case they arrive now.

Yours faithfully,
J. Joghi
Proprietor

Sample 16: Having placed an order with Mumbai Toy Traders, you want to cancel the order on the ground that there is sufficient stock and that the order was the result of an error.

Vridhachalam Novelty Stores

22, Junction Road,
Vridhachalam – 606 101
22nd February 2011

The Mumbai Toy Traders,
77, Sri P.M.Road,
Fort, Mumbai– 400 002

Dear Sirs,

We confirm our telegram sent today which reads as follows:

"Cancel Order 66 - Letter follows"

We regret that we have to cancel our order No. 66 of 15th February for the supply of assorted varieties of toys.

A thorough check of stock reports and a physical verification thereof have disclosed that the order was the result of an error on the part of our store-keeper.

Since we have sufficient stock of the items we had ordered for, we are constrained to cancel our order.

We know how greatly you will be inconvenienced and sincerely apologise for this cancellation. We assure you that we will be happy to place a large order with you, once the present stock gets exhausted.

Yours faithfully,
K. Kolanjiappar
Manager

Sample 17: Vasudevan & Sons cancel their order for 10 dozen Mirzapur Woollen Carpets given two days earlier to Thiruveni Carpets Co., Allahabad, since they have learnt in the meantime that the customer for whom the carpets were ordered has become insolvent.

Vasudevan and Sons

20 Kamaraj Road,
Vandavasi – 604 408.

5th January 2011

Thiruveni Carpets Co.,
Jawaharlal Nehru Road,
Allahabad – 211 005

Dear Sir,

We placed an order with you for the supply of 10 dozen Mirzapur woollen carpets. We now confirm the following telegram sent by us today.

"Cancel Order 25 dated 3rd January for woollen carpets"

We are compelled to do this as we have learnt that the customer for whom the carpets were ordered, has become insolvent. We are sorry for the inconvenience this cancellation would have caused you. We request you to stop dispatching the goods and we assure you of large order in a month's time which will make good the loss of this order.

Yours faithfully,

Rishab Dev

Sample 18: Gurusingh Trading Corporation, Amristar, Punjab, writes to M.S. Olympia Trading Company, Chengalpet stating that they have to claim damages to the extent of ₹ 2000 if the contract for the supply of sports goods is cancelled. However, they express their willingness to store the goods for three months at a rent of ₹ 500, but they desire payment within one month of the order, as arranged. Draft a reply to the letter of cancellation.

Gurusingh Trading Corporation

77, G.N. Road,
Amritsar,
Punjab – 143 001

2nd July 2011

M/s. Olympia Trading Company,
Church Road,
Chengalpet – 603 001

Dear Sir,

We regret to learn from your letter of 30th June that you are compelled to cancel your order No. 234 for the supply of sports goods on account of expected shortage of storage space.

Unfortunately, to cancel the order at this stage causes difficulties to us also as we have booked your order for execution to meet your special requirements. You may have to be charged a penalty of ₹ 2000 to cover the expenses we have already incurred. Alternatively, we will be glad to store your goods in our godown at a rent of ₹ 500 if you so desire. This will save you ₹ 1,500.

However, we hope to receive payment of the amount due within one month of completion of the order as arranged.

We trust that you will take advantage of the alternative we have suggested and hope to receive your reply within a week.

Yours faithfully,

M.Tara Singh

Manager

SUMMARY

A letter placing an order is to acknowledge acceptance of the quotation. It includes the type of goods, price of goods, quantity of goods, mode of transport, time and delivery instructions and mode of payment.

Confirmation letters contain the number and date of the order, description of goods, terms and conditions, request for missing information by means of an acknowledgement letter and possibility of delay in order execution.

Defective orders needs clarification. It should thank the buyer for the appreciation shown in goods, seek missing information and promise immediate action once the missing information is given. No offensive words should be used.

Reasons for cancellation of orders include insolvency of the customer, fall in market price, undue delay in execution and price hike by the seller.

Cancellation letters should contain reasons for cancellation, expression of regret and assurance to place orders in the future.

REVIEW QUESTIONS

Part A: Short Questions

1. What is an order letter?
2. What is a confirmation letter?
3. What is a defective order?
4. What is a cancellation letter?
5. What is an execution letter?

Part B: Paragraph Questions

1. State the points to be noted while writing an order letter.
2. What are the points that should be kept in mind while writing a confirmation letter?
3. What are the points to be considered while writing a letter pointing to the defects?
4. State the circumstances leading to cancellation of orders placed.
5. What are the points to be highlighted while explaining the delay in execution of an order?
6. State the circumstances under which an order may not be executed.

Part C: Essay Questions

1. Write a letter regretting your inability to supply the pens your customer wants and inducing him to buy the ones you can supply.
2. You have received an order for goods which you no longer stock. Write a tactful reply trying to get the customer interested in a substitute.
3. Draft a letter expressing inability to book orders on account of heavy orders on hand.

4. Draft a letter intimating inability to supply as the order arrives after expiration of firm offer.
5. Write a letter refusing the order on technical grounds.
6. State the circumstances resulting in cancellation of orders placed earlier.
7. Write a letter stating that the order was the result of an error.
8. Write a letter cancelling the order on the ground that the customer has become insolvent.

Part D: Objective Type Questions

State whether the following statement are true of false

1. Letter ordering goods is a contract. Ans: True
2. Letter expressing setter's inability to execute the order is cancellation letter. Ans:True
3. Confirmation letter is an acknowledgement of order letter. Ans:True
4. A letter of order is written by seller. Ans: False
5. An order placed by telegram or phone need to be confirmed by writing. Ans:True

Choose the correct answer

1. Order letter is a

   a Contract   b. Contingent contract   c. Void contract   (Ans: a)

2. Confirmation letter drawn by the seller is

   a. Acknowledgement   b. Circular Letter   c. Order letter   (Ans: a)

3. Cancellation letter is drawn by

   a. Buyer   b. Seller   c. Both   (Ans: a)

4. Delay in execution of an order is communicated by

   a. Buyer   b. Seller   c. Official   (Ans: b)

5. Order placed by telegram or phone need to be confirmed by a

   a. Written letter   b. Return telegram   c. Return call   (Ans: a)

6. Letter written to confirm the order placed is

   a. Defective letter   b. Cancellation letter   c. Acknowledgement letter   (Ans: c)

7. Order lacking any essential information is a

   a. Confirmation letter   b. Defective lette   c. Execution letter   (Ans: b)

8. A letter intimating the dispatch of supply of goods

   a. Defective letter   b. Confirmation letter   c. Execution letter   (Ans: c)

Fill in the blanks

1. Letter ordering goods constitutes a contract of ___________. (purchase)
2. Acknowledgement letter sent in response to an order letter is __________. (confirmation letter)
3. Defective order letter is ___________. (defective orders)
4. Letter expressing inability of seller to execute the order is __________ letter. (cancellation)
   Oral orders by telephone needs a ______________ confirmation. (written)
5. Order lacking in some essential information is __________ order. (defective)
6. A letter written to confirm the order placed by the buyer letter is ______________. (acknowledgement/confirmation)
7. Letter written dispatching the ordered goods is _____________. (execution letter)

11

CHAPTER

COMPLAINTS AND ADJUSTMENTS

INTRODUCTION

Owing to the complexities of modern business, occasions often arise when customers have to complain. For example, delayed execution of orders, supply of inferior goods, goods delivered not corresponding to samples, machinery supplied not performing as promised. All these causes force a customer to make complaints.

Customer Satisfaction — the Supreme Goal of Modern Business

The modern businessman regards the customer as the pivotal point around which the business moves because it is customer's satisfaction that is at the bedrock of a successful business. Goods supplied must satisfy customer requirements and machines sold should perform as promised. If they fail, customers write to the firm.

COMPLAINTS

Unless the failure of the goods is brought to the notice of the supplier, no action can be taken to rectify the mistake and satisfy the customers. It is the complaint letters which bring the attention of the supplier to the dissatisfaction suffered by customers. Hence, a good businessman welcomes letters of complaints.

A Check on the Quality of Service and Products

On account of the laziness or inefficiency of employees or due to the incivility of staff, customers get faulty goods, delayed supplies or discourteous treatment. Customer complaints open the eyes of the supplier to the inefficiency of his own staff. Complaints and claims offer a good check on the quality of service or merchandise. Continuous monitoring of complaint letters act as a control mechanism for their products and services.

An imaginative executive welcomes complaints because it is he who understands the challenges that are there in the company, in his products and in the attitude and performance of his staff. It is always better to discover a fault than to let it continue unsuspected.

A Potential Threat Turned into an Opportunity for Growth

Nothing is more detrimental to good public and business relations than a discontented or dissatisfied customer. If he writes directly to the company and thereby gets his complaints adjusted, the company is converting a potential threat into an opportunity for growth. A potential liability becomes a sales booster because the complainant will spread the word to all his friends and acquaintances that even a trivial complaint is well-attended by the particular company which views its customer as its kingpin.

An enlightened businessman views the complaint letters of his customers as an eye-opener to the realities of the situation and as a goodwill booster. To regard them as nuisance is to gradually lose one's customers—and ultimately the business itself—to his competitor.

The views of top businessmen on complaint letters:

I make it a rule to answer every letter of complaint that I can personally handle. If a schedule prevents me from doing this, an associate takes care of the letter for me; but the point is every letter is answered.

(John C. Whitaker, President, R. J. Reynolds Tobacco Company)

It has been our invariable policy to let people know we appreciate hearing from them if they are dissatisfied in any way. We have always recognized the customer's right to expect our products to fulfill any claim we made for them in our advertising.

(M.F. Jones, Vice-President, Compell Soap Company)

Thus it becomes clear that a good businessman welcomes complaints instead of resenting them by throwing light on the weaknesses, the firm can take steps to remove irritants and deficiencies and fortify customer relations, so that the organization grows in stature and strength.

Careful Choice of Words—an Essential Ingredient

To stimulate the correct type of reaction, a careful choice of words is of fundamental importance. An angry outburst will not solve the problem but will only worsen the situation.

Avoid accusation: The claim letter should avoid anger, sarcasm and accusation. In short, it should not give the impression that at the first opportunity, complaint is levelled against the company. It should appear as if he is forced to write the letter as a last resort.

Avoid being vague and pinpoint the specific complaint: Vague accusations will not lead to adjustment of complaints. The specific complaint must be pinpointed with all details furnished so that the recheck is easily facilitated.

Indicate the consequential loss: The claim letter should also state the inconvenience or the loss that has resulted from the error.

Suggest the remedial measure: Adjustment or compensation that is desired must also be indicated.

When soft words do not succeed: When milder methods have failed to prevent recurrence of grievances, the complaint letter should be sternly worded. But on no account should it be drafted impolitely or rudely.

In the Case of Imaginary Grievance

The error pointed out may be the result of misinterpretation or misunderstanding on the part of the complainant. In such a case, the use of strong abusive epithets will apply to the writer himself.

In view of what has been mentioned above it is clear that while the complaint must be voiced in clear terms for getting the grievance addressed, it should not impair business relations.

Reasons for Complaint Letters

There are various occasions that give rise to letters of complaints (or claims). Though every effort should be made to reduce the percentage of errors, occasions may arise when complaints are lodged by customers. The reasons for complaints can be:

1. Delay in the execution of order.
2. Supply of inferior quality goods or goods not corresponding to samples.
3. Supply of goods not ordered for or shortage of supplied goods.
4. Goods may arrive in a damaged condition.
5. Goods being delivered at the wrong place.
6. Machines procured not giving the expected result or promised service not provided.
7. Incivility (discourtesy) of staff when the customer visits the office.
8. Misunderstanding over discounts, credit terms, etc.
9. Letters written to bring these errors to the attention of the firm responsible are called *claim letters*.

Hints on Writing Letters of Complaint

Letters couched in angry tones defeat the very purpose for which they are written. They should be drafted in such a way that grievances are redressed. The following hints are worth noting:

- The claim letter should avoid anger, sarcasm and accusation.
- It should be fair and tolerant. Courtesy, rather than angry outbursts, stimulates favourable action.
- Complaints should be based on facts alone; vague accusations must be avoided.
- It should contain an explanation of what or where the problem is. It should also give complete information, date, order number, invoice number, size, colour, etc., which may make a recheck easier.
- It should pinpoint the inconvenience or loss that has resulted from the error.
- The complainant's exact requirement should be stated clearly. It should appeal to the reader's sense of fair play and honesty.
- However, when milder methods have failed to get complaints adjusted, a claim letter can be worded firmly. In no case should it be drafted impolitely.

ADJUSTMENTS

The reply to a complaint letter is called an *adjustment letter*. It assuages the injured feelings of a complainant by rectifying the committed mistake or by adjusting suitably. It builds up the image and goodwill of the company.

The following points must be borne in mind while drafting a letter of adjustment:

1. A delayed adjustment letter embitters business relations. Hence, even when investigation is necessary, the complaint should be acknowledged first.
2. The reply must be factual, polite and courteous. It should not take a critical attitude. For example, it should not say that no one else has had any cause for complaint.
3. It should not humiliate the complainant by doubting the veracity of his complaints. It should not be forgotten that *one good word quenches more heat than a bucket of water*. The attitude that the customer is always right should be reflected in an adjustment letter.
4. It should never contain vague statements like *company policy prevents us from doing this*.
5. It should contain an expression of regret over the inconvenience caused but should not be over-apologetic. It should first thank the complainant for the pains he has taken to bring the complaint to their notice.
6. There should not be any passing of the blame to someone else; buck-passing must be avoided; but the letter can explain the cause of the error.
7. The adjustment letter should not repeat the mistake complained of. It is enough if it suggests what adjustment is being made.
8. It should not give any assurance that such mistakes will not be repeated in future. But it can suggest that every effort would be made to prevent such occurrences in the future.
9. Even when the complaint is due to a misunderstanding on the part of the customer, the adjustment letter should not point out his carelessness or hasty judgement. The facts overlooked must be stated with utmost courtesy and friendliness.
10. If the complaint is unreasonable, the adjustment letter should express its inability to grant the adjustment.
11. The letter should reflect the feeling of sympathy that the firm has for the customer and that it is trying to accommodate them.

SAMPLE COMPLAINT AND ADJUSTMENT LETTERS

Sample 1: Letter protesting against delay in the delivery of goods urgently needed, explaining the adverse effect of the delay and indicating the action envisaged if it continues beyond a specified time.

Sundar Traders

77, Main Bazaar,
Neyveli – 607 801

26th May 2011

The Cool Concentrates Ltd.,
111, R.N. Tagore Road,
Chennai - 600 017

Dear Sir,

We placed an urgent order with you on 8th April for the supply of 10 gross bottles of summer cool concentrates of different varieties. We are very much distressed to tell you that these goods have not reached us yet.

This is causing us considerable loss of business and threatens the loss of one of our valued customers for whom the order is largely intended.

You are aware that summer is the best period for the sale of your products and with it drawing to a close, it will become a slow-liner.

We have had to complain of delay in the execution of our orders several times. We can continue to place orders with you only if you undertake to fill our orders promptly in the future.

We trust you will take steps to hasten the despatch. If we do not receive the goods before 5th June, we shall be compelled to cancel the order.

Yours faithfully,
S. Rajakannu

(If this mild form of complaint fails, then a strongly worded letter threatening legal action may be better. In such a situation, **instead of the last two paragraphs the following two paragraphs can be inserted.)**

Please remember that the order was placed with you on your specific undertaking to deliver the good on or before 15th May. Your inordinate delay under the circumstances gives us the right to sue you for damages. However, we do not want to resort to this extreme step and are prepared to wait till 6th June.

We hope that you will take the necessary steps for expediting the despatch and avoid legal action which is unpleasant for both of us.

Sample 2: A conciliatory reply to the above letter

Cool Concentrates Ltd.

111, R. N. Tagore Road
Chennai – 600 017

3rd June 2011

M/s. Sundar Traders,
77, Main Bazzar,
Neyveli – 607 801

Dear Sir,

We thank you for your letter of 26th May complaining of delay in the execution of your order and we also confirm a telegram sent to you today which reads as follows:

'Goods Despatched Second June. Regret Delay'

We are very sorry to inform you that a devastating fire broke out in our godown destroying a greater part of our finished stock and put our despatch schedule into complete disarray.

In addition to our dislocation caused by this fire accident, our machinery also broke down thereby forcing complete stoppage of production. We are glad to say that we resumed normal production a week ago. Despite overtime work put in by our workforce, it was not possible for us to have effected delivery of your goods much earlier.

We fully understand the extent of inconvenience and hardship suffered by you because of our delayed despatch and we sincerely apologise.

We trust you realise our utter helplessness in the matter and we assure you of our prompt service in the future.

Yours faithfully,
For Cool Concentrates Ltd.,
M. Seran

Sample 3: Anbazhagan & Co, Attur, complains about the consignment of varnish received from Evershine Paints, 77, Mint Street, Chennai, alleging that it is too thick and almost unfit for use. They offer to retain the goods, however, on condition that an allowance of 10°% is made in the price, failing which they suggest that Evershine Paints should take back the goods.

Anbazhagan & Co.

70, Salem Road,
Attur – 636102

10th April 2011

Evershine Paints,
Mint Street,
Chennai – 600 001

Dear Sirs,

We thank you for the consignment of 100 1kg tins of Ever shine Varnish sent on 1st April.

We have to tell you that we have received a number of complaints from our customers that the quality of this consignment is far from satisfactory and that it does not correspond with the previous one. The varnish is said to be too thick and is not fit for economical use. We are, however, prepared to retain the goods provided an allowance of 10% is made on the price as we feel that a similar allowance by us to our customers will go a long way in retaining their loyalty by compensating them for the loss.

If an allowance is not provided, we will have to return the 80 tins remaining with us. We shall hold on to the goods till we hear from you in this regard.

Yours faithfully,
K. Mathiazhagan
Manager

Sample 4: Evershine Paints attribute the condition of the varnish to the fact that it has been in stock for a long time and say that the defect can be removed by heating it immediately before use. They say that though there is no ground for a claim or any reason to return the goods, they will make an allowance of 3%.

Evershine Paints

77, Mint Street,
Chennai- 600 001

13th April 2011

Anbazhagan & Co,
70, Salem Road,
Athur – 636 102

Dear Sir,

We thank you for your letter of 10th April, bringing to our notice the dissatisfaction of your customers with the quality of varnish supplied by us.

An examination of a sample from the same stock disclosed no defect except for the thickness which can be liquified by heating it before use. The thickness of the varnish is due to the fact that it has been in stock for a long time. Since the quality of our varnish is not inferior by any standards and the complained thickness is remediable, it does not warrant an allowance of 10% price reduction or a right to return the goods.

However, keeping in view our long connection, we are prepared to make an allowance of 3%. Our margin of profit does not allow anything beyond this.

We trust you will convince your customers on these lines and appreciate this special gesture shown to you.

Yours faithfully,
S. Senthil
Managing Partner

Sample 5: Jamal Chinawares Company received from Tulsidas Brothers, Mumbai, Chinawares in a damaged condition. Draft a letter asking for replacement of goods.

Jamal Chinawares Company

11, Evening Bazaar,
Chennai – 600 001

2nd July 2011

M/s. Tulsidas Brothers,
22-A Tilak Road,
Mumbai – 400 012

Dear Sirs,

We thank you for your consignment of 200 sets of chinawares which we had ordered on 19th June.

On opening the crate, 50 sets were found in a damaged condition. Since they appear unsaleable, we request you to provide replacement.

Yours faithfully,
A. Suresh

Sample 6. Reply to a complaint letter regarding damaged goods granting the request.

Tulsidas Brothers

22-A Tilak Road,
Mumbai – 400 012

8th July 2011

Jamal Chinawares Company,
11, Evening Bazaar,
Chennai – 600 001

Dear Sir,

We regret to learn that 50 sets of the chinawares despatched by us on 25th June were so badly damaged that they have to be replaced.

An enquiry conducted by us proved that because packing was entrusted to a new, inexperienced employee on account of heavy work pressure, some sets were damaged. A warning has been issued to the packing department to be more careful in future.

We have despatched 50 new sets of chinawares today to replace the damaged ones. We offer our apologies for the inconvenience you have suffered.

Yours faithfully,
S. Mohandas
Proprietor

Sample 7: M/S Bharathi & Co, Pondicherry complain that the Camel Hair Rugs supplied by Modern Trading Co., Delhi are much inferior in quality to the provided sample which led to the placing of the order. The hair is rough with bad finish and the appearance repels the buyer. They return the goods and want immediate adjustment.

Bharathi & Co.

78, Bharathidasan Road,
Pondicherry – 605 002

22nd February 2011

The Modern Trading Company,
78, Daryaganj,
New Delhi – 110 002
Dear Sir,

We regret to inform you that your recent consignment of Camel Hair Rugs is far from satisfactory. We placed the order only on the basis of samples sent to us along with your letter of offer. But the rugs supplied are far inferior in quality and they do not tally with the samples. They are rough with a bad finish and the appearance unattractive.

As we fear that sale of such inferior goods will damage our reputation, we are returning them. We will be pleased to have goods of better quality corresponding to the samples sent.

Yours faithfully,
Mrs. K. Punitham
Proprietress

Sample 8: Modern Trading Company, Delhi state in reply that owing to an unfortunate oversight, rugs of an inferior quality were sent, that the error was detected soon after and the required quality sent. Write an adjustment letter.

The Modern Trading Company.

78, Daryaganj,
New Delhi – 110 002

25th February 2011

Bharathi & Co,
78, Bharathidasan Road,
Pondicherry – 605 002

Dear Madam,

We regret to note that you are forced to return the camel hair rugs supplied by us as they were found inferior in quality. In spite of our best efforts not to cause any hardship to our customers through any slip while filling an order, this happens once in a while. They supply of rugs of inferior quality was owing to an unfortunate oversight and a re-check after despatch disclosed this. We are sorry for having blundered on your order causing you a lot inconvenience. We have already despatched goods required strictly as per samples and we hope this will win your approval.

We are taking steps against recurrence of such lapses in future and we trust you will give us further opportunities to serve you better.

Yours faithfully,
M. Malhotra
Partner

Sample 9: One of your customers complain of defects in the goods you have just supplied. A tactful letter to him pointing out that you are unable to accept any liability till your representative has inspected the goods and assure him of fair treatment.

Balu Trading Company

11, Cutchery Road,
Erode – 638 009

4th January 2011

Bangalore Tailors,
7, Mahatma Gandhi Road,
Avinashi – 641 653

Dear Mr. Venkat Rao,

We have your letter dated 2nd January and note with regret that two Kala Sewing Machines you bought from us two weeks ago arrived in a damaged condition.

You will appreciate that we can admit no liability until we have made an on-the-spot inspection of the machines. Our representative will call on you on 8th January between 11 a.m. and 1 p.m.

Please feel assured that steps will be taken so that you will suffer no loss owing to any fault of ours.

We are sorry that we have caused some inconveniences and offer our sincere apologies.

Yours faithfully,
S. Pandian
Proprietor

Sample 10: The Seaco Watch Company receives an angry letter from a customer who had purchased an electric wall clock a fortnight ago. He now claims that the clock arrived in a damaged condition and demands a new one. A tactful reply from The Seaco Watch Company to the customer explaining why it is not possible has been drafted.

The Seaco Watch Company

327, N.S.K. Road,
Chennai – 600 001

19th October 2011

The Anna Clock House,
7, Pachiayappa College Road,
Kanchipuram – 631 501

Dear Sir,

We are sorry to learn from your letter of 16th October that three electric wall clocks were received in a slightly damaged condition.

We never hesitate to replace any goods which our customer receives in a damaged condition. But the claim for damages should have been preferrably written within a week of receipt of the goods. We have made this clear in all our invoices. Only then can we make a counter-claim on the transport company which is actually responsible for the damage.

Since you intimated us about the damage to clocks three weeks after taking delivery, thereby depriving us of all chances of getting compensation from the transport company, we regret our inability to replace them. However, in view of our long association, we are prepared to bear 50% of the cost of repairs.

We request you to co-operate with us in future by referring claims promptly whenever the need arises.

Yours faithfully,
For Seaco Watch Company,
V. Ruthrapathy
Sales Manager

Sample 11: You have recently purchased a T.V. Set from a local dealer. You are dissatisfied with the performance of the set. The dealer has refused to look into the matter. Write a letter stating your specific complaints to Southend T.V. Ltd, Bangalore.

Prof. K. Gopalakrishnan,
134, East Car Street,
Chidambaram – 608 012

2nd June 2011

The Southend T.V. Ltd.,
4, G.M. Road,
Bangalore – 560 059

Dear Sir,

I deeply regret to have to inform you that a Southend T.V. Set Luxury Model purchased from your dealer Microtronics at 7, West Car Street, Chidambaram vide invoice No. 374 dated 26th May does not perform well. The picture is distorted and fuzzy, which makes it difficult to watch any programme.

We approached the local dealer who sent his repair man but the performance has not improved even a wee bit.

I chose Southend T.V. only because of my conviction that it would give me greater satisfaction by ensuring clarity of the picture and that your service centres manned by qualified technicians would attend to even minor repairs. But I am most distressed to say that your dealer in Chidambaram does not care once the sale is closed and treats complaints as nuisance.

Since all my efforts to set matters right locally proved to be of no avail, I deemed it wise to approach you.

I request you to instruct your dealer to do the repair work more thoroughly so that the T.V. set can give a trouble-free performance or else replace it with a new set.

Since customer satisfaction has been an important reason behind your success story, I am sure you will agree with me that it is neither luxury to expect your T.V. sets to be in perfect condition nor charity to get proper after-sales service.

Yours sincerely,
K. Gopalakrishnan

Sample 12: M/S Murugan & Co bought a system from you 2 years ago. He now claims that the service is unsatisfactory and returns the system asking for an exchange. The system has obviously been carelessly handled. Write to him refusing to exchange it but agreeing to repair it.

Electronic Pradise Ltd.

88, Poonamalle High Road
Chennai – 600 034

9th September 2011

M/s. Murugan & Co,
77, Junction Road,
Thirunelveli – 627 756

Dear Sirs,

We thank you for your letter of 2nd September. We carefully examined the system which you have returned to us.

The report from our service department indicates that the system appears to have been handled carelessly due to which some of ICs in mother board are broken. Further, it appears as if it has not been serviced for months together.

Since our guarantee covers only defects in workmanship or materials, we are unable to assume responsibility for service necessitated due to improper care. We are sorry we cannot grant your request to repair your machine without charge.

If you agree to pay only ₹ 5000 towards the actual cost of the circuits, we shall be glad to repair the computer within a few days and bring it to an excellent working condition.

Yours faithfully,
Kamalahasan
Manager

Sample 13: Make a complaint of shortage of goods received and submit a claim to the Railway Authorities.

Velu Brothers

7, Nehru Street
Mayiladudurai – 609 007

10th August 2011

The Chief Traffic Manager,
Southern Railway,
Trichi – 620 010

Sir,

Sub: Shortage of goods received–goods booked from Chennai–claim submitted

I regret to inform you that a consignment of 1000 pairs of sunglasses booked to me by Messrs Shah Opticals, 75, Park Lane, Broadway, Chennai, under RR No 45321 dated 2nd August at Railway Risk arrived here in a most unsatisfactory condition..

The broken condition of the packing cases was immediately brought to the notice of the Station Master and an open delivery of the consignment was requested. This was given on 18th August and as the report to the Railways Claims Inspector would confirm, the case contained only 900 pairs of sunglasses instead of 1000 pairs despatched. Necessary entries have been made in the Railways Delivery Book.

In view of the goods been booked at Railway Risk, please make good the loss ascertained as given below:

	₹ P
Cost of 100 missing pairs of sun glasses.	75,000.00
Add Loss of Profit @ 10% of the cost	7,500.00
Proportionate Freight	500.00
	83,000.00

A copy of the consignor's invoice is enclosed in support of my claim. I request you to admit the claim and arrange for an early payment.

Yours faithfully,
V. Sen
Proprietor

Sample 14: Draft an adjustment letter to a customer who complains of incivility and inattention when he visited your premises.

Cuddalore Paper Ltd.

111, Lawrence Road,
Cuddalore – 607 005

22nd July 2011

M/s. Ilavazhagan Paper Merchants,
First Main Road,
Nellikuppam – 607 105

Dear Sir,

We are surprised and deeply distressed to learn from your letter dated 19th July that you have had reason to complain of incivility and inattention on the part of our office staff. We thank you for the pains you have taken to bring the incident to our notice.

We have immediately ordered an investigation of the matter and found that Mr. M.Muthu, who attended on you yesterday, has behaved rather rudely and used discourteous words, quite unbecoming of an Office Assistant. He has admitted his guilt that he lost his mental balance in the midst of pressing work due to personal problems about which he repented later.

We have severely reprimanded him and apprised the fact that even the slightest discourtesy to any visitor would be looked at as a serious breach of discipline and stern action will be initiated without any further warning.

We offer our sincere apologies for the unpleasant occurrence.

Yours faithfully,
S. Palanisamy
Secretary

SUMMARY

Causes for a complaint letter are delay in order execution, supply of inferior goods, shortage in supply, arrival of goods in damaged condition, delivery at wrong address, not getting the service promised, incivility of staff, misunderstanding over discount and credit terms.

Hints for drafting a complaint letter are, avoid anger, sarcasm and accusation, be fair and tolerant, base your complaint on facts, do not be vague, provide an explanation of what is wrong, pinpoint the inconvenience caused, request what needs to be done and appeal to the reader's sense of fairness.

Hints for writing adjustment letter are, reply to a complaint should be prompt, polite and courteous, not to take critical attitude or humiliate the complaintant, should not contain vague statements, express regret but not blame others assurance to avoid recurrence and express inability in case of unreasonable complaint.

Art of writing complaint letters includes choice of words, avoid accusation, avoid vague statement, indicate the consequential loss, suggest remedial measure and use milder words.

The attitude of business correspondance is to remember that customer satisfaction should be the goal and take it as an opportunity to take a check on quality of service and product and by turning the threat into an opportunity.

REVIEW QUESTIONS

Part A: Short Questions

1. What is a complaint letter?
2. What is an adjustment letter?
3. What is a complaint?

Part B: Paragraph Questions

1. Specify the occasions that gives rise to complaints or what are the causes of complaint letters?
2. What are the points to be borne in mind while writing a complaint letter?
3. What are the points to be borne in mind while writing an adjustment letter?

Part C: Essay Questions

1. Complaints are not routine letters. The writing of a complaint letter requires tact. Do you agree with the statement? If so, give your reasons.
2. What should be the attitude of a businessman when a complaint letter is received?

Part D: Objective Type Questions

Choose the Correct Answer

1. Complaint letter is drafted by

   a. Customer   b. Seller   c. Both   (Ans: a)

2. Adjustment letter is drafted by

   a. Customer   b. Seller   c. Competitor   (Ans: b)

3. Which letter requires more tact?

   a. Letter refusing adjustment   b. Letter granting adjustment

   c. Both   (Ans: a)

Fill in the Blanks

1. _______ Letter is drawn in response to a complaint. (Adjustment)
2. _______ Letter is drawn by a customer expressing dissatisfaction on goods bought. (Complaint)
3. _______ Letters needs more tact. (Letter refusing adjustment)

Rewriting Badly Drafted Letters

1. Rewrite the following badly-worded passage found in a letter of complaint.

What would happen if all others emulates your example of doing business? Your promise to deliver the goods on 2nd June is yet to be carried out. A month has already gone and how many more months you will take for executing our order, God alone knows!

I don't understand as to why you should keep mum! You may apologise. What is the earthly use of your apology?

I don't understand as to why you should keep stone silence! Can your silence deliver the goods?

Please note that if I do not receive the goods in five days time you can treat the order as cancelled and you need not expect any order from us hereafter.

The letter couched in a courteous tone:

We placed an order with you on 2nd June for the supply of 10 dozen polyster shirts (Pattern No. 75) and requested delivery before 20th June. You also acknowledged receipt of our order on 8th June.

Unfortunately we have not yet received them nor have we received any intimation from you about their dispatch.

Any further delay is sure to cause loss of business for us. Hence, if we do not receive the goods within a week, we regret to say that we shall be obliged to cancel our order.

2. Rewrite the following sentences so that they are polite and tactful.

> Don't you know that it is humanly impossible for any dealer under the sun to supply goods within the scheduled time when workers decide to strike even on frivolous grounds and stop production?

The rewritten form of the letter:

> We are extremely sorry for the delay. We could not get supplies from the manufacturer because of strike in the factory and consequent stoppage of production. Now that production has resumed, we assure you of supply before 15th January.
>
> We quite understand the inconveniences our delay in despatch would have caused you and regret it very much.

3. Rewrite the following paragraph from a letter:

> You are complaining that one of our salesmen was very discourteous and behaved rudely to you. Don't you think that it is but natural that one loses temper in the midst of enormous work? Can you point out anyboby in the world who is calm and composed even when people like you use harsh **words?** Learn to be patient.

A courteous way of expressing oneself would be:

> We are very sorry to learn that you have a reason to complain of incivility of one of our employees and thank you for taking the trouble of bringing it to our notice.

12 CHAPTER COLLECTION LETTERS OR DUNNING LETTERS

INTRODUCTION

Credit sales form a significant portion of the total turnover of any business these days. Collection letters which aim at recovering the amount due from debtors, thereby facilitating regular flow of funds for uninterrupted business operations, assume paramount importance.

It must be remembered that not all customers pay promptly. Many do not even pay after the first reminder. A lot of persuasion and cajoling is required to make customers pay their bills. Hence, collection letters must be drafted in such a way that it stimulates the necessary instinct in the debtors to settle their accounts. This means that they must be polite as well as persuasive.

While politeness is an essential ingredient in any type of business letter, that alone will not pave way for the success of sales letters. Since there are customers who may flare up at the mere demand of payment, a good deal of tact is necessary. Letters should be written in such a way that their egos are not offended.

There are others who will not pay by mild letters. A series of follow-up letters reminding and persuading their sense of pride must ensue. These series of letters written periodically must be worded differently and drafted efficiently.

Some may continue to default despite reminders and appeals. Mild words may prove to be useless. Letters with stern warning indicating the hardened attitude of the creditor may have to be sent.

The technique of collection varies greatly with the individual debtor who will probably be classified in one of the three general groups of *good, fair or poor credit risks (Prompt pay, slow pay and poor or uncertain pay)*.

It is clear that the tone of a collection letter depends upon the particular situation and the type of customers. This requires a thorough knowledge of the customer's behaviour and his background. One must know where it pays to be rigid and where it pays to rely on one's trade practices. In short, the collection letter must be drafted to suit the circumstances of each case. It must be understood that while collecting the amount, the customer must not be lost. It implies that recovering the amount due should not be the sole objective of a collection letter. Collection must be painless. If the customer feels that the collection letter has shattered his prestige, he will not place any further order with the company. The business loses his patronage. The collection letters have twin objectives, namely keeping the customer even while collecting what is due from him. So it is correct to say that *the function of a collection letter is not merely to collect money but to collect it painlessly*. Hence they must be drafted in such a way that the debtor never likes to snap his business ties with the firm even after effecting payment.

The collection letter should sell the idea to the debtor that it is to his own advantage to pay. Instead of a dull, routine notice of payment due, the collection letter should therefore assume all the sales arguments and the attention-arousing techniques which are the features of a sales letter. In the words of Robert L. Shurter, "*Many a collection man has discovered that if he can entertain or amuse his debtor, the chances of payment increase.*"

All these point to the fact that collection letters require the greatest amount of care, tact and use of psychological appeals and that loosely worded letters have the risk of losing a customer. Hence it is stated that the most delicate and difficult business letters are those which deal with the collection of accounts. One should also agree with the statement that of all routine letters the collection letter is the hardest to write.

OBJECTIVES OF COLLECTION LETTERS

The twin objectives of collection letters are (1) To collect the overdue amount (2) To retain customers.

Tone of Collection Letters

If letters reflect a harsh tone even in the first instance, it will irritate the customers. They may decide to clear off the past due and never to place orders thereafter. Thus, the tone of the letters make them react in a different way. No doubt the amount is to be collected but it must be remembered that customers are not to be lost in the process. This is the side effect of a badly drafted collection letter. Another equally important goal of a collection letter is to retain the customer.

Painless Collection

The objective of retaining customers can be better achieved if the collection letter is aimed at collecting the amount painlessly. It should sell the idea to the debtor that it is in his own interest to pay. In short, it should contain sales arguments and attention-arousing techniques of a sales letter.

If the collection letter is polite and persuasive, the collection process will not be painful to the debtor. There are customers who may flare up even at the mere demand of payment. If letters are drafted in such a way so as not to offend their ego, dues will be settled but the customers will continue to patronise.

Badly Drafted Collection Letters

On the other hand, if customers feel that their prestige has been shattered by a badly drafted collection letter, they may not hesitate to snap their ties with the firm. The business relation becomes strained and ultimately comes to an end.

Hence to achieve the twin objectives of collecting the pending amount and keeping the customer, a thorough knowledge of the customer's behaviour and the particular situation in which he is placed are absolutely essential.

The collection letter must carry a strong appeal to the customer's self-interest or to his sense of fair play. It must be drafted on the theory that most people want to pay their debts; that persuasion and perseverance are the best means to get bills collected and that the feeling of anger and sarcasm merely annoy the debtor and antagonize him permanently. If this theory is kept in mind while drafting a sales letter, the amount can be collected and the customer can be retained.

STAGES INVOLVED IN WRITING A COLLECTION LETTER

Collection letters are not routine letters, but they have to be sent in a series. Collecting the amount is a painful process but it has to be effected in a painless way. If the very first letter demanding payment is written in a harsh tone, the amount may sometimes be realised but the customer may be lost. Hence, a series of letters are sent varying the tone of each letter so that the self respect of the customer is not hurt but he may be motivated to pay the bill. In short, this series of letters rests on the belief that the customer will pay if he is reminded regularly and with increasing insistence that his payment is due.

The Collection Series

First stage: Reminder

The initial remainder stage consists of the following:

First Reminder: This is a printed routine letter sent to remind the customer of the debt, enclosing a statement of account.

Second Reminder: This also encloses a statement of account, but the brief letter expresses the assumption that the statement of account sent earlier has perhaps been overlooked. Or it may even suggest that the first reminder has not reached the customer.

Third Reminder: This urges the customer to settle his account early.

Second stage: Enquiry

From now on the tone of the letters becomes serious.The letter indicates that the firm is puzzled at the inaction of the debtor and expresses that all previous assumptions—that the default to pay was a result of work pressure—have been proved wrong. Payment is demanded firmly.

Another letter may be sent after a suitable interval of time enquiring about the debtor's difficulties and offering some adjustment. This is done because some unexpected misfortune or depression might have really affected the business of the customer. The offer to help must be stressed.

If even this letter offering help fails to evoke any response, then it indicates irresponsibility on the part of the customer. Hence, another letter is sent after a short interval of time expressing regret at the customer's continued carelessness and appealing to his sense of fairness. This letter contains some sales talk on sound credit.

Final stage: Warning or Threat

If even this appeal to fairness falls on deaf ears, the collection routine enters the last stage. Here usually, three letters are sent.

The first one demands settlement of account, the alternative of which is to face legal action. No definite date is specified.

The second letter instructs payment before a particular date, threatening legal action on further default.

The third and the last of the series merely informs the debtor that papers have been handed over to an attorney for legal action.

It must be remembered that no set pattern of series is followed uniformly by all business establishments. Series are modified or cut short depending upon the circumstances of each case. But the one important rule that is inviolable and must never be scarified is that the collection letter at no stage should be rude and uncouth, though it can be firm and sterner in tone.

POINTS TO CONSIDER WHILE DRAFTING COLLECTION LETTERS

It must be remembered that collection letters are the hardest to write and a good deal of tact and skill is required to do it. This is because it has two objectives to achieve, namely collection of the overdue amount and retaining the customer. The following points are to be borne in mind while drafting collection letters:

1. A collection letter should be polite and persuasive. There are customers who may flare up even at the mere demand of payment. Hence it should be drafted so carefully that the debtor's self-respect is not wounded.
2. A collection letter should be courteous. Any rudeness will impair business relations and the collection process would then become tedious and protracted.
3. Though a collection letter must be courteous, it should not be apologetic. The creditor asks no favour when he requests payment.
4. The collection letter should be drafted in the belief that the customers want to pay their bills; on the other hand, if it reveals that the customer is considered hopeless, he may decide not to pay at all.
5. '*Collect the amount but keep the customer*' must be the guiding principle for drafting a collection letter. For this, collection should be painless and it would be painless if debtors are approached psychologically.
6. The collection letter can also contain some of the features of a sales letter which is attention-arousing.
7. Since customers are of varied types—prompt payers, slow payers and uncertain payers—letters must be drafted differently to appeal to the different type of customers. No uniform pattern can be followed. The circumstances surrounding the customer and the type of customer addressed must be considered before setting the tone of the letter.
8. When reminders fail to evoke any response, it can appeal to his self-interest. The letter should bring home the fact that it is in his own interest to pay.
9. The letter must exhibit a real concern in the debtor's prosperity. Because of unforeseen depression, unwise purchase decision or locking up of funds in expansion programmes, the debtor may find it hard to settle the account. The letter should seek to know what exactly holds up the payment so that he can be helped, if possible.
10. The letter should contain an offer to help him to come out of his business difficulty by suggesting any workable adjustment. It may even offer to assist him in disposing of bought goods.

11. A collection letter should contain the threat of legal action only after exhausting the entire collection routine; when persuasion and perseverance, offer of help and appeals fail to evoke the necessary response.

SAMPLE COLLECTION LETTERS

Sample 1: Draft a collection series, four in number, beginning with a formal notification of the debt and ending with a hint at legal proceedings.

Reminder–I

Pallavan Publishers

Karamanikuppam,
Varakalpattu – 607 109
2nd June 2011

M/s. Abdulkuthoos Brothers,
128, Kutcheri Road,
Erode – 638 002

Dear Sirs,

May we draw your attention to your account showing a balance of ₹ 2,500. We enclose a statement of account and will be pleased to have your remittance as early as possible.

Yours faithfully,
R. Annamalai
Partner

Encl:1

(only body of the letter is given hereafter)

Reminder–II

23rd June 2011

Dear Sirs,

We have not received any reply to our letter of 2nd June demanding settlement of account. We presume that our communication has not probably reached you.

We enclose a duplicate statement of account and we will appreciate your sending us a cheque as early as possible.

Yours faithfully,
Annamalai

Reminder–III

15th July 2011

Dear Sirs,

We regret to inform you that we have not received any reply to our letters of 2nd and 23rd June demanding early settlement of your account.

As you have considerably exceeded the term of credit normally allowed by us, we must now insist on your settling the account by 30th of this month.

Will you allow your credit to be tarnished by ignoring our repeated request for early payment?

Yours faithfully,
Annamalai

Reminder–IV

2nd August 2011

Dear Sirs,

We very much regret to find that our earlier letters have evoked no response from you. We have to demand payment by 17th August. In case of any further default, we shall be compelled to file a suit against you for enforcing payment.

We trust you will not force us to take this unpleasant step.

Yours faithfully,
Annamalai

Sample 2: A letter to your debtor who had purchased goods from you some six months ago. He has neither responded to your reminders nor had he sent any remittance. A letter holding out a legal threat, if you do not hear from him within ten days is written as under.

Kannan & Co.

78, Radia Street,
Chennai – 600 004

2nd June 2011

M/s. Kuselar & Sons,
6, Main Road,
Krishnagiri – 635 109

Dear Sirs,

We very much regret that we have received any payment in your past due account for ₹ 9000 with respect to the merchandise despatched to you six months ago, and that our repeated reminders demanding payment remain unanswered. You have not taken notice of even our well intentioned letter of 15th May offering to assist you in case you face any difficulty. Your non-payment as well as your irritating silence leaves us no choice but to place this matter in the hands of our solicitors.

However, we like to give you one more opportunity to settle the account in full within 10 days or else we shall be forced to take an action which, we frankly dislike.

Yours faithfully,
R. Kannan
Proprietor.

Sample 3: Martin & Sons, a customer of Jayam & Co has neither settled his account with them nor given any reply to their reminders. Jayam & Co writes a sympathetic letter to Mr. Muthusamy, inquiring whether he is in any difficulty and suggesting payment by instalments.

Jayam & Co.

326,Rajaji Salai,
Chennai - 600 001

9th September 2011

M/s Martin & Sons,
34, Saraswathi Nagar,
Cuddalore - 607 002

Dear Sirs,

We are surprised to note that you have allowed your account to remain three months overdue. What worries us most is that you have not replied to any of our reminders.

You have always paid your bills with us promptly in the past. Therefore, we know there must be some special reason for non-payment in this instance.

We would appreciate if you write to us frankly as to what exactly holds up the payment as we, on our part, would try to assist you in getting over the difficulty.

We are willing to accept payment by instalment, if you are facing financial stress at the moment. In case you find any difficulty in disposing off the goods, please feel free to write to us so that we can accept the return of unsold goods. We can together work out some plan whereby you can settle your account without causing too much strain on resources.

We hope to hear from you soon.

Yours faithfully,
Stephen
Sale Proprietor

Sample 4: M/s Martin & Sons explains why be has not been able to settle the account, appreciates the mode of payment suggested by Jayam & Co and encloses a cheque to cover a third of the debt.

Martin & Sons

34, Saraswathi Nagar,
Cuddalore – 607 002

12th September 2011

M/s Jayam & Co,
326, Rajaji Salai,
Chennai – 600 001

Dear Sirs,

We thank you for your letter of 9th September.

Our desire to pay your account in full is the reason for not having responded to your letters so long. But we regret to say that we are unable to fulfill our desire because we ourselves are unable to collect what is due to us from a large number of customers owing to depression in our trade.

Our efforts to collect, however, does not leave us sufficient funds to settle our account by a single remittance. Hence, we propose to make fortnightly payment of ₹ 1000 starting with an initial payment of ₹ 2000 which is a third of the total dues.

Since we have decided to dispose off the stock even at a nominal profit to secure ready cash, we do not want to cause inconvenience to you by accepting your suggestion to return the unsold stock.

We hope our plan to clear our arrears will meet with your approval, though it involves further extension of time.

We thank you for all your kindness and sympathy.

Yours faithfully,
S. Martin
Partner

Sample 5: All your reminders and offers have failed to evoke any reply from Messrs P.S.K Brothers who have a payment due of ₹ 10,000 for goods bought 5 months before. Write a letter to them appealing to their credit reputation.

V.S.TEX .

7, Thiruvalluvar Road,
Karamanikuppam
Cuddalore – 607 109

4th June 2011

M/s P.S.K. Brothers,
Kanchi Road,
Cheyyaru – 604 407

Dear Sir,

We are sorry to say that our several reminders about your overdue account for ₹ 10,000 have evoked no response from you.

Usually we do not extend credit for more than a month and your bill is outstanding since January 2011.

The credit references you cited at the time of opening our account showed that you did enjoy a good credit record. We have no doubt that you continue to enjoy this reputation even now. We are proud of it. We hope you will consider how important and invaluable an asset your credit standing is. Undoubtedly you will place a far high value on it than the amount you owe us.

Non-payment combined with silence does not inspire confidence in creditors. Do you not think that your credit rating suffers as a result of delayed payment? When we are asked to give our opinion on your handling of credit account with us, we hardly know what to say.

We trust you will live upto your reputation and settle your account within this week.

Yours faithfully,
S. Rajakannu
Partner

Sample 6: A tactful letter to a customer who is in the habit of deducting discount even though his payments are made too late for it.

Vep Oil Mills

Katpadi Road,
71, Gandhi Nagar,
Vellore – 632 006

10th June 2011

The Seran Oil Stores,
22, First Agraharam Road,
Salem – 636 001

Dear Sir,

We thank you for your letter of 8th June enclosing a cheque for ₹ 980. You have deducted ₹ 20 towards discount.

We regret to state that you have deducted 2% towards discount even though payment is effected late, which is against our trade practice.

As you know, we permit a 2% discount to customers who pay their bills within ten days of the date of their bill. We maintain this policy because it enables us to earn similar discounts by paying our own bills promptly. We pass on the discount earned by us to our own customers as a reward for their promptness.

The amount of ₹ 20 is in itself a trivial matter, but fairness to all customers demands that we should adhere to a consistent policy without permitting deviation.

Will you not object if we grant certain favourable terms to other customers while denying them to you? Will you not like us to treat everybody fairly and consistently?

Now that the facts are with you, we do hope that you will take advantage of our discount policy by paying within the prescribed period and by not deducting discount when you are not eligible.

Please co-operate with us.

Yours faithfully,
V. Ruthrapathy
Credit Manager

Sample 7: Inform a customer that owing to his repeated delay in paying his dues, you are compelled to deal with him on cash basis only.

Pallavan Auto Spare Parts

79, Thiru Vi Ka Road,
Villupuram – 605 602

5th June 2011

Messrs. Habu Brothers,
123, Jinjee Road,
Tindivanam – 604 001

Dear Sirs,

We have your letter of 28th May, 2011, requesting supply of goods on credit.

You are aware that credit accounts lock up working capital. Delayed payments bring business to a standstill and all of us suffer. If credit period is scrupulously followed and payment made within prescribed dates, credit can be extended. But we regret to say that in the past you have allowed your accounts to remain overdue for a long time on several occasions and settled them only after repeated reminders. This has caused us quite a lot of inconvenience.

In the circumstances, we are compelled to deal with you on cash basis only. If you let us have the necessary remittance, we will fill your order without delay on our part.

Yours faithfully,
For Pallavan Auto Spare Parts,
K. Pallavan
Sole Proprietor

SUMMARY

Characteristics of a collection letter are inevitability of credit sales warranting the writing of collection letters, to be drafted in a way to stimulate the debtors' instinct to settle accounts, letter to be drawn in a way not to offend the debtor. Collection letters need to be written in series depending on the attitude of debtors. Tone of collection letter varies with the situation. It should conform to principles for writing collection letter and stress the advantages of settlement in time to debtor.

Guiding principles for writing collection letters are collection of the overdue amount, keeping the customer and keeping the cost of collection to a minimum.

Letters drafted in various stages of collection are

Stage 1– Reminder, second reminder, and third reminder.

Stage 2 – Enquiry and discussion, appeal and urging.

Stage 3 – Demanding settlement within a specified time with a warning to take legal action. If not settled within the time specified, informing the legal action initiated.

Points to be observed in writing collection letter are to be polite and persuasive, to be courteous, not to be apologetic, to be written on the belief that customer wants to pay, observe the principles like 'collect the amount and keep the customer', to contain some of the features of a sales letter, letter to appeal to self–interest of a debtor when reminders evoke no response, to express concern in debtor's prosperity, to include an offer to help and to include a threat to take legal action after exhausting the routine.

REVIEW QUESTIONS

Part A: Short Questions

1. What is a collection letter?
2. How would you classify the customers?
3. State the guiding principles of collection.

Part B: Paragraph Questions

1. Spell out the collection strategy for different types of customers.
2. Enumerate the points to be kept in mind while drafting a collection letter.

Part C: Essay Questions

1. Outline the characteristics of a collection letter.
2. Elaborate on the guiding principles for drafting a collection letter.
3. Bring out the various stages involved in writing a collection letter.

Part D: Objective Type Questions

Choose the correct answer

1. With which letter is it difficult to unlock the amount locked with debtors

   a. Circular letter   b. Collection letter   c. Complaint letter

   (Ans: b)

2. Specify the principles of a collection letter

   a. Collecting the amount and keeping the customer

   b. Keeping the collection cost to a minimum   c. Both

   (Ans: c)

3. With whom should a threat of legal action be insisted

   a. Slow payers   b. Defaulters   c. Fraudulent customers

   (Ans: c)

Fill in the blanks

1. __________ letter is drawn to unfreeze the amount locked in debtors. (Collection)
2. The principles of collection letters are__________ (Keeping the collection cost minimum, collection of the amount and keeping the customer)
3. __________ is the first stage of collection. (Sending statement of accounts)
4. __________ is last stage of collection. (Sending warning)

13 CHAPTER SALES LETTERS

INTRODUCTION

A letter written with the immediate objective of inducing sales of merchandise or service is called a *sales letter*.

Though any business letter like reply to an enquiry, trade circular etc., may ultimately result in a sale, only those letters which have their immediate objective as sales of goods or services are called sales letters.

PURPOSE OF A SALES LETTER

Business people use sales letters for the following purposes:

- To make direct sale.
- To test the reaction of the prospects to new products.
- To know the queries and doubts of the prospects.
- To promote an image for a new product.
- To strengthen dealer's sales efforts and to attract new dealers.

ADVANTAGES OF A SALES LETTER

The advantages of a sales letter include:

- It serves as a cheaper medium of advertisement.
- Sales advertisements are not mixed with advertisement of other sponsors.
- It is a personal appeal and hence it carries weight.
- Even distant places can be accessed through sales letters.
- Since it is sent to a lot of customers the impact can be measured immediately.

STRUCTURE OF A SALES LETTER

A sales letter aims at inducing the right reaction in the recipient. Hence its structure is designed to achieve this objective by closely following the four stages of the selling process. In short, the AIDA formula needs to be observed. AIDA means Attention, Interest, Desire and Action. Sales letter needs to be written in pursuance of the formula.

1. Attracting the reader's attention.
2. Creating an interest in the products.
3. Convincing the reader that this product will ideally suit his requirement and thereby triggering his desire.
4. Motivating action.

Attracting attention

The opening paragraph must be so cleverly drafted so as to get sufficient attention of the reader. If it fails to arouse curiosity, the whole sales letter fails.

- The routine opening like *"We have pleasure in informing you"* must be totally avoided.
- If it can appeal to the reader's self-interest, it can start with a question. For example:

  Are you satisfied with the amount of money you save?

  Have you seen any cheap watch that is good?
- A courteous command is another technique used to arouse attention. For example:

  Don't waste your time and energy in a sweltering office when you can enjoy the cool comfort of air conditioning.
- A split beginning is another device used to attract maximum attention. For example:

  We can't make all the T.V. Sets. So we just make the best of them.

  Arrest declining income! Our financial service is designed to do just that.
- A statement of significant fact or a quotation from an eminent authority will also focus on attention. For example:

  No pain, no gain is the proverb. We plan to disprove it.

Anecdotes are also frequently used as attention arousing device. But to be effective, the story told should not divert attention from the main objective of the sales letter. It should have some connection with the message.

Creating an interest in the product or service

This depends upon the type of prospect to whom the letter is addressed and also on the understanding of human desires and feelings. For instance, if a sales letter is sent to a dealer, it should emphasise on profits, exposition of its mechanism etc. If it is written to the general public, it will concentrate on the joys of air-conditioned homes and offices.

The choice of the appeal also depends upon the type of product to be sold. While an appeal to reason will be effective in the case of necessities, appeal to emotion will be the best for luxuries and novelties.

It is stated that there are 25 reasons why people spend money. It is to make money, to save money, to enjoy comforts, to enjoy good health, to be popular, to attract the opposite sex, to protect their family, to satisfy their appetite, to emulate others, to take advantage of an opportunity etc. By appealing to one or more of these reasons, a sales letter can create the necessary desire for the product or service in the reader.

Convincing the reader by winning his confidence, thereby firing his desire

The third part of the letter should show facts to prove that the claims made for the product are true.

Expert testimony: Opinions of qualified experts in the field constitute a sound sales argument. Opinions of satisfied customers are also given.

Facts: Details regarding the number of sales effected within a specified period, actual cost of operation, number of satisfied customers etc., give factual support to the claims made for the product.

The use of logic: A sample offer of the product, giving guarantee cards etc., may appeal to the readers' reasoning.

Examples:

1. Our Summer Softs (Soft drink) has won the gold medal at the International Food For Health Exhibition held in New Delhi last year.
2. You need not go by the word of any expert. A sample tin of our milk powder is waiting to be sent to you. Just mail the enclosed postage-paid card with your signature on it.
3. This fan will meet your expectations in every respect. If you are not completely satisfied, our money-back guarantee entitles you to return it and get your money back.

Motivating Action

The concluding paragraph of the sales letter should not only stimulate action on the part of the reader but should also show how he would benefit by it. Business reply paid envelopes (which do not require payment of postage) must be enclosed. The reader should be prodded to act and to act quickly.

Examples:

1. You have nothing to lose-perhaps a lot to gain by using the enclosed card.
2. Check the item that interests you right now. We will gladly send you a sample of each.
3. Walk into any of our authorised dealer's shop with the enclosed coupon and get your 1kg packet of snow white washing powder at 20% discount. The offer expires on the 7th.

It must be remembered that the success of a sales letter is reflected in a large number of its readers taking the suggested course of action.

SALES SERIES OR WEAR-OUT SERIES

Like the collection series, the sales message is conveyed in a series of letters using fresh arguments so that the reader is induced to act ultimately. Since they are designed for constant repetition to 'wear out' the reader's sales resistance, they are also known as the *wear-out series*.

They are used only to sell costly products. Though the number of letters to be included in this series cannot be dogmatically stated, three or four follow-up letters after the original message will suffice.

The sales series should be brief. They can be used for trying different appeals.

The interval between any two follow-up series should not be unduly long. A ten to fifteen day interval is considered reasonable.

An argument use in the earlier letter must not be repeated in the subsequent series.

SAMPLE SALES LETTERS

Sample 1: Draft a sales letter introducing a new electronic typewriter.

The Standard Electronics Ltd.

5/1000 Abdul Rehman Road,
Karol Bagh,
New Delhi - 110 005

25th August 2011

The Chitra Commercial House (P) Ltd,
170, Nehru Nagar
Karaikal – 609 602

Dear Sirs,

19th February, 2011
In Japan EX-53 comes off production line.
18th May 2011
The incredible EX-53 arrives in
India and the dividing line has been drawn.

The elite corporate in this country is going to be divided into the 'haves' and the 'have-nots'.

Those who have the EX-53 Electronic typewriter and those who do with just an electric typewriter.

The electronic typewriter arrived and overnight the electric typewriter yielded its place in all the advanced countries of the world.

Yes, our EX-53 has been created through a totally new concept in electronic typewriter technology. It has been widely acclaimed in Japan within weeks of its introduction. It is natural, because the users there have recognised the unique features of EX-53 that make it such a versatile and adaptable machine. It is complete with memory in which it can store upto six typewritten pages.

It allows you to make any number of corrections on the display panel before the copy-matter appears on the paper. Copy block capabilities, word search and replace-all features are packaged into this machine that is so simple and so easy to operate.

Even at a glance, the visual impact of the printed pages from Ex-53 are so much superior! The chances of breakdown are 200% less.

Well, which side of the dividing line are you going to be?

Seeing is Believing. It is impossible to talk about all the features that Ex-53 offers.

Why don't you call us a for a free demonstration? The machine is so advanced that nothing else can match it's versatality. We promise that you wont be disappointed.

Yours faithfully,
A. Sundaresan.
Sales Manager

Sample 2: A sales letter introducing a new scooter.

Windspeed Auto Ltd.

Ennore,
Chennai – 600 105

30th July 2011

Dear Customer,

If someone asks you to name India's largest motor cycle manufacturer, whose name would come to your mind first?

Definetely Windspeed Motor Cycles. What will equal this matchless motor cycle; It is our own Windspeed scooter!

Yes, to cope up with the mounting pressure on scooters, Windspeed Auto Ltd., which has received the prestigious productivity award for 2011, has recently put on India's roads its Windspeed scooter.

Deployment of the most advanced technology and stringent quality control at every stage of production has made Windspeed scooter a functional beauty.

We are always conscious that India is not the West; our roads are not perfect, petrol is not cheap, service and spare parts are not available at every corner. That is why, we have designed and built the Windspeed scooter which will admirably suit our Indian conditions.

It gives a mileage of 70 km per litre. Easily availabile low-cost spares, largest service and spares network for easy maintenance, constant upgradation of technology are the chief features of our brand.

Surely, the Windspeed scooter, with its style, strength and looks, is going to capture the fancy of millions of our countrymen as the most economical, lowest-priced mode of conveyance.

Yours faithfully,
For Windspeed Auto Ltd.,
A. Sasikala
Sales Manager

Sample 3: A sales letter introducing a Mixer Grinder.

The Shiva Kitchen Appaliances

Avenue Road,
Bangalore – 560 002

1st October 2011

Ratha Appliances & Co,
5, Kumbakonam Road,
Panruti – 607 106

Dear Sir,

Some of our new appliances will be terrific in your kitchen! The wearisome housewives are sure to heave a sigh of relief. Our Mixer Grinder is tougher. It is safer. It is international standard brought for the Indian kitchen, yet moderately priced.

Our Shiva Mixer Grinder is a sleek, compact, different looking appliance. This means that what inside lies is not a mere imitation but a number of improvements on the existing models. Why you should go in for our Mixer?

i. The imported circuit breaker protects the motor against overloads.
ii. The blades are made of specially hardened steel for better performance and longer life.
iii. It has solid controls that ensure superority in all aspects.
iv. High quality couplers are used for smoother operation and have a long life.
v. The safety 'Silver' switch ensures that the mixer operates only when the jar is locked in place.

Like all our other appliances, our mixer grinder will soon prove be a fast selling line since it has the solid backing of our image.

Please use the enclosed card to tell us when our representative can call you at your convenience and with absolutely no obligation.

Yours Sincerely,
P. Sivanesan
Manager

Sample 4: A sales letter introducing an LED T.V. Set.

Paragon Electronics Ltd.

78, Ambattur Road
Chennai – 600 012

2nd June 1986

Dear Customer,

Which would you prefer – Less for More or More for Less?

The PEL T.V. Sets give you more pleasure at lesser costs because they come from the house of pioneers in electronic equipments.

Before you buy your LED T.V., make sure it meets the highest standards.

Does your T.V. incorporate the latest LED technology? Will It give you the refinement of an Automatic Fine Tuner and Auto De-gaussing unit for undisturbed viewing?

Does it ensure the perfection of flawless colour? Will it give you quality reproduction? Will it come with the assurance of expert service at a moments notice?

If there is one T.V. that passes the test with flying colours, it is PEL. You can see even the minute details like the eyelashes and pimples on the face of a newsreader.

The automatic noise cancellation circuit in PEL LED variety keeps the picture from rolling and makes televiewing a pleasure.

All PEL LED models, including the economy set, have a pick-up facility that enabels you to listen to music when there are no T.V. programmes. They add zest to hi-fi sound. PEL LED Televisions will certainly be the pride of your living room.

We have a panel of specialists to fall back on at all important centres. Above all, it carries a name that stands for a tradition of innovation.

Remember that in the quest for excellence, we are always a step ahead! Our guarantee card is an assurance that this will meet your expectations in every respect.

Which models would you like to see? Fill in the enclosed card, send it directly to us or contact your nearest dealer.

Yours faithfully,
S. Karthikeyan
Sales Manager

Sample 5: A sales letter introducing 'Sufloil' (sun flower oil) stressing its value for preventing heart trouble.

Vegetable Oil Industries (P) Ltd.

77, Broadway
Cochin – 628 001

14thNovember 2011

Dear Sir,

Long years of research and study have confirmed the deadly link between high cholesterol and heart disease.

The more you lower cholesterol and fat in your diet, the more you reduce the risk of heart disease.

What is cholesterol?

Cholesterol is a waxy substance. It is mostly produced in the liver. About 20% to 30% of it comes from the food we eat. The normal cholesterol level for the average Indian adult is 150 to 250 mg. Excess of it leads to thickening of the arteries and eventually to heart trouble.

How to reduce cholesterol level?

A subtle change in diet works wonders among other things. Fats should account for no more than 30% of your total daily calories. Out of this 30%, only less than 10% can be saturated fat. Ghee, butter, vanaspathi and coconut oil contain a high amount of saturated fats. Hence, cook with oil containing more polyunsaturated fat. This has the following benefits:

'Sufloil' has the highest percentage of polyunsaturated fats and the lowest content of saturated fat. It has the following benifits:

- It reduces blood cholesterol level and keeps it in check. It is pure, refined sunflower seed oil.
- Light and easy to digest.
- Can be used for cooking, baking and frying. Sufloil is good for your heart and health. It is good for your entire family.

Please ask us for a free, colourful informative folder. Fill in the postage-free coupon and mail it to us with absolutely no obligation.

Yours Truly,
for Vegetable Oil Industries (P) Ltd,
V. Karikalan
Secretary

Sample 6: Festival offer.

Bulkiwala Home Appliances

16, Kadar St,
Dindugul – 624 001

15th December 2011

Dear Customer,

You would be very much delighted to learn that we offer excellent discount on all home appliances sold in our shop. We have a wide range of Music systems, Television sets, Computers of different configuration, Washing machines, Refrigerators, and Air-conditioners in various brands. We also offer exchange value and take your old items at the best possible price. Our discounts range from 5% to 15% depending upon the brand value of the products.

The discount season is on till 15th January. I am enclosing an invitation for the inauguration of the discount fortnight on Jan 1st at 9 a.m. The shop will be open from 9 a.m. to 9 p.m. on all days and you can avail of a special gift on your purchase.

Yours faithfully,
Solanki
Senior Manager

SUMMARY

Purpose of a sales letter is making direct sale, obtaining enquiries, testing the reaction of a customer, reaching out for more prospects and reinforcing dealer's sales effort.

Advantages of a sales letter are cheaper mode of advertisement personal appeal not mingled with advertisement of others, outreach to far-flung areas and accurate measurement of result.

Structure of a sales letter should aim at attracting attention, creating desire, convincing the reader, motivation and action.

REVIEW QUESTIONS

Part A: Short Questions

1. What is a sales letter?
2. What is wear-out series?
3. What is sales series?

Part B: Paragraph Questions

1. What are the purposes of a sales letter?
2. State the advantages of a sales letter?

Part C: Essay Questions

1. What points should be noted in drafting a sales letter?
2. What is the structure of a sales letter?
3. Draft a sales letter introducing a T.V. Set.
4. Draft a sales letter introducing a new electronic typewriter.
5. Draft a sales letter introducing a new scooter.
6. Draft a sales letter introducing a Mixer Grinder.
7. Draft a sales letter introducing 'Sufloil' (sun flower oil) stressing its value for preventing heart trouble. Let your sales letter appeal to health benefits.

Part D: Objective Type Questions

Choose the correct answer

1. Letter written to induce the potential buyer is

    a. Collection letter   b. Sales Letter   c. Circular letter

    (Ans: b)

2. Which formula needs to be observed while drafting sales letter

    a. AIDA   b. BIDA   c. ABC

(Ans: a)

Fill in the Blanks

1. Letter written to induce the potential customer to buy goods/service is ___________. (Sales Letter)
2. Sales Letter promotes a new__________. (Image)
3. Writing a sales letter using____________. formula would create an impact on the reader. (AIDA)

14

CHAPTER

CIRCULAR LETTERS

INTRODUCTION

A circular is a letter addressed to a large number of customers conveying the same message. For example: Opening of a new branch. The letters are photocopied or printed, as multiple copies are required.

Occasions When Circular Letters are Sent

The usual occasions when circulars are sent to customers are mentioned below:

- When a new branch is opened
- When a new department is added
- When a new business is set up
- When new goods are introduced
- When business is moved to a new premises
- When a partner retires from a firm or dies
- When a new partner is added
- When a partnership is converted into a joint-stock company
- When a power of attorney is given
- When an agency is obtained
- When clearance sales are effected

CHARACTERISTICS OF CIRCULAR LETTERS

The general characteristics of a circular letter are as follows:

1. All copies of circular letters convey the same information.
2. They are addressed to a large number of people.
3. They are generally photocopied, printed or lithographed.

4. They are not addressed personally to a recipient since the message to be conveyed is common to all.

5. Such letters are usually not signed, since a very large number of them are sent.

6. They contain information which the customers need to know.

7. Since they are mass produced, inside addresses are entered at the time of mailing.

8. Since they are sent to different types of customers such as individuals, partnerships, companies etc., the salutation is general such as 'Dear Customer', 'Dear Manufacturer' etc.

9. They are pleasantly worded and in the nature of inspiring confidence.

TYPES OF CIRCULAR LETTERS

Circular Letters Announcing the Establishment of a New Business

The primary object of a circular letter announcing the establishment of a new business is to wean the customers away from their previous dealers. Therefore, the letters should be drafted so as to win the confidence of the customers.

1. The letter should convince that the firm has necessary experience in the particular line of business. It can also show the connections that the firm has with the manufacturers.

2. The price quoted should be competitive. Initial low price is likely to attract the customers to make the first contact. The letter should also mention the facilities the organisation is offering to customers such as free delivery, special discount allowed and the period it is offered, its central location, shopping conveniences etc.

3. The name and style of its business address.

4. Date of commencement of business, nature of the business.

5. Details about the proprietor or partners and their experience in the line.

6. Capital at your disposal. The exact amount need not be mentioned.

7. A request for a trial order which will convince the recepient of the circular about the claim made in the circular.

8. Such a letter should enclose an invitation to the inauguration ceremony.

Circular Letters Intimating the Opening of a Branch

Points which a circular letter must contain while announcing the opening of a branch are stated below briefly:

- The complete address and location of the branch.
- The date from which the branch will be functioning.
- The name of the Manager together with his specimen signature.
- The letter should recall with gratitude the patronage extended so long and with an appeal to extend it.
- A brief mention of the conveniences offered to customers as a result of opening of the

branch.

- An invitation to the customers to visit the new showroom on the opening day ceremony.

Circular Letters Announcing the Shifting of the Business to a New Premises

The points given in the previous heading must be reproduced and the following ones must be stressed:

- The letter should also state how the inconveniences exhibited in the old place has been removed in the new premises.
- The benefit of central location, vastness of accommodation, shopping conveniences provided, transport facilities available all must be stated.

Circular Letters announcing Addition of a New Department

- State how consumers can get all their requirements satisfied under one roof.
- It must be stressed how the persistent demand of numerous customers to have such goods in their own shops has been fulfilled by the creation of the new department.
- The experience and efficiency of the person who heads the department.
- An assurance to provide a variety of standard goods at competitive prices.
- The usual invitation to the customers to visit the department.

Circular Letters Intimating the Death or Retirement of a Partner

Since a circular letter announcing the death or retirement of a partner involves change in the constitution of the firm necessitating depletion of financial resources, it must be drafted with a view to retain the confidence of the customers.

- The letter should contain expression of regret at the loss of the retiring or deceased partner.
- It should acknowledge the services rendered by such a partner.
- It should assure that this change does not result in the depletion of capital and that the business would continue to be run on the same lines as before.
- If there is any change in the name of the firm, it should be pointed out.
- It should also state whether the vacancy will be filled in by a new partner.
- It should give the specimen signature of an incoming partner, if any.
- It should end with soliciting customers' continued patronage.

Circular Letters Announcing the Conversion of a Partnership into a Private Limited Company

A circular letter announcing the conversion of a partnership into a private limited company must contain the following points:

- The letter must point out that the very conversion into a private company is an evidence of its substantial growth.
- The continued expansion has made it necessary for mobilising greater capital.
- The name and style under which it will function after conversion.

- The date from which it will start functioning as a private limited company.
- The letter should also stress that despite this change, it will continue to have its personal relations with the customers and that customer satisfaction will be its main motto.
- It should end with an appeal to continue their patronage.

Circular Letters Announcing the Obtaining of an Agency

A circular letter which announces that an agency has been obtained must stress the following points:

- The area of agency operation.
- A reference to qualities of the product.
- A hope that orders would be more promptly executed.
- It should also refer to the wide publicity given through various media so as to make the product a fast selling line.
- The competitive price advantage that the product enjoys.
- The benefit of brand image that the product carries with it.
- Such a circular letter can be accompanied by samples stating that the claim made in the letter can be tested.
- If any special discount is offered at the time of introduction of the product in the market, it should be stressed.
- The letter should conclude with a hope that the dealer would unhesitatingly co-operate in pushing the sales of the product.

SAMPLE CIRCULAR LETTERS

Sample 1: Kalpana Cloth Centre is opening a new cloth business in Pondicherry. A circular letter announcing the setting up of this business is drafted.

Kalpana Cloth Centre

30, Nehru Street,
Pondicherry – 605 007
26th May 2011

Dear Sir/Madam,

It gives us great pleasure to inform you that we are opening a high class cloth centre on Friday, June 6, 2011, in the above address under the name of 'Kalpana Cloth Centre'.

Mr. Balu who was formerly associated with big cloth merchants like V.S. Tex, Chitra Mills Cloth House and Alankar will be our Purchase Manager. His wide and varied experience in the line will help us a great deal in selecting the excellent and the most fashionable textiles and in running the business most efficiently.

The capital at our disposal is sufficient to enable us to stock large varieties of textiles from popular mills.

Since we recognise the sovereignty of the consumers, we adopt a pricing policy which aims at realizing a low margin of profit. Our prices are most competitive.

Our shop is fully air-conditioned and our courteousness will make shopping a pleasant affair.

We trust your visit will convince you of this. May we have the pleasure of meeting you soon?

Yours faithfully,
for Kalpana Cloth Centre,
R. Alalasundaram
Proprietor

Sample 2: Draft a circular letter intimating the opening of a branch.

Chitra Shoe Mart

69, Anna Salai,
Kanchipuram – 631 502

15th September 2011

Dear Customer,

You will be pleased to know that we are opening a new branch at 85, Periyar Nagar, Thiruvarur for the convenience of our customers with effect from 1st October.

Our Assistant Manager, Mr. K.Karunanithi who has been looking after the orders received from that region quite successfully for a fairly long time will be in-charge of that branch. We have no doubt that under his stewardship, the branch will be in a position to cater to the needs of our patrons from Cuddalore, Thiruvarur, Thanjavur, Pudukkottai and Trichi Districts in a more effective way.

Please pay a visit to our branch and place orders for all your requirements from 1st October directly at our Thiruvarur Branch. Your orders will be attended more promptly by our branch with savings in freight.

We take this opportunity to thank you for your patronage and we assure you that our branch in Thiruvarur will make every effort to give you continued satisfaction.

Yours faithfully,
G.M. Vasantha
Managing Partner

Sample 3: A circular letter announcing the admission of a new partner.

Seran - Sozhan Papers

73, Anderson Street,
Chennai – 600 001

30th July 2011

Dear Customer,

We have pleasure in informing you that owing to the expansion of our business, we have today included Mr. S. Pandyan, our Branch Manager at Madurai, as a partner.

Mr. S. Pandyan has been associated with us for the last fifteen years serving in responsible positions.

Besides his rare talents and rich business experience, he is investing ₹ 25,00,000 as capital. His admission as a partner will therefore prove to be of immense value to us in expanding our business activities to areas so far untouched and in ensuring prompt and better service.

We will henceforth trade under the name and style of Seran, 'Sozhan and Pandyan Papers' in the same premises.

There will be no change in the policy of the firm due to the admission of Mr.S. Pandyan.

We thank you for your business in the past and look forward to your continued patronage.

Yours faithfully,
V. Seran
Managing Partner

Sample 4: A circular letter announcing the retirement of a partner of your firm.

Ram, Rahim, Robert & Company

7, Mosque street,
Trichy – 621 714

10th June 2011

Dear Customer,

We are sorry to inform you that Mr. Robert, a senior partner and one of the founders of the firm is retiring owing to ill-health and old age. He has been advised by his family doctor to take complete rest.

His business acumen and pleasant disposition has undoubtedly contributed a great deal to the present growth of our firm. No doubt we will be missing his active association hereafter.

However, on account of Mr. Robert's continued ill-health for the last two years, his work has been completely taken over by our young and energetic partner, Mr. Mathew whose capacity for hard work you are well aware of. There will be no change in the policy of the firm and we assure that we will continue to serve you to your complete satisfaction as in the past.

Due to the retirement of Mr. Robert, we will function under the name and style of Ram, Rahim, Mathew & Company.

Our financial resources will not suffer because of the withdrawal of capital by Mr. Robert as the deficiency has been made good by contributions from the other partners.

We thank you for your confidence in the past and we hope enjoy your continued patronage.

Yours faithfully,
V. Ram
Managing Partner

Sample 5: Fair Deal Traders is a firm of general merchants and commissioning agents. Mr. N. Ganesan has died and his son, Mr. G. Sukumar has been made a partner in the firm. The firm will continue under the old name. A circular letter giving this information to the customers of the firm is drafted as follows.

Fair Deal Traders

49, Kamaraj Street,
Viruthunagar – 626 001

9th September 2011

Dear Customers,

I regret to inform you of the sad and premature demise of my partner Mr. N. Ganesan, one of the founders of the firm. I am sure that but for his experience and business knowledge, our firm would not have reached its present position.

To fill this gap, I have admitted Mr. G. Sukumar, the son of the late Mr. N. Ganesan into partnership. Mr. G. Sukumar has been working with us for the last ten years in various responsible capacities, showing keen interest in its growth.

We will continue to trade under the same name and style and on exactly the same lines as before.

We trust that the change in the constitution of the firm will not stand in the way of enjoying your patronage in the years to come.

Yours faithfully,
For Fair Deal Traders
V.K. Murugaiyan
Managing Partner

Mr. G. Sukumar will sign as under:
(Signature)

Sample 6: A circular letter for Messrs Paari Brothers, announcing the conversion of the partnership into a private limited company under the style of Paari & Co (P) Ltd.

Paari Brothers

Manufacturers of Auto Spares

73/2 Lingi Chetty Street,
Chennai – 600 001

8th December 2011

Dear Customer,

We are pleased to inform you that we have decided to convert our firm into a private limited company.

Having completed all legal formalities connected with this conversion, the name and style of the new company which will come into existence with effect from 1st January, 2011, will be,

Paari & Co (P) Ltd.

We have five directors on the Board who are well-versed in different fields of activity.

The need for additional capital as well as greater managerial capacity warranted by the ever-expanding activities of our business has made us think in terms of this conversion.

Though the legal structure of our organisation has changed, the personal touch running through our relationships will remain unaltered. Your interests will continue to be supreme to us whether we are a partnership or a company.

We take this opportunity to thank you for the confidence you have placed in us all these years and we look forward to its continuance.

Yours faithfully,
For Paari Brothers,
K. Paari
Managing Partner

Sample 7: A circular letter in the name of the Sales Manager, Washers India Ltd, Bangalore to their customers about a new washing powder recently introduced in the market by them is drafted as follows, soliciting trial orders, enclosing a catalogue and an order form.

Washers India Ltd.

Manufacturers of High Class Washing Powder

77, Grant Road,
Bangalore – 560 001

17th November 2011

Dear Patrons,

We are pleased to inform you that months of patient and tireless research by our staff has at last borne fruit. We have prepared a new washing powder, 'Snow White' which will be in the market by the end of this month.

Our Snow White washing powder washes woolen, silk and synthetic fabrics besides cotton clothes. While it removes the dirt without rubbing or scrubbing, it retains the original whiteness. It simply requires the soaking of clothes for half an hour after which it must be rinsed with water. Washing is completed without any effort or exertion in a few minutes.

Our publicity campaign to be launched soon, together with the reputation that our other products enjoy will make selling easier. Meanwhile, we are sending samples of Snow White in 25g packets for trial and we will be thankful if you let us know how you feel about our new achievement.

The Snow White powder is packed in 450g and 900g cartons and are moderately priced. We have enclosed a price list and trade terms. In addition to the usual discount of 15% we allow on our other products, we offer a special extra discount of 5% on the trial orders received before the end of this month.

We hope that you will extend your co-operation in the marketing of this new product which, we trust, will prove to be a fast selling line.

Yours faithfully,
P. Satyamurthi
Sales Manager

Sample 8: Messrs B.S. Bangarappa & Co, New Delhi, have obtained the sole agency for Tamil Nadu for television which is produced by West End Electronics Ltd., Mumbai. A circular suitable for notifying the retailers of this fact is drafted.

B.S. Bangarappa & Co.

150, Connaught Place,
New Delhi-110 001

17th November 2011

Dear Customer,

It gives us great pleasure in informing you that we have obtained the Sole Distributing Agency for the sale of the famous Telesona LED Television sets manufactured by the West End Electronics Ltd, for the states of Tamil Nadu and Kerala. All orders are to be executed through us only.

As you know, the Telesona LED T.V. sets are well received throughout India and they stand for a tradition of innovation. Incorporating the latest 3D technology, they have already created history in sales volume.

We stock all varieties, right from the plain vanilla type to the most sophisticated ones.

Since the products of West End Eletronics Ltd, have already proved to be a fast selling line, you will not have any difficulty in selling the Telesona LED T.V. sets despite a variety of models from a host of manufacturers flooding the market. You will not have to wait for long as we will be in a position to serve you promptly, since we have agreed to keep a fairly large stock of their products.

We have enclosed an illustrative catalogue and the latest price list.

Our representative Mr. S. Kutty will also call on you next week for booking orders.

We solicit your co-operation and patronage as in the past.

Yours faithfully,
M. Rathinam
Sales Manager

Sample 9: As the Manager of a publishing firm, write a letter addressing college teachers announcing the publication of a new book on 'Social Obligations of Commercial Banks' mentioning all its attractive features.

Pallavan Publishers

22, Pondy Road,
Cuddalore – 607 003

1st May 2011

Dear Sir/Madam,

A number of books are published every year on Banking. Another outstanding addition to the long list of standard books is the one recently published by us, 'Social Obligations of Commercial Banks' written by the renowned author Dr. K. Gopalakrishnan, Professor of Commerce, Annamalai University, Chidambaram, Tamil Nadu.

As you all know, Dr. K.G., as he is affectionately called, needs no introduction. Several books authored by him already adorn the shelves of college teachers and libraries.

The chapter on the 'Concept of Social Obligation and its Relevance to Banking Industry' in the present title bears eloquent testimony to his distinguished scholarship and erudition.

The concluding chapter on 'The Applicability of Social Obligation Concept to Indian Commercial Banks' is superb and absorbing. Advanced arguments have been statistically based and conclusions wisely and logically drawn. The views expressed are so novel and logical that they constitute a separate school of thought.

You all will agree with us that his lucid, simple style makes reading interesting. It will undoubtedly be of tremendous value to those who want to enrich their knowledge. This book, in fact, fills a long felt need, as titles on this particular aspect of banking are fewer in number.

Please fill in the enclosed card and mail it. We will be sending a free copy of the book for your personal use.

We hope you will willingly and unhesitatingly recommend it to your students studying banking and research scholars besides placing orders for your departmental as well as college library.

Yours truly,

Dr. P. Kaliyaperumal
Sales Manager

Sample 10: The expansion of your business has made it necessary for you to move to larger premises. Draft a circular letter to announce this fact to your customers. Give details of your new premises, explaining how the customers are likely to benefit by the change. Let your circular letter have some of the characteristics of a sales letter.

Cauvery Department Stores

77, Maduri Road,
Trichirappalli – 621 717

10th June 2011

Dear Customer,

Yes, we have grown!—grown with you or rather because of you!

Your continued patronage, increasing demand on varieties and your confidence in us that we supply only quality goods which people like you demand, have all necessitated our shifting to a larger premises.

The old premises has become so congested because of stupendous increase in the number of customers we serve every day that we have had to keep you waiting, before attending on you. You will not have this wearisome waiting any longer. We have acquired a newly-constructed large building at

75, Bazaar Street,
Trichirapalli-8

to which we will be moving effective from 24th June, 2011. It is situated in the business centre of the town well connected by all modes of transport. The building consists of five storeys and contains 15 halls in all besides the basement.

There is ample space for parking. Another pleasant convenience we offer our customers is that the entire building is air-conditioned.

The exterior of the building has an imposing appearance while the interior display is pleasing to the eye.

We have more departments now to satisfy the requirements of our customers. We also provide you a high class Snack Bar.

We have no doubt that Cauvery Department Stores will be a pleasant shopping centre where you buy goods with pleasure.

Your visit will convince you of the veracity of our claim.

Yours faithfully,
For Cauvery Department Stores,
B. Kasthuri Rangan
Managing Partner

Sample 11: A circular letter on behalf of Bharat Electricals, the wholesaler in electrical appliances, drawing attention of the retailers to the new stock, special discount and concession for three months is drafted as follows. The special offer is on account of the Silver Jubilee celebrations of Bharat Electricals.

Bharat Electricals

60,Anna Salai,
Chennai – 600 002

3rd February 2011

Dear Customer,

A splendid offer with incredible concessions is what we are offering our customers.

You will be glad to learn that we stocked a large quantity of electrical goods of all types so as to offer them to our valued customers at the best affordable terms for a period of three months during this year as part of the Silver Jubilee celebrations of our company.

We have also added a verierty of electrical appliances so that you can get all your requirements of electrical goods from us under one roof thereby reducing your ordering cost.

In addition to the usual discount of 15%,we offer a specical discount of 5% on all orders received from the 1 St of March to 31 st of May. Further, we will be dispatching them to you F.O.R your station.

We trust you will not miss this opportunity to avail yourself of this unbelievable concession by ordering large quantities. We look forward to hearing from you.

Yours faithfully,
A. Sundaresan
Proprietor

Sample 12: A circular letter announcing a clearance sale.

Vasanthi Readymade Garments Center

134, East Car Street,
Chidambaram – 608 001
9th September 2011

Dear Sirs,

Rush in to buy cheap!
Prices have
Reached rock bottom!
Unbelievable
Yet true!

You will be gald to know that we have decided to effect a clearance sale of our stock commencing from 17 th September.

We enclosed a copy of our price list showing the orginal as well as the reduced price. You will be pleased to note that price in men's garments, nylon stocks and georgette sarees have been salshed; they are as low as 50 percent.

The sale will remain open only for ten days between 9 a.m .and 9 p.m without lunch break so that you can choose to buy when it is most convenient to you. Please come early to secure the best of the bargains.

Yours faithfuly,
G.Ramanan
Proprietor

Sample 13: Messrs Bhagawan Dass & Sons (P) Ltd.,Agra wants to inform their customers that Mr.A.K Murugan,their representative in Tamil Nadu,is no longer in their employment and that they will not be bound by any receipts given or representations made by him. A suitable circular is drafted on behalf of a Dass& Sons (p) Ltd.as given below.

Bhagawan Dass & Sons (P) Ltd.

77, Taj Road,
Agra – 282 002

11th October 2011

Dear Sirs,

We would like to inform you that Mr. A.K. Murugan, our representative in Tamil Nadu has resigned with effect from 8th October, 2011 and is no longer in our employment.

We, therefore, advise you not to deal with him in future and any receipts given by him or representations made by him will not bind us.

We will soon be appointing a new representative in his place and we request you to bear with us for the inconvenience caused.

Yours faithfully,
Bhagawan Dass
Sales Director

Sample 14: Draft a circular announcing the grant of Power of Attorney to your Manager.

Mahalingam & Co.

(Dealers in Home Appliances)

74, Town High School Road,
Kumbakonam – 612 001

24th December 2011

Dear Customers,

On account of the continued expansion of my business, I had to be away from Kumbakonam quite frequently. This has been inconveniencing my suppliers and customers a good deal. Hence, I have this day granted power of attorney to my manager, P.R.S. Rajan who has been associated with me for well over a decade.

I request you to treat anything done by him as done by self.

Please note Mr. P.R.S. Rajan's signature given below.

Yours faithfully,
P. Mahalingam
Proprietor

Mr. P.R.S. Rajan will sign as
Per Pro P. Mahalingam & Co,
Signature

SUMMARY

Occasions to write circular letters include opening of a new branch new department, admission of a new partner, retirement of a partner, death of a partner, shifting of existing business to new location, conversion of partnership into a company, giving power of attorney, obtaining agency and clearance sale announcements.

Characteristics of a circular letter are to convey the same information; it is addressed to a large number of people, generally printed, not generally signed, pleasantly worded, saluation is general, for example, Dear customer, Dear manufacturer etc., and the inside address is written at the time of mailing.

Circular letter announcing establishment of a new business should contain name and style of business address, date of commencement of the business, details about the proprietor and his experience, capital at his disposal, reference to the specimen signature and a request for trial order.

Letter announcing a new branch should contain address of the new location, date of functioning, name of the manager, the patronage received, mention about the conveniences provided at the new place and an invitation to the customer for the inauguration of the new premises.

Letter announcing shifting of business to a new location should include stressing the inconveniences of the old space, benefits in the new location, like transport, space, air-conditioning, toilet, lift etc.

Letter announcing adding a new department includes getting all requirements under one roof, experience and efficiency of the person leading, the department, assurance to provide a variety of standard goods and the usual invitation to customers to visit the department.

Letter announcing the death of a partner contains expression of regret, acknowledgement of the services rendered, stress the adequacy of capital, change in the name of the firm should be pointed out, stating whether vacancy is to be filled up, give specimen signature of the incoming partner and to solicit customer's continued patronage.

Letter announcing conversion of a partnership firm into company should contain the fact that conversion is an evidence of growth, state that expansion needs capital, name and style after conversion to be stated, date of functioning to be stated, assurance of sustained personal attention to customers even after conversion and end with an appeal to continue patronage.

Letter announcing the obtaining of an agency includes the area of operation, reference to maintained quality, assurance of prompt execution of order, reference to the wide publicity given via media, stress price advantage, highlight the benefit of brand image, accompanied by samples if possible, special discounts offered need to be highlighted and end the letter with hope of getting continued patronage.

REVIEW QUESTIONS

Part A: Short Questions

1. What is a circular letter?

Part B: Paragraph Questions

1. State the occasions when circular letters are drafted.
2. Point out the objectives of a circular letter.

Part C: Essay Questions

1. What are the general characteristics of a circular letter?
2. What characteristics must a circular letter announcing the starting of a new business contain?
3. What points should be included while drafting a circular letter intimating the opening of a new branch?
4. What points are to be included while drafting a circular letter announcing
   a. Shifting of business to a new premises.
   b. Adding a new department.
5. What points must be stressed while drafting a circular letter intimating the death or retirement of a partner?
6. What points must a circular letter, announcing the conversion of partnership into a private company, contain?
7. What point must a circular letter announcing the obtaining of an agency contain?

Part D: Objective Type Questions

Choose the correct answer

1. A letter addressed to a large number of customers conveying the same message is

   a. Collection letter b. Circular letter c. Agency letter d. Sales letter

   (Ans: b)

2. To announce the change in the location of business, which of the following letter is drawn?

   a. Circular letter b. Sales letter c. Agency letter d. Insurance letter

   (Ans: a)

3. To announce the admission of a new partner which of the following letter is drafted?

   a. Sales letter b. Agency letter c. Circular letter d. Dunning letter

   (Ans: c)

4. To announce the establishment of a new business, which letter is suitable?

   a. Circular letter b. Sales letter c. Collection letter d.agency letter

   (Ans: a)

5. To announce a clearance sales which letter is to be drafted?

   a. Sales letter b. Circular letter c. Agency letter d.dunning letter

   (Ans: b)

Fill in the blanks

1. Letter addressed to many customers conveying a message is _________ letters. (Circular)
2. Letter announcing the establishment of a new branch is _________ letter. (Circular)
3. Letter announcing clearance sale is _________ letter. (Circular)
4. Letter announcing new product is _________ letter. (Circular)
5. Conversion of firm into company is conveyed through _________ letter. (Circular)

PART 3

SPECIAL BUSINESS CORRESPONDENCE

15 CHAPTER

BANK CORRESPONDENCE

INTRODUCTION

Banks are the catalyst of economic development of a country. It serves different types of clients in the process of delivering a variety of its financial services. Tremendous development in information technology and electronics has transformed the style of banking. Contemporary and modern banks have diversified their services apart from the traditional services. Mechanization and automation have addressed a plethora of problems experienced in the banking sector. Yet, customer grievances continue to mar the services provided by the banks, and the banks' grievances regarding the customers and their head office do not augur well with the allround developments enveloping the banking environment.

One of the powerful means of communication is letters. The significance of letters in banks has not lost its sheen even after the advent of technology. On various occasions, the bank has to write letters, depending on persons with whom it has to communicate. When customers write letters to banks, the banks reply to them, clarifying the queries and redressing the grievances of customers. It has to periodically send statements to its head office, regional office and corporate office. It also has to interact with other government agencies, public utility-service providers, staff members, unions and other banks. This chapter deals only with bank correspondence with customers, head office and other branches.

TYPES OF BANK CORRESPONDENCE

It is grouped into two categories:

Formatted Letters

In order to ensure uniformity in the format, banks supply pre-printed letters like account opening forms, loan application forms and credit reports. In other words, standardized forms are supplied by the banks to the customer. Since it is pre-formatted, it requires no elaborate discussion and illustration.

Individual Letters

It represents letters written by individuals on different occasions. They are not standardized. This type of letters requires a lot of tact. Therefore, letters of this type are illustrated. The following are the sub-categories of individual letters:

Letters between banker and customer

It is further subdivided as follows:

a. **Letters from banker to customer:** Banks have to answer the queries and doubts raised by the customer. It aslo has to redress the grievances of the customer.

b. **Letters from customers to banks:** Customers communicate with banks through letter requesting opening of an account, seeking clarification for certain charges, interest etc., requesting loans and overdraft.

Letters between banks

This relates to status enquires, negotiation of bills, clearance of cheques etc.

Letters between head office and branch office

a. These include letters from head office to its branches which deal with matters of administration, and convey its policy decisions.

b. Letters from branch office to head office include:
   - Monthly, quanterly and half-yearly reports submitted by the branch manager.
   - Branch manager suggesting measures to improve business.
   - Letters recommending appointment, promotion and transfer of staff.
   - Letters disclosing the volume of advance.
   - Letters explaining some unconventional decisions.

Occasions for correspondence increases as the operation of the banks widens. The reports of branch managers should be logically arranged and substantiated with facts and figures.

CHARACTERISTICS OF BANK CORRESPONDENCE ADDRESSED TO CUSTOMERS

Though there are formatted letters used by banks with respect to routine matters, occasions often arise when letters have to be addressed with a personal touch. Great care should be exercised while drafting such letters. They should possess the following characteristics:

Courtesy

Courtesy is the most important characteristic that should never be lost sight of by a banker. Just because a customer approaches a bank for a loan or other facilities, the banker should not assume superiority.

Tact

Even when the customer is wrong and writes irritating letters, the banker should not reply in the same manner. Letters contradicting the presumptions of the customers must be drafted with utmost tact so that while attempting to convince the customers, no offence to their sentiments is caused.

Conviction and building custom

Letters rejecting loan applications or other favours should make the stand of the bank clear, so that the applicants will continue to be its customers.

Not to divulge secrets

The letters should not divulge secrets or any vital information about other customers. While replying to letters of status enquiries, it should be brief and to the point. The bank should not indicate the balance standing in their accounts.

To be intelligible to all

The letter should be free from the use of banking jargons. They should be intelligible to persons of ordinary education.

Correct information

Bank letters should not be vague, nor should they contain incorrect figures.

Brevity

Bank correspondence should be brief.

KEY POINTS TO REMEMBER

Points to be noted while acknowledging a letter demanding stoppage of payment for a cheque

- The letter from the bank should acknowledge the receipt of intimation regarding *stop payment order*.
- It should state that the bank has instructed its staff not to pay the cheque in question.
- It should also make it clear to the drawer that the bank should not be held responsible in the event of the cheque being paid through oversight despite the notice of stop order.

Points that should be included on intimating the rejection of loan application of a customer

- The letter should acknowledge receipt of the loan application.
- It should explain the bank's general policy of not allowing loan on personal security.
- It may ask for a guarantor so that the applicant may be financially accommodated.
- The letter should state that while the bank considers the applicant among its valued customers, it could not comply with his request only because of the rigid rules.

LETTERS BETWEEN BANKER AND CUSTOMER

Sample 1: A letter to your banker giving standing instruction for paying your life insurance premium periodically.

Panruti Emporium

78, Vandipalayam Road,
Tirupapuliyur – 607 002

22nd February 2011

The Branch Manager,
The Goodluck Bank Ltd.,
Cuddalore – 607 001

Dear Sir,

I request you to kindly pay my life insurance premium to the Cuddalore Branch of the LIC as and when they fall due in respect of my policies detailed below:

S.No	Policy No.	Due date	Amount ₹
1.	K 7480032	4th of January, April, July and October	350.00
2.	M 342645	10th of March June, September and December	400.00
3.	A 400765	Annual Premium	960.00

The premium amount paid by you as well as your charges thereon may be debited to my current account no. C 746.

I undertake to keep sufficient balance in my account to enable you to comply with this standing instruction.

Yours faithfully,
R. Annamalai
Sole Proprietor

Sample 2: You have received intimation about the loss of a draft issued to K. Somasundaram & Co and a request from him for the issue of a duplicate draft in its place. As the Manager of bank, draft the reply, explaining your stand in such a situation.

Bank of Pondicherry

123, Nehru Street,
Pondicherry – 605 001

14th March 2011

Messrs. K. Somasundaram & Co.,
4/66 Rodier Mill Street,
Mudaliarpet.
Pondicherry – 605 007

Dear Sir,

Sub: Loss of your draft

We have received your letter of 12th March reporting loss of the D.D. No. D3456 for ₹ 7,500 favouring Messrs Kalpana Electricals, on our Hyderabad branch and requesting to stop its payment.

We have advised our Hyderabad branch to exercise caution in case it is presented for payment. We regret, however, to inform you that we cannot stop payment of the draft at our Hyderabad branch, as under the Negotiable Instruments Act, a holder who has acquired a draft in good faith and value is entitled to claim payment from the drawee bank, notwithstanding the notice of its loss.

With regard to your request for the issue of a duplicate draft, we enclose an Indemnity Bond which you have to fill and return to us duly signed by you and by two other securities. The bond should be stamped with court fee stamps with a value of ₹ 2.50. This is to protect the bank from any loss which it may suffer by paying the original draft under circumstances indicated in paragraph 2 above.

The duplicate draft will be issued on getting confirmation from our Hyderabad branch that the lost draft has not been paid by them, and on receiving the Indemnity Bond duly completed from you.

Yours faithfully,
R. Balu
Manager

Sample 3: As the manager of a bank, draft a letter in reply to a customer's letter in which the customer had complained about the item 'Bank Charges' appearing in his pass book at the end of the last half-year.

Calicut Bank Ltd.

32, Triplicane High Road,
Chennai – 600 005

8th August 2011

The Bombay Shoe Mart,
8, Pycrafts Road,
Chennai – 600 005

Dear Sirs,

Sub: Current Account No. 123 - Bank Charges

We have your letter of 5th August in which you have complained about the debit of ₹ 100 in your pass book as bank charges for the half-year ending 30th June.

While we agree with your contention that banks profit from current accounts on which no interest is paid, we have to point out that we do not ordinarily debit your account with charges for maintaining accounts, stationery involved etc. Only when a specified minimum balance is not maintained, it is customary for banks to charge a small amount for their services on accounts.

We would also like you to refer to our Rule No.5 of the Regulations governing current accounts, wherein it has been made clear that bank charges will be levied on currents accounts if the minimum balance of ₹ 5000 is not maintained. We trust that we have made our stand clear to you.

Yours faithfully,
K. Sundar
Branch Manager

Sample 4: Ask your bankers to explain why they have dishonoured a cheque drawn by you in spite of the fact that a cheque for ₹ 5,500 had already been credited into your account which should have raised your balance sufficiently to cover the dishonoured cheque.

Radha Silk Emporium

7, V.O.C. Road,
Tuticorin – 628 001

30th July 2011

The National Bank of India,
Bazaar Branch,
Tuticorin – 628 004

Dear Sirs,

Current Account No. 326

We regret to note that you have dishonoured our cheque No. BA/736256 dated 15th July for ₹ 1000 issued in favour of City Cloth Centre, Madurai with your remark, 'Insufficient Funds'.

We would like to point out that we have paid into our account on 12th July for collection and credit a cheque no. A/7 32124 for ₹ 5,500 drawn in our favour from Canara Bank, Bangalore.

The amount of the cheque together with the balance standing as credit in our account was sufficient to pay the cheque in question.

Your unjustifiable dishonouring has put us in an awkward position and we would like to hear from you the reason for your return of the cheque.

Yours faithfully,
R. Krishnan
Manager

Sample 5: You have received a complaint from your customer that a cheque was dishonoured, even though a cheque deposited by him earlier into his account would have been sufficient to pay it. As the Manager of a bank, draft a suitable reply.

The National Bank of India

(Regd. Office: Mumbai)

77, Main Bazaar,
Tuticorin – 628 004

2nd August 2011

The Radha Silk Emporium,
7, V.O.C. Road,
Tuticorin – 628 001

Dear Sirs,

Current Account No. 326

We regret to note from your letter of 30th July, that you have been greatly embarrased by our refusal to pass your cheque No. BA/7 36256 dated 15th July issued in favour of City Cloth Centre, Madurai.

We have to inform you that the cheque for ₹ 4000 which you have deposited for credit on 12th July was from Canara Bank, Bangalore. Cheques from banks in other States usually take at least 4 days to collect. Further, there were two intervening bank holidays in Karnataka and this caused further delay. Hence, the proceeds of the cheque could not be credited to your account till 17th July before which date your cheque for ₹ 5000 was presented to us. Consequently, we had to return the cheque unpaid in the absence of any previous arrangement for overdraft facilities especially because the amount involved was fairly large.

We trust the position is clear to you and we assure you our best attention at all times.

Yours faithfully,
K. Maran
Branch Manager

Sample 6: Write a letter to your bankers to confirm a telegram stopping payment of one of your cheques issued two days ago.

Prabakar Hardwares

11, South Car Street,
Pennadam – 605 105

2nd May 2011

The Branch Manager,
The Goodwill Bank Limited,
77, Junction Road,
Virudhachalam – 606 001

Dear Sirs,

Sub: Current Accout No. 423 Countermanding of payment.

We confirm our telegram sent to you today, which reads as follows:

'Stop payment—cheque No. S 7564 dated 30th July for ₹ 3500—Prabakar Hardwares'

The above cheque was issued to M/S Balu Brothers, Salem two days ago. A subsequent scrutiny of our accounts revealed that actually no payment was due to them, and through oversight on the part of our accountant, a cheque was sent to them.

Hence, I request you to stop payment of the above cheque. We very much regret the inconvenience caused. I request you to confirm your action.

Yours faithfully,
E. Prabakaran
Sole proprietor

Note : If payment is stopped on account of the cheque being lost, the second paragraph of the letter can be modified as follows:

As the above cheque has been lost before its despatch to the party concerned, I have to request you to stop payment of the cheque. I request you to confirm action.

Sample 7: As the Manager of a bank, write a letter to your customer stating the action taken on his advice to stop payment of the cheque.

The Goodwill Bank Ltd.

77, Junction Road,
Vridhachalam – 606 001

3rd May 2011

Messrs. Prabakar Hardwares,
11, South Car Street.
Pennadam – 605 105

Dear Sirs,

We have received your telegram as well as your letter of 2nd May asking us to stop payment on cheque No. S 7564 dated 30th July for a sum of ₹ 3,500 issued in favour of Messrs Balu Brothers, Salem.

Necessary instruction has already been issued to the staff to stop payment on presentation.

However, we would like to draw your attention to Rule No 10 of our Current Account Rules which makes it clear that though we will register instructions from the drawer regarding countermanding of payment, the bank should not be held responsible if payment of the cheque is made through oversight or inadvertence.

Yours faithfully,
M.S. Srinivasan
Manager

Sample 8: A businessman writes to the local bank that owing to excellent business prospects on account of the approaching Deepavali festival he should be allowed overdraft facilities to the extent of ₹ 40,000 without security. Draft the letter.

Bharathi Textiles

78, Arani Road,
Vellore – 632 001.

3rd August 2011

The Manager,
The Goodluck Bank Ltd,
23, Main Road,
Katpadi – 632 007.

Dear Sir,

Current Account No. 123

With the approach of Puja and Deepavali festivals, we expect considerable increase in our business. The wholesalers are unable to extend credit to us because ours is a small concern.

We, therefore, approach you with a request to grant us overdraft facilities up to ₹. 40,000 which we will clear in a period of two months.

We have no security to offer but I am prepared to execute bonds. We look forward to your favourable disposal.

Yours faithfully,
for Bharathi Textiles,
A. Bharathi
Proprietor

Sample 9: Draft the bank's reply to the above letter explaining its inability to grant overdraft on personal security.

The Goodwill Bank Ltd.

23, Main Road,
Katpadi – 632 007

6th August 2011

Messrs Bharathi Textiles,
78, Arani Road,
Vellore – 632 001

Dear Sirs,

We have received your letter dated 3rd August requesting grant of overdraft facility of ₹ 40,000 in your Current Account No. 123 against your personal security.

We consider you among our valued customers and find it difficult to refuse your request. But guidelines issued by the Head Office are very specific and they cannot be deviated. Overdraft exceeding ₹ 20,000 can be granted only against some tangible securities, and below ₹ 20,000 against guarantor in exceptional cases. We hope you appreciate our difficulty in complying with your request.

Yours faithfully,
K. Paari
Branch Manager

Sample 10: Write to your bankers for an advance against your Life Insurance Policy, stating the amount you require and the period for which you require it.

Poompuhar Cloth Centre

77, Kumbakonam Road,
Mayiladudhurai – 609 001

7th July 2011

The Progressive Bank Ltd,
112, Car Street,
Mayiladudhurai – 609 004

Dear Sirs,

Current Account No. 156

With the festival season starting from October, we like to build a large stock of clothes by obtaining supplies from a variety of mills. This bulk order will also enable us to avail ourselves of specially favourable terms. We are, therefore, in need of large funds during the months of October, November and December, and we request you to kindly grant us overdraft facilities to the tune of ₹ 50,000. We assure you that we will place our account in credit by the end of January 2011.

We propose to deposit my life insurance policy for ₹ 50,000 as a cover for the overdraft.

We do hope that you will find the security acceptable and grant us the overdraft.

Yours faithfully,
for Poompuhar Cloth Centre,
V. Prasanna

Sample 11: Draft a reply from the bankers stating that a loan up to the surrender value of the policy will be considered, provided the applicant has his age admitted by the company and that he assigns the policy to the bank by way of mortgage.

The Progressive Bank Ltd.
(Regd. Office: Chennai)

112, Car Street,
Mayiladudhurai – 609 004

10th July 2011

Messrs Poompuhar Cloth Centre,
77, Kumbakonam Road,
Mayiladudhurai – 609 001

Dear Sirs,

Sub: Your application for overdraft facilities.

We have your letter of 7th July and we would very much like to sanction the grant of overdraft facilities up to ₹ 50,000 you had asked for. But in the case of life policy which is offered as security, it is the policy of the Bank not to grant an overdraft in excess of 75% of the surrender value of the life policy. Further, its acceptability as security also depends upon your age being admitted by the Life Insurance Corporation. The policy should be assigned in favour of the Bank and you should undertake to pay the insurance premium regularly. We hope we have made our position clear to you.

Yours faithfully,
M. Muthuveeraganapathy
Branch Manager

Sample 12: A letter drawing attention to an overdrawn account was addressed to a valued client whose account was in credit. Draft the bank manager's letter of apology and explanation.

The Kanchi Bank Ltd.

378, Anna Salai,
Chennai – 600 002

15th July 2011

Messrs Nathan & Co,
77, Velacherry Road,
Chennai – 600 014

Dear Sirs,

We have your letter of 12th July and we very much regret to note what an embarrassment our letter of 7th July has caused you.

The letter should have been addressed to another customer of ours bearing a name similar to yours, and whose account was in debit for quite a long time. It was addressed to you through oversight and we offer our unconditional apology for the error and the inconvenience it has thereby caused you.

Yours faithfully,
N. Elavazhagan
Branch Manager

Sample 13: As the manager of a bank, write a tactful letter to a lady customer whose financial position is believed to be good but who persists in overdrawing her account without making any previous arrangement.

The Bank of Tamil Nadu

(Regd. Office: Kanchipuram)

78, Netaji Road
Cuddalore – 607 010

18th November 2011

Mrs. K. Punitham,
Proprietress,
Pallavan Publishers,
Karamanikuppam – 607 109

Dear Madam

We would like to inform you that yesterday a cheque for ₹ 5,000 drawn by you was presented for payment, though the balance credit in your current account was only ₹ 4,850. We had no hesitation in honouring it as we felt that the insufficient balance was due to oversight.

We very much regret to tell you that on previous such occasions also we had brought this to your notice. It is not the usual practice of this bank to honour cheques drawn in excess of balance standing to the credit of an account,but we have made an exception in your case.

We would, however, like to inform you that in case you require overdraft facilities for future payment, we shall be only too glad to arrange them for you against adequate security. If you are interested in the suggestion, you are welcome to discuss with me.

In the meanwhile,will you please arrange to deposite sufficient amount not only to adjust the debit balance but also to keep enough funds in your current account.

Yours faithfully,
Kumara Raj
Manager

Sample 14: One of your customers requires urgent overdraft facilities. As the Branch Manager of bank, write to the Head Office recommending sanction of the overdraft facilitiy even though the security offered is inadequate.

The Dowell Bank Ltd.

(Regd. Office: Mumbai)

25, Cross Street,
Besant Nagar,
Chennai – 600 090

2nd June 2011

The General Manager,
The Dowell Bank Ltd,
35, Apollo Street,
Mumbai – 400 001

Dear Sir,

Mr. Ismail Maraiker, proprietor of The Crescent Stores dealing in stainless steel vessels approached me yesterday with a request for a loan of ₹ 1,00,000.

He has finalized a contract for bulk purchase with a stainless steel manufacturer in Mumbai to take advantage of a special offer. As he has recently diverted large business funds for acquiring a building in T.Nagar area, he now finds himself tight financially and is in need of ₹ 1,00,000 to pay for the contract concluded recently. He promises repayment within a period of six months from the date of its receipt.

Mr. Ismail Maraikeir offers the following securities as a cover against the loan:

1. Charge on 7.5% Government of India 2000 Loan Bonds of the face value of ₹ 50,000 (the present market value is ₹ 40,000).

2. A charge on his stock-in-trade in his shop valued at ₹ 50,000.

Mr. Ismail Maraiker is our customer for over ten years and has been fulfilling all his commitments. He enjoys sound reputation in business circles and his association with us has secured us a number of profitable accounts.

In view of what has been stated above, though the securities offered by him are not sufficient to cover the advance completely, I strongly recommend that his request for a loan of ₹ 1,00,000 be granted.

In view of the urgent nature of the proposal, I am not submitting the loan proposal in the usual L6 form.

Yours faithfully,
M. Subramaniam
Branch Manager

Sample 15: Reply from the Head Office to Sample 14. Draft a suitable reply from the Head Office sanctioning loan only up to 60% of the value of security offered.

The Dowell Bank Ltd.

(Regd Office: Mumbai)

35, Apollo Street,
Mumbai – 400 001

7th June 2011

The Branch Manager,
The Dowell Bank Ltd,
25, Cross street,
Besant Nagar,
Chennai - 600 090

Dear Sir,

We have your letter of 2nd June recommending a loan of ₹ 1,00,000 to Mr. Ismail Maraiker.

As you know, it is the invariable practice of our Bank to advance loans only up to 60% of the value of stainless steel products. In the context of the declining price trend in the stainless steel market, even this margin of 40% appears risky and we are unable to relax our stipulations on any ground.

In view of Mr. Ismail Maraiker's unblemished record and credit reputation, we, however, sanction a loan of ₹ 60,000 subject to the condition that the market value of stock hypothecated to us should never fall below ₹ 50,000 during the period of loan.

Yours faithfully,
B. Vaidhya
Credit Manager

Sample 16: Your customer's security has depreciated. As the Manager of a bank, advise him to reduce the overdraft or to furnish additional security.

The Cuddalore Bank Ltd.

(Regd. Office: Cuddalore)

17, Lawrence Road,
Tirupapuliyur – 607 002

17th June 2011

M/S Vijaya Electricals,
23, Beach Road,
Cuddalore – 607 001

Dear Sirs,

You will recall that you have been granted overdraft facilities to the extent of ₹ 20,000 against the shares of ABC Limited, which were then valued at ₹ 25,000. During the last few months, there has been a sharp decline in the market value of securities deposited with us. They have fallen to ₹ 10,000. Since it is the invariable practice of the Bank not to grant overdraft in excess of 60% of the market value of the securities, we are constrained to request you to reduce your overdraft limit to ₹ 7,000. We shall, however, be glad to continue the limit upto ₹ 10,000, provided you see your way to deposit similar additional securities of the market value of about ₹ 15,000. We hope you will comply with our requirement.

Yours faithfully,
S. Rajakannu
Branch Manager

Sample 17: A customer of yours enjoys an overdraft facility to the extent of ₹ 2 lakhs but has not availed himself of this facility for the last one year. Draft a letter telling him that the bank has decided to charge him a certain minimum interest whether or not he avails himself of this facility.

Thillai Bank Ltd.

(Regd. Office: Chidambaram)

77, Avani Moola Veethi
Madurai – 625 003

9th September 2011

Messrs Ratha Jewelleries,
North Masi Street,
Madurai – 625 007

Dear Sirs,

Sub: Your overdraft arrangement with us

You were allowed overdraft facilities to an extent of ₹ 2,00,000 against N.S. Certificates of the value of ₹ 4,00,000. A study of the operation of your account revealed that you have made use of the overdraft facility very rarely and that too for sums not exceeding ₹ 80,000.

Your account has been showing credit balance for a greater part of the year. The Bank finds your overdraft account quite unremunerative because while a sum of ₹ 2,00,000 is to be always kept ready for your use, the interest earned on overdraft actually availed of is very low.

Since you have been our valued customer for over 15 years, we do not want to request you to close the overdraft account, but we would like to let you know that we have to charge a minimum interest on the limit sanctioned.

This arrangement will enable you to utilize overdraft facility up to ₹ 2,00,000 and at the same time enable the bank to benefit.

Yours faithfully,
Mrs. K. Punitha
Branch Manager

Sample 18: One of your customers who is influential in the town frequently overdraws the current account, and has the habit of issuing post-dated cheques and also stopping payment of cheques when there are insufficient funds in the account. Write a suitable letter to the customer pointing out the various objectionable features of his account and threatening to close it if he does not conduct it in a proper manner in the future.

The Chennai Bank Ltd.

Private and Confidential

28, Avvai Shanmugam Road,
Chennai – 600 004

3rd February 2011

Mr.A. Thanikachalam,
78, Station Way Road,
T. Nagar,
Chennai – 600 017

Dear Sir,

I regret to inform you that your cheque for ₹ 500 dated 27th January drawn in favour of Pothigai Pathippagam had to be returned unpaid owing to insufficient funds.

Since October 2011, it became necessary for us to dishonour seven of your cheques on the same ground. Besides, you also countermanded payment of your cheques whenever there were no adequate funds.

Another disturbing aspect is that you issue post-dated cheques quite frequently.

You will agree with us that such irregular conduct of the bank account not only reflects badly on your credit but harms the reputation of the bank too. Our directors, therefore, view this mode of operation very seriously and I am constrained to observe that unless you conduct your account properly, I will have to request you to close your account.

I hope you will cooperate with us by operating the account on proper lines.

Yours faithfully,
R. Selvaraj
Branch Manager

Sample 19: Letter from the bank which regrets the inconvenience caused to the customer owing to delayed collection of outstation cheque.

Bank of Allahabad

(H.O. 111 Nariman point, Mumbai 400 801)

Lake Avenue Branch

12th June 2011

Your ref: Letter dt. 10 June 2011
Our ref: YGP/I/23

Banu Sekar
110, Fort Avenue,
Mumbai – 400 112

Dear Sir,

I was taken aback by your letter. dt. 10th June 2011, detailing the stress that the delayed collection of the cheque has caused you. We know pretty well that you have been one of our esteemed customers enjoying good relationship with us for over 20 years. It is a matter of serious concern that there was an inordinate delay this time in the collection of outstation cheque.

I had a discussion with the staff concerned in the matter. I am convinced that the delay could have been avoided. I have given necessary instructions to the staff concerned. You will appreciate that you never had such an occasion in the past. Since we consider customer service an uppermost priority in our growth agenda, we ensure you that this sort of incidents will not recur. We regret the inconvenience caused to you and express sorry for the delay.

Yours faithfully,
Banerjee
Branch Manager

Sample 20: A customer of your bank has to pay penal interest for belated payment of insurance premium which should have been paid by bank under standing instruction. Write a suitable reply.

Punjab National Bank

Ref : Your letter dt. 10th July 2011
Our ref: CVS/YSC/INS/SB/08/2011

12, Mosque Street,
Vaniyambadi Branch,
Tirupattur – 635 601

July 12 2011

Anamulla
23, Lake Avenue,
Vaniyambadi – 635 751

Dear Sir,

I apologise for the belated remittance of your insurance premium for the year 2011. I have written to our head office, enquiring whether our branch can bear the penal interest you have paid for the belated premium remittance. I would let you know as soon as I get advice from the H.O. in this regard. Absolute shortage of staff forces us to engage the services of temporary staff, who have committed the lapse in your case. Yet, I do know that such an excuse should not absolve the branch of its responsibility to its customers. You would appreciate the fact that we have not given room for such a complaint in the past 20 years of your association with us. We assure you, sir, of our sustained satisfactory service. We will take care that such incidents will not recur.

Yours faithfully,
for Union Bank of India,
S.Kumar
Manager

Sample 21: Letter regretting delay in realization of outstation cheque

Bank of Baroda

14, Kennet Avenue,
Parry's Corner,
Chennai – 600 001

September 5, 2011

Your ref: Sep.1 2011
Our ref: Ye1Y./CYZ/So/112

Charles
42, Seaward Road,
Thambuchetty Street,
Mannady,
Chennai – 600 107

Dear Sir,

We regret the delay caused in the realization of three of your outstation cheques drawn on Union Bank of Ceylon, Chandini Chowk branch, Delhi. The normal time for collection of an outstation cheque is two weeks. But it has taken more than a month to realize them. Unfortunately, the postal strike has compounded the matter. Though the excuse in our part is unjustifiable, I would like to bring to your notice the reason for the delay. We assure you, sir, that we would carry out your instructions promptly in future. I have also written to our head office seeking clarification as to bearing the interest charge by us for the period of delay. Though this may not mean much to you, we wish to sustain your loyalty by owning up our responsibility.

Yours faithfully,
Martin
Branch Manager

Sample 22: Write a tactful reply to a customer who has complained rude behaviour of the cashier.

Oriental Bank of commerce

14, High Court Road,
Nagpur – 300 008

April 3, 2011

Samuvel
53, Gurduwara Road,
Old Town,
Nagpur – 300 001

Dear Sir,

I received your letter dt. 30th March 2011, and noted the contents. I have taken personal interest in your complaint and enquired Premkumar, cashier of our branch. He explained to me that the whole situation has been misunderstood by you when he sought to explain his inability to comply with your request at the peak hour of business. However, you, as one of our esteemed customers, are not in the wrong when you insisted your point. Of course, such situations can lead anyone to lose their temper. The whole situation could have been avoided if you had sought my help to address the problem. In this context, I feel it would be nice to treat the matter as closed and not to continue any hostility by pursuing complaints to the senior management. I have also advised him to keep his cool in such situations. I will see to it that such a situation does not recur.

Yours faithfully
Paniker
Branch manager.

Sample 23: Letter to a customer whose cheque is dishonoured.

ICICI Bank

14, Temple Car Street,
Cuddalore - 607 107

10th March 2011

Manickavasagam
12, Big Street,
Tirupapuliyur,
Cuddalore - 607 026

Dear Sir,

We draw your attention to the dishonouring of a cheque vide 127652 for ₹ 10,000 issued by you and presented by Abubaker of Nagercoil, due to inadequate funds in your current account no. AZ 1257. As per current account rules, customer has to have sufficient balance to enable us to honour a cheque. Last month also one of the cheques issued by you was dishonoured for want of funds and you had tendered assurance that such an incident would not recur. Despite the assurance, the same problem has resurfaced. We request you to cooperate with us to render good service to our clients.

Yours faithfully,
Appar
Branch Manager

Sample 24: Bank seeking collateral security.

Dena Bank

10,Nehru Street,
Pondicherry - 605 008

10 April 2011

Doss
17, Asarkan Street,
Lawspet,
Pondicherry - 605 002

Dear Sir,

I wish to inform you that our H.O. has turned down your application seeking loan for want of adequate security. As banks are grappling with the problem of non-performing assets, RBI has restricted the commercial banks from sanctioning loans without proper security.

I hope that you would appreciate our position in this regard. We would be happy to process your loan application, if you could arrange to give some more securities in the form of LIC policies, document of titles etc. I am sorry to stress this point, but it is only for our mutual advantage.

Yours faithfully,
Thanikodi
Branch Manager

LETTERS FROM CUSTOMERS TO THE BANK

Sample 25: Letter requesting opening of an account.

Padi Electronics & Co.

212, Whites Road,
Anna Nagar,
Chennai – 600 008

August 10, 2011

The Branch Manager
Karur Vysya Bank Ltd,
23 Cross Road,
Anna Nagar,
Chennai – 600 008

Sir,

Sub: Account opening

We are dealers in electronic goods both imported and locally manufactured. We are functioning in the name of Padi Electronics & Co, a partnership firm. The average annual turnover of our firm is ₹ 50,00,000. We would like to open a current account with an overdraft facility in your bank and agree to maintain the minimum balance insisted and also to other terms and conditions. I am enclosing a filled-in application form and all other documents required in their regard. Mr. R. Elango will be the person authorized to operate the account. We are sending ₹ 1,00,000 through our messenger Mr. Rathinam to deposit in the account to be opened.

Yours faithfully,
R.Selvan
Managing Partner

Enclosure:

1. Certificate of Registration
2. Partnership Deed
3. Certificate of the proposal of the firm for opening current a/c
4. Two references
5. Specimen signature of R.Elango
6. Filled-in application from

Sample 26: Mr. Martin writes to Dravidian Bank asking for extention of time for payment of his carloan.

24 Loydes Road,
Tambaram,
Chennai – 600 046

1st April 2011

The Manager
Dravidian Bank,
Selaiyur,
Chennai – 600 047

Dear Sir,

Sub: Request for extention of time for loan repayment

Ref: Car loan a/c no. 1178777

I availed myself of a car loan of ₹ 3,50,000. I have been paying EMI of ₹ 10,000 towards the loan up to March 2011. Owing to financial emergencies, I am sorry to state that I will not be able to pay EMJ for the next two months. I request you, I sir, to kindly arrange for extension in the repayment period for 2 months. I agree to pay the interest for the extended period.

Yours faithfully,
Martin

Sample 27: A letter from a customer to a bank requesting transfer of SB account to another branch.

18, North Mada Street,
Villiavakkam,
Chennai – 600 021

19th May 2011

The Branch manager
XYZ Bank,
Luthern Church St,
Villivakkam,
Chennai – 600 021

Dear sir,

Sub: Transfer of SB account

I have an account with your branch since May 2009, and my SB account no. is 127052. As I have been transferred to Trichy and shifting my residence there, I request you to transfer my SB a/c to your Palakarai Branch, Trichy. I am returning the unused cheque leaves.

Yours faithfully,
Philip

Sample 28: A letter from a customer complaining wrong debits in his account.

15, Writers Road,
Vanavil Nagar,
Pondicherry – 605 003

December 3, 2011

The Manager
Kerala Bank,
Radha Nagar,
Pondicherry – 605 007

Sir,

Sub: Request to correct wrong debit in SB a/c no. 1275SA

I have a Savings Bank account no. 1275SA. I had my passbook updated on December 1, 2011. On my verification of entries therein, I was shocked to note a wrong debit of ₹ 10,000. As per my records, there is no issue of cheque to any party for the amount. Therefore, I request you to rectify the wrong debit made in my account. Such a wrong debit is likely to lead to dishonoring of cheques issued by me. I request you to see to it that such a lapse do not recur. I would like to hear from you as early as possible.

Yours faithfully,
Premchand

Sample 29: Customer giving standing instruction to pay insurance premium.

22, Valluvar Street,
Chidambaram – 608 002

December 2, 2011

The Branch Manager
Karnataka Bank,
North Street,
Chidambaram – 608 002

Sir,

Sub: Standing instruction to pay premium for my endowment policy number 2017257.

I have taken an endowment policy in my own name from TVS insurance company. The policy number is 2017257. The premium is payable half-yearly, on 14th July and 10th January every year. Kindly pay my premium by debiting my SB a/c 175727 with ₹ 6000 on the 1st day of July and January every year, and remit the premium to the TVS insurance, 17, James Road, Alwarpet, Chennai – 600 018. I shall undertake to keep sufficient balance in my account.

Yours faithfully,
Rupram Gupta

Sample 30: Customer assigning LIC policy as a collateral security.

Your Ref: Loan a/c 17277
Our ref: LIC/Assign/021/2011

14, Nixon Street,
Tiruppapuliyur,
Cuddalore – 607 109

10th Jan 2011

The Branch Manager
Simson Bank,
Cuddalore – 607 101

Sir,

Sub: Assignment of insurance policies as collateral

I am lodging the following life insurance policies duly assigned in your favour as collateral for the loan a/c cited in the reference. I authorize the bank to collect the benefits of the policy in the event of defaulting to repay the loan amount in the period stipulated.

1. LIP no. 12T217 Maturity value ₹ 1,00,000
   Date of maturity 17-7-2014
2. LIP 1212125 Maturity value ₹ 50,000
   Date of maturity 21-2-2015

Yours faithfully,
Gulam Ali

Sample 31: As the Manager of Mullai Bank Ltd, write a letter to Marutham Bank Ltd seeking confidential enquiry as to the status of a client.

The Mullai Bank Ltd.
Private and Confidential

138, Raja Street,
Coimbatore – 641 001

2nd July 2011

The Manager,
The Marutham Bank Ltd,
11, Oppanaikaran Street,
Coimbatore – 641 005

Dear Sirs,

We understand that you have had dealings with the party whose name is given below. We request you to furnish your opinion as to his means, standing and respectability.

Any information you may provide us will be treated as strictly private and confidential.
We shall be glad to reciprocate when a similar request comes from you.
Name: Mr.K. Jones
Business: Proprietor, Paalai Auto Spares
Address: 111, Old Jail Road, Coimbatore

Yours faithfully,
R. Sengodan
Branch Manager

Sample 32: You have received an enquiry regarding the standing of one of your customers. Draft an unfavourable reply to sample 31.

The Marutham Bank Ltd.

Private and Confidential

11, Oppanaikaran Street,
Coimbatore – 641 005

4th July 2011

The Manager,
The Mullai Bank Ltd,
138, Raja Street,
Coimbatore-641 001

Dear Sirs,

We have your enquiry dated 2nd July and have pleasure in enclosing our report.

This report is sent in the strictest confidence and without any liability on the part of the bank or any of its employees.

Yours faithfully,
P. Jamal Mohamed
Branch Manager

The Report

The Marutham Bank Ltd.

Private and Confidential

The opinion given below must not be taken as a guarantee. It is strictly private and confidential, and is given by the bank without prejudice and on the condition that no liability shall be attached to the Bank or any of its officials. We further stipulate that the name of the bank should not be disclosed in the event of our report being communicated to any of your customers.

Opinion

We have been informed that Mr.K. Jones of Paalai Auto Spares Coimbatore, is having a hard time of late. He does not enjoy confidence in the local market. He has ceased to enjoy overdraft facilities from us since November last.

LETTERS BETWEEN HEAD OFFICE AND BRANCH OFFICE

Sample 33: Proposal to start extension counter of Moovendar Bank.

Ref: YS/121/41/02

Sholinganallur Branch,
Old Mahabalipuram Road,
Chennai – 600 056

1st June 2011

The General Manager
Moovendar Bank,
12, Maidan Street,
Mysore – 560 001

Dear Sir,

The entire stretch in old Mahabalipuram is studded with a number of educational institutions. The Neppiyar Education Trust founded in 1989 in Sholinganallur has been witnessing a phenomenal growth. At present, they have an Engineering college, Polytechnic, Paramedical, Dental and Arts and Science colleges. There are around 10,000 students and 700 staff members working in this institution.

Sholingnallur is a small town wherein most of the resident students are staying. The Neppiyar Educational Trust is holding its account in two banks in Sholinganallur. The trust has promised to transfer one of its accounts if we open an extension counter in their campus which is located just 2 kilo meters away from our service branch. There are also bright prospects of the extension counter being upgraded into a full-fledged branch in the course of time. In this context, I request you, sir, to permit me to open an extension counter with just one clerical staff and one cashier at the temporary accommodation provided by the Trust. I solicit urgent action with regard to this proposal.

Yours faithfully,
Maran
Branch Manager

Sample 34: Write a letter to H.O regarding shortage of ₹ 1,00,000 in your branch.

Pallai Bank Ltd.

12, Lawrence Road,
Cuddalore New Town – 607 105

10th February 2011

The General Manager
14, Cholan Street,
Sowcarpet,
Chennai – 600 020

Dear sir,

Sub: Shortage of cash reported

We have sent you a fax regarding this. While closing the accounts for the day, the head cashier reported shortage of ₹ 1,00,000 at 5.15 p.m. One bundle of ₹ 1000 is found missing. As soon as I confirmed the shortage, I telephoned the Superintendent of police, Cuddalore circle and lodged a police complaint. The police also arrived at the branch immediately and made a thorough search, but to no avail.

Our head cashier, Mr. R. Uthaman took the responsibility and remitted the amount before closing the vault in accordance with the rules of the bank.

There was heavy disbursement at the counter since it was the first week of the month. Mr. R.Uthaman was very busy making disbursement that he could not recollect the image of any person who transacted with him today. But he could recall some chaos in the queue, and he had to intervene to calm the queue. According to my suspicion, someone in the waiting line could have deliberately created an unrest to get access to the bundle of notes kept on the counter by diverting the attention of our cashier.

I have warned Mr. R.Uthaman for his negligence. In this regard, I would like to add that this is the first misfortune in his career spanning 20 years in our bank. His conduct and character are beyond question till date.

Yours faithfully,
Harichandran
Branch Manager

Sample 35: Letter from the Branch Manager to H.O. asking for change in the working hours.

Seran Bank

Guduvancherry Branch,
12, Clock Tower Road,
Guduvancherry – 603 202

10th Jan 2011

The General Manager
Seran Bank,
Head Office,
Raymond Street,
Mumbai – 400 002

Dear Sir,
Sub: Change in working hours.

Our branch opened in Guduvancherry locality six months ago with work time as 10.00 a.m. to 2.00 p.m. I am constrained to inform you that we could not achieve our branch target as our working time was unsuitable to the public.

Guduvancherry, though rural in outlook, has a number of factories, small industries and educational institutions. More than 50 per cent of local population is working in these places, of which 25 per cent of the population comprises of residents located in this stretch. A survey conducted by the branch revealed the fact that most of local people could not avail themselves of branch's service due to time unsuitability. Besides, when we met the local people at a trade fair, they expressed their willingness to deposit with us if we could start our operations at 8.00 a.m. Moreover, during our door-to-door canvassing for deposits, we were convinced of the integrity of the people. Therefore, we have potential to advance loans without any recovery constraints. In light of the above facts, we suggest that the working hours of this branch be changed as follows on week days (Mon-Sat):

Morning—7.00 a.m. to 9.30 a.m.

Evening—3.30 p.m. to 7.00 p.m.

We honestly believe that we can attract a majority of the local population through our courteous service. The general tendency of rural people is to give their word-of-mouth publicity if they are impressed with our service.

We also understand that some leading banks have written to RBI for permission to open branches at Guduvancherry. It is our wish that we should secure maximum clients before that. We await your earliest possible response, accepting the change in working hours.

Yours faithfully,
Ramachandran
Branch Manager

Sample 36: Letter from Branch Manager to Head Office asking for more manpower.

Vijaya Bank

Jammala Madugu,
Cuddappah Dist - 530 444.

April 1, 2011

The General Manager
Vijaya Bank,
Head Office,
Park Avenue,
Mysore - 650 002

Dear Sir,

I have already submitted a detailed report on the volume of work in our branch. Out of the seven staff members, three are on medical leave. As a result, the existing staff are overloaded and they too are suffering from health problems due to hectic work. Counter staff have to face the wrath of customers due to the slow service. I request you to send two more assistants on deputation to our branch to clear up the pending work and continue to serve the customers satisfactorily.

Kindly treat this as most urgent.

Yours faithfully,
Rose
Branch Manager

Sample 37: Letter to the Head Office notifying an urgent advance without sanction

Bank of Cholan

101, J.N. Road,
Madurai – 636 001.

10th May 2011

The General Manager,
Bank of cholan,
Mumbai House,
Flora Fountain,
Mumbai – 400 010

Dear Sir,

Sub: Paav & Co. – Advance of ₹ 8,00,000/-

I enclose a complete advance form with respect to Paav & Co's application for an urgent advance of ₹ 8,00,000. Owing to the urgency of the case, I have taken the liberty of allowing Paav & Co. to draw the required amount in anticipation of a sanction from you.

Paav & Co. is one of our oldest customers and has a wide network of chain stores in our State. His need was immediate and urgent, because he wanted to firm up a big deal today. His connection with the Bank has been very remunerative and has brought several very good accounts to this branch.

All the details are fully outlined in the application form from which you will see that it was a good business deal to grant his request for the advance.

I trust that this explanation will be accepted in justification of the procedural lapse on account of the emergency of a special customer.

Yours faithfully,
Thomas
Branch Manager

Sample 38: Letter to the Head Office recommending the confirmation of a Probationary Assistant.

Cheran Bank

101, Evening Bazzar Street,
Chennai – 600 004

18th May 2011

The General Manager,
Cheran Bank,
Manipal – 576 119

Sir,

Sub: Mr. B. Sivanesan – Completion of probation.

Mr. B. Sivanesan, who was appointed as a probationer in our bank on 18th November 2010, today completes his six-month term of probation and we have pleasure in submitting our report favourably on his ability, diligence and conduct

The officers of the various departments in which B. Sivanesan has worked have given satisfactory reports on his performance, character, attitude and aptitude for learning and work. He has keen interest in learning the essentials of every new job entrusted to him.

Mr. B. Sivanesan celebrates his twenty-first birthday next September. Though young, he has acquired valuable social connection. He has an excellent character. By nature, he is enthusiastic and hardworking. If right opportunities are given, he will prove to be an asset to our bank.

I recommend that Mr. B. Sivanesan be confirmed.

Yours faithfully,
Sivasakthi
Branch Manager

Sample 39: Letter recommending renewal of an overdraft facility.

Pandian Bank

72, Riche St,
Pondicherry – 605 001

10th May 2011

The General Manager,
Pandian Bank,
Mumbai House,
Mumbai – 400 001

Dear Sir,

Sub: Renewal of overdraft of M/S Arvind & Co. for ₹ 75,000/-

The overdraft facility with a limit of ₹ 75,000 sanctioned to Messrs. Arvind & Co., expires on the 31st of this month. I have been approached by the firm for the continuance for this facility. I request you to sanction its renewal for another year, as their transactions are satisfactory and profitable to the bank.

The partners of the firm are people of reputation and means, and they devote their full attention to their businesses.

The security they deposited with us in the form of debentures of Ahmedabad Electricity Co., have a present market value of ₹ 1,75,000/-.

I, therefore, have no hesitation in recommending the renewal of the overdraft limit of ₹ 75,000 for one more year.

Yours faithfully,
Parithi
Branch manager

SUMMARY

The characteristics of banking correspondence are courtesy, tact, conviction, not to divulge secretst, to be intelligent, to give correct information and brevity.

Types of bank correspondence include:

i. Çorrespondence from customer to banker

ii. Reply to customer's correspondence by the bank

iii. Correspondence between banks

iv. Correspondence between banks and head office

v. Correspondence between banker and outside agencies.

REVIEW QUESTIONS

Part A: Short Questions

1. What is bank correspondence?
2. What is overdraft?
3. What is countermanding of payment?
4. What are collaterals?
5. What is advance?

Part B: Paragraph Questions

1. Highlight the characteristics of bank correspondence.
2. What are the points a banker should keep in mind while writing a letter rejecting a loan application of a customer?
3. What are the different types of bank correspondence?

Part C: Eassay Questions

1. As a customer, draft a letter to your banker giving standing instruction for paying your life insurance premium periodically.
2. You have received intimation about the loss of a draft issued to K. Somasundaram & Co., and a request from him for the issue of a duplicate draft in its place. As the Manager of the Bank, draft the reply explaining your stand in such a situation.
3. As the manager of a bank, draft a reply to a customer's letter in which the customer had complained about the item 'Bank Charges' appearing in his passbook at the end of the last half year.
4. Ask your bankers to explain why they have dishonoured a cheque you had drawn, inspite of the fact that the last cheque for ₹ 15,000 paid into your account should have raised your balance sufficiently to cover the dishonoured cheque.
5. You have received a complaint from your customer that a cheque was returned dishonoured,

even though a cheque deposited by him earlier into his account would have been sufficient to pay for it. As a Manager of a bank, draft a suitable reply.

6. Write a letter to your bankers to confirm a telegram stopping payment of one of your cheques issued two days ago.
7. As a Manager of a bank, write a letter to your customer stating the action taken on his advice to stop payment of the cheque.
8. A businessman writes to the local bank that owing to excellent business prospects due to the approaching Deepavali festival, he should be allowed overdraft facilities to the extent of Rs. 10,000 without security. Draft the letter.
9. Draft the bank's reply to the above letter explaining its inability to grant overdraft on personal security.
10. Write to your bankers for an advance against your Life Insurance Policy, stating the amount you require and the period for which you require it.
11. Draft a reply from the bankers stating that a loan up to the surrender value of the policy will be considered, provided he assigns the policy to the bank by way of mortgage.
12. A letter drawing attention to an overdrawn account was addressed to a valued client whose account was in credit. Draft the bank manager's letter of apology and explanation.
13. Write a tactful letter from the manager of a bank to a lady customer whose financial position is believed to be good, but who persists in overdrawing her account without making any previous arrangement.
14. One of your customers requires urgent overdraft facilities. As a Branch Manager of a bank, write to the Head Office recommending sanction of the overdraft facilities even though the security offered is inadequate.
15. Draft a suitable reply from the Head Office sanctioning loan only up to 60% of the value of security offered.
16. Your customer's security has depreciated. As a Manager of a bank, advise him to reduce the overdraft or to furnish additional security.
17. A customer of yours enjoys an overdraft facility to the extent of ₹ 2 lakhs, but has not availed himself of this facility for the last one year. Draft a letter telling him that the bank has decided to charge him a certain minimum interest whether or not he avails himself of this facility.
18. One of your customers who is influential frequently overdraws from the current account and is in the habit of issuing post-dated cheques and also stopping payment of cheques when there is insufficient funds in the account. Write a suitable letter to the customer pointing out the various objectionable features of his account, and threatening to close it if he does not conduct it in a proper manner in future.
19. As the Manager of Mullai Bank Ltd, write a letter to Marutham Bank Ltd seeking confidential enquiry as to the status of a client.
20. You have received an enquiry regarding the standing of one of your customers. Draft an unfavourable reply.

Part D: Objective Type Questions

Choose the Correct Answer

1. Account held by business people is

   a. savings a/c   b. Recurring a/c   c. Current a/c

   d. Fixed deposit a/c

   (Ans: c)

2. Collective name of securities to be given by the customer for a loan

   a. Hypothecation   b. Collaterals   c. Mortgage

   d. Non of the above

   (Ans: b)

3. Loan given on the basis of C's is

   a. Clean Loan   b. Secured loan   c. Mortgage

   d. Non of the above

   (Ans: a)

Fill in the blanks

1. Letters supplied by bankers is __________. (formatted letter)
2. Amount drawn over and above the credit balance of a customer is__________. (overdraft)
3. Customer instructing the bank to stop payment is__________. (countermanding)

16 CHAPTER INSURANCE LETTER

INTRODUCTION

Insurance is a mechanism through which loss of a few is shared by many in a given plan. Insurance contract is founded on the principle of *uberrimae fidei* (good faith). Hence, both the insurer and the insured have to exchange correct, complete and accurate information about the subject matter, plan, mode of settlement, terms of policy, profile of the policy-holder etc. Non-disclosure of any material information renders the insurance contract void at the option of the affected party. Insurance facilities are available for all subject matters like human life, health, accident, motor vehicle, crop, animals, building, etc. All these fall into two categories: Life insurance and Non-life Insurance. Non-life Insurance is further sub-divided into fire insurance, marine insurance and general insurance. Insurance services are provided by both public sector and private sector insurance companies. Different types of insurance correspondence include enquiring policy details, surrender value, notification of loss, opting for change in premium period, revival of a lapsed policy, acceptance of claim, rejection of claim etc.

FIRE INSURANCE

Sample 1: Write a letter to your insurer notifying them of a small fire at your business premises. Ask them to arrange for an early inspection to enable you to put things right as soon as possible.

Maruthi Cloth Centre

32, Raja Street,
Coimbatore – 641 005

22nd February 2011

The Bharat Insurance,
145, E. P. Road,
R. S. Puram,
Coimbatore - 641 002

Dear Sirs,

Fire Policy No. F 3040

I regret to inform you that a fire broke out at about 11.30 p.m last night in my godown at 16, R.S. Puram, destroying stock-in-trade insured under the above policy for ₹ 1,50,000.

The night watchman called the fire brigade immediately, which arrived within ten minutes. Because of our strenuous efforts, use of fire extinguishers and the fire brigade, the fire was put out at about 12.30 a.m, and we were able to salvage a major portion of our stock.

According to our estimate, loss of stock on account of fire is ₹ 35,000. Further, we have incurred an expenditure of ₹ 1,200 in extinguishing the fire. We have also obtained the necessary voucher. Please send your surveyor to inspect the damage. As we have to repair the godown urgently for accommodating large supplies which are expected to arrive soon, we request you to settle our claim as early as possible.

Yours faithfully,
V. Chandra Prakash
Partner

Sample 2: A reply letter from the insurance company intimating that they would be sending their surveyor soon.

The Bharat Insurance Company

145, E.P. Road.
R.S. puram,
Coimbatore – 641 002

23rd February, 2011

Messrs Maruthi Cloth Centre,
32, Raja Street,
Coimbatore – 641 005

Dear Sirs,

Your Claim under Fire Policy No. F 3040.

We regret to note from your letter dated 22nd February that there was a fire in your godown, destroying goods insured under the above-mentioned policy.

Our surveyor Mr.S. Balasubramaniam has been instructed to visit your premises to assess the damage caused. Please make your account books, stock registers available to him. A claim form is enclosed for return to us, after it is duly filled in.

We will proceed further in the matter on receipt of claim form and the surveyor's findings.

Yours faithfully,
K. Sundar
Manager

Sample 3: The Bharat Insurance Company replies to Messrs Maruthi Cloth Centre effecting settlement of the claim. Draft the reply.

The Bharat Insurance Company

145, E.P. Road,
R.S. Puram,
Coimbatore – 641 002

15th March 2011

M/S Maruthi Cloth Centre,
32, Raja Street,
Coimbatore – 641 005

Dear Sirs,

Settlement of claim: Fire Policy No. F 3040

We have received our surveyor's report on the loss caused by fire to your stock covered under the above policy. We find your claim form correct in all respects. The loss has been estimated as follows:

	₹
Stock on 21.02.11- date of fire as per your books	2,50,000
Less: stock salvaged	2,15,000
Stock destroyed by fire	35,000
Add: Salvage expenses	1,200
Claim Admitted	36,200

Accordingly, we enclose a cheque for ₹ 36,200 in full settlement. Please send a stamped receipt for the amount for our record.

Yours faithfully,
K. Sundar
Manager

Encl: Cheque

Sample 4: Cuddalore Silk Yarns transfers a stock of yarn covered by fire policy from their godown at 20, Sankar Naidu Street to 35, Bodi Chetty Street, Cuddalore, and informs the insurance company. Draft the letter.

Cuddalore Silk Yarns

25, Bharathi Road
Cuddalore – 607 106

2nd June 2011

The New Bharat Assurance,
77, Arcot Woodlands Buildings,
Cuddalore – 607 108

Dear Sirs,

Sub: Transfer of stock covered by Fire Policy No. F 326

We have shifted the entire stock of silk yarn (valued at ₹ 40,000) stored at 20, Sankar Naidu street to another godown at 35, Bodi Chetty street. The goods will remain in the new godown for the rest of the period covered by the above policy.

The godown now warehousing our stock is new and has R.C.C. roofing. Fire extinguishers have also been installed in all the two floors. We, therefore, request a reduction in the premium rate.

We request you to send your surveyor to inspect the new premises for early confirmation of coverage for goods in the new godown. We enclose our fire policy for necessary endorsement and return.

Yours faithfully,
For Cuddalore Silk Yarns,
K. Raman
Manager

Encl: Fire policy

Sample 5: Draft a reply on behalf of the insurance company advising reduction in the premium rate by 0.5 per cent from the date of transfer.

The New Bharat Assurance

77, Arcot Woodlands Buildings,
Cuddalore – 607 108

10th June 2011

The Cuddalore Silk Yarns,
25, Bharathi Road,
Cuddalore – 607 106

Dear Sirs,

Sub: Stock transferred to new godown. Fire policy No. F 326

As desired by you in your letter of 2nd June, we return the above-mentioned policy with the necessary endorsement confirming cover for the goods shifted.

As our surveyor has informed us, after the inspection of your new godown at 35, Bodi Chetty Street, that the new building is rated high, we are pleased to reduce the premium rate by 0.5 per cent. Accordingly, we enclose a receipt form for ₹ 200 towards the refund of the excess premium already paid by you. Please return it duly signed.

Yours faithfully,
K. Maran
Manager

Sample 6 : Draft a reply on behalf of the insurance company raising the premium rate on the ground of increased risk in the new godown. (Another model)

The New Bharat Assurance

77, Arcot Woodlands Building,
Cuddalore – 607 108

10th June 2011

The Cuddalore Silk Yarns,
25, Bharathi Road,
Cuddalore – 607 106

Dear Sirs,

Sub: Stock transferred to new godown-Fire Policy No. F 326

As desired by you in your letter of 2nd June, we return the abovementioned policy with the necessary endorsement confirming cover for goods shifted.

After the inspection of your new godown at 35, Bodi Chetty street, our surveyor has informed us that it is adjacent to a warehouse containing hazardous goods. To add to this, there is an oil store room just behind yours. In view of the higher risk, we are unable to concede to your request for a reduction in the premium. We are, on the other hand, compelled to charge one per cent more applicable from the date of transfer.

You are, therefore, requested to kindly remit a sum of ₹ 200 as extra premium charges before 22nd June for covering risk in the new premises.

Yours faithfully,
For The New Bharat Assurance,
K. Maran
Manager

MARINE INSURANCE

Sample 7: Draft a letter to Nav Bharat Insurance Company asking for a marine policy to cover a shipment of tea valued at ₹ 6,00,000. Give all the necessary details.

Darjeeling Tea Ltd.

375, Dr. B.C. Roy Road,
kolkata – 700 005

2nd July 2011

The Nav Bharat Insurance Co,
35, Chittaranjan Avenue,
kolkata – 700 052

Dear Sirs,

We are shipping a consignment of tea valued at ₹ 6,00,000 in the account of Messrs. Duncan Brothers, London by s.s. *Jaldoot* sailing from Kolkata to London on 22nd July. Please issue in our name an F.P.A. all risks policy to cover this shipment of cargo.

The goods will be packed in five lead-lined cases. The cases will be marked TAL and numbered 1 to 5.

We hope to receive the policy as early as possible, as we have to send it to our consignee along with other shipping documents.

Yours faithfully,
M. Syed
Manager (Exports)

Sample 8: Draft a letter to your insurance broker to arrange for a floating policy to cover marine risks giving details of its working.

Tamil Nadu Handlooms

138, Harrington Road,
Chennai – 600 037

30th July 2011

Messrs. Rauther & Sons,
Insurance Brokers,
27, First line Beach,
Chennai – 600 054

Dear Sirs,

We have secured substantial orders from our overseas buyers and we shall be making regular shipments of handloom goods to Australia from this August to April next year.

We would like to know whether you would arrange to get us a floating policy for ₹ 8,00,000 with respect to shipments by approved steamers.

Goods will be shipped in containers with waterproof paper and will be metal-strapped.

Please quote your lowest rates and also outline the working of such a policy.

Yours faithfully,
For Tamil Nadu Handlooms,
K. Paari
Managing Partner

Sample 9: M/S Rauther & Sons write to the Tamil Nadu Handlooms agreeing to arrange for a floating policy (open policy). Draft the reply outlining the features of the policy. (Reply to sample 8)

Rauther & Sons
(Insurance Brokers)

27, First Line Beach,
Chennai – 600 054

2nd August 2011

The Tamil Nadu Handlooms,
138, Harrington Road,
Chennai – 600 037

Dear Sirs,

We thank you for your enquiry dated 30th July, regarding open policy for shipments of handloom goods from Chennai to Australia from this August to April next year.

The lowest rate that we can arrange for your shipments is between 2 to 3% to different ports.

To start with, you have to pay the premium at 3 % on the policy amount, and any difference between the amount paid and the amount due will be adjusted on the expiry of the policy.

Along with the policy, you will be supplied with Declaration Forms. You have to complete them giving details of shipment, number of packages, value, marking destination, name of the ship, etc., sign it and send it to the insurance company every time a shipment is made. A certificate of insurance for each shipment will be issued by the insurers after making entries on the duplicate policy retained by them. After the policy is fully run off, the duplicate policy will be returned to you and any surplus will be carried forward to a new policy.

It must be noted that any shipment will be covered by the policy only if the Declaration Form is received by the shipper before the ship sails. We trust to hear from you soon for arranging an open policy (Floating policy) for you.

Yours faithfully,
For Rauther & Sons,
Md. Ibrahim
Partner

Sample 10: The Tamil Nadu Handlooms which has taken up a floating policy of marine insurance informs their insurers to declare off the policy shipments of certain handloom goods. Draft the letter on behalf of the Tamil Nadu Handlooms.

Tamil Nadu Handlooms

138 Harrington Road,
Chennai - 600 037

9th September 2011

The Manager,
Marine Department,
The National Insurance Co. Ltd.,
22, Lingichetty Street,
Chennai - 600 001

Dear Sir,

Sub: Floating Policy No. 35

We are shipping the following goods on 12th September. We request you to declare them off the above policy.

A.K. & Co	5 Bales of handloom cloth
Melbourne	s.s. *Atlantic* to Melbourne
23/87	Value ₹ 2,00,000
R.A & Co	4 Bales of handloom cloth

Sydney s.s. *Ocean Princess*
42/125 Value ₹ 1,60,000

The above shipments leave an undeclared balance of ₹ 4,40,000 on the above policy. Please confirm.

Yours faithfully,
K. Paari
Managing Partner

Sample 11: The National Insurance Co. Ltd., writes to the Tamil Nadu Handlooms that the floating policy issued by them has been run off (fully declared) and asks them if it is to be renewed. Draft the letter.

The National Insurance Co Ltd.

22, Lingichetty Street,
Chennai – 600 001

10th April 2011

The Tamil Nadu Handlooms,
138, Harrington Road,
Chennai – 600 037

Dear Sirs,

Sub: Floating Policy No. 35-Run off

With the issue of Certificate of Declaration No. 75 on 1st April 2011, your Floating Policy No.35 for ₹ 8,00,000 is run off. The details of shipments covered by us under the above policy are given below:

1. To Melbourne by s.s. *Atlantic*
   on 12th September. Value ₹ 2,00,000
2. To Sydney by s.s. *Ocean Princess*
   on 15*th* September. Value ₹ 1,60,000
3. To Perth by s.s. *Jalusha*
   on 17th November. Value ₹ 2,40,000
4. To Melbourne by s.s. *Ocean Princess*
   on 8th December Value. ₹ 2,50,000
5. To Sydney by s.s. *Jalusha*
   on 10th April. Value ₹ 2,50,000

Total Value ₹ 10,00,000

We wait your instructions to issue a fresh floating policy. We assure you of our prompt services at all times.

Your faithfully,
for National Insurance Co Ltd,
K. Pallavan
Manager

Sample 12: A merchant has taken an open policy of marine insurance on shipments of Kashmir silks from Mumbai to London. He writes to his insurers claiming damage to one of his shipments. Draft his letter.

Bombay Textiles

15,Beach road,
Mumbai – 400 012

2nd May 2011

The National Insurance Co Ltd.,
Mumbai – 400 005

Dear Sirs,

Sub: Marine Policy No. 456 – Declaration No. 5

We regret to inform you that we have received a report from our consignee at London, saying that 4 out of our 7 bales of Kashmir silks which we had shipped by s.s. *Jalusha* on 10th April, were received by them in a very damaged condition, having suffered damage by heavy seas. This shipment was covered by your floating policy No. 456 Declaration No.5.

Your authorised surveyor Mr. B. Robertson has also surveyed the damage and his report is also enclosed. We request you to arrange for early settlement of our claim as detailed below:

	₹
Value of 4 bales of Kashmir silk damaged by sea-water and rendered useless	40,00,000
Add 10% of the invoice for estimated loss of profit	4,00,000
Add surveyor's fees (Receipt enclosed)	40,000
Total claim ₹	44,400,000

We have also enclosed a copy each of our invoice, bill of lading, original insurance policy, and damage certificate from the ship's captain.

Yours faithfully,
For Bombay Textiles,
K. Murfi
Manager

Sample 13: A consignment of cotton, shipped from Port Said to Chennai per s.s. *Sultana* by Messrs Karimboy & Co, Cairo on your behalf suffered damage during the transit. Submit a claim for the damage, giving every relevant detail and supply all necessary documents.

Note: This should be written on similar lines as given in the answer to the previous question.

The difference is that the person to whom goods are shipped writes this letter to the insurance company in the exporter's place. You have to state that you have received the goods in a badly damaged condition and submit the claim as in the previous letter.

Sample 14: You have received a claim from a merchant in Kolkata for damage by heavy seas to a consignment of sugar while being taken to the shore in small boats from the steamer standing at some distance from the shore. Reply to the merchant that you have official evidence that on the day in question, the sea was dead calm with no wind, and that the claim cannot be considered unless the two conflicting statements are reconciled.

The National Insurance Co. Ltd.

15, Park Street,
Kolkata – 700 011

11th October 2011

Messrs Ajoy Mukherjee & Co,
74 Lake View Road,
Kolkata – 700 006

Dear Sir,

Sub: Claim under Policy No. 567 Declaration No. 4

We received your letter dated 5th October, regarding damage to your consignment of sugar covered under the above policy shipped by S.S. *Jaldoot* on 5th September.

According to your report, this damage was caused on the afternoon of 1st October by heavy seas, off Sydney, while the shipment was being taken in small boats from the ship which was standing at some distance from the shore.

The Meteorological Report, however, states that the sea was dead calm with no winds on the day in question.

In the context of these conflicting statements, we regret to say that we are unable to admit your claim.

Yours faithfully,
for the National Insurance Co. Ltd.,
A. Ramalingam
Marine Manager

LIFE INSURANCE

Sample 15: Write a letter on behalf of the LIC to a policy holder, who wishes to convert his policy to a paid-up one, dissuading him from doing so.

Life Insurance Corporation of India

145, Temple Street.
Thiruchendur – 628 215

21st February 2011

Mr. A. Karikalan, B.Com (Hons),
140, Main Road,
Thiruchendur – 608 217

Sub: Policy No. 740006 - own life

We regret to note that from your letter of 14th February that you intend to convert your policy into a paid-up one, because of certain financial strain.

We would like to make it clear that you will get back the amount paid-up only on maturity of the policy, even if it is converted into a paid-up one. The immense benefit that a life policy in force confers upon you, needs no emphasis..

Though your policy for ₹ 20,000 has lapsed for non-payment of premium amount, it can be revived. The total amount that you have to pay including the fine and revival fee amounts to ₹ 1,024. Further, you have to produce a medical report from a medical practitioner authorised by LIC.

You can raise a loan on your policy from LIC and tide over your temporary difficulties.

We hope you will take steps to revive your policy rather than convert it into a paid-up one.

Yours faithfully,
A. Panneerselvam,
Branch Manager

Sample 16: A life insurance policy holder wants to know the surrender value of his policy. Draft the LIC's reply explaining why the policy has no surrender value.

Life Insurance Corporation of India

154, Imperial Road,
Cuddalore – 607 107

30th July 2011

Mr. P. Karpakavinayagam,
234, Bharadhidasan Street,
Nellikuppam – 603 108

Dear sir,

Sub: Loan on Policy No. 76542 - Own life.

We have received your letter of 22nd July, requesting the grant of a loan of ₹ 10,000 on the security of your life policy. We regret our inability to advance the loan, since it has not acquired any surrender value.

We like to draw your attention to the condition no.7 appearing on the policy issued to you. The condition clearly states that a policy will start acquiring a surrender value only after the premiums have been paid for at least three years. 'The minimum surrender value allowable under this policy is equal to 30 per cent of the total amount of the premiums paid excluding the premium for the first year.' Since you have to pay one more premium for any surrender value to accrue and since the surrender value will be too meagre to entitle you to the grant of a loan you ask for, we are unable to grant it.

Yours faithfully,
M. Selvarasan
Branch Manager

Sample 17: Draft a letter on behalf of the LIC to a policy holder intimating the amount of loan that can be granted and incorporating some of the terms and conditions of the loan.

Life Insurance Corporation of India

5, Railway Feeder Road,
Chidambaram – 608 007

1st July 2011

Prof K. Gopalakrishnan,
134, East Car Street,
Chidambaram – 608 006

Dear Sir,

Loan on your Life Policy No. 765432 - regarding sanction.

We are glad to inform you that a loan of ₹ 25,000 has been granted to you on your above policy.

The terms and conditions of the loan are as follows:

i The policy must be assigned absolutely to the Corporation which will hold it as a security till the loan is repaid, together with interest accuring thereon.

ii. Interest on the advance shall be paid at 10% compounding half-yearly.

iii. The Corporation is entitled to call back the loan with interest by giving three months' notice.

iv. In case you fail to pay as advised, the policy shall be forfeited to the Corporation and the surrender value applied for adjusting the dues from you.

v. In case the policy matures or becomes a claim by death, the Corporation is entitled to deduct the amount of the advance outstanding, together with the interest from the policy money.

Please send the following documents for preparing the loan bond:

i) Your original life policy.

ii) Proof of your age, if it has not been already admitted.

Yours faithfully,
K. Palanisamy
Divisional Manager

Sample 18: Write a letter on behalf of the LIC to a policy holder, who wants to surrender the policy, advising against surrender.

The Life Insurance Corporation of India

215, Kasi Street,
Pudukkottai – 622 504

9th September 2011

A. Sundaresan,
7, Raja Street,
Pudukkottai – 622 501

Dear Sir,

We regret to note from your letter dated 1st September that you are thinking of surrendering your policy on account of adverse financial circumstances.

As you know, the amount you get on surrendering your policy is far below than what you have paid as premium. The immense benefit that a life policy in force confers upon a policy holder, needs no emphasis. In case you decide to take out a policy later on, the rate of premium will be higher because it is related to your age at the time of taking out the policy.

We can suggest an alternative course to you. You can get a loan up to 90% of the surrender value and tide over temporary difficulties, keeping the policy in force at the same time.

If, however, you stick to your decision to surrender the policy, you have to send the following documents:

1. The original policy
2. Proof of age, if it has not been admitted earlier.

Yours faithfully,
Abdual Razak,
Divisional Manager

Sample 19: A letter from the policy holder opting to surrender his policy.

14, Keneddy St,
Mannadi,
Chennai – 600 002

January 12 2011

The Manager
Birla Sunlife insurance,
17, Adithi Street,
Alwarpet Junction
Chennai – 600 018

Dear Sir,

Ref: Policy No YGP 717171.

I have taken an endowment policy for 15 years in January 2006, from your insurance company and I have been paying premium annually since then. Due to my financial exigency, I am unable to keep the policy alive and wish to surrender the policy. I request you to send me the surrender application.

Yours faithfully,
R. Ravanan

Sample 20: Letter from the insurance agreeing to the surrender.

Birla Sunlife Insurance

17, Adithi Street,
Alwarpet Juction,
Chennai – 600 018

January 14, 2011

R. Ravanan,
14, Keneddy Street,
Mannadi,
Chennai – 600 002

Dear Sir,

Sub: Surrender of policy

We are sorry that you have decided to surrender the aforesaid policy. Your decision will be carried out. The company will pay you 12% of the premium paid along with bonus accrual on this policy. A transaction fee of ₹ 300 will be charged for surrendered policies. I request you to provide all the details relating to the policy in the surrender application enclosed with this letter to enable us to process you application faster and settle the value.

Yours faithfully,
P. Vaiko
Branch Manager

Encl: Surrender application

Sample 21: A letter informing the customer of maturity of a policy

Delpi Insurance company

Your Ref: Letter Mat/End/1212121

17, Pawar Street,
Tata Nagar,
Mumbai – 400 036

15th May 2011

Mr. Vilasmukh,
19, Temple Street,
M.G. Nagar,
Navi Mumbai – 400 012

Dear Sir,

The endowment policy mentioned in the reference matures on June 1, 2011. The maturity value and the accured bonus are payable to you on that day. I request you to kindly fill in the discharge form enclosed with this letter to enable us to send you the maturity cheque.

Yours faithfully,
K. Anilkumar
Manager

Encl: Discharge form

Sample 22: A letter to LIC requesting claim settlement

19, Kabaleswaran Koil St,
Triplicane,
Chennai – 600 005

March 12, 2011

The Divisional Manager,
Royapettah Division,
LIC of India,
Anna Salai,
Chennai – 600 002

Dear Sir,

Ref: Policy No. YGR 1212121

I am pained to inform you that my husband Mr. Tapar, the holder of the policy specified in the reference, passed away on March 10, 2011 at Chennai. I am enclosing the copy of policy and the death certificate issued by the hospital. I am the only nominee on the policy and I request you to send me the claim form.

Yours faithfully,
Trisha

Sample 23: Letter for revival of a lapsed policy

24, Potters Street,

Little Kancheepuram,

Kanchipuram – 631 501

10th March 2011

The Branch Manager
LIC of India,
Kancheepuram Division,
24, North Street,
Kancheepuram – 631 504

Dear Sir,

Ref: Policy No YSR 241274/Adigamen

I took the aforesaid money-back policy in 2004. As I got an appointment abroad in 2006, I could not pay the premium since then. Consequently, the policy has lapsed. Now I wish to have the policy revived, and am willing to pay the premium due including penal interest thereof and other charges due in this connection. I request you, sir, to issue me a form to renew the policy. I am enclosing a photo copy of the policy.

Yours faithfully,
Kalaivanan

Encl: Photocopy of the policy

Sample 24: Reply to the Sample 23.

LIC of India

Kancheepuram Division,
24, North Street,
Kanchipuram – 631 504

15th March 2011

Kalaivanan
24, Potters Street,
Little Kanchipuram,
Kanchipuram – 631 501

Dear Sir,

Your Ref: Letter dt. 10/3/2011

Our Ref: Renw/LIFE/ PIVN/12/2011

It is a matter of great pleasure to renew your lapsed policy. Besides the regular formalities, renewal of policies for Non-Resident Indian involves some additional formalities. The premium for non-resident Indians are higher. In your case, you have to undergo medical examination with our empanelled doctor. The premium and period of the policy will have to be revalued. Therefore, I request you to kindly meet us at our office on any convenient date.

Yours faithfully,
Gopalakrisha Gokale
Branch Manager

GENERAL INSURANCE

Sample 25: A letter from policy holder to an insurance company, stating his claim under a policy covering burglary.

90, Punniakodi Street,
Arumbakkam,
Chennai – 600 024
Tel: 32787214

February 2, 2011

The Branch Manager
ICICI Lambard insurance,
17, TTK Road,
Alwarpet,
Chennai – 600 018

Dear Sir,

Sub: Burglary of house article notified.

Ref: Household policy no: YP1712127

I regret to inform you that my house located at the above address was burgled on Feb 1, 2011, when I was out of station for a couple of days.

The following articles were stolen:

1. Gold jewellery worth 50 sovereigns
2. Two pairs of platinum ear-studs
3. 1 Kg of silver
4. Electronic items
   (a) Sound system
   (b) Digital camera

All the aforesaid items were covered under the burglary policy mentioned in the reference. I have lodged a police complaint at Arumbakkam police station. I am enclosing a copy of FIR filed, along with the complaint letter for your perusal and speedy action.

Yours faithfully,
Krishnan

Enclosed: (1) Copy of policy YP 1712127
(2) Copy of FIR
(3) Complaint letter

Sample 26: Reply to Sample letter 25.

Alpha insurance Company

Your Ref: Letter dt. 2nd Feb, 2011
Our Ref: YCP/BURG/ATpe/091/2011

17, TTK Road,
Alwarpet,
Chennai – 600 018
15th February 2011

Mr. Krishnan,
90, Punniakodistreat,
Arumbakkam,
Chennai – 600 024

Dear Sir,

We are extremely sorry to learn of the burglary that took place in your residence. We can understand and appreciate the mental trauma you are undergoing in the aftermath of the burglary, besides the monetary loss with respect to the valuables stolen. We will do our best to compensate the loss within the framework of the insurance contract. Our spot inspector Kapil Sibel will inspect your residence and assess the loss and help you complete the formalities prescribed in this regard. As soon as an assessment report is received, we would process your application and arrange to settle your claim.

Yours faithfully,
K.S. Kodumudi
Branch Manager

Sample 27: Letter from insurance co. accepting the claim.

Bilroth Insurance Company

Your Ref: Letters dt. 1Aug 2011

24,Garrington Road,
Kalkata – 700 112

Our Ref: YSR/PROP/12P/881

10th Aug 2011

Mr. Rablindra Sadan,
1212 Dav Ganj,
Kalkata – 700 022

Dear Sir,

We are happy to inform you that your claim for the damaged property located at 23, Samdha Nagar, is accepted in full. We have enclosed a cheque for ₹ 2,50,000. As per the lease agreement you have with Bikanir & Co. (Lessee), we have to recover the loss from the lessee. I request you to send us immediately the letter of subrogation to enable us to claim the amount from the lessee.

Yours faithfully,
Choudry
Branch Manager

SUMMARY

Insurance is classified into life insurance and non-life insurance.

Non-life insurance is sub-divided into fire insurance, marine insurance and general insurance

Life insurance is provided by public and private sector insurance companies.

Insurance correspondences include enquiring policy details, surrender value, notification of loss, opting for change in premium period, revival of a lapsed policy, acceptance of claim and rejection of claim.

REVIEW QUESTIONS

Part A: Short questions

1. What is insurance?
2. What is life insurance?
3. What is fire insurance?
4. What is marine insurance?
5. What are the various types of insurance?
6. What is surrender?
7. What is revival?
8. What is nomination?
9. What is premium?

Part B: Objective Type Questions

Choose the correct answer

1. Sum assured is paid on attaining specified age or his death is

    a. Endowment policy b. Whole life policy c. Joint life policy

    (Ans: a)

2. Sum paid as consideration by the policy holder for risk coverage given by the insurer is

    a. Surrender value b. Premium c. Bonus

    (Ans: b)

3. Practice of designating a person for receiving the benefit of policy in the event of death is

    a. Assignment b. Claim c. Nomination

    (Ans: c)

4. Demand made by the policy holder or his legal heir in case of a risk is

    a. Claim b. Surrender c. Bonus

    (Ans: a)

5. The term assurance is used in

    a. Life insurance b. Marine insurance c. Fire insurance

    (Ans: a)

Fill in the blanks

1. Policy covering more than one life is________. (Joint life policy)
2. Sum assured is paid to the nominee on the death of the policy holder under________. (Whole life policy)
3. The amount the insurance company undertakes to pay on the discontinuance of premium by the policy holder is________. (Surrender value)
4. Transfer the right to receive the policy amount is______. (Assignment)

17

CHAPTER

SECRETARIAL CORRESPONDENCE

INTRODUCTION

The term *company secretary* is derived from the Latin word *secetarius* meaning *confidential officer*. There has been a growing appreciation for a company secretary in the company's administration, with the growth of the corporate sector.

DUTIES OF A COMPANY SECRETARY

It can be divided into two categories:

Statutory duties

Specific duties under the Companies Act include:

- Signing copies of annual returns
- Authenticating balance sheet and P&L account
- Signing copies of balance sheet and P&L account
- Signing statutory declaration at the time of incorporation.
- Verifying statutory declaration
- Publishing the name of the company and outlining business place
- Delivering return of allotment to the Registrar
- Issuing share certificates and debentures
- Registering charges with the Registrar of Joint Stock Companies
- Maintaining statutory registers
- Sending out copies of the audited balance sheet and P&L account.

General Duties

These are further subdivided into:

Duties to Director

i. Dealing with correspondence requested by the directors
ii. Issuing notice and agenda for the Board meeting, Annual General Meeting, etc.
iii. Acting as a liaison between the Board and the shareholders
iv. Ensuring submission of statutory returns
v. Keeping calendars of due dates and checklist of meetings

Duties to shareholders

i. Working on details all connected with issuing share certificate, prospectus, application form, allotment letter, etc.
ii. Maintaining non-statutory books
iii. Arranging funds for interest payment
iv. Arranging for issuing dividend warrant
v. Issuing notice/agenda for AGM and class meetings
vi. Attending meetings and maintaining the minutes of the meeting

Duties to the organization

i. Communicating the instructions and orders of the Board to other heads
ii. Coordinating the activities of other departments
iii. Assisting HR in recruitment and training

CLASSIFICATION OF SECRETARIAL CORRESPONDENCE

Secretarial correspondence can be to a wide range of people. They can be classified into three categories as follows:

Correspondence with the Directors

Occasions warranting correspondence with directors are:

- Sending notice of board meeting
- Giving reply to directors concerned on the instruction of the chairman
- Absentee director seeking proceedings of a meeting
- Replying to the director who wants inclusion of a particular item in the agenda
- Replying to the director whose proposal is unacceptable and not in the interest of the company

Correspondence with the shareholders

Correspondence of secretary to the shareholders relates to the following matters:

- Reply to complaints from the shareholder on dividend
- Reply to shareholder's complaint relating to non-receipt of notice of the meetings, share certificate, transfer deed, etc.
- Convey change in the address of the company or schemes of reconstruction

Correspondence with the Registrar and the Company Law Board

Correspondence with the aforesaid authorities relates to:

- Sending periodical statements and returns.

POINTS TO REMEMBER WHILE DRAFTING SECRETARIAL CORRESPONDENCE

The points that must be looked into by a secretary of a company while drafting a letter are:

To the Directors

- The secretary should show politeness and courtesy in his letters
- He must be very tactful especially when he has to write letters which are distasteful to the directors.
- Even while pointing out their mistakes or carelessness, he should draft it in such a way that he does not mean any offence to them.
- He should be impartial.

To the Shareholders

- He should be helpful and friendly in his attitude.
- He may have to answer certain indiscreet request from the shareholders. For instance, a shareholder may seek the opinion of the secretary regarding the likely rate of dividend, why a higher rate of dividend has not been paid despite a large profit earned, or he may claim special consideration to a tender submitted by him. In all these cases, the secretary should politely refuse the requests.
- He should never divulge any confidential information favouring any particular shareholder.
- He should not offend the sentiments of the shareholders by pointing out to their ignorance in company affairs.
- He should never enter into any verbal duel or indulge in long arguments.

Sample 1: A shareholder complains that a larger dividend than that recommended by the directors is justified by the profits for the year. Draft the Secretary's reply.

The Pumpuhar Export Corporation Ltd.

Kovalan Illam,
72, Royapettah High Road,
Chennai - 600 014

2nd July 2011

Prof. K. Pachaiyappan,
22, Anna Salai,
Chengalpet - 602 025

Dear Sir.

I have your letter of 30th June. I am to inform you that before deciding the declaration of dividend of 12 per cent, the Board gave careful consideration to all the points you have raised. In the context of the present trading trend and in the larger interests of the shareholders, it was decided to strengthen the financial position of the company by appropriating a larger share of profit to Reserves and by limiting the rate of dividend to the rate recommended.

You will hear more on this at the Annual General Meeting of the company to be held on 30th July.

Yours faithfully,
T. Velayutham
Secretary

Sample 2: A shareholder writes inquiring about the company's business and if there is any likelihood of an increased dividend this year. He also writes that he is thinking of buying a few more shares and he would like to know if you would advise him to do so. Write the letter as written by the share holder.

Dr. A. Selvaraj
27, Nehru Street,
Pondicherry - 605 110

2nd June 2011

The Secretary,
Auro Food Ltd,
Pilliarkuppam,
Pondicherry - 605 107

Sir,

I have been a shareholder of your company for the past eight years, and I find the company making steady progress.

As I intend to increase my shareholding in your company, I would like to know whether there is any good prospect for the company with its diversified expansion programmes and whether there is a likelihood of a larger dividend being declared this year.

By virtue of your post as its Secretary, you are in a better position to help me in this regard.

Yours faithfully,
S. Selvaraj
Dr. A. Selvaraj

Sample 3: Draft a suitable reply as the Secretary of the company to the above letter.

Auro Food Ltd.

Pilliarkuppam,
Pondicherry – 605 107

10th June 2011

Dr. A. Selvaraj,
27, Nehru Street,
Pondicherry – 605 110

Dear Sir,

I recevied of your letter dated 2nd June, in which you have sought my opinion on the prospects of the company and on the likely rate of dividend for the current year. To divulge an information which I gain by virtue of my position as Secretary of the company, is a gross abuse of my authority. You will quite agree with me that to favour a few with any confidential information is to prejudice a vast majority of the shareholders.

A study of the Directors' report and other published financial statements will enable you to form an opinion on the present position and future prospects of the company. Further, your stock-brokers will be in a position to help you with the information you seek.

Yours faithfully,
A. Sundaresan
Secretary

Sample 4: As the Secretary of a car manufacturing company, reply to a letter of a shareholder who asks for an explanation of a rapid fall in the market price of the company's shares.

India Motors Ltd.

Tambaram,
Chennai – 600 070

2nd May 2011

Mr. B. Kasthuri Rangan
77, Anna Nagar,
Tiruchirappalli – 620 010

Dear Sir,

I have your letter of 30th April, concerning the rapid fall in the market price of our company's shares.

A reference to the Stock Market quotation would have pointed to the steady decline in the price of auto shares in the country for the past nine months. This is because there is, at present, a slump in the auto mobile industry arising due to general trade conditions, restlessness on the labour front, spiraling increase in the administered price of petroleum products, etc. But economic experts are of the firm opinion that the situation compares favourably with that in foreign countries, and that a quick reversal of trend may be expected at an early date.

Yours faithfully,
T. Thirugnanam
Secretary

Sample 5: A shareholder urges that because of his connection with the company, special consideration should have been given to a tender he has submitted. A reply as the Secretary of the company is drafted as below.

Madura Cotton Mills Ltd.

Pandyan Nagar,
Madurai – 625 011.

22nd February 2011

Mr. K. George,
22, Arignar Anna Street,
Kambham – 517 216.

Dear Sir,

We thank you for your letter of 19th February and we regret our inability to accept your tender for the building of the company's new factory at Madura, as it was very much above several others. While considering the tenders, directors are guided solely by the company's interests, and no shareholder is shown any concession in the matter.

The records prove beyond doubt that the directors allowed no personal bias to cloud their judgement; they acted purely on commercial considerations for the benefit of the shareholders as a whole.

Yours faithfully,
Valarivan
Secretary

Sample 6: Reply letter of the Secretary to a shareholder who complains that he did not receive proper attention on the occasion of a recent visit to the company's office.

Decan Papers Ltd.

111, Kuthoosi Gurusamy Road,
Cuddalore – 607 005

22nd July 2011

Mr. N. Elavazhagan,
48, Main Road,
Nellikuppam – 607 105

Dear Sir,

I am surprised and deeply distressed to learn from your letter dated 19th July that you have had reason to complain of incivility and inattention on the part of our office staff.

We thank you for the pains you have taken to bring the incident to our notice.

I have lost no time in ordering an investigation of the matter, and found that Mr. Velu who attended on you behaved rather rudely and used discourteous words, which are quite unbecoming of an office assistant. He has himself admitted of his guilt that he lost his mental balance in the midst of pressing work, because of certain personal problems, and repented later..

I have severely reprimanded him, and have brought home the fact that even the slightest discourtesy to any visitor would be looked upon as a serious breach of discipline, and stern action will be initiated without any further warning. I offer my sincere apologies for the unpleasant occurrence.

Yours faithfully,
P.S. Lakshmanan
Secretary

Sample 7: As the Secretary of a company, draft a circular letter to share holders, offering new shares for subscription pro rata to their holdings.

Chennai – 600 034

2nd June 2011

Dear Sir/Madam,

Issue of 80,00,000 equity shares of ₹ 10 each at par.

It is indeed my privilege to be instructed to present to you a great investment opportunity in the modernization of our company's plant.

In view of the vastly expanding market for the product of our company, the directors, after a careful consideration of all issues involved, have concluded that a favourable opportunity for expansion is currently presenting itself. They have, therefore, decided to modernize the plant and equipments in the company, besides expanding their factory at Nellikuppam. This will enable the company not only to take full advantage of the larger demand, but also to secure substantial benefits from reduced cost of production.

To carry these projects into effect, an additional ₹ 8,00,00,000 of capital will be required. The Board has decided to raise this by means of an issue of 80,00,000 equity shares of ₹ 10 each and to offer these shares at par to the existing equity share holders of the company, pro rata to their holdings. As the market price of the company's equity shares is as high as ₹ 40, this offer represents a valuable and profitable investment opportunity to the share holders.

If you desire to participate in the issue, kindly forward the application form attached, to reach this office before 19th June.

Your holding in the company entitles you to apply and have allotted to you 80 new shares.

By Order of the Board,
A. Thanikachalam
Secretary
42, Grahams Road,

Sample 8: A letter from the company secretary to the director who could not attend a Board meeting.

Kamalini Tubes Ltd.

Regd. Office:
77, Bright Road,
Bangalore – 560 002

19th March 2011

Mr. Kamal
Director
12, Main Road,
Anna Nagar,
Bangalore – 560 040

Dear Sir,

I am enclosing a brief extract of the minutes of the board meeting held on 3rd March 2011. The detailed minutes will be sent to you soon. Most of the decisions taken pertain to the modernization of the plant and office. There was unanimity on all matters and the resolutions adopted were also unanimous. Pending matters have been put off till the board meeting to be held on 25th April 2011.

Yours faithfully,
Kalaivanan
Secretary

Sample 9: Letter to a director on conducting an AGM.

Alpha Corporation Ltd.

Regd. Office:
17, Kenneth Lane,
Georgetown,
Mysore – 570 001

February 20, 2011

Ms. Jasmine
Director
73, Greams Road,
Nirmal Mukarjee Nagar,
Kalkata – 700 005

Dear Madam,

Your suggestion to conduct the AGM of our company on April 7, 2011 at Ooty is well taken. But rules governing the conduct of such meetings read:

'The AGM shall be held either at the Registered office of the company or at some other place within the same city/town or village in which the registered office is situated. Therefore, Board has no power to change the venue of the meeting.'

Yours faithfully,
Saleem
Secretary

Sample 10: Letter to a director on the inclusion of an item in the agenda.

Violet Ltd.

Corporate Office
12, Nett Road,
Sambalpur,
Cuddapah – 516 004

February 20 2011

Mr. Venkat Rengan
17, Chamiyar Road,
West N.T.R. Nagar,
Guntur – 522 403
Andhra Pradesh.

Dear Sir,

I am directed by the Chairman to inform you that the item you have sought to get included in the agenda of the Board meeting cannot be done at this stage. However, it will be included in the next board meeting. The Chairman hopes you will appreciate the situation and agree to get it deferred for the next meeting.

Thanking you,

Yours faithfully,
Desai
Secretary

Sample 11: One of the directors of your company has not obtained the share qualification specified in the Articles of Association. Write to him drawing his attention to the relevant section of the Companies Act, 1956, by which the office of the director has to be vacated if he fails to obtain the qualification within two months of his appointment.

The Cauvery Cements Ltd.

Cauveri Illam
Anbil,
Tiruchi District – 620 007

30th June 2011

Mr. K. Sengunthar
77, Madura Road,
Tiruchirapalli – 620 010

Dear Sir,

I have been directed by the Chairman to draw your attention to the fact that you have not yet acquired 100 equity shares, prescribed as the qualification shares for directorship under Regulation No: 40 of the Articles of Association of our company. You have to obtain these shares before 22nd July, as a period of two months expires on that day since the date of your appointment as director.

I would like to bring to your kind notice that a director who fails to acquire his qualification shares within a period of two months of his appointment, is deemed to have vacated his office automatically under section 283 (i) of the Companies Act, 1956. He is also punishable with a fine which may extend up to ₹ 50 per day under section 272.

I hope you take immediate steps for acquiring the qualification shares within the prescribed time and inform me of your action.

My sole aim in writing this letter is just to avoid the unpleasantness of attracting these provisions of the Companies Act.

Yours faithfully,
for The Cauvery Cements Ltd,
Udayar
Secretary

Sample 12: As a secretary of a company, write a letter to a director requesting him to attend an important Board meeting.

The Tamil Nadu Sugars Ltd.

Pettavaithalai – 639 112
8th December 2011

Thiru M. Pillai,
77, Thillai Nagar,
Tiruchirapalli – 620 005

Dear Sir,

I invite your attention to item no. 5 of the agenda for the next meeting of the Board, a copy of which has already been forwarded to you. It is obvious that this important item deals with the appropriation of a larger balance from the Profit and Loss account. In view of the expansion schemes that the company has on hand, whether a larger appropriation to reserve fund and recommendation of lower rate of dividend would be an appropriate policy, must be discussed in depth.

In view of the importance of the matter, you are earnestly requested to attend the meeting and give your views to the Board.

Yours faithfully,
for The Tamil Nadu Sugars Ltd,
V. Iyer
Secretary

Sample 13: As a secretary of a company, write a letter to one of its directors, giving a brief account of the proceeding at the Board meeting from which he was compelled to absent himself.

National Constructions Ltd.

1/78 Napier Road,
Chennai – 600 011

17th, November 2011

Sri V. B. Naidu,
123, M. G. Road,
Bangalore – 560 005

Dear Sir,

I have your letter of 14th November, and I am enclosing for your perusal a copy of the minutes of the Board meeting held on 10th November. I would like to invite your attention to item no. 5 dealing with the purchase of 5 acres of land by the company adjacent to our factory at Manali at a cost of ₹ 10 crores.

The move that the company should purchase the land was made by Mr. B. Bava Mohideen, and it was seconded by Mr.M. Thennarasu.

The motion met with stiff opposition from three members, who argued that this amount would be better spent on other proposals yielding better returns, and to invest such a huge amount on land is equal to locking it up in a barren asset. To this, the Chairman replied that Mr.M. Bava Mohideen's proposal must be looked upon as a long-term investment. The locality is developing so fast that a remarkable increase in its value could be expected soon. This piece of land adjacent to our factory can be utilized for expansion programme envisaged to happen in a few years. It may not be available then and at such a low price.

After the Chairman's convincing reply, the motion was carried unanimously. Other items in the minutes are of routine nature. I shall, however, be glad to explain any further points, if you so desire.

Yours faithfully,
for National Constructions Ltd,
Reddy
Secretary

Sample 14: A director has been absent for two consecutive meetings of the Board. As a Secretary, draft a letter informing him of the consequence of his continued absence from the Board meetings.

Coimbatore Textiles Ltd.

24 D, Naidu Street,
Coimbatore – 642 154

2nd July 2011

Dr.M. Ezhavan
99, Periyar Nagar,
Madurai – 625 002

Dear Sir,

I enclose the notice of the meeting of the Board of directors of our company to be held on 25th July, together with an agenda.

I would like to draw your kind attention to the fact that you were absent without leave at the two preceding Board meetings held on 15th April and 2nd June, maybe because of your hospitalization. If for any reason, you find it inconvenient to attend the meeting fixed for 25th July, I request you to obtain permission from the Chairman for a leave of absence.

Doing so,you will not attract the provisions of section 283 of the Company's Act which states that the office of a director will fall vacant automatically when he does not attend three consecutive meetings of the Board or does not attend all meetings of the Board for three months, whichever is longer, without obtaining leave of absence from the Board.

Yours faithfully,

for Coimbatore Textiles Ltd,

Nair

Secretary

Sample 15: A director of your company has a certain interest in an important contract that is to come up for discussion at the next Board meeting. As a secretary of the company, write a courteous letter, requesting him to disclose his interest as required by law.

Moovendar Silks Ltd.

123, Pandiyan Road,
Kanchipuram – 631 504

11th October 2011

Dr.M. Seran,
75, Old Jail Road,
Coimbatore – 642 156

Dear Sir,

According to the Board resolution dated 9th September tenders for the construction of an additional building for our company were invited. We have received tenders from five parties, including one from M/S Pallavan Construction Company, Chengalpet.

These tenders will be taken up for consideration and finalization in the forthcoming Board meeting to be held on 20th October.

As it is learnt that you have a personal interest in this particular company, I am writing to you unofficially to know the truth. In case this is true, under section 299 of the Companies Act, you are required to disclose the nature of your interest at the Board meeting and also not participate in the discussion or vote on this contract.

My aim in writing this letter is only to avoid the unpleasantness which may result, in case you fail to disclose your interest.

Your correspondence will be treated with the utmost confidence.

Yours faithfully,

M. Sozhan

Secretary

Sample 16: Write a letter to a well-known business person, inviting him, on behalf of the Board of directors, to join the Board of your company.

Windspeed Auto Ltd.

75 Ennore High Road,
Chennai – 600 056

25th August 2011

Thiru V. Gowda,
Palm Grove,
37, Mowbrays Road,
Chennai – 600 018

Dear Sir,

I am requested by the Board of directors to extend to you a cordial invitation to join the Board of this company in place of the late Mr. Joseph Parker.

As a shareholder of many years' standing, you are well acquainted with the financial position and the present growth of the company.

I enclose a copy of the company's Memorandum and Articles of Association, together with the latest published balance sheet, in case you would like to refer to any matter contained therein.

The Chairman Mr. E. Prabakaran feels that your presence on the Board will help remarkably in the diversification and expansion programmes the company has planned to embark upon soon. He would welcome an opportunity to discuss this matter with you in person on a day most convenient to you.

Yours faithfully,
Thomas Buckitt
Secretary

Sample 17: Letter of allotment of shares.

The Hitech Ltd.

Registered Office:
20, Willington Road,
Perambur,
Gwalior – 475 110

21st June 2011

Mr. Nalli
Prakasam Road,
C.I.T. Nagar,
Bangalore – 560 111

Dear Sir,

The company is pleased to allot to you 100 shares at ₹ 125/- each. Since you had applied for 1000 shares and have paid with the application, the balance will be refunded to you, after adjustment. Please keep this letter of allotment until the share certificates are sent to you..

Name of the Shareholders	No. of shares applied	Amount in credit	No. of shares allotted	Value of share	Balance
Nalli	1000	1,25,000	100	₹ 12,500	₹ 1,12,500

Yours faithfully,
Patnaik
Secretary

Sample 18: Letter regretting the non-allotment of shares.

Balfour Ltd.

23 Pentafour Industrial Estate,
White fields,
Andhra pradesh – 500 086
Regd Office: 14 Cannaught Circle,
Vijayawada – 520 005

20th Jan 2011.

Ms. R. Radha
17, East Kamaraj Street,
Thirumullai vasal,
Kodanadu,
Nilgiris – 643 217

Dear Madam,

The Board of directors regret that the shares you have applied for have not been allotted to you, as the issue has been oversubscribed. The amount you have remitted for the shares is refunded to you. A cheque drawn on Canara Bank, Bangalore for ₹ 10,000 dated 10th Jan. 2011 is enclosed with this letter.

We thank you for your interest in our company, and request you to mail the duly signed receipt.

Yours faithfully,
Aruvi
Secretary

Sample 19: Reply to a shareholder's letter asking for higher dividend.

EID Parry Confectioneries and Toffees Ltd.

Regd Office:
17, Boulevard Road,
Kolar Gold Field,
Bangalore – 500 004

March 10, 2011

Mr. Nambudri
23, Gandhi Road,
Annamalaipuram,
Kottayam – 686 010

Dear Sir,

Your concern and anxiety about the non-enhancement of the usual dividend, in spite of profits, is appreciated. But there is a valid reason behind it. The Board of directors had decided last year that the company was required to buy two new estates at Moonar Hill Station, and this has necessitated a greater allotment to capital funds. You would appreciate that, in the long run, this move would prove to be wiser.

This explanation is offered at the direction of the board, which has anticipated such clarification being sought by our shareholders.

Yours faithfully,
Panicker
Company Secretary

Sample 20: Letter indicating the issue of bonus shares.

The Dunlop Ltd.

Regd. Office:
23, Whites street,
First Line Beach Road,
Mumbai – 400 069

September 20, 2011

Mr. Raman
78, Beach road,
Visakhapatnam – 530 007

Dear Sir,

Sub: Issue of bonus shares to shareholders

The Board of Directors of The Dunlop Limited has resolved to allot bonus shares to existing shareholders in the ratio 1:1. This entitles you to one additional share for every share held by you. The breakup of allotment and certificates will be sent to you shortly.

Yours faithfully,
Mannen
Company Secretary

Sample 21: Reply letter written by the company secretary to a complaint from a shareholder

Camel India Ltd.

56, Gandhi road,
Anna salai,
Chennai – 600 002

17th January 2011

To
Mr. Ricksan
47, Sydenhams Road,
Vepery,
Chennai – 600 007

Dear Sir,

We acknowledge your letter dated January 1, 2011. On verification of our records, we have found that the Dividend Voucher No. MsQ 47453 for ₹ 7262/- was dispatched through Professional Couriers Ltd, and the same has been returned to us with the note 'door-locked'. We request you to confirm your mailing address by letter or telephone so that we can arrange to re-send it. The voucher is valid for six months and can be exchanged at par in any branch of the State Bank of India.

Yours faithfully,
Ulmer
Secretary

Sample 22: A letter to a shareholder regarding transfer of shares.

Tyson Corporation

Regd. Office:
17, Second line Beach,
Georgetown,
Chennai – 600 001.

14th December 2011

Mr. Sheldon
77, Randals Road,
Vepery,
Chennai – 600 007

Dear Sir,

We appreciate your idea of transferring the shares between your two daughters. Though these shares are freely transferable, it cannot be done without some formality being completed.

The contractual relationship between you, a member of Tyson Corporation and the company, makes it obligatory that an instrument of transfer be presented to the authority mentioned in the enclosed format, on a blank paper. Then, the instrument of transfer shall be presented to the company along with the share certificates. The instrument will be executed by the transferer, in this case, Mr. Sheldon in favour of his daughters Ms. Rose and Ms. Mary, the transferees. It is mandatory that we complete this exercise within two months. Please forward the instrument of transfer duly signed to enable us to do the needful.

Yours sincerely,
Wilson
Secretary

SECRETARIAL CORRESPONDENCE WITH GOVERNMENT AGENCIES AND OTHERS

Sample 23: Letter for certificate of incorporation.

20th Jan 2011

To
The Registrar of Companies
Shastri Bhavan,
Mumbai – 400 004
Maharastra

Dear Sir,

Sub: Documents for registration of Laurel Hardy Private Ltd. (a food processing industry) – Filing fees.

Ref: Registrar's letter dated 3.1.2011

I am enclosing the following documents for the registration of Laurel Hardy Private Ltd. (a food processing industry) with corporate office at 17, Alsoor road, Alsoor, Bangalore – 500 008.

1. Filing fees: A pay order for ₹ 50,000/-
2. Power of Attorney in stamp paper of ₹ 20/-
3. Power of attorney in stamp paper of ₹ 20/- (to receive letter of incorporation)
4. Memorandum of Association and Articles of Association
5. Name available letter in Original
6. Form No. 1
7. Form No. 18

Kindly issue the certificate of incorporation at the earliest.

Your faithfully,
Franklin
Secretary

Sample 24: Notice of the Annual General Meeting.

Levincare Ltd.

Banjara Hills,
Hyderabad – 575 009

June 1, 2011

Notice is hereby given that the 25th Annual General Meeting of the Members will be held at 2.00 p.m. on Monday, 23rd June 2011 at Flower House, 17 Railway Feeder Road, Hyderabad – 575 003, to transact the following business:

i To receive and adopt the Director's Report, audited balance sheet as on 30th March 2011 and the profit and loss account for the year ended 31st March 2011.

ii. To declare dividends for shareholders.

iii. To appoint a director in the place of Mr. Varunkumar, who retires by rotation and is eligible for reappointment.

iv To appoint an auditor for the company and fix his renumeration.

v. To transact any other business, for which prior notice has been given by any shareholder.

By Order of Board
B. Bedi
Secretary

Sample 25: Letter for raising of authorized capital.

12th May 2010

To
The Registrar of Companies
Shastri Bhavan,
Navi Mumbai – 400 004.

Dear Sir,

Sub: Raising the authorized capital

Ref: Your letter no. 337 – 03/05 dated 5/2/2010

By the direction of the letter cited above, we confirm that we have raised the authorized capital from ₹ 8,00,000/- to ₹ 50,00,000/-. We request you to allot the same name as per our application dated 1.01.2010 be made available to us.

Yours faithfully,
Sharma
Secretary

Sample 26: Submission of Annual Report.

5th June 2011

To
The Registrar of Companies
Shastri Bhavan,
Chennai – 600 006

Dear Sir:

Sub: Submission of Annual Report

Ref: Appasamy Constructions Pvt. Ltd

I am enclosing the following documents related to Appasamy Construction Pvt. Ltd.

1. Schedule V–2 copies

2. Notice of AGM

3. Company's report – 3 copies

4. Auditor's report – 4 copies

5. Balance sheet as on 31.3.2011

I am also enclosing the filing fee of ₹ 10,000 with DD No. 113210 dated 5th June 2011 drawn on Indian Bank.

Yours faithfully,
Peter
Secretary

Sample 27: Letter to the stock exchange for listing of shares.

Jasmine Hospital Ltd.

24 III Lane,
Writers Road,
Madurai – 625 004

10th August 2011

To
The Secretary
Mumbai Stock Exchange Ltd.,
17, Jail Road,
Navi Mumbai – 400 104

Dear Sir,

Jasmine Hospitals Ltd., Madurai, has been incorporated vide Registrar of Companies which is enclosed with this letter. The board of directors, at the meeting, have resolved to apply to your exchange to list equity and preference shares in the market. I am enclosingnecessary application and prescribed fee of the stock exchange. We request your board to give their consent and send it to us at the earliest.

Yours faithfully,
S. Susmitha Reddy
Secretary

Enclosed: 1. Application form
2. Prescribed fees

SUMMARY

Points to be noted while drafting a letter to directors are: to show politeness and courtesy, tactfully point out an unpalatable message, be impartial and tactfully point out the mistakes or carelessness of a director.

Points to be noted while drafting a letter to shareholders are: adopting a friendly and helpful attitude, answering indirect questions, never divulging confidential information, not offending the sentiment of shareholders and not entering into a verbal quarrel with them.

REVIEW QUESTIONS

Part A: Short Questions

1. Who is a secretary?
2. What is secretarial correspondence?
3. List any four occasions when the secretary has to correspond with the Registrar of Joint Stock Companies.

Part B: Paragraph Questions

1. State the occasions when a secretary has to correspond with the directors.
2. What are the circumstances necessitating correspondence between shareholders and the secretary.
3. Highlight the points to be kept in mind while corresponding with the directors.
4. What are the points to be noted while corresponding with the shareholders?

Part C: Essay Questions

1. As the secretary of a company, write a letter to a director requesting him to attend an important Board meeting.
2. Reply of the company secretary to a complaint received from a shareholder.
3. Letter to a director on the inclusion of an item in the agenda.
4. A letter from the company secretary to the director who could not attend a Board meeting.
5. As the secretary of a company, draft a circular letter to shareholders offering new shares for subscription pro rata to their holdings.
6. A shareholder complains that a larger dividend than that recommended by the directors is justified by the profits for the year. Draft the secretary's reply.

Choose the Correct Answer

1. The term company secretary is derived from

   a. Latin word b. French word c. Japanese word

   (Ans: a)

2. Issuing share certificate and debenture is

   a. General duty b. Statutory duty c. Administrative duty

   (Ans: b)

Fill in the Blanks

1. The term company secretary means ______________.(confidential officer)
2. Duties to be discharged by company secretary as per law are called ____________duties. (statutory)

18 CHAPTER GOVERNMENT CORRESPONDENCE

REPRESENTATION

A representation is essentially an upward communication drawing the attention of those in authority to a grievance, an injustice or simply a requirement. A representation is mostly in writing.

Pre-requisites of Representation Letters

- Since the purpose of a grievance is redressal, it should clearly point out the issue.
- Facts must be stated.
- Government orders, regulations or provisions of relevant Act must be quoted and their extracts attached thereto as documentary support.
- Things represented must be stated politely, persuasively, clearly and concisely.

Structure of a Representation Letter

- A representation is usually made on a plain paper with the writer's address given at the bottom of the left-hand margin.
- If it is a group representation and they have a letterhead of their own, it can be used for this purpose.
- The saluatation is generally *Sir* or *Madam*. The president or the governor is addressed as *Your Excellency*.
- The usual complimentary close is *Yours faithfully*.

Sample 1: Representation presented by the staff of a company, requesting for provision of adequate facilities in the office and an indoor games room.

1st July 2011

The Manager,
Pondicherry Chemicals Ltd,
Kudikadu,
Cuddalore – 607 003

Sir,

We, the members of staff of our office, request your kind attention to the following problems faced by us and seek an early solution.

The halls which house our Accounts section and Establishment section are so dingy and without ventilation, so working there in summer is very unbearable.

Lighting in these halls is also inadequate . The staff working a few metres away from the windows get very little natural light. Many members of the staff suffer quite often from eye strain.

Toilet facilities for a staff strength of 100 are also inadequate. Water connection gets disrupted quite frequently, with the result that they become totally unusable.

We have made several representations separately for providing an Indoor Games Room where we can play table tennis, carrom, chess, etc., after a day's hard work. Games contribute significantly to the building up of a good physique, which helps to keep us healthy and cheerful.

No one can deny that expenditure on these items which go a long way towards providing a better and healthier work atmosphere, is a good investment. It is amply-rewarded in the form of greater work turnout.

We do hope that you will take immediate steps for removing the handicaps with which we have to work. Since our oral representation has had no effect, we have it put it in writing.

An early action is sure to strengthen the bonds of loyalty, which alone can result in greater productivity.

Yours faithfully,
V. Singaravelu
Secretary

Enclosed: Signatures of all the members of staff are attached.

Sample 2: Representation to be submitted to the Honourable Minister for Health on the problem of air pollution in your town.

The Hon' ble Minister for Health,
Government of Tamil Nadu.

Sir,

We, the residents of Manali, present the following facts for your kind consideration and favourable disposal.

The problem of air and water pollution caused by the mushrooming growth of industries in this area, is assuming alarming proportions. Unless the problem is tackled early it would prove to be an unimaginable health hazard.

Our representations to the Municipal authorities and to our representative in the assembly have fallen on deaf ears, as nothing worthwhile has been done to enforce observance of anti-pollution regulations by factories located here.

Companies such as D.M. Chemicals Ltd, Chemequp Ltd as well as some 20 other smaller chemical units are already causing enough havoc. Both the air and water of Manali have become so heavily polluted that every fourth child in this town has chronic bronchial asthma. Doctors are unable to cure lung diseases such as tuberculosis, since their medicines have no effect in an atmosphere laden with chemical pollution.

Our frequent appeals to authorities and visits to the secretariat were equally fruitless. No objection certificate is issued by the Municipal authorities to these companies, with utter disregard to the representations made by various bodies.

A visit to the Housing Board colony will convince the force of our argument. The galvanised iron pipes of all the overhead water tanks are severely corroded. Because of chemical pollution, residents in these buildings have to keep their windows permanently shut.

Children frequently become unconscious when exposed to this high levels of pollution and need periodic medical treatment.

Incidence of paediatric tuberclosis have gone up. Twenty-four doctors practicing in Manali town have submitted a report, saying that this mist of pollution is causing irritation to the skin and the respiratory tract, and repeated common colds not responding to treatment.

In the fervent hope that you will pay personal attention to this serious matter concerning the health of the citizens and take appropriate action swiftly, we have ventured to make this representation to you. We need not point out that this is a serious problem requiring immediate attention to save us from destruction.

Yours faithfully,
ABC
On behalf of residents
of Manali

Enclosed: Signatures of the citizens of Manali

OFFICIAL (GOVERNMENT) CORRESPONDENCE

An organization or a business person has to deal with Government officials and send correspondence to them on a regular basis in their way of work. Hence, a lot of thought has to go into these letters.

Structure of an Official Letter

The structure of an official letter is as follows:

- The name of the government and the department sending the letter must appear at the top-centre.
- Reference number must appear at the top left-hand side.
- Date and place must be written at the top right-hand side.
- The words *From* and *To* must be prefixed to the sender's address and to the address of the person to whom the letter is meant.
- The salutation is *Sir* or *Madam*.
- After salutation, a very brief mention of the subject under discussion is mentioned as *Sub*.

Correspondence with the State Government

Every businessman has also to deal with the following departments of the State Government:

- Commercial Tax Department
- Police Department
- Registration Department
- Transport Department
- Revenue Department
- Labour Welfare Department

Besides these, he also has to deal with other local bodies.

Hints on Drafting Letters to the Government

Basically, government correspondence is a type of business communication and, therefore, to be written based on the main principles of a business letter. The following points are especially more important in drafting letters to the government departments:

- The letter should be addressed to the officer concerned with the subject matter. He should not be addressed by his name even if he is intimately connected with the correspondent.
- The best form of salutation is *Sir* and *Dear Sir*.
- The complementary close should be *Yours faithfully*.
- The letter should contain the subject and reference part for easy identification.
- The matter should be precise, clear and complete.

Large business houses employ experts and tax consultants to deal with the government departments on their behalf. Even small businessmen may employ them when the matter concerned is complicated. With routine matters, the correspondence is generally completed by filling in the printed forms available in the office.

However, there are certain transactions which require some originality on the part of the correspondent. Since the occasions are many and the number of departments to deal with is also more, we have provided only a few specimen letters that are required to be written by a trader on certain important issues.

General layout of an official letter

Government of Tamil Nadu
(Ministry of Education)

No ... Chennai

From April 10, 2010.

The Commissioner and Secretary to the Government of Tamil Nadu.

To

The Registrars of all Universities

Sir,

Sub: Grant of scholarship -Research Scholars-clarifications issued.

Ref:......................

Body of the letter ....

....

Yours faithfully,
for Secretary

Sample 3: Letter to the postmaster about a money order already sent.

K.F. STORES

20, C.N.K. Road,
Chepauk,
Chennai – 600 005

10th May 2010

To
The Post Master,
Triplicane Post Office,
Triplicane,
Chennai – 600 005

Sir,

Sub: Money order sent on 25.04.2010 – Non-Receipt by the addressee – reported and action requested.

Ref: M.O. Receipt No. 654321 dt. 26.06.2010.

We sent a money order for ₹ 500 (Rupees five thousand only) to M/s. Ramesh & Co., Chennai, on 25th April 2010 (vide your receipt No. 654321). But we are surprised to note that the payee has not yet received the amount. We shall be thankful to you, if you can make the necessary enquires and see that the amount is paid to the payee without any further delay.

Yours faithfully,
For K.F. Stores,
S. Kannan
Manager

D.O. LETTERS

D.O. letter means *Demi Official letter*. It is issued with a view to get the required information or action quickly without the formality of the prescribed procedure. It receives the personal attention of the individual addressed.

Circumstances under which a D.O. Letter is Usually Issued

A D.O. letter is not a regular letter. It is issued during special situations like:

- When the matter dealt with is of an urgent nature
- When the matter is of a very confidential nature
- When an explanation is offered to supplement an official letter
- When the matter is to be brought to the personal attention of the officer to whom it is addressed, after reminders have failed to evoke the necessary response

Characteristics of a D.O. Letter

A D.O. letter has the following characteristics:

- A D.O. letter must be addressed to an officer by his or her name
- It should be written in the first person singular and in a friendly tone
- The appropriate salutation is 'Dear Mr..............'
- The usual complementary close is 'Yours sincerely'

Sample 4: A specimen of a D.O. letter

Dr. R. Muthian, M.Com, Ph.D.
Principal

Office of the Principal
Periyar Arts College
Cuddalore – 607 004

10th June 2010

D.O. No 208/70/1
Dear Mr. Pattabiraman,

Please refer to this office letter No. 470/p/86 dated 30th April and 27th May, regarding the salary details of Thiru C. Ragavan, Professor of Mathematics during the period he was in your college. As refixation of his pay is pending for a long time, please let me have these particulars at an early date.

With kind regards,

Yours sincerely,
R. Muthian

To
Prof. S. Pattabiraman,
Principal,
Govt Arts College,
Chidambaram – 608 001

Sample 5:Another specimen of a D.O.letter

From
Thiru R.A, M.A.B.T.,
Principal,
Government Arts College,
Chennai – 600 002

To
The Principal,
Arignar Anna Govt Arts
College for Men,
Namakkal – 637 007
Salem District

Rc. No. 344/B/70 – dated 5-12-2010

Sir,

Sub: T.E.S.S, Thiru A.K.R, former

Asst. Prof. of Commerce of this college, L.P.C

Ref: Your Rc. No. 208/A/2010 - dated 17-11-2010

With reference to your letter cited, I have to state that the Last Pay Certificate of Thiru A. K. R, former Asst. Prof. of Commerce has been forwarded to the Accountant General, Chennai in this office Rc. No. 344/B/70/ dated 11-11-2010.

Sd
Principal

MEMORANDUM IN GOVERNMENT INSTITUTIONS

A memorandum or a memo is a letter written between different departments. This form of communication is used

- between departments of equal standing
- while replying to petitions
- when letters are to be sent to subordinates

- when a reminder is to be sent
- when the matter dealt with is not very important

Characteristics of a Memo

A memo has the following characteristics:

- It is written in third person singular.
- It has neither a salutation nor a complimentary close.
- It is signed by the officer sending the letter or his immediate subordinate officer.
- Designation of the person signing the memo must be mentioned below the signature.
- It does not begin with the phrases such as 'I am directed', 'I am to state', etc.
- The address of the person to whom it is addressed must be written on the left-hand corner after the signature.

Sample 6: A specimen of a memo

Government of Tamil Nadu
Department of Health

Chennai - 600 005
2nd July 2010

Office Memorandum

Sub: Permission to purchase motor cycle for own use.

With reference to the application dated 2nd June, Dr.K. Jayachandran, Medical Officer, Primary Health Centre, Varakalpattu, is permitted to purchase a motor cycle for his use out of his savings.

Dr. K. Sundar
Director of Medical Service

To
Dr. K. Jayachandran,
Medical Officer,
Primary Health Centre,
Varakalpattu - 607 109

Sample 7: A specimen of a memo intended to be addressed to a large number of officers

Government of India
Ministry of Finance

No. 2345

New Delhi - 110 010

8th August 2010

Memorandum

Attention is invited to the Memo of this Ministry of number 2240 dated 5th January 2010 banning purchase of costly furniture. It has come to the notice of the Ministry that this is not being observed in many cases. Any violation of this order will, therefore, be viewed very seriously and the officers concerned will be held personally liable.

For Deputy Secretary,
Kamal Gupta
(Finance)

To
All Heads of Departments

ENDORSEMENT

An endorsement is not the original letter. It is a method by which the original letter emanating from another office or from a higher officer is circulated amongst people for whom it is intended. When a copy of the letter received from another office is to be communicated to a particular officer, the intermediate officer sends it to him for necessary action.

Similarly, when the head of an office has to send a letter submitted by his subordinate officer to a superior officer, the head of the office just notes on the letter that it is forwarded to the superior officer. No opinion is usually expressed in the endorsement.

It is written at the end of the original letter. It is dated and numbered.

For example,

No. ....

Office of the Revenue Divisional Officer,

Udupi Division, Mangalore

11th October 2012

Forwarded for information and necessary action.

Signature
Revenue Divisional Officer,
Mysore

Even where the original is returned to the applicant himself, an endorsement is made with the remark.

'Returned with a request to send this representation through proper channel'.

NOTIFICATIONS

Notifications are announcements of a general nature intended for the general public, usually published in Government Gazettes. Appointments, promotions, transfers, enactment of new laws, etc., are notified through this.

They bear the signatures of the Heads of Office issuing them. They also carry reference number and date.

Sample 8: Specimen of a notification.

Government of Kerala.

Abstract

Kerala Educational Service - Arignar Anna Government Arts College for Men, Triuvandram - Professor of Commerce Appointment - Notified.

Education Department

G.O. Ms. No... Dated: 19th October 2010

Read: -

From the Director of Collegiate Education, letter

Rc. No....... dated 5.8.70.

Order:

The following appointment is notified:

Notification

Appointment

Under rule10 (a) (i) of the General Rules for the Kerala State and Subordinate Services, Thiru A.Kumara Raj, Assistant Professor of Commerce, Government Arts College, Trivandram is appointed temporarily as Professor of Commerce in Arts Colleges in Kerala Educational Service and posted at Arignar Anna Government Arts College for Men, Kottayam with effect from the date of taking charge.

The above appointment is ordered under emergency provisions as there are no approved candidates available for regular appointment.

The Director of Collegiate Education is requested to take action for making regular appointment to the post at an early date.

Sd.

Secretary to Government of Kerala

Sample 9: Specimen of the notification issued by the Public Works Department for acquiring certain lands for a public purpose.

Public Works Department

G.O. Ms. No. 2345 Dated 6.6.2010

Notification

As it appears to the Government of Andhra Pradesh that the land specified in the schedule below and situated in Kotturu Village,Nellore District, is needed for a public purpose, for the excavation of Gadilam Branch Canal under Gadilam Improvement scheme, notice to that effect is hereby given to all to whom it may concern in accordance with the provisions of sub section (1) of section 4 of the Land Acquisition Act 1894 (Central Act of 1894).

Now, therefore, in exercise of the powers conferred by sub-section (2) of section (4) of the said Act, the Governor of Andhra Pradesh hereby authorizes the special Tahsildar (Land Acquisition), Gadilam Improvement Scheme, Nellore, his staff and workmen, to exercise the powers conferred by section 3 of the said Act. The Government of Andhra Pradesh, hereby appoints special Tahsildar Gadilam Improvement scheme, Cuddalore to perform the functions of Collector of Cuddalore Distrit under section 5 - A of the Act.

The Schedule.

District: Nellore, Village: Kongarayanur Government Wet R.S. No. 185, Belonging to Thiru K. Subramaniam Mudaliar, S/o A Kattimuthu Mudaliar. Bounded on the North by R.S. No. 185/8A, West by Narayanamagalam village, East By R.S.No. 186/1A1, South By R.S.No. 186/1A2, Total Extent to be acquired: 0.005 hectare.

R. Maran
Joint Secretary to Government of Karnataka

SUMMARY

Pre-requisites of representation letters are: the point of issue to be clearly stated, facts must be provided, Government orders and regulations must be clearly quoted, be polite, persuasive and concise.

Structure of an official letter includes name of the Government and the Department, reference number, date and place, salutation, 'From' and 'To' to be prefixed and subject line.

Demi official letter is issued when the matter is of urgent nature, confidential nature, supplements an official letter and when personal attention of an officer is required on a matter of importance.

A memorandum or memo is written between departments of equal standing, as a reply to petitions, as letters to subordinates, reminders and when the matter is not very important.

Charasteristics of a memo are written in third person singular, no salutation or complimentary close, sign of the officer sending it, designation has to be mentioned and address of the person is written after the signature in the left-hand corner.

Endorsement is not an original letter. Letter from another office or seniors is circulated amongst people for whom it is intended.

Notification are announcements of general nature for the general public issued by Government Gazettes.

REVIEW QUESTIONS

Part A: Short Questions

1. What are the pre-requisites of a representation letter?
2. State the structure of a representation letter.
3. Give the structure of an official letter.
4. What is a memorandum?
5. What are the characteristics of a memo?
6. What is an endorsement?
7. What is a notification?
8. What is a D.O. letter?

Part B: Paragraph Questions

1. Write a note on Government correspondence.
2. What are the points to be remembered while drafting letters to the Government?
3. Write a note on D.O. letters.

Part c: Essay Questions

1. What are the various types of Government correspondence?

Part D: Objective Type Questions

Choose the correct answer

1. A representation is essentially a

   a. Downward communication   b. Diagonal communication

   c. Upward communication

   (Ans: c)

2. It is issued with a view to get immediate action without formality

   a. Endorsement   b. D.O. letter   c. Representation

   (Ans: b)

3. They are letters of general nature

   a. Endorsement   b. D.O. letter   c. Notification

   (Ans: c)

Fill in the blanks

1. A representation is essentially a/an ___________ communication. (Upward)
2. ___________ addresses an officer by his name. (D.O. letter)
3. ___________ is written between departments. (Memo)
4. ___________ are announcements of general nature. (Notifications)
5. ___________ is not the orginal letter. (Endorsement)

19

CHAPTER

AGENCY LETTERS

APPLYING FOR AN AGENCY

While applying for an agency, the applicant should convince the principal that he could carry out the agency work profitably. For this purpose, he should stress the following points in his application:

1. If the application is made on his own initiative i.e. in the case of an unsolicited application for an agency, the applicant should show that there is a good market for the manufacturer's goods in the region and that it can be exploited.
2. In case it is made in response to an advertisement, he should stress his ability to promote the sale of his goods by pointing out
   a. his experience in the line
   b. his knowledge of the local market
   c. his wide business connections and personal contacts
   d. the special facilities he has like showroom, his sales force travelling and counter salesmen, possession of delivery vans, etc.
3. He should also convince the principal that he is financially sound.
4. He can support these points by making references of firms of which he is the agent. He should also furnish bank reference.
5. He should state the commission on which he is prepared to work.
6. He should also state as to how the accounts would be settled.
7. The letter should end with an optimism that a mutually beneficial connection will be established.

DRAFTING AN AGENCY LETTER

A letter offering an agency should contain the following points:

1. An expression of thanks for the offer of agency and acceptance.
2. The area of agency operation.
3. If the agent himself has offered certain terms, agreement with the terms of offer or modification of certain terms.
4. In case the agent's application seeks to know the terms and conditions, the offer letter by the principal should specify all the terms and conditions like
    a. Commission on sales effected
    b. del credere commission, if such a responsibility is entrusted
    c. period of agency
    d. the share of advertising expenses to be borne by the principal
    e. settlement of accounts
    f. maintenance of Stock Registers
5. An expression of hope that this will result in the development of a mutually profitable trade relations.

SAMPLE AGENCY LETTERS

Sample 1: The National TV Distributors, Chennai apply to Premier Electronics Ltd, Bangalore for sole agency for the whole of Tamil Nadu to distribute its premier TV sets. Draft the application.

The National TV Distributors

178, Anna Salai,
Chennai – 600 002

19th November 2011

The Premier Electronics Ltd,
100, Chowdeshwari Temple Road,
Bangalore – 560 005

Dear Sirs,

We are pleased to bring to your kind notice that Tamil Nadu offers an excellent market for the sale of your Premier LED TV sets. We therefore, offer ourselves to act as your sole selling agents for all the districts of Tamil Nadu.

We have established ourselves as wholesale dealers in FM radios, laptops, audio systems, home theatres, etc., for the last twenty years. We have built up extensive and valuable connections, besides establishing a large number of our branches in a number of towns throughout Tamil Nadu.

At present, we hold the sole agency for English Electrical, Kolkata. But as they do not manufacture TV sets, their products will not compete with yours.

We have spacious accommodation required for sales, attractive window display points and also godown facilities.

We have technically qualified sales officers, who will periodically visit our branches and agents in the districts and market the sales of your TV sets, despite different varieties from countless competing units flooding the market. We are, therefore, confident of achieving a large turnover of your products.

We are pleased to furnish the following trade references:

i. United Commercial Bank, 77, Anna Salai, Chennai - 2

ii. The English Electrical, Kolkata

In case you are willing to appoint us as your sole selling agents, please let us know your terms and conditions for the agency.

We would make the payment every quarter. We are prepared to take up the del credere responsibilities also at 2% over and above your regular rate of commission.

Should you grant us the sole agency, it shall be our endeavour to increase the sales of your TV sets to our mutual advantage.

Yours faithfully,
J. Manravanan
Sales Manager

Sample 2: A reply from The Premier Electronics Ltd, Bangalore to the above letter granting sole agency to The National Electronics Distributors.

The Premier Electronics Ltd.

100, Chowdeshwari Temple Road,

Bangalore – 560 005

2nd December 2011

The National Electronics Distributors,

178, Anna Salai,

Chennai – 600 002

Dear Sirs,

We thank you for your letter of 19th November, and we are favourably impressed by your offer to act as our sole selling agents for our Premier LED TV sets. We are pleased to appoint you as our sole selling agents for all models of our TV sets for Tamil Nadu.

The agency agreement enclosed contains the terms and conditions of appointment.

As will be observed therefrom, we agree to pay you a commission of 20% on the net value of all orders received by us either through you or direct from any part of your agency area. However, orders directly received by us will be executed only after referring them to you.

The period of agency will be for two years in the first instance.

We agree to share 50% of your advertising expenses to popularise our products, provided your advertising plans and the estimated costs are approved by us.As regards del credere commission, we are prepared to accept your offer of 2%.

We shall be sending display articles along with the first consignment.

We expect all our agents to maintain an up-to-date stock register and send us a monthly report as soon as we have your approval of the terms.

We are looking forward to a long and multually profitable relationship with you.

Yours faithfully,
E. Nijalingappa
Sales Manager

Sample 3: The Manager, Chennai Cosmetics Ltd, Chennai offers an agency for distribution of their talcum powder 'Flora' to M/s Alfares Trading Company. Draft the letter.

Chennai Cosmetics Ltd.

432, Sterling Road,
Chennai-600 034
22nd February 2011

M/s Alfares Trading Company
Damman P.O. Box No. 1543,
Saudi Arabia C.R. 2612

Dear Sirs,

We are the manufacturers of Flora talcum powder and perfumes, which are acclaimed all over the world as high class cosmetics.

We are already doing a considerable volume of business with different buyers in Saudi Arabia. We are now contemplating the appointment of another commission agent for further development of our trade. Your name as an agent has been suggested to us by M/S Abubaker & Co of Mumbai, and we are glad to offer you an agency in Saudi Arabia.

We manufacture a large variety of perfumes and talcum powders in different fragrances. We use expensive perfumes for fabulous, fresh fragance. Our prickly heat powder is efficacious in fighting prickly heat, and we have special powder to protect the soft skins of babies too. We also use herbs for clear complexion and to act as antiseptics. So, it is natural that we command a high market share.

Since we are aware of the hurdles you have to face in introducing a new product to your local buyers, we are willing to pay a commission of 15% on the F.O.B. value of sales besides a del credere commission of 3%.

We are enclosing our price list. Goods will be consigned according to your instructions, since you are the best judge of the tastes and particular requirements of your local customers.

If this offer interests you, please let us have your reply. We trust that this relationship will grow to be mutually profitable.

Yours faithfully,
K. Pallavan
Manager

Sample 4: Two Wheelers Ltd. offers an agency to M/S Bharat Auto Distributors for distribution of their newly introduced moped in Karnataka.

Two Wheelers Ltd..

111, Royapettah High Road,
Chennai-600 004

11th October 2011

M/s Bharat Auto Distributors,
76 Kamath road,
Bangalore – 560 007

Dear Sir,

As you are aware, we are the India's largest motor cycle manufacturers and our matchless Wind Speed Scooter is a household name in India.

Our Windspeed Scooter of 200 cc recently introduced will admirably suit our Indian conditions. With its lowest petrol consumption, trouble-free service along with its elegant look, it is going to be the favourite of the moped-riding public.

Since we are not adequately represented in Karnataka which has a very good market potential, we are contemplating the grant of agency to some firms. M/S Bava Mohideen Auto Service of Kerala has kindly suggested your name for our agency.

We trust that the image our two-wheelers carry, which is suitably backed by a powerful advertisement campaign, will make your sales efforts easier.

We are also prepared to maintain, at our cost, a showroom for the display of our products under your supervision and control. We are willing to allow you a commission of 15 per cent on net sales.

It is our earnest belief that this connection would prove mutually beneficial and we will be sending you our contract forms on hearing from you.

Yours faithfully,
V. Jayakumar
Marketing Manager

Sample 5: A tactful letter to an applicant for agency, pointing out that you are already represented adequately in Tamil Nadu and Pondicherry, but state that his application is being filed for reference.

The Premier Electronics Ltd.

118, Miller Road.
Bangalore – 560 052.

24th November 2011

The National Electronics Distributors,
178, Anna Salai,
Chennai – 600 002

Dear Sirs,

We thank you for your letter of 19th November, offering your agency services for

Tamil Nadu and Pondicherry. We regret to state that, since, at present we have already given agency to three firms in these States, we are unable to consider your application favourably.

However, we are keeping your name in our records. With substantial rise in demand, we may resort to re-allocating the areas in the near future and we will correspond with you then in this regard.

We thank you once again for your offer.

Yours faithfully,
E. Nijalingappa
Sales Manager

Sample 6: Draw your agent's attention tactfully to a decline in his sales and insist on his forwarding reports more regularly. Point out that this is also for his own interests.

Chennai Biscuits Ltd.

177, Thiruvotriyur High Road,
Chennai-600, 019

5th January 2011

M/S Siva Agencies,
99, Srinivasapuram,
Rajaraja Sozhan Nagar,
Thanjavur – 613 003

Dear Sirs,

We regret to note from your reports that half-yearly sales show a sharp decline in your territory, and also there is a considerable delay in forwarding of your monthly reports. Our biscuits sell quite well even in your neighbouring districts and the returns of our agents there, are in excess to what they were during this period last year.

We feel that there must be some specific problems you are confronting. We will be glad to help you in all possible ways in overcoming these difficulties and in changing this unsatisfactory state of affairs. We, therefore, ask you to give us a detailed report together with your suggestions for reviving the business.

We would also like to impress upon you the necessity of sending the monthly report more regularly in future, as it would facilitate early action in arresting decline in sales, which is in our mutual interest.

We do hope that with your renewed efforts, the sale of our products will pick up significantly.

Yours faithfully,
For Chennai Biscuits Ltd,
B. Ashok
Marketing Manager

Sample 7: Draft a defensive reply to the above letter.

Siva Agencies

99, Srinivasapuram,
Rajaraja Sozhan Nagar,
Thanjavur – 613 003

9th January 2011

The Chennai Biscuits Ltd,
177, Thiruvotriyur High Road,
Chennai – 600 019

Dear Sir,

We have your letter of 5th January and we share your concern for the sharp fall in sales during the past half-year.

During the period under review, the havoc wrought by the ravaging floods in the area was so heavy that very little purchasing power was left with the people. In this context, alarming rise in the prices of food materials and other basic necessities of life, the amount spent on purchase of biscuits naturally dwindled significantly.

Now with the expectation of bumper harvest this year, our sales are picking up as revealed by our last monthly report and we hope to show better results during the current half-year.

Because of the time-consuming effort of personally visiting the innumerable shops spread in the far-flung hamlets, there was some delay in the despatch of monthly reports. They will be sent regularly hereafter.

We assure you that there will be no let-up in our efforts in pushing the sale of your products and that there would be improved sales performance in the months to come.

Yours faithfully,
P.M. Rathinam
Proprietor

Sample 8: Write a letter from an agent drawing the attention of the principal to the delay in, forwarding the goods, pointing out the damage it causes to your sales.

Arasu Agencies
Distributors of Milton Baby Food

129, Sarang Street,
Cuddalore – 607 003

26th October 2011

The Milton Products Ltd.
4, K. Urs Road,
Mysore – 570 004

Dear Sirs,

We deeply regret to write to you that you take unduly long time in forwarding the goods ordered by us. Such occasions have become frequent in the past three months. We deem it our duty to bring this to your notice.

Late arrival of goods causes out-of-stock situation. This is an invitation for the competitor's goods to occupy the dealers' shelves. Since our Milton Product is a baby food, consumers will go in for other suitable alternatives rather than wait for it.

In view of the fact that delay in order-filling is causing considerable damage to the sales volume of our products, we request you to avoid it in the future.

We trust that you would be prompt in your despatches in the future, which would be in our mutual interest.

Yours faithfully,
V. Arasu
Sole Proprietor

SUMMARY

Hints for drafting application for agency include application to be made on the prospective agent's initiative, ability to market should be stressed, financial soundness needs to be highlighted, references of firms with which he is dealing should be mentioned, method of account settlement to be stated and should end the letter with optimism that business relations will blossom.

Letter offering agency should contain expression of thanks for offer of agency and acceptance, area of agency to be stated, whether the terms offered by the agent is accepted in full or in part, other terms and conditions be stated and end with the optimism that business relations would flourish.

REVIEW QUESTIONS

Part A: Short Questions

1. What is an agency letter?
2. Who is a broker?
3. Who is a factor?
4. Who is a Del credre agent?
5. Who is an underwriter?
6. Who is a commission agent?
7. Who is a auctioneer?

Part B: Paragraph Questions

1. Highlight the points to be included in drafting an application for an agency.
2. What points should a letter offering agency contain?

Part C: Essay Questions

1. Write a letter from an agent drawing the attention of the principal to the delay in forwarding the goods, pointing out the damage it causes to your sales.
2. Draft a defensive reply to the previous question.
3. Draw your agent's attention tactfully on the decline of his sales and insist on his forwarding reports more regularly. Point out that this is also for his own interests.
4. Reply to an application for an agency.
5. A letter by a principal offering agency within the country.
6. The Manager, Chennai Cosmetics Ltd, Chennai offers agency for distribution of their talcum powder 'Flora' to M/s Alfares Trading Company. Draft a letter.
7. Draft a reply for The Premier Electronics Ltd, Banglore granting soke agency to the National Electronics Distributors.

Part D: Objective Type Questions

Choose the correct answer

1. A person employed to do an act for another is

    a. Principal b. Agent c. Consignor

    (Ans: b)

2. A person employed to sell goods by inviting bids at a public sale

    a. Broker b. Auctioneer c. Consigree

    (Ans: b)

3. A person appointed to take up shares not subscribed to by the investing public

    a. Del credre agent b. Factor c. Underwriter

    (Ans: c)

4. A person possessing goods and selling it in his own name without the principle's name is

    a. Factor b. Commission agent c. Warehouse keeper.

    (Ans: b)

Fill in the blanks

1. ______________ letter is written to request the manufactures to sell their goods. (Agency)
2. ______________ is a connecting link between buyer and seller. (Broker)
3. _____________ is employed to buy and sell goods at foreign location. (Commission agent)
4. _____________ is the person clearing goods for the importer. (Clearing agent)

20

CHAPTER

LETTERS RELATING TO IMPORTS AND EXPORTS

INTRODUCTION

Buying and selling goods in international trade involves a lot of formalities. They have to pass through a series of stages viz. making enquiries, obtaining quotations, getting an order, execution of the order, etc. Besides, importers and exporters are subjected to a lot of control with respect to trading in certain items. The foreign trade policies keep changing depending upon the business dynamics. In all these situations and at each stage, correspondence is required. This chapter gives certain specimen letters in different contexts. It is desirable for the students to know certain terms used in foreign trade.

INDENTS

An *indent* is an order for goods placed by an importer to a foreign exporter. It contains details of goods ordered, the price, packing and shipping instructions, date of shipment, insurance, the name of the ship by which goods are to be shipped.

Types of Indents

Indents can be of three types. They are:

Open indent: When the source from which goods to be bought and shipping instructions are not specified, it is called an *open indent*. It means that they are left to the discretion of the agent in the foreign country.

Closed indent: When detailed description of the goods required, brand, price, and full shipping instructions are mentioned in the indent, it is known as a *closed indent*.

Confirmatory indent: When price is to be confirmed after negotiation, the indent specifying the price finally agreed on is called *confirmatory indent*.

INDENT HOUSES

Indent houses are firms which act as intermediaries between local importers and foreign exporters. When the importer does not possess adequate knowledge about the exporter from whom he can get his goods, he approaches an indent house.

These indent houses have wide connections with foreign manufacturers. Their representatives abroad, collect market information and ascertain sources of supply. They even show samples received from abroad to local merchants.

CLEARING AGENTS

A clearing agent is a specialized agent who is entrusted with the work of clearing the imported goods from the port.

They examine the quality and quantity of goods, arrange for their warehousing and finally dispatch them to the importer.

COMMISSION AGENTS

Commission agent engaged in foreign trade acts in his own name. For instance, when a commission agent in India receives orders from an American importer, he will get quotations from different manufacturers. He then chooses the cheapest source and places order. He also sees to it that goods are exported within the specified time.

LETTER OF CREDIT

A commercial Letter of Credit (LC) is a document issued by a banker in the importer's place authorizing his own branch, or an other banker acting as his agent at the exporter's place, to honour or accept bills drawn by a named exporter up to a stated amount who then charges the total payment to the issuing banker.

In other words,

- The importer's banker agrees to honour the bill drawn by the exporter.
- The bill itself may be drawn either in the name of the importer or the banker himself.
- The letter of credit contains details regarding the amount up to which bills will be honoured, terms of credit, documents to accompany the bill, etc.

Types of Commercial Letters of Credit

Documentary letter of credit: When shipping documents such as bill of lading, marine insurance policy, consular invoice, certificate of origin, etc., are to be attached to the bill drawn by the exporter, it is known as a documentary letter of credit.

Clean or open letter of credit: When the banker opens an LC undertaking to accept the bills or honour them without the shipping documents accompanying them, it is known as clean or open letter of credit.

Fixed letter of credit: When a letter of credit is issued for a specified amount up to which bills can be drawn within a stipulated time, it is called a fixed letter of credit. Once bills are drawn and paid up to this amount, the credit is exhausted. Hence, no further credit is allowed.

Revolving letter of credit: Under this type, the maximum amount specified relates not to the amount up to which bills can be drawn, but the amount up to which bills can remain unpaid. Credit becomes available to the extent of the bill paid.

Revocable letter of credit: A letter of credit which can be cancelled any time by the issuing authority without the consent of the beneficiary (the exporter), is known as revocable letter of credit.

Irrevocable letter of credit: A letter of credit which cannot be revoked without the consent of the beneficiary is called irrevocable letter of credit.

Confirmed letter of credit: When the advising banker in the exporter's country adds his own confirmation in addition to the undertaking of the issuing banker, the letter of credit is known as confirmed letter of credit.

This confirmation is given at the request of the issuing banker. It cannot be revoked without the consent of the beneficiary as well as the confirming banker.

Unconfirmed letter of credit: A letter of credit which does not contain the undertaking of the advising banker is called unconfirmed letter of credit.

BILL OF ENTRY

A *bill of entry* is a form which declares that goods of a specified quality and value are entering the country from abroad.

Separate Bills of Entry are used for free goods, dutiable goods and bonded goods.

BILL OF SIGHT

When the importer is not in a position to supply detailed information regarding goods imported, he is required to fill in *bill of sight* instead of the *bill of entry*. He furnishes in the bill of sight whatever information he has and declares that he is unable to state other details about the goods on board the ship. In such a situation, on arrival of the ship, he will be permitted to examine them in the presence of the customs officials and complete the bill of entry.

D/A BILL

This means *Document Against Acceptance Bill*. If the shipping documents are to be handed over to the importer on his accepting the bill drawn by the exporter, it is known as D/A Bill.

D/P BILL

This means *Documents Against Payment Bill*. In this case, all the shipping documents sent by the exporter will be handed over to the importer only on his paying the amount of the bill drawn by the exporter.

MATE'S RECEIPT

Mate's receipt is a document issued by the captain of a ship or his assistant (mate) acknowledging receipt of goods on board the ship.

If the packages are found defective, he will mention this fact in his receipt. Such a receipt is called *dirty mate's receipt* or *foul mate's receipt*.

A mate's receipt without any such adverse remark is called a *clean mate's receipt*.

BILL OF LADING

Bill of lading is a document issued by the shipping company and signed by the captain of the ship. It contains the terms and conditions of the contract for carriage. It also serves as an acknowledgement of receipt of goods on board the ship.

The person named in the bill of lading is entitled to the ownership of the goods. Thus, it serves as a document of title to goods.

The contents in a bill of lading are:

a. The name of the person who is shipping the goods

b. The name of the ship

c. The place of loading

d. Description of goods shipped

e. The name of the consignee to whom goods are to be delivered

f. The port of destination

g. Freight payment details.

CERTIFICATE OF ORIGIN

Certificate of origin is a document frequently used in export trade. It testifies the place where the exported goods have grown or where they have been manufactured.

To take advantage of the lower import duty between countries under trade agreement, this certificate which furnishes proof as to the origin of goods exported, is enclosed.

CONSULAR INVOICE

In a country where import duty is levied *ad valorem* (i.e. on the basis of value of goods), the customs authorities must be satisfied with the accuracy of the invoice amount.

It is the consular invoice which authenticates the correctness of the invoice amount.

A consul is an official stationed in a foreign country to look after the commercial interests of his country.

When the consular invoice is produced, import duty is assessed without opening all the packages.

PRICE QUOTATIONS USED IN FOREIGN TRADE

The common price quotations used in foreign trade are given below:

Loco

Loco price gives the cost of the goods at the place of purchase. This type of quotation is very rare. This is also referred to as ex-warehouse price.

F.A.S

This means *Free Alongside Ship*. This quotation means that the price quoted includes expenses to be incurred till goods are delivered alongside the ship or wharf. The subsequent expenses will be separately charged.

F.O.B

This means *Free on Board*. According to this, the invoice price of goods is inclusive of expenses till the goods are delivered on board the ship. The buyer assumes liability for both insurance and freight.

C.I.F

This is *Cost, Insurance and Freight*. This type of price quotation denotes that the price quoted will cover the cost of the goods and also the expenses of insurance and carriage. Apart from the cost of the goods, the price quotation includes expenses such as carriage to port, dock charges, loading charges, export duty (if any), freight and insurance. Thus the importer has to incur only expenses such as landing charges at his port, customs duties and other delivery expenses.

Franco

This is sometimes referred to as *rendu* or *free*. When goods are quoted on these terms, the price includes all charges including delivery to the buyer's address.

SHIPPING ADVICE

It is a letter from the exporter informing the importer that he has effected shipment of the goods ordered. He furnishes details regarding the ship carrying the goods, probable date of arrival at the port of destination and the mode of payment.

Sample 1: Messrs Bava Mohideen & Co writes a letter of enquiry to MIS AI-Fares Trading Corporation for the purchase of dry fruits. Draft the letter.

M/s Bava Mohideen & Co.

128, Bunder street,
Chennai – 600 001

31st July 2011

M/S AI-Fares Trading Company,
A1-Khobar,
C.R. 1234 P.O. Box 212,
Saudi Arabia.

Dear Sirs,

Messrs Ismail & Co, Mumbai has recommended your firm to us as a large exporter of dry fruits.

There is a good demand here for dates, especially of the seedless variety and also other dry fruits. We would like to place large orders with your company in case your prices are competitive.

Please let us have your terms and quotations at the earliest, as we would like to have the goods with us in the first week of September, well before the festival season.

Yours faithfully,
M. Bava Mohideen
Sole Proprietor

Sample 2: The Eximp Traders, Kolkata has received an enquiry from Messrs Abu Baker & Sons of Singapore for the supply of woollen flooring carpets. Draft quoting rates.

Eximp Traders

35, Chittaranjan Avenue,
Kolkata – 700 005

25th January 2011

Messrs Abu Baker & Sons
Singapore.

Dear Sirs,

We thank you for your enquiry dated 22nd January. We have sent today, in a separate cover, samples of our woollen flooring carpets and we quote our rates for the different qualities:

i) Sun 4x25 @ sh 40 per square metre

ii) Moon 4x25 @ sh 35 per square metre

iii) Beauty 3x20 @ sh 30 per square metre

The price are C.I.F.

Please note that these woollen carpets are specially prepared from hand-spun woollen yarn for trade in your market. The carpets can be made in any design or colour.

It is because of the large size of your order that we have quoted these exceptionally low prices.

We trust you will find our rates favourable and our samples quite satisfactory. In case you decide to purchase, we request you to open an LC in our favour with Indian Bank. We look forward to a lasting business relation with you.

Yours faithfully,
Per pro Eximp Traders,
R.L. Gupta

IMPORT/EXPORT CORRESPONDENCE

Sample 3: Direct Enquiry with the manufacturer

Mangalore Electronics Ltd.

Regd. Office: Dhan Building, Annasalai

Chennai – 600 002

1st March 2011

Messrs. Samsang Electronics Ltd.
156, Parker Avenue,
Tokyo,
Japan.

Dear Sirs,

We have been manufacturing plastic products of a very wide variety for the last twenty years. The use of electronic products in our country has been increasing rapidly in the past few years. So we plan to increase our production capacity by installing four new models of washing machine.

Your name was suggested to us by the Trade Commissioner of your country during his recent visit to Chennai. We have already obtained import licence as actual users. Will you please send us an illustrative catalogue of your latest machines for use in the production? We expect a very reasonable quotation from you.

An early reply will be greatly appreciated.

Your faithfully,
For Mangalore Electronic Pvt.Ltd,
K. Artha Naarishwaran

Sample 4: Reply to sample 3.

Samsang Electronics

Administrative Office

156, New Bazaar,
Tokyo,
Japan.

25th March 2011

The Director (Purchases),
Mangalore Electronics,
Dhan Building, Anna Salai,
Chennai – 600 002
India.

Dear Sir,

We are thankful for your enquiry regarding the Samsang washing machines. We have pleasure in enclosing an illustrated catalogue of our products. The machines of your requirement are illustrated on pages 10 to 25, which are the latest addition to our products.

Our research department consisting of the most competent technical staff who have invented these machines of superior design, simple handling and maximum capacity of turn-out. These machines are highly suitable for the manufacturing activity you are engaged in particular. We recommend to you our Sansui Machine with designing part adjustable for different designs. For each machine, we give you five different design patterns which you can fix according to your requirements. Besides that, the in-built patterns provide you block, cubes, plates, wires, balls and other usual items for manufacturing different products separately.

We give you two-year guarantee on all these machines. The enclosed Proforma Invoice shows the trade discount, packing description and other details. The rate mentioned is firm for 30 days only. While placing your order you are requested to deposit with us 25% or above of the invoice value. The balance of the invoice will have to be paid to the banker of your firm through whom you will be receiving the D/P bill and other documents.

We shall be pleased to book your order for delivery within 15 days from the receipt of the order.

Yours faithfully,
Sui Lee

Enclosed: 1. Proforma Invoice
2. Catalogue

Sample 5: National Wool Traders, Mumbai place an order with Messrs Thomson & Co, Melbourne, Australia for 5000 kg of knitting wool. Draft the letter enclosing an indent, giving instructions for shipment, settlement of account, etc.

National Wool Traders
Importers & Exporters

784, Babar Street,
Mumbai – 400 011

8th December 2011

Messrs Thomson & Co,
Melbourne,
Australia.

Dear Sirs,

We thank you for your letter of 1st December, and we have sent the samples separately. We now enclose our Indent No. 326 for 5000 kg of knitting wool. We will be glad if you ship the goods as early as possible but not later than 15th January 2012.

We are enclosing the letter of credit issued by the Central Bank of India, D.N. Road, Mumbai.

Please draw on us a D/P bill through our bankers, the Central Bank of India, Mumbai.

If goods prove suitable, we trust to do contriving business with you.

Yours faithfully,
K.S. Patel
Partner

Sample 6: Messrs Thomson & Co, Australia, advises National Wool Traders, Mumbai that they have shipped 5000 kg of knitting wool ordered by them. Draft the advice of shipment.

Thomson & Co.

Melbourne,
Australia.

12th January 2011

National Wool Traders,
784, Babar Street,
Mumbai – 400 011.

Dear Sir,

We thank you for your letter of 8th December, together with your indent No. 326. We are glad to say that we have been able to effect shipment of 5000 kg of knitting wool by s.s. *Nav Bharat* which sailed on 11th January, and we enclose a copy of our invoice.

The shipping documents, i.e., the invoice, D/P bill, bill of lading and insurance policy have been sent through the Chartered Bank of India, Australia and Hongkong to your banker to be handed over to you on payment of our draft. We trust the shipment will reach you in perfect condition. We look forward to receiving further orders from you.

Yours faithfully,
per pro Thomson & Co
Thomas Brown

Sample 7: The Tamil Nadu Hosieries, Tirupur writes to their Clearing Agents in Chennai to clear the consignment of Egyptian cotton from s.s. *Chidambaram* and to send it to them by passenger train. Draft the letter.

The Tamil Nadu Hosieries

25, Kumaran Street,
Tirupur – 640 602

3rd March 2011

M/S Dhanaraj & Co,
77 N.T. Gramani St.,
Tondiarpet,
Chennai – 600 014

Dear Sirs,

We have received a consignment of Egyptian cotton by s.s. *Chidambaram* scheduled to berth in Chennai harbour on 10th March. We enclose the related bill of lading and marine insurance policy.

We request you to clear the goods from the port and despatch them to us by passenger train as early as possible. We will remit your charges on receipt of your bill.

Yours faithfully,
for The Tamil Nadu Hosieries,
R. Shanmugan
Partner

Sample 8: The importer orders through the agent.

Kingston Cotton Mills Ltd.

15 Banerjee road,
Muharji Nagar,
Kolkata – 700 001.

1st April 2011

M/s Manik Chand & Sons,
Commission Market,
Ahmedabad – 380 025
Gujarat.

Dear Sirs,

Many thanks for sending us samples of Egyptian cotton of assorted quality. We are pleased to place our Indent No. 453 with you for supply of order entirely at our risk and account, the following goods:

S.No	Description	Qty.	Terms
1.	Pattern No. EC/ Ahuluva/50.12	25 Bales	Price C.I.F. Mumbai
2.	Pattern No. EC/ Ahuluva/13	15 Bales	Special Packing at extra charges.

Others terms of business: as printed on the back-side of the Indent. Kindly acknowledge receipt.

Yours faithfully,
for Kingston cotton Mills Ltd.,
Shiraji
Purchase Manager

Sample 9: The exporter informs about shipment of goods to the importer.

Sheikh & Co.

Head Office: Ahuluva Building,
Cairo.

20th April 2011

The Purchase Manager,
Kingston Cotton Mills Ltd.,
15, Banerjee road,
Muharji Nagar,
Kolkata – 700 001

Dear Sir,

Ref: Your Indent No. 53 through Manik Chand & Sons.

Forty bales of cotton as mentioned in your indent were shipped yesterday, the 19th April by s.s. *Saudi Arabia*.

As desired by you, the bales have been specially packed to resist the hazards of a long voyage with no additional charges. Further, the bales are insured 'Warehouse-to-Warehouse', so the risk is covered all through the transit up to your factory. We hope that the goods will meet with your approval.

The D/P bill, original invoice, consular invoice and insurance policy have been sent through Bank of India. You are requested to honour the bills when presented and take delivery of the documents.

We appreciate your interest in our products and assure you of our best service.

Yours faithfully,
for Sheikh & Co.,
Theikh Jarookh
Proprietor

Encls: Four documents as mentioned above.

Sample 10: The banker informs the buyer (Import correspondence).

State Bank of India

Head Office: Mumbai, India

116, N.S. Bose Road,
Kolkata – 700 001

1st May 2011

The Secretary,
Kingston Cotton Mills Ltd.,
15, Banerjee road,
Muharji Nagar,
Kolkata – 700 001

Dear Sir,

We hold a D/P bill in your name received from Messrs. Syed & Co, Cairo. This is in respect of 20 bales of Egyptian cotton that you have bought from them. The bill is for ₹ 1 crore and the bank's commission thereon is ₹ 3 lakhs.

Kindly arrange to pay the above amount and take delivery of the documents within 20 days. You can avail yourself of our special service of foreign trade customers in the matter of clearing of goods.

Please let us know, by return of post, whether you wish us to arrange for the clearing of the bales from Mumbai harbour and storing them in a duty-paid warehouse. If you wish so, please remit, or allow us to debit your account with ₹ 99,750 towards duty and clearing charges.

Yours faithfully,
for State Bank of India,
Madavan Nair
Manager

Sample 11: The importer requests the banker to open an irrevocable letter of credit in favour of the exporter.

Kingston Cotton Mills Ltd.

15, Banerjee road,
Muharji Nagar,
Kolkata - 700 001

27th March 2011

The Manager,
State Bank of India,
116, Titan square,
Kolkata - 700 001

Dear Sir,

We request you to kindly open by cable an Irrevocable Documentary Credit in favour of Messrs. Sheikh & Co., Cairo for the amount of ₹ 1 Crore (Rupees one crore only) available to them by draft at 45 days by your agent in Cairo.

This credit is in respect to a shipment of Egyptian cotton bales as mentioned in the enclosed sheet..

The draft to the beneficiaries should accompany the following documents:

- Bills of Lading (2)
- Commercial Invoice (3) to verify shipment of cotton bales as specified in the enclosed sheet
- Insurance Policy (1)
- Consular Invoice (1)
- Certificate of Origin (1)

The credit is to be established in local currency with your Cairo correspondents to be availed of by the beneficiary. The credit is to be confirmed to:

Messrs Sheikh & Co.,

Head Office: Ahuvalia Building, Cairo, and shall cease to be valid after 31st July 2011.

Part shipment not allowed.

Invoice to be made C.I.F. Kalkata and to include the bank commission also. Special instructions: Documents to be forwarded to us by air mail.

Yours faithfully,
for Cotton Mills Ltd.,
Kingston

Sample 12: The importer informs the exporter of the arrangements being made to open an irrevocable letter of credit in his (exporter's) favour.

Kingston Cotton Mills Ltd.

15, Banerjee road,
Muharji Nagar,
Kolkota – 700 001.

27th March 2011

Messrs Sheikh & Co
Head Office: Ahuluvlia Building,
Cario.

Dear Sirs,

Many thanks for your letter accepting our order dated 1st March, 2011. We are pleased to inform you that we have instructed State Bank of India to open an irrevocable letter of credit for ₹ 1 crore in your favour, available in your local currency and valid up to 31st July 2011.

This credit will be confirmed by the Cairo branch of the State Bank of India. They will accept your draft on them for 30 days.

Please attach the following documents to your draft and surrender them against acceptance:

- Bills of Lading (2)
- Commercial Invoice (3)
- Insurance Policy for Rs.30,000
- Consular Invoice (1)
- Certificate of Origin (1)

The invoice should be made to include C.I.F Kolkata and the bank commission.

Please advise us by air mail immediately on the dispatch of goods.

Yours faithfully,
for Kingston Cotton Mills Ltd.,
Maxmuller

Sample 13: The foreign correspondent of the importer's banker (who himself is a banker) informs the exporter that the credit is available and the exporter can draw on him.

This is the procedure to the credit. Such information is also generally in the form of a printed proforma, which is completed with necessary details and sent to the exporter. However, if a letter is to replace such a printed proforma, it will be in the following style:

Bank of India.

Head Office: Mumbai (India).

24/12, Central Avenue,
Cairo.

4th June 2011

Messrs. Sheikh & Co.,
Ahuluva Building,
Cairo.

Dear Sirs,

The Kolkata Branch of the State Bank of India has instructed us to open an Irrevocable Credit for 65,000 dinars in your favour, valid till 31st July 2011

We are pleased to inform you that you are authorized to draw on us for 30 days against this credit. Please send your draft to us for acceptance immediately after the despatch of goods to Kingston Cotton Mills Ltd., Kolkata, as specified in the enclosed list.

You are requested to enclose the following documents with your draft for its acceptance:

- Bills of Lading (2)
- Commercial Invoice (3)
- Insurance Policy for ₹ 30,000
- Consular Invoice (1)
- Certificate of Origin (1)

Please note that your draft is to include all charges to Mumbai and our commission at 5%.

Yours faithfully,
R.K. Govind
Manager

IMPORTING THROUGH INDENT HOUSES

The intending buyer buys goods through indent houses. An illustrative series of such correspondence is as follows:

Sample 14: Letter from the importer to the indent house.

Vijay Nicole (P) Ltd.,
Booksellers & Publishers

22, Borivali,
West Mumbai – 400 092

Ref: GR/NR/Imp

6th January 2011

To
The Marketing Officer,
M/s Max Muller Ltd.,
New Kamani Chambers,
32, Nicol Road,
Mumbai – 400 001

Dear Sir,

Sub: Indent for 'Gateway Natural Tracing Paper' for total value: C.I.F equivalent to ₹ 40,000.

We request you to kindly forward a copy of our order to your principal

M/s. Wiggins Teape Overseas Sales Ltd., Belgrave House, Basing Views, Basingstock (U.K.) for the supply of Gateway Tracing Paper extra smooth finish in size 40"x20 Yards. Quantity: Approx. 926 rolls.

1. 50% - 60/65 gsm, and
2. 50% - 85/90 gsm.

Against our import Licences Nos. P/L2711016/C/XX/53/B/37-38 of 2.10.98 & P/L2718283/C/XX/55/B/39.49 of 30.12.99.

We shall open an irrevocable letter of credit with our bankers, Bank of India, Kalbadevi Branch, Mumbai – 400 002, for ₹ 40,000 in favour of your Principal through the London Office of Bank of India.

Thanking you and awaiting your reply.

Yours faithfully,
for Vijay Nicole (P) Ltd.,
Madavan
Sales Manager

Encl: Indent

Sample 15: Letter from the indent house enclosing the indent.

Max Muller Limited

A member of the Teape group

New Kamani Chamers,
32, Nicol Road,
Mumbai – 400 001
Phone: 2754776
Email: Tribeni@eth.net

Ref: VV/OM/GWT

8th January 2011

Dear Sirs,

We thank you for your order worth ₹ 40,000 and are pleased to enclose our formal indent B-4697 for your signature. Kindly return one copy of the indent duly signed for our records.

Please arrange to open a letter of credit for this order as per particulars furnished in the attached sheet as early as possible.

On receipt of your credit details, we shall arrange to forward your order to our associates to process the same at the mill for an early shipment.

Yours faithfully,
for Max Muller Ltd,
Vembar
Marketing Officer

Encl: As stated above.

16. Letter of the indent house intimating acceptance of the indent.

Max Muller Ltd.

New Kamani Chambers,
32, Nicol Road,
Mumbai – 400 001
Phone: 275477
Email: Tribeni@eth.net

6th February 2011

VV/OM/GWT
M/s. Vijay Nicole (P) Ltd.,
22, Borivili West,
West Mumbai – 400 092

Indent No. B-4697
L/C No. K.40/47

In connection with the above we are enclosing herewith our Associate's acceptance letter Ref: VSR/s.c. dated 29th January 2011 in original for your information.

Our Associates have received your letter of credit and released the order to the mill, and they anticipate having the paper ready for shipment by the end of March 2011. We trust you will find this in order.

We now request you to amend your letter of credit to read as all bank charges are for openers account. Please arrange to make the above amendment as early as possible.

We now look forward to receiving your amendment advice for the above.

Yours faithfully,
for Max Muller Ltd.
Vembar
Marketing Officer

Sample 17: Letter from the exporters confirming the order received and acknowledging LC arrangement.

Taylor Overseas Sales Ltd.
Lincoln's, in Fields, London.
(Successors to the business of Charles Morgan & Co.Ltd.)

Distributors for: Rickson & Co. Ltd.,

Teape (Stationery) Ltd.,
P.O. Box 88, Belgrave House,
Basing View, Basingstoke,
Aamshire RG21 2EE.
Telephone: (0256) 20262
Telegrams & Cables: Wigteape Basinstoke
Telex 858628/9

Ref: VSR/SC

27th February 2011

Vijay Nicole (P) Ltd.,
22, Borivili West,
Mumbai – 400 092
India.

Dear Sirs,

Indent Number B-4697 – Our OV/65877/F/IN

We acknowledge with thanks the receipt of your Letter of Credit No. K40/47 for a sum of £ 1,295.18 through the Bank of India.

We have accordingly instructed our mill to proceed with this order, and they anticipate having it ready for dispatch by the end of March 2011.

Please note that all bank charges covering the above letter of credit are for the account of openers. Enclosed is our official order confirmation, which we trust is to your satisfaction.

Yours faithfully,
for Taylor Overseas Sales Ltd.,
Simson
Zone F

Encl: Official Order Confirmation.

Sample 18: Letter intimating shipment and negotiation of documents

Max Muller Ltd.

New kamani chambers,
32, Nicol road,
Mumbai – 400 001
Phone: 275477
Email: Tribeni@eth.net

Ref: UV/OM/GNT

15th March 2011

Vijay Nicole (P) Ltd.,
22, Borivili West,
Mumbai – 400 092

Dear Sirs,

Indent No: B-4697 L/C. No. K40/47

We have pleasure in enclosing herewith shipping documents covering the above indent expected to arrive by 1.4.2011, for your information.

1. Copy of Non-negotiable bill of Lading No. 18
2. Copy of Invoice No. WF/UK/1328 dated 26.2.2011
3. Copy of Insurance Certificate
4. Copy of the Packing List

Please note that the original and duplicate invoices and duplicate insurance certificates and two copies of Bills of Lading have been forwarded to Bank of India, Mumbai – 2, along with a sight draft for £ 1,294.18 drawn against your letter of credit.

We trust you will receive the consignment shortly.

Yours faithfully,
for Max Muller Ltd.,
Vembar
Marketing Officer

Sample 19: Letter of the importer requesting the banker to retire the Bill of Exchange

Vijay Nicole (P) Ltd.

22, Borivali West,
Mumbai – 400 092

1st April 2011

The Manager,
Bank of India,
Foreign Exchange Department.,
Kalbadevi Branch,
Mumbai – 400 002

Dear Sirs,

Ref: LC No. K/40/47 for £ 1,294.18

Favouring: M/s. Wiggins Teape Overseas Sales Ltd., London.

We request you to retire the sight Bill of Exchange for £ 1,294.18 + £ 6.01 = £ 1,300.19 of the above beneficiary and release the documents under intimation to us.

Enclosed herewith Foreign Remittance application form A duly filled in and signed. The exchange copies of relevant 'Import Licences' are already with you.

Yours faithfully,
For Vijay Nicole (P) Ltd.,
G.R. Sharma
Marketing Manager

Encl: As above.

SUMMARY

The types of indents are open indent, closed indent, and confirmatory indent.

Terms used in foreign trade are indent houses, clearing agents, commission agent, Letter of Credit (LC), bill of entry, bill of sight, D/A bill, D/P bill, mate's receipt, bill of lading, certificate of origin, consular invoice and shipping advice.

Types of commercial letters of credit includes documentary LC, clear or open LC, fixed LC, revolving LC, revocable LC, irrevocable LC, confirmed LC and unconfirmed LC.

Price quotations used in foreign trade are Loco, F.A.S., F.O.B., C.I.F and Franco

REVIEW QUESTIONS

Part A: Short Questions

1. What is an indent?
2. What is an open indent?
3. What is a closed indent?
4. Who is a clearing agent?
5. Who is a commission agent?
6. What is a letter of credit?
7. What is an indent house?
8. What is a bill of entry?
9. What is a bill of sight?
10. What is a D/P bill?
11. What is a D/A bill?
12. What is a mate's receipt?
13. What is a certificate of origin?
14. What is a consular invoice?
15. What is a bill of lading?
16. What is shipping advice?
17. What is price quotation?
18. What is F.A.S?
19. What is C.I.F?
20. What is Franco price?

Part B: Essay Questions

1. Messrs. Harrison & Co of London have effected sale of tea received from the South India Tea Trading Co. Ltd, Nilgiris and despatched the proceeds. Draft a letter of advice of sale.
2. The South India Tea Trading Co. Ltd. Nilgiris, informs Messrs. Harrison & Co, Mayo Street, London, E.C. 7, of the shipment of a consignment of 50 chests of Queen Tea by I.N.S. *Jalpadma* due at London on 15th November. They enclose the bill of lading and request their Commission Agent to effect a profitable sale.
3. The Tamil Nadu Hosieries, Tirupur writes to their Clearing Agents in Chennai to clear the consignment of Egyptian cotton from s.s. *Chidambaram* and to send them by passenger train. Draft the letter.
4. The Central Bank of India, Mumbai writes to the National Wool Traders about the receipt of shipping documents from Thomson & Co of Australia. Draft the letter requesting them to clear the documents.

5. Messrs Bava Mohideen & Co write a letter of enquiry to MIS AI-Fares Trading Corporation for the purchase of dry fruits. Draft the letter.
6. The Eximp Traders, Kolkata has received an enquiry from Messrs Abu Baker & Sons of Singapore for the supply of woollen flooring carpets. Draft a letter quoting rates.
7. The National Wool Traders, Mumbai place an order with Messrs Thomson & Co, Melbourne Australia, for 5000 kg of knitting wool. Draft the letter enclosing an indent giving instructions for shipment, settlement of account etc.
8. Messrs Thomson & Co, Australia, advise the National Wool Traders, Mumbai that they have shipped 5000 kg of knitting wool ordered by them. Draft the advice of shipment.

Part C: Objective Type Questions

Choose the correct answer

1. Order placed by an importer is

   a. Indent b. L.C. c. Franco

   (Ans: a)

2. Detailed description of goods is found in

   a. L.C. b. Open indent c. Closed indent

   (Ans: c)

3. Clearing of goods is done by an agency

   a. Commission agent b. Importer c. Clearing agent

   (Ans: c)

4. Intermediary acting for a foreign principal

   a. Factor b. Commission agent c. Broker

   (Ans: b)

5. L.C. is issued by banker in

   a. Importer's place b. Exporter's place

   c. Place where neither exporter nor importer are present

   (Ans: a).

6. Which document specifies goods of specified quality entering a particular country?

   a. Consular invoice b. Mate's receipt c. Bill of entry

   (Ans: c)

7. Documentary evidence of goods of a specific description produced in particular country.

   a. Certificate of origin b. Bill of entry c. Bill of lading

   (Ans: a)

8. Document stating goods have been shipped as per order is

   a. Bill of lading b. L.C. c. Shipping advice

   (Ans: c)

9. Official stationed in a foreign country to take care of commercial interest of his country is

   a. Customer officer b. Mate c. Consul

   (Ans: c)

10. Price of goods includes expenses till the goods are loaded aboard a ship

    a. F.O.B b. F.A.S c. C.I.F

    (Ans: a)

11. Cost of the goods at the place of purchase is

    a. Franco b. Loco c. C.I.F

    (Ans: b)

12. All charges up to the point of delivery to the buyer are included in

    a. Franco b. Loco c. C.I.F

    (Ans: a)

Fill in the blanks

1. Order for goods placed by an importer is ________. (Indent)
2. Indent specifying negotiated price is ________. (Confirmed indent)
3. Work of clearing the goods is undertaken by an agent called ________. (Clearing agent)
4. Agent employed in foreign location to buy/sell goods for a principal is ________. (Commission agent)
5. ____________ document evidences the nationality of goods. (Certificate of origin)
6. Shipping document is handed over to the importer on his paying the amount of the bill under. This is known as ________. (Document against payment)
7. Document issued by the mate acknowledging the receipt of goods on board is ________. (Mate's receipt)
8. Through ________, an exporter informs the importer that he has shipped the goods as per the terms agreed. (Shipping advice)
9. ____________ is stationed in foreign country to take care of the commercial interest of his country. (Consul)
10. Expenses up to the ship are borne by exporter price quotation under ________. (F.A.S)

PART 4

REPORTS AND PROPOSALS

21
CHAPTER

REPORTS – STRUCTURE AND LAYOUT

INTRODUCTION

The various parts that constitute a report have been standardized over a period of time by virtue of custom and convenience. However, the structure of a report varies according to purpose, scope and contents of a report. Various elements form the front matter, main body and back matter of a report. The order in which these elements are organized is given in Figure 21.1

Structure of Report

A. Front Matter

- Cover
- Front Piece
- Title Page
- Copy Right Notice
- Forwarding Letter
- Preface
- Acknowledgement
- Table of Contents
- List of Illustrations
- Abstract and Summary

B. Main Body

- Introduction
- Discussion
- Conclusion
- Recommendation

C. Back Matter

- Appendices
- List of References
- Bibliography
- Glossary
- Index

Fig. 21.1 Structure of a Report

Front Matter

1.Cover 2. Front piece 3. Title page 4. Copyright notice 5. Forwarding letter 6. Preface 7. Acknowledgement 8. Table of contents 9. List of illustrations 10. Abstract and summary

Main Body

11. Introduction 12. Discussion 13. Conclusion 14. Recommendation

Back Matter

15. Appendices 16. List of references 17. Bibliography 18. Glossary 19. Index

All these elements should be present in long reports. Inclusion of any element depends on its usefulness. Inclusion of unnecessary elements are likely to impede the flow of communication. Out of the 19 elements, title page, introduction and discussion are mandatory.

FRONT MATTER

The front matter of a report includes the following parts:

Cover

Cover protects the manuscript from damage and it imparts a neat appearance. Some organizations use pre-printed coverpage wherein name and address of the organization is found. The cover page should include the title of the report, number if any, the date and the classification (secret or confidential). The name of the author preparing the report is also given in some cover pages.

Front Piece

It generally appears in bound reports meant for wide circulation. It serves as a window that kindles the readers' curiosity.

Title Page

Title page is the first right-hand side page of the report.

Report Number 326

GRACE STEEL CORPORATION

Varun Nagar
Chandpura – 326917

A Report

on

Installing a New Production Plant

Prepared For
The Managing Director

By
K. Paari
Assistant Engineer (Production)

Approved by
Sri Maran
Production Manager

17 January 2001

Fig. 21.2 Example of Title Page

Where there is no prescribed form, the sample as shown in Figure 21.3 will be appropriate.

Project Number	E42	Report Number	R319

A Report

On

Combating the Noise Pollution in

Engine Model No. Lexa981

Prepared For

The Direction of Research Okay Engineering Works
Dadabhai Road
Mumbai

By

T. Punitham
Senior Technical Assistant

15 January 2001

Fig. 21.3 Another Example of Title Page

In figure 21.3, the whole page has been divided into four sections. Project number is written on right-hand side, the nature of report i.e whether it is confidential or ordinary is given in the left-hand side. The second section gives the title of the report. The third section indicates the authority for whom the report is prepared. The last section groups two items, namely, the author (name and designation) and the date of submission. One inch margin is allowed on all four sides and an extra half-an-inch on the left side for binding.

Copyright Notice

If the report is published, copyright is given inside the title page. The following note is added:

All rights reserved. No part of this report may be reproduced in any form or by any means without permission in writing from the publisher.

Forwarding Letter

This is of two types, namely covering and introductory. The covering letter does not form part of the report. It is written for transmission of the report.

However, the introductory letter performs the function similar to a preface written for a book. It is written to establish a rapport with the reader and to bring him into a receptive mood. One should mention the authorization under which one did the work and acknowledge the assistance received in various forms from the persons and organizations in carrying out the work. The transmittal letter is usually placed after the title page and bound with the report.

19 September 2010

Dear Secretary of State,

I have the honour to present the Report of the Committee set up by your predecessor, Mrs. Vasanta, in 2010 to inquire into teaching, reading and writing of English. As the Committee's Chairman, I would like to place on record, the great help I have received from Mr. Ravi, who has acted as Vice-Chairman throughout the inquiry. The Committee's debt to its Secretary, Mr. R. Radha, HMI, is acknowledged in the introductory chapter. I would also like to express my personal appreciation for the assistance given by him to the Chairman and the close cooperation with which we have worked.

Yours sincerely,

Radha

(Chairman)

The Rt. Hon. Reg. E. Prentice J.P., M.P.

Fig. 21.4 Example of Forwarding Letter

Preface

Preface introduces the report and not the subject matter. The content of the preface has been explained in the previous point and also in figure 21.4. The preface is different from foreword. The former is written by the author and the latter is written by an authority or expert in the field commending the work done.

Acknowledgement

This section recognizes and records the assistance of various inputs received from different persons in preparation of the report. If permission has been obtained for reproduction of copyright material, it should be mentioned in this section. If published material is included, it has to be indicated mentioning the source. A separate sheet may be added if the list of sources is long.

Table of Contents

If the report is lengthy, i.e., more than 10 pages, table of contents is essential. Reader gets an overall view of the report by reading this segment. It also helps the reader to go to a particular section or topic in the report. Sub-headings are also given with the respective page number.

TABLE OF CONTENTS

Fig. 21.5 Structure of Table of Contents

List of Illustrations

A separate list of illustrations is given after the table of content for tables and figures. The number, title and page reference of each illustration is given. When there are more illustrations, it is better to divide it into two parts. List of tables and list of figures are mentioned as separate headings.

Abstract and Summary

Synopsis or gist of the report is called an *abstract* or *summary*. The summary presents the report in a nutshell without any illustration or explanation. Abstract is shorter than summary. It is better to accommodate just 5 per cent of the original content in an abstract. The purpose of this is to help the busy reader gather important highlights without going through the whole report.

MAIN BODY

The main body contains the subject of the report and is divided into the following parts:

Introduction

It provides a starting point to the reader who is not familiar with the subject of a report. This section familiarizes the reader with the content of the report. The following items are included in this section:

a. Historical and technical background

b. Scope of study specifying its limitations and qualifications

c. Methods of data collection and sources of data

d. Authorization for the report and terms of reference

e. Organization of the material

f. Definition of technical terms, symbols and operation

In short, introduction gives a picture of what the author intends to discuss in a right manner.

Discussion

It deals with the main business of the report. It accommodates most of the report and contains all the illustrations. This part presents the information in an organized form, discusses its significance and analysis, and the results that flow from them. Inference is given at the end of each analysis. If the data is vast and likely to impede the explanation or flow of discussion, it is better to include it in the appendix. There is no hard and fast rule for writing discussion. Many report writers, however, follow backward order. This means that they first state the results and then describe how they were arrived at. As the reader is more interested in knowing what happened finally than knowing how they had happened, the report writers prefer this approach.

Conclusion

This part brings the discussion or description to an end and signals to the reader that they have reached the end. The term conclusion refers to logical inference drawn and the judgement formed on the basis of analysis of data presented in the report or to the findings of the investigation made.

All conclusions should be supported by what is present in the discussion so that nothing new needs to be incorporated at this phase. In some reports, mini conclusion is drawn at the end of the discussion of each topic and arranged in the descending order of their importance.

Recommendations

In some reports, recommendations and conclusions are clubbed together. This is done in short reports. The function of recommendation is to suggest the future course of action. Busy executives, sometimes, read only this part of the report and take decisions. Suggestions should be made only after examining all parts in the report. The terms of reference would usually indicate whether the investigator has the authority to tender recommendations. If the terms of reference given requires the investigator to investigate, then it is not wise to give recommendations. Giving recommendation in such cases would hurt the readers who may mistake that the investigator has assumed the authority which rightly belong to them. Therefore, the investigator has to act according to the terms of reference. If recommendations are invited, in terms of reference, then the investigator arranges them in descending order of their importance under different headings and sub-headings.

BACK MATTER

The back matter contains materials to support the subject matter presented in the main body. It includes:

Appendices

It represents the materials used to support the main body of the report. This section helps the reader who wants to examine the supporting material in detail. The following points determine which materials should be sent to the appendix:

- Whether the material sustains the theme and forms an integral part of the subject.
- Whether inclusion of the material in the main body disturbs the flow of readers' thought. Normally, questionnaires, statistical data, specimen forms, data sheet, detailed calculations, illustrations, workings, derivation of questions, tables of definition, circulars, correspondence, symbols, summaries of results achieved by other organizations, perspectives of others concerned with the report, etc., would be included here for record.

List of References

It is not only customary but also decency to acknowledge the work (published or unpublished) used or quoted in the report. Such references are alphabetically listed at the end of the report. If the number is small, they can be cited at the foot of each page. The attention of the reader is drawn by printing a printer's mark like a star or an asterisk. The report has to observe meticulously the method of citing and quoting the work.

Bibliography

It is a serially numbered list of published and unpublished works consulted before or during the preparation of a work. It is different from the list of reference in the following aspects:

Table 21.1 Comparison of Bibliography and Reference

	Bibliography	Reference
1.	It lists the work which the authors have read and to which they feel indebted for ideas or information.	It points to specific location of an idea or a piece of information in the original source.
2.	It recommends certain works for further study.	It does not do so.
3.	It may be annotated. It indicates the content and usefulness of the work cited.	It indicates only the sources.

4.	Bibliography has to be selected depending on their relevance to the theme.	It is general. It need not be selected or be relevant to the theme.
5.	It is always in alphabetical order	It may be recorded in the sequence in which they have been cited in the report.

The following points deserve mention in connection with bibliography:

- Order of writing the names and surnames of authors
- The sequence of details
- Punctuation mark
- The layout

Glossary

The list of technical words or jargon is accommodated in this part. However, the inclusion of glossary depends on the types of readers. When the reader is an expert in a given field, there is no need for glossary. If the report is meant for diverse category of audience, it is better to provide a glossary.

Index

It serves as a quick guide to the material in the report. It enables the reader to easily locate the topic, sub-topic or other important aspects of the contents. There is a need for index in the case of bulk reports where the table of contents does not suffice. The entries in the index are made in an alphabetical order and cross-referenced.

SUMMARY

The layout of the report includes cover, front matter, main body and back matter.

The front matter contains front piece, title page, copyright notice, forwarding letter, preface, acknowledgement, table of contents, List of illustration, abstract and summary.

The main body has introduction, discussion, conclusion, recommendation.

The back matter has appendices, list of references, bibliography, glossary and index.

REVIEW QUESTIONS

Part A: Short Questions

1. What is a preface?
2. What is an acknowledgement?
3. What is an index?
4. What is a bibliography?
5. What is a reference?
6. What is an appendix?

7. What is an introduction?
8. What is a table of contents?
9. What is a copyright notice?
10. What is a glossary?

Part B: Paragraph Questions

1. Illustrate a table of contents.
2. Distinguish bibliography and reference.
3. State the contents of introduction.
4. What points are to be remembered while preparing bibliography?
5. Write a note on recommendation in a report.

Part C: Essay Questions

1. Discuss the layout of the report.

Part D: Objective Type Questions

Choose the correct answer

1. The following section introduces the report

   a. Preface   b. Appendix   c. Acknowledgement

   (Ans: a)

2. Which of the following helps the reader to locate a particular topic

   a. Foot note   b. Table of contents   c. Acknowledgement

   (Ans: b)

3. Illustrations are provided after

   a. Acknowledgement   b. Table of contents   c. Bibliography

   (Ans: b)

4. Which provides the whole information in the report

   a. Abstract   b. Table of content   c. Main body of the report

   (Ans: c)

5. Several sections grouped under heads and subheads comes under

   a. Discussions   b. Recommendations   c. Conclusion

   (Ans: a)

Fill in the blanks

1. The window display for a report is __________. (Front piece)
2. Warning about duplicating the copy is given under _________. (Copyright notice)

3. Types of forwarding letter include ________ and ________. (Covering and introductory)
4. Credit attribution for various people who helped in report preparation is given in __________. (Acknowledgement)
5. Overall view of the report is given in __________. (Table of contents)
6. Judgement formed on the basis of analysis of data is written in ________. (Conclusion)
7. The various materials that have helped in the report making are included in ________. (Appendices)
8. The list of works cited in an alphabetical order is accommodated in ________. (Reference)

22 CHAPTER BUSINESS REPORT WRITING

INTRODUCTION

Reports are drafted not only in business but in all fields. A great deal of business decisions are made in terms of information presented or recommendations made by experts. Reports help in the following ways:

- Facilitates an executive to perform the functions of planning and controlling various types of resources.
- Informs about the department, company or individual's progress.
- Reveals the performance gap by comparing the actual with the standards established.
- Helps in decision-making on a proposed new venture.

A business report is an orderly presentation of factual information—data, records or events about a specific business incident, activity or programme. A business report, therefore, contains not only facts collected but also conclusions and recommendations based on the analysis of such facts.

TYPES OF REPORTS

Business reports can be classified into different types. The classification is as follows:

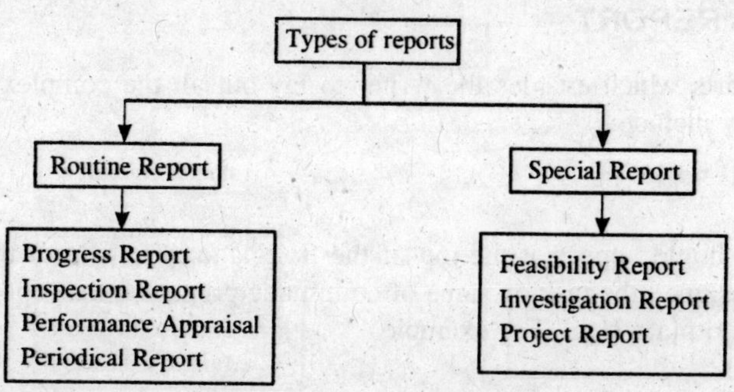

Fig. 22.1 Types of Reports

Routine Reports

These reports are used in day-to-day routine by an organization. They are classified as:

Progress report: This report enlightens the progress made in a given project or in a task under progress. For example, construction projects, manufacture of a new product.

Inspection report: This report is prepared after investigating and inspecting the work performed. It is necessary to figure out irregularities or deviations from the targeted performance. Internal audit report, report by site engineer in a civil project, inspection of buildings under construction are some examples of inspection report.

Performance appraisal report: This report is prepared after reviewing the performance of employees. The appraiser has to give his assessment of each individual worker's performance periodically. This helps the top management to decide on pay hike, increment, promotion, etc.

Periodical report: This report is prepared at regular intervals on the functioning of a particular portfolio such as incremental deposits, loans sanctioned, credit recovery, etc., in banks.

Special Reports

Special reports are prepared only when required and asked for. They are sub-divided into:

Investigation report: It is prepared after a thorough investigation and enquiry of the case entrusted. This report contains the genesis of the problem and suggestions for solving it. For example, report on falling sales, declining deposits in a bank, customer complaint, loss in a branch. Preparation of this type of report requires a great deal of time, energy and resources for thinking, deliberation and considerations.

Feasibility report: This type of report is prepared when an organization intends to launch a new product, new service or make changes that may impact the customers, etc. This report specifies the area or field where survey is conducted, conditions observed, factors examined, state policy intervention, probable expenditure to be made, attitude of stakeholder if relevant, etc. In short, this report throws light on conditions favourable or adverse to undertaking a venture.

Project report: This report is written after a proposal takes shape and completion of preliminary survey. It describes the proposal, significance of the study, financial implication of a project, expected results, etc. It is prepared for convincing the funding agencies for ensuring sufficient funds.

STRUCTURE OF A REPORT

A report has several parts which enables the writer to lay out all the complex information in an easy-to-read form. They include:

Title

The title of the report should appear at the top of the first page. The title of the report, name of person who has been assigned the task or name of committee preparing the report, month and year of submission should find place here. For example,

Report of Alpha Committee

Appointed to Investigate the Decline in Sales in

Tamil Nadu

Between January and June 2010

If it is an individual's report, title is in the form of subject line indicating only the topic. For example,

Subject: Decline in Sales in Tamil Nadu Between January 2010 and June 2010

Terms of Reference

This section accommodates the details of assignment, purpose and scope of the study.

Name of the assignor, date of submission, mode of appointment of members of committee/ individual, names of members, request for recommendations, if needed, should be mentioned. For example,

A committee was appointed by the resolution adopted at the board of directors meeting, held on 8th July 2010.

Resolved that a committee consisting of Mr. C.N. Annadurai (convener), Mr. Kovalan and Mrs. Mathavi be and are hereby appointed to investigate the decline in sales in Tamil Nadu between January 2010 and June 2010 and to report the recommendations in one month's time.

If the assignment is given through a letter by the CEO or any other authority, terms of reference must give the number, date of letter, name and title of appointing authority, purpose of the report and the time allowed. For example,

According to D/O no 7787, dated 10th June 2010 from Mustaba, M.D., a committee consisting of Mrs. Janifer, Mr. Rosario and Mr. John was formed to examine the complaints of customers in Tamil Nadu region. The committee is asked to submit its findings and recommendation in three weeks.

Procedure

This section deals with the methods of data collection depending on the nature of the study. Some procedures followed are:

a. Records of the organization.

b. Observing certain phenomena involved in problems, and recording what is systematically observed.

c. Interview is conducted with experts with the interview schedule. If the number of persons targeted is small, interview method is apt; questionnaire method is suitable, if large number of people are to be covered.

d. References to books, directories, journals, magazines, reports, research studies, etc., are used to gather information.

e. Visits to sites are necessary in the case of survey.

f. Experimentation is done through various tests for certain kinds of enquires.

Therefore, the report must indicate the method of data collection.

Findings

The data collected is analysed and divided for easy and readable presentation. Each division needs to be numbered, titled and sub-titled. Charts, diagrams, graphs, photographs, maps, drawings, etc., can be used to make the presentation of data more effective. The statistical data can be tabulated. Each table needs, to be numbered, titled and divided into columns and rows. Summary of findings for each division needs to be given.

Recommendations

The last section is dedicated for recommendations. The recommendations should be in the order in which problems have been analysed.

Other parts of a Report

A long report is divided into several chapters or divisions.

a. Table of contents

- It is given after the title page
- List of chapters is given with page numbers

b. Acknowledgement

Names of persons who were helpful in the study need to be acknowledged.

c. Appendix

Copy of questionnaires, plans, any other information which will arouse the interest of the reader needs to be given in the appendix.

d. Bibliography

Sources of information consulted for the study need to be mentioned. It may be from books, magazines, newspapers, websites, reports, documents, etc. The rules relating to citation and footnotes need to observed.

ORGANISING THE REPORT

There are three different ways of organizing reports are:

- Simple letter form
- Simple memorandum form
- Letter-cum-text form

Simple Letter Form

When a report is to be made on a simple subject and requires only a few pages, it is presented in a letter form. This letter type report has to conform to all the mechanics of letter writing i.e date, inside address, salutation, the body, complementary close and signature. The body of letter should contain:

Introduction: This part should accommodate the origin of a report. It should specify about the authorisation given or invitation made to person concerned for making a report.

Findings: This part should contain the findings.

Recommendations: This part has recommendations.

Report were discussed already under the heading "Order of contents".

Sample 1: Simple letter report

Report on Apprentice Unrest in

Madras Engineering Company Limited

25, N.S.C. Bose Road,
Chennai – 600 001

12th May 2011

The Directors,
Madras Engineering Co.Ltd.,
25, N.S.C. Bose Road,
Chennai – 600 001

Gentlemen,

Report on Apprentice Unrest at the Company's Training Center

In accordance with the instructions given to me on May 9, 2011, I visited the training center of the company to find out the causes and extent of unrest among the apprentice trainees.

I interviewed the instructors, plant-workers and forty apprentices selected at random in this connection.

There seems to be widespread unrest amongst apprentices. Several foremen pointed out that the number of incidents of breach of discipline and general non-co-operative attitude has gone up considerably. Foremen expressed the view that the situation has worsened and serious outbreak of misbehaviour might result.

The apprentices, on their part, had some complaints too. According to them, the supervisors were inadequate; the apprentices were given long hours on the production line and skilled workmen were not eager to explain the working of the machinery to them.

There were other avoidable defects which the apprentices presented. The skilled workmen, to save their time, leave the machines dirty which the apprentices have to, clean. Safety precautions in the machine room are continually being ignored. The belief is widespread that the rates paid to the apprentices are the lowest in the area.

I am of the opinion that immediate action must be taken to prevent further disturbances. It is also felt that there is evidence that all the complaints are well-founded. Especially, ignoring safety precautions is an offence under the Factories Act and it must be stopped.

Regarding pay and allowances, it is necessary to bring to the notice of the apprentices that our rates compare favourably with those paid to apprentices in other similar factories. It is, therefore, my considered opinion that the following suggestions will go a long way towards reducing the discontent:

- A training officer may be appointed to draw up a balanced training programme.
- All supervisors must be strictly advised to keep the machinery clean and observe all safety precautions.
- The personnel officer must point out to the apprentices that the rates of pay enjoyed by them in this factory are very favourable.

Yours faithfully,
Pegan
Personnel Officer

The Memorandum Form

The same report can be presented in the systematic form with sub-headings for different points. This form is used mostly in committee reports where the subject matter is complex. But even in reports by individuals, this form can be used. We give below the same report in this form:

Sample 2: Report on Apprentice Unrest at the Company's Training Center

Terms of Reference: In accordance with the instructions given to me on May 9, 2011, I visited the training center of the company in order to find out the causes and extent of unrest among apprentice trainees.

Procedure: In this connection, I interviewed the instructors, plant workers and twenty apprentices selected at random. I found out the following facts which are responsible for this unrest.

Findings: There seems to be widespread unrest amongst apprentices. Several foremen pointed out that the number of incidents of breach of discipline and general non-co-operative attitude has gone up considerably. The foremen expressed the view that the situation has worsened and serious outbreak of misbehaviour might result.

The apprentices, on their part, had some complaints too. According to them, supervisors were inadequate, the apprentices were given long hours on the production line and skilled workmen were not eager to explain the working of the machinery to them. There were other avoidable defects which the apprentices present. Skilled workmen, to save their own time, leave the machines dirty which the apprentices have to clean. Safety precautions in the machine room are continually being ignored. Again the belief is widespread that the rates paid to the apprentices are the lowest in the area.

Conclusion: I am of the opinion that immediate actions must be taken to prevent further disturbances. There are reasons to believe that all the complaints were well-founded. Deliberately ignoring the safety precautions is an offence under the Factories Act and so it must be stopped.

Regarding pay and allowance, it is necessary to bring to the notice of the apprentices that our rates compare favourably with those paid to the apprentices in other similar factories.

Recommendations: It is therefore my considered opinion that the following suggestions will go a long way in reducing the discontent.

1. A training officer may be appointed to draw up a balanced training programme.
2. All supervisors must be strictly advised to keep the machinery clean and observe all safety precautions.
3. The personnel officer must point out to the apprentice that the rates enjoyed by them in this factory are fairly competitive.

May 12, 2011.

H. Kanshiram,

HR Manager

Note:

1. In this form, note that the usual letter structure, is not followed; that is, the address, salutation, etc., are not used.
2. At the end, the name and designation of the report writer are put on the right-hand side.
3. The date is written on the left-hand side.

Letter-Cum-Text Form

Long and lengthy reports are prepared like this. When the subject needs an elaborate discussion, this form is adopted. It should be prepared in a structured fashion. This has been addressed in this chapter under the head structure of report.

CHARACTERISTICS OF A GOOD REPORT

The characteristics of a report are as follows:

Objectivity: The report should adhere to the objectives stated in the terms of reference.

Focus: Report should focus on the main issue without straying away.

Conciseness: The report should be precise. There in no place for jargon.

Clarity: The findings and recommendations should be presented in unambiguous terms. It should not leave any room for presumptions and assumptions.

Completeness: The issues raised should be discussed thoroughly and should not be left incomplete and inconclusive, leading to redoing the investigation.

Timeline: The report should be submitted in the stipulated time frame for effective action. Otherwise, unnecessary delays may defeat the purpose of the report.

Disinterestedness: Report should be free from prejudice, bias and parochialism. It should adopt a neutral tone and language.

CLASSIFICATION OF A REPORT

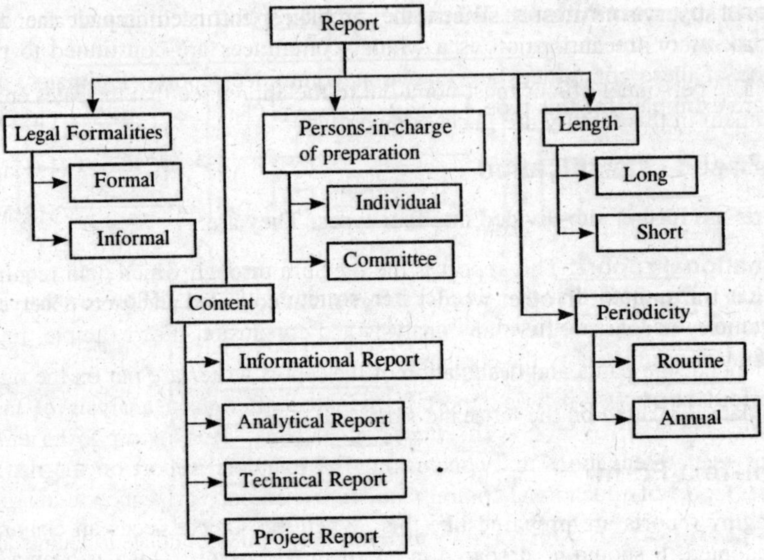

Fig 22.2 Classificatio of a report

Reports can be classified into:

Classification Based on Legal Formalities

This is futher sub-divided into formal and informal reports.

Formal report: It is prepared according to the prescribed format, established procedure and submitted to the authority designated. It is classified into statutory report and non-statutory report.

Statutory reports: Statutory reports are prepared according to the provisions of the Act concerned. Auditor's report, director's report and annual returns come under this category.

Non-Statutory reports: These are reports prepared by subordinates or experts as per the instruction given by their superiors. They have no specific form or standardised procedure. For example,

- Reports by the committee of directors
- Report by a departmental head
- Report by the committee of experts appointed by the company

Informal report: They are more or less like non-statutory reports.

Classification Based on the Person-in-charge of Preparation

These reports are sub-classified into reports by individuals and reports by committees.

Report by individuals: Reports submitted by individual officers like auditor, secretary, manager, foreman, etc., are known as report by individuals.

Reports by committees: When the problems entrusted impact the interest of many departments or the institution as a whole, committees are constituted to probe into them. Reports of these committees are known as committee reports. Estimates, director's report, etc., are examples for this type.

Content-Based Classification

These reports are further sub-divided into four types. They are:

Informational report: This report is the medium through which data required for decision-making is transmitted. In other words, information collected and facts observed are sent to the management. It does not have any analysis and conclusion. For example, reports on training programmes conducted by the company.

Analytical report: Analytic report is prepared after deep analysis of facts and figures, interview and interrogation with connected persons. This report is an exhaustive one. It contains recommendations and conclusion. For example, report on the marketing of a new product, report of educational commission, report on poor grievance redressal.

Technical report: It is prepared by experts or domain specialists in technical language using diagrams, charts and illustrations. This type of report can be understood by the technical employees concerned. For example, report on the success of laparoscopy surgery, report on law commission, report on new design of a car ready for launch.

Project report: This report is prepared after the completion of a project. For example, project report on creation of new machinery, computerisation of banking services, civil and construction project, research projects undertaken by scholars. They are narrative, informative and analytic.

Periodicity-Based Classification

These reports are prepared based on duration. They are of two types:

Routine report: These reports are submitted periodically to designated authorities. Banks, insurance companies, financial companies, government offices, corporates, etc., periodically submit certain reports to their head offices. Confidential report, progress reports, appraisal report are examples for routine reports.

Annual report: Limited companies and voluntary organisations submit annual reports covering company's performance, profit and loss, financial status, dividend disbursal, success, failure, challenges ahead, goals attained, etc.

Length-Based Classification

Reports can be classified based on their length as:

Short report: When top management perceives a particular problem in the organization, it may want to know about it. In such a case, it may designate an official to report on the subject. For example, report on alcholism, absenteeism, labour turnover, labour unrest, sexual harassment.

Long report: Long reports are prepared by experts appointed for the investigation of a major issue. It consists of one chairman and members. The appointing authority provides all sorts of support services to facilitate smooth enquiry. The committee members divide the work among themselves and undertake tours and field visits to collect information. They make references to books, journals, past records, repositories, newspapers, past research work. They interview all those persons connected with the problem under investigation. They analyze the information gathered and give recommendations and conclusion. These reports need to be prepared according to rules prescribed for the layout of a structured report.

REPORTS BY INDIVIDUALS

Sample 3: There has been a remarkable fall in sales in the business of Smellwell Cosmetics Limited. As a secretary, you have been asked to investigate the causes of decline and offer suggestions for arresting the decline. Draft a report to be submitted to the Board of directors.

The Smellwell Cosmetics Ltd.

59, Anna Salai,
Chennai - 600 002

2nd June 2011

The Board of Directors
The Smellwell Cosmetics Limited,
Chennai - 600 002

Gentlemen,

Sub: Report on the decline in the sales of our cosmetics

In accordance with the instructions contained in your letter dated 1st May 2011 I have made a thorough enquiry into the causes of the decline in the company's business for the past one year, and I now submit my report.

Decline in the quality of our products: The questionnaire points to the dissatisfaction of our customers with the quality of our products. While our shampoos leave the hair rough, our talcum powder does not serve as an effective deodorant. The steady erosion in quality is the cause of sagging demand for our cosmetics.

Competition: Many giant units have entered the cosmetics market and have priced their products far below ours. Consumer preference for cheaper products is quite natural.

Poor advertisement and publicity policy: Our publicity programme is outdated and hence unable to catch up with the latest trends. Coupled with this, ineffective salemanship has hastened the process of decline.

Recommendations: The costing department must be instructed to review whether reduced prices can be quoted at least till we are in a position to match the fierce competition.

i) Our talcum powder must come in different sizes so as to attract even those in the lower strata of society.

ii) Finer varieties must also be made available to satisfy the sophisticated section of the society. By this process of broad basing our varieties, the entire market segment can be tapped to our advantage.

iii) A very powerful and sustained advertisement campaign must be undertaken.

iv) Smart, experienced and well-trained sales people should be asked to periodically visit our dealers and win back their customers.

v) Market information with regards to credit and discount rates offered by our rival companies must be obtained and we should not hesitate to offer similar terms to get shelf-space for our products.

vi) Since the only factor that can secure brand loyalty even in the context of severe competition is quality, every effort must be made to see that our products never fail on the score of quality. The inspection department has a greater role to play in this regard.

vii) Follow-up correspondence must be maintained with all our former customers so as not to lose the company's connections.

I am quite confident that if these suggestions are carried out, the unfavourable climate will soon disappear and sales of our products will pick up gradually and we may not have any cause for concern.

Yours faithfully,
Rathinam
Secretary

Sample 4: Report of a manager who has been asked to find suitable premises for the company.

ABC Papers Limited.

148, Anna Nagar,
Cuddalore – 607 002

30th July 2011

The Board of Directors,
ABC Papers Limited,
Cuddalore – 607 003

Gentlemen,

Sub: Proposed Premises for our office

In accordance with the instructions contained in your letter dated 2nd July 2011, I have inspected a number of suitable premises in the neighbourhood and after careful consideration, I recommend the building at 110, South Car Main Road as the most suitable for our office. This building was still recently occupied by a small boarding school.

The proposed building is situated near the business centre of the town and is proximate to the railway station and bus terminal. By shifting to the new premises, our customers will not be in any way inconvenienced. As for our employees, it is within ten minutes walk of the company's present work site.

The building consists of a two-storeyed apartment. It has 30 rooms, all well-lighted and airy and has an imposing appearance.

The large hall on the ground floor can be conveniently used for setting up the counters needed. The other two rooms can be used for record-keeping and storing stationery items. As there are only two floors, lifts will not be required.

Being in the midst of busy thoroughfare, noise and dust is likely to mar concentrated work. But this disadvantage is more than offset by the many advantages it possesses.

Some structural alteration may have to be made. It is necessary to demolish two dividing walls so as to make four of the rooms on the first floor into two large offices for the accounts department and establishment department. On the ground floor two medium-sized rooms can be made into one so as to use it as a reception hall. For this purpose, the dividing walls must be removed.

Mr. Arasu., the owner of the building has consented to let out the building on a monthly rent of ₹ 50,000 initially for a period of five years. Though the rent of the building appears be a little high, I unhesitatingly recommended that this offer can be availed of without delay. I have verified that the building is free from all encumbrances. Estimates for the proposed structural alterations and a letter of consent offering the building on rental basis are enclosed.

Yours faithfully,
R. Annamalai
Manager

Sample 5: The report of the company secretary on the reorganization of the office.

The Coimbatore Electricals Ltd.

111, Avinasi Road,
Coimbatore - 641 101

10th June 2011

The Board of directors,
The Coimbatore Electricals Ltd.
Coimbatore - 642 104

Dear Sirs,

In accordance with the instructions given to me at the last Board meeting held on 2nd June 2011, I have carefully examined the proposal submitted by the Chief Office Superintendent for the re-organisation of the company's office, and I would like to report as follows:

1. The volume of company's business has increased tremendously, almost six-fold increase since the inception of the company a decade ago. With the diversification of business line and stupendous increase in turnover, the work of the accounts department, sales department, and correspondence and records department has increased significantly. However, the share transfer department and the public relations department are overstaffed.

The total number of staff is now 200 against 140 four years ago. But office accommodation has remained the same and the congestion in the office is very acute.

Hence, there is an urgent need, not only for transfer of surplus staff to understaffed departments but also for change of accommodation.

Suggestions

1. Room no.17, presently used for dumping unwanted materials can house accounts

Department. The dumped materials can be shifted to the unused room just below the staircase.

2. Room no.15, a fairly bigger hall presently used by the share transfer department can be allotted to the sales department, and the share transfer department can move to room no.4, occupied at present by the sales department.

3. Mr. V.Robert, now working in share transfer department, and Mr. Vargeese of the public relations department can be transferred to Accounts Department as junior Accountants.

4. Mr. Thomas of share transfer department can be transferred to correspondence department as dispatch assistant, while Mr. Basheer of the Public Relations Departments can be transferred to sales department as sales officer.

I must mention, in this connection, that the heads of departments concerned have also agreed to my suggestions.

I am sure that these changes will ensure efficient functioning of our office while removing congestion in office accommodation.

Yours faithfully,
Choudri
Secretary

Sample 6: Report on heavy book debts.

The Tip Top Ltd.

Guntur – 522 403
Andhra Pradesh.

30th June 2011

The Directors,
The Tip Top Ltd.,
Guntur – 522 409
Andhra Pradesh.

Dear Sirs,

In accordance with the instructions issued to me by the Board, I have made a thorough investigation into the fact that the outstanding book debts are heavier and I have come to the following conclusions:

The total of the book debts as on 31st March 2011 stood at ₹ 1,13,50,000 as compared to ₹ 76,00,000 on 31st March 2010 and to ₹50,00,000 on 31st March 2009.

The interviews with the travelling sales people confirmed that due to the drought condition prevailing continuously for the last two years, the customers are finding it difficult to collect amounts owing to them and that they themselves are carrying heavier debts.

The general increase in the volume of our trade has also contributed to the increase in the amount of outstanding debts.

The credit and collection department is not to blame and they have granted credit only to well-established customers and others whose credit worthiness is beyond doubt. They have updated their credit reports.

It is, therefore, felt that no change in the policy hitherto followed is called for and credit should not be curtailed as our customers are all of good standing and their difficulties are only temporary.

The trend has already begun to correct itself, as the outstanding debts on 31st May totalled ₹1,10,00,000 and the situation is expected to improve significantly soon.

Yours faithfully,
Gowri
Financial Manager and Secretary

REPORTS BY COMMITTEES

Sample 7: The Cuddalore Sugars has appointed a sub-committee of directors to look into the workers' unrest at their factory at Karamanikuppam. The report of the sub-committee submitted to the Board of the directors of the company can be drafted as follows.

The Cuddalore Sugars Ltd.

Sugar House
Beach Road,
Cuddalore – 607 005

17th September 2011

The Board of directors,
The Cuddalore Sugard Ltd.,
Cuddalore – 607 002

Gentlemen,

Sub: Report on workers' unrest at our factory in Karamanikuppam

In pursuance of the resolution of the Board dated 25th August, we have carefully examined the various causes of the workers' unrest at our sugar factory in Karamanikuppam, and we enclose our report together with our recommendations for remedying the situation.

Yours faithfully,
S. Charles
Chairman.
Mohamed Farook
S. Peter
Members

Encl:
Report

Report on Worker's unrest at our Sugar Factory in Karamanikuppam

Terms of reference:

A sub-committee was constituted in accordance with the following resolution passed by the Board of directors in their meeting held on 25th August:

'That a sub-committee consisting of Mr. S. Charles as its chairman and Messrs Farook and S. Peter as its members be formed to enquire into the causes of workers' unrest at our factory in Karamanikuppam and to suggest suitable measures for amicable settlement.'

Procedure:

i) The sub-committee met the works manager twice and held detailed discussions.

ii) It had meetings once, each with the assistant manager, foreman and labour officer.

iii) Twenty five workers selected at random were interviewed personaly.

iv) It had detailed discussions with the union leaders.

v) A study of the workload and grievance procedure in action was also made.

Findings:

There were signs of unrest and outbursts of frayed tempers in the month of March

Group meetings were subsequently held, followed by slogan shoutings after working hours.

Labour officer initiated steps and held dialogues with them in April.

On the works manager's refusal to meet the labour leaders, workers had resorted to adopt go-slow tactics twice in the month of June.

A representation submitted by agitating workers on 5th June had not been forwarded to the Board.

An interview with the foremen and union leaders revealed their firm conviction that unless quick remedial action is taken by the management, the situation will soon become explosive and a total strike cannot be averted.

Causes of unrest:

i) Inadequacy of bus facility from the railway station.

ii) Even a few minutes' late arrival was marked absent and wage cut is resorted to.

iii) The present works manager's dislike of union activities.

iv) Lack of improvement in canteen facilities despite growth in labour force.

v) Sanction of educational advance of ₹ 5000 to each worker for financing the education of sons and daughters of the workers.

Conclusion:

i) On account of infrequent bus service and terribly overcrowded buses, workers have to walk the distance quite often. This results in their late arrival by a few minutes.

ii) Similarly, their grievance over inadequate canteen facilities is also justified. What was started for a work force of 400 cannot obviously serve the present strength of 750. They have to wait for at least half an hour for their turn to occupy a seat in the canteen.

iii) The present works manager who took charge on 2nd January is a tough task master who appears to believe that stern action and severe punishment alone will make workers behave properly.

Refusal to meet workers or use of harsh words cannot get things done these days when workers expect to be treated with dignity.

iv) The labour officer has adopted an unhelpful attitude. He has initiated steps only when the situation became serious.

Recommendation:

i) The company itself should operate bus service between the factory and the railway station.

ii) On completion of the new building, the store room will be shifted there and the store room which is very spacious can be allowed to be converted into a canteen. The food served there is also far from satisfactory. The canteen contractor should be warned to serve quality food.

iii) Educational advance of Rs.5000 to each worker on production of a certificate from the head of the institution should be granted. This can be recovered in ten equal monthly instalments.

iv) An explanation should be called for from the labour officer, who was not alert atthe initial stage and disciplinary proceeding initiated for having allowed a mole-hill to become a mountain.

v) The works manager should be instructed to change his outlook and to adopt a more humane attitude towards the workers. While discipline should be strictly enforced, he should be asked to treat workers with dignity and attend to the genuine grievances of the workers.

S. Charles
Chairman.
Mohammed Farook
S. Peter
Members

Sample 8: A sub-committee has been constituted by the Board of directors of India Sugars Ltd, Bangalore to find a suitable site for another factory in Tamil Nadu. Draft the report of the committee.

India Sugars Ltd.

143, M.G. Road,
Bangalore – 560 070

1st July 2011

The Directors
India Sugars Ltd,
Bangalore.

Gentlemen,

Sub: Report of the sub-committee on the proposed site for our sugar factory in Tamil Nadu

In pursuance of the resolution passed at the Board meeting held on 2nd May, we submit our report on the possibility of setting up a sugar factory in Cuddalore District, Tamil Nadu.

Yours faithfully,
Sundar (Chairman)
Maran (Director)
Paari (Director)
Pallavan (Secretary)

Encl: Report

Report of the sub-committee on the proposed site for a sugar factory in Cuddalore district, Tamil Nadu.

Terms of Reference:

The members of the sub-committee were appointed in accordance with a resolution of the Board at their meeting held on 2nd May.

'That a sub-committee be constituted to explore the posibilities of setting up a sugar factory in Cuddalore district of Tamil Nadu, India.

That the sub-committee consists of Thiru K. Sundar (Chairman), Messrs L. Maran and M. Paari (Directors) and Thiru N. Pallavan (Secretary).'

Work done:

The sub-committee held four meetings on 5th and 20th May, and 7th and 25th June.

The members of the committee visited Keerapalayam, Vandipalayam, Vellappakkam and Villupuram and saw serveral industrial sites.

The members also met the government officials and the local authorities to study the facilities available such as water, power connections, etc.

Findings:

Panruti town presents a good opportunity for a sugar factory. Thirunavalur area, just 10 km from Panruti town is an ideal site for the industrial location. It is on Panruti-Kallakurichi trunk road surrounded by fertile lands suitable for sugarcane cultivation. Cuddalore district is noted for using the largest number of pumpsets and with good water resources, sugar can be cultivated in a vast area.

Present position and- raw material availability: A large number of plots in surrounding villages already grow sugarcane and supply them to E.I.D Parry Limited at Nellikuppam or to a Cooperative Sugar Factory at the far-away Mundiampakkam, incurring heavy freightage.

A very large number of agriculturists spontaneously welcomed the idea of a sugar factory near their door-steps.

Sugar recovery rate of sugarcane cultivated in these areas is stated to be very high.

Availability of skilled workers: Skilled and unskilled labour is available in plenty. Many people have experience in factories, after having worked as casual labourers in the nearby sugar factories.

Power and water: Government and local authorities have promised to give adequate power supply and water connections.

Site: There are two suitable sites ideal for industrial location, one on the road to Ulundurpet and another on the road to Panruti. 5 to 10 acres are available for outright purchase.

Recommendations:

The sub-committee makes the following recommendations:

i) One of the sites can be chosen after consultation with the company's architects.

ii) Steps can be initiated immediately for acquiring the selected site.

iii) The secretary is required to keep in touch with the Government of India for necessary licence for importing the related equipments.

K. Sundar (Chairman)
L. Maran (Director)
M. Paari (Director)
N. Pallavan (Secretary)

Date: 1st July 2011
Place: Bangalore

PRESS REPORTS

Press report is a report prepared by a reporter, correspondent or by any news agency for publication in newspapers or journals. It covers any type of activity—the political or economic policy of the government, its actual implementation, pitfalls noticed in their implementation, social inequalities and atrocities, investigative enquiries into the shady deals of top people, cultural activities, trade developments, etc.

The Characteristics or Requisites of a Press Report

Accuracy: The report should be based on facts and not on hearsay or wild rumours just to arouse curiosity. If it involves data, correct figures should be collected and presented.

Faithful reproduction: It should be a faithful reproduction of what has been observed or heard from reliable quarters. The events should not be distorted.

Comprehensive: The report should be complete so that readers can understand the course of events correctly.

Lucid style: The expression should be lucid, devoid of technical jargon and bombastic words. It should be easily understandable.

Attractiveness: The structure should be logically arranged with attractive headings, divided into paragraphs under suitable sub-titles.

Fearlessness: Just to get favours, the report should not suppress facts which are distasteful to the government but should expose misdeeds fearlessly.

At the sametime, it should be devoid of prejudice or passion. It should not aim at appealing to the basic emotions of people.

Mobilising public opinion: Reporting with a view to mobilising public opinion on current issues is most welcome, as it promotes healthy reading habit and develops vigilant citizens essential for the preservation of democracy.

The Structure of a Press Report

A press report consists of the following structure:

The caption or the headline: Any press report should have an attractive caption. It is the caption which induces a reader to read the report. But it should not mislead the public. For example,

University makers go haywire

The place and date: The place and date of reporting must be mentioned. It usually appears on the right top comer of the report. For example,

New Delhi, August 16

The lead: The introductory sentences or the first one or two paragraphs of the report are called the *lead*. This may reveal the gist of the message to be conveyed and has to be in an attractive tone.

Narration: The details of the discussion must be presented under suitable paragraph headings.

Concluding paragraph: A summary of the report should be furnished in the last one or two paragraphs. For example,

So the next time you try for a school admission, do your home work; apply on time and make the right moves. With a little bit luck, you can give your child a good start.

Sample 9: General report for the press on the havoc wrought by a storm.

Storm leaves 4 dead in Jaipur

Visakapatnam May 27, 2011

With reports of three more deaths from village, Bejat, 20 km from here, the toll in last night's storm lashing the city and the adjoining areas rose to four today. While three died due to electrocution, the other died in a wall-collapse.

At least two persons were reportedly blown off the roof tops and have been admitted to a hospital in a serious condition.

A high velocity storm with a speed of 110 kmph, disrupted all telecommunication links, power supply, rail, road and air services. PTI

Sample 10: Press report on the inauguration of the Head Office of a Regional Rural Bank in Cuddalore.

Regional Rural Bank in Cuddalore opened

Cuddalore, June 21, 2011

Vallalar Grama Bank, the third regional rural bank in the State was inaugurated here on Thursday.

Mr. M.S. Nambiyar, Director of the Bank of Tamil Nadu and Adviser to the RBI, who declared open the head office of the Grama bank, said the concept of grama bank was evolved to fill the gaps left by the counterseal and cooperative banks in the sphere of rural lending. Stating that the Bank of Tamil Nadu, which has sponsored this bank, also had approached the State government for clearance to start similar regional rural banks in Vellore and Salem districts. Mrs. Tolstoy, Director of Vallalar Grama Bank, appealed to the rural folk to utilise the services of the bank effectively.

The third Regional Rural Bank in the State:

Mr. M. Aristotil Shah, Executive Director of the Bank of Tamil Nadu, said the Vallalar Grama Bank was the third regional rural bank to be sponsored by the Bank of Tamil Nadu in the country.

Mr. R. Panicker, Chairman of the Vallalar Grama Bank, received a cheque for ₹ 8.25 lakhs from Mr. M. Bernard Shah as the sponsoring bank's contribution to the paid-up capital for the new bank.

The paid-up capital of Grama Bank:

The Grama Bank is being started with a paid-up capital of ₹ 25 lakhs, 50 per cent of which is borne by the Central government. The State government will meet 15 per cent, while the sponsoring bank provides the other 35 per cent of the paid-up capital.

District Collector Ms. Theresa, Mr. Ram Monohar Lokiya, Deputy Secretary, Institutional Finance and others spoke. Loans to the tune of ₹ 1.45 lakhs were distributed to the weaker sections at the function.

Vailalar Grama Bank has plans to open two more branches in the district in the next five years and has a target of ₹ 10 crore for the same period, according to a press release from the Bank. The bank plans to open about ten branches with in the current financial year-end with a weaker section loan target of ₹ 50 lakhs.

Sample 11: Specimen report for the press on the speech made by Mr. Maraimalai Adigal, the Union Industry Minister at the 66th Annual General Meeting of the Associated Chambers of Commerce and Industry.

Industry not passing benefits: M.A.

From Our Special Correspondent

New Delhi, June 3, 2011

The Union Industry Minister Mr. Maraimalai Adigal, on Tuesday, regretted that the benefits derived by industries from operating in a competitive environment and from the various liberalization measures taken by the government, were not being passed on to the consumers.

The Minister emphasised that competition invariably means that some will lose in the race. Now, such units should not expect succor from the government to bale them out of their own failure to compete, he told the 66th Annual General Meeting of the Associated Chambers of Commerce and Industry here.

"It is strange that some people constantly talk of more liberalisation but are not themselves prepared for the resultant steps which must be taken to modernise and enhance quality and productivity."

"Such units continue to demand all types of protection and concessions. While for the interim period we may have to help them in certain matters, it is up to the management to take decisive, time-bound and firm steps to achieve the desired result."

Corporate responsibility: Mr. Maraimalai reminded the gathering comprising captains of the industry, that corporate responsibility is extended to many areas.

The first responsibility, he observed, was project implementation. Entrepreneurs had to be more businesslike and committed to converting their intentions to invest into actual projects more expeditiously than they had been accustomed. Another responsibility was in relation to technology development and R & D because the viability of the industrial strategy is dependent on their ability to adapt and innovate with respect to technologies acquired from abroad.

The third responsibility was in relation to the environment and industry which left room for improvement. The fourth responsibility is related to industrial dispersal and the fifth to modernization, which was proceeding in spite of generous incentives.

MARKET REPORTS

A market report is one which indicates the state of market of a commodity on a particular day or for a specified period.

Contents of a Daily Market Report

A daily market report contains the opening, the highest and the lowest rate of the previous day. It indicates the market tone.

Structure of a Market Report

A market report consists of the following parts:

Introduction: The name of the market such as stock exchange, jute market, etc., must be mentioned at the top.

Opener: Here an attractive headline is given. It indicates the tone of the market. For example,

Silver drops, gold easy.

Castor futures drop.

Precious metals firm up.

Place and date: It is given on the right-hand corner of the report. For example,

Mumbai, May 20, 2011

Body: The body of the report indicates whether it is a daily or weekly report. This includes

Particulars of business: Activities must be briefly surveyed with emphasis on those items which have fluctuated. All the items or commodities need not be individually reviewed.

Volume of business transacted, nature of business (spot or future), nature and extent of demand and supply must be reported. The opening and closing quotations must be stated.

Closer: The closing paragraph embodies the opinion of the writer. Based on the present market condition and the previous report, opinion must be expressed as to the future course of events.

Advantages of Market Reports

The advantages of market reports are:

1. Market reports furnish accurate and up-to-date information on business transacted in a particular market during a particular period.
2. They are the index to the future price movements and to the demand and supply position of a commodity.
3. They provide data necessary for speculative trading.

4. The publication of rates prevailing in different markets enable the dealers to indulge in arbitrage operations. They even out the price differences and stabilise prices in all the markets.
5. They enlighten the readers on the various avenues of profitable investment.

Commodity Market Report

A commodity market is a permanent place where persons meet for the purpose of doing business in a commodity, which may be a natural product of the soil (such as jute, cotton, wheat, tea, etc.) or a mining product (such as gold, silver, copper, etc.) or a manufactured article (such as sugar, cotton textiles, etc.).

The principal commodity markets in our country are jute markets of Kolkata, cotton markets of \, bullion markets of Mumbai, Kolkata & Delhi, and hides & skin markets of Chennai and Kanpur.

Explanation of certain terms

Ready business: This is *trading in actuals*. When a commodity is purchased and sold for spot delivery, it is called ready business.

Forward business: Contracts for forward delivery are termed as *futures*. Terms of the contract are settled, but delivery of goods will be made at some future date mutually agreed upon by the buyer and the seller.
The seller, in such a transaction, is stated to be *selling forward* and the buyer is said to be *buying forward*.

Bull: The speculator who buys commodities anticipating a rise in its price so that he may subsequently sell it at a profit is known as a *bull*.

Stale bull: When the expectation of a bull goes wrong and the price does not rise, the bull is then known as a *stale bull*, a *tried bull* or a *disappointed bull*.

Staunch bull: A speculator who always acts as a bull and never as a bear.

Bear: Anticipating a fall in price, the speculator who sells in the present so that he may buy it cheap in the future is called a *bear*.

Bull support: Purchase by the bull operator, it is also called *bullish activity*.

Bullish tendency: When owing to rising prices, the market becomes dearer, it is known as *bullish tendency*.

Bull campaign: When the price moves against a bull, the speculator tries to influence the price movement spreading hopeful rumours. Such an activity is called *bull campaign*.

Stark bear: It refers to a speculator who always acts as a bear and never as a bull.

Bearish sentiment: It refers to the feelings among speculators that price will go down.

Bear account: This refers to a oversold position in a market because of the preponderance of bear transactions over bull operations.

Nervous bear: When the expectation of a bear speculator goes wrong and prices rise instead of falling, the bear becomes a nervous bear.

Square deal: A bull selling what he has purchased, or a bear purchasing what he has sold already is called square deal.

Snatching: It refers to heavy buying in a commodity because of prevalence of low prices.

Speculative bout: This refers to the tug-of-war between bulls and bears to bring the market under their respective influence.

Undertone: This refers to a future tendency of the market price.

Offerings: Commodities put up in the market for sale by the sellers are called offerings.

Glut: It means the over-supply of a commodity.

Lackluster trading: Not much business was done or the atmosphere of the market was dull owing to lack of demand. This is called *lackluster trading*.

Upcountry centres: Small consuming centres, feeder markets.

Arrivals: Supplies brought to the market.

Hedging: Process of risk transference.

Rigging the market: Organised transactions by bulls to manipulate prices.

No resistence: There are no buyers.

To go short: A speculator acting as a bear.

To go longer: A speculator acting as a bull.

Setback: Falling of prices after brisk business.

Kerb trading: Buying and selling of futures outside the fixed hours of a produce exchange.

Trapped bull: The bull being forced to sell at a lower price because of his overbought position.

Offtake: The volume of business done as shown by purchases by traders.

Overnight: In the morning.

Dip: Sudden fall in prices.

Jumpy: Unsettled situation.

Slump: Period of falling prices and low business.

Spurt: Sudden jump in prices.

Advice: Information received from other markets.

Bottom fallen out: Sudden collapse of prices.

Bullion: Gold or silver in bars.

Counter: A particular share.

Electricals: Shares of electricity companies.

Shippings: Shares of shipping companies.

Gained ground: Recovery of prices after a fall.

Groundnut oil hardens: The prices of groundnut oil rises.

Holding the baby: Parties being obliged to hold unsold securities.

Nibble: A dealer showing interest in a particular security.

Rally: Revival after falling prices.

Scattered realising: Note spread over.

Short selling: Sale by bears without actually possessing them.

Meaning of certain expressions

The tone of the market is dull: The number of sellers is more than the buyers.

The market opened cheerful: The prices were showing an upward tendency when sale or purchase started in the market.

The market closed hesistant: The demand was less at the close of the market. Hence the prices were showing a downward tendency.

The oil seeds market opened on a steady note: The oil seeds market opened with increased prices.

Groundnut oil opened steady but reacted slightly on weaker Gujarat advice.

i) **Opened steady:** The ground nut oil market opened at prices a little higher.

ii) **Reacted slightly:** Prices fell from the highest level reached.

Groundnut rules firm due to reduced arrivals: The prices of groundnut were quite high because supplies were less.

In Kolkata Stock Exchange, government securities were dull, Tata industrials opened very steady at Rs.81, but the closing was easy. plantations were unchanged. Textiles were dull.

i. **Dull:** No business was transacted.

ii. **Closing was easy:** Prices showed a downward tendency.

iii. **Tata industries:** Shares of Tata Group of industries.

iv. **Plantations:** Shares of plantation companies like rubber, tea, etc.

v. **Textiles:** Shares of textile companies.

Sample 12: A specimen bullion market report.

Mumbai June 14, 2011

The precious metals showed a further improvement in Mumbai on Saturday. Gold opened firm and moved up owing to fresh demand from jewellers and stockists at lower levels.

The arrivals were limited. Silver, on the other hand, resumed lower owing to greater offering but firmed up to close with nominal gains.

Sample 13: Specimen commodity market report for (a) groundnut oil (b) cotton (c) jute.

a) Groundnut oil hardens

Mumbai May 20, 2011

Groundnut oil hardened further in a firm oil seeds and oil market here today. The rise in the commodity was mainly attributed to brisk local buying.

Groundnut oil rose to ₹ 182 (kg) from ₹ 179.92.

b) Cotton Steady

Mumbai June 20, 2011

In restricted activity due to weekend, cotton prices exhibited a steady trend in Mumbai on Saturday. Scattered demand was noted to stray lots of selected qualities like 707, Sankar-4. Hardly 3000 lakhs changed hands.

c) Jute rules dull

Kolkata, June 18, 2011

Dull dealings were in evidence on Wednesday on the spot market in Kolkata, where jute goods remained stagnant at their opening levels due to lack of interest.

Stock Market Report

Stock market is a term used to describe the physical location where the stocks are bought and sold and also to the overall market activity within a country. A report on these activities is a stock market report.

Stock Market Terminology

Stag: Stag is a speculator on a stock exchange who applies for the shares of a new company without any intention of actually becoming its shareholder. He hopes to sell them at a premium to investors and is therefore called a *premium hunter*.

Lame duck: When a bear struggles hard to meet his commitments to deliver securities because of their non-availability, he is called a *lame duck* in the market.

Short selling: The selling of security by a bear on a stock exchange which he does not possess is termed as *short selling*.

Ready delivery: When the contract for buying or selling of securities is to be settled by cash payment, and delivery of securities on the same day or within a week, it is called a *ready delivery contract*.

Forward delivery contracts: If contracts for buying or selling of securities on a stock exchange are settled on fixed settlement days, they are referred to as *forward delivery contracts or forward dealings*.

Option dealings: The term *option dealings* refers to the securing of a right to buy or sell certain securities within a certain time at a certain price.

Call option: *Call option* denotes the securing of a right to buy certain number of securities within a certain time at a certain price.

Put option: *Put option* refers to securing the right to sell certain number of securities within a certain period at a certain price.

Arbitrage: *Arbitrage* is a speculative activity undertaken to make profit out of difference in the price of a security in two different markets. It consists of buying a security in the cheaper market and quickly selling it in another market where a higher price prevails for the same security.

Wash sale: *Wash sale* consists of selling a security and buying it at a higher price through another broker thereby creating a false opinion about the price of the security. As a result of this misleading opinion, the price may move up and the speculator will then sell his holdings at a higher price, thus making profits.

Daily official list: The stock exchange's *daily official list* is a list of prices at which business is done. This list is published by the managing committee of the stock exchange.

Sample 14: Specimen Stock Exchange Market Report.

Reliance Debentures in lime light

Mumbai June 10, 2011

Equities pulled back from a weak opening and closed steady to better on the Mumbai Stock Exchange on Monday after speculative support. Business volume was, however, restricted.

Brokers said concern over the fluid political situation in many States overshadowed trading at the beginning.

Indian Rayon & Tata Steel attached enquiries for 15,000 shares each and gained ground. On buying of 2000 shares, Gujarat Fertilizer rose 10 points. Buying was also good in Premier Auto.

Reliance 'F' series debentures were in much demand and shot up to a high of ₹ 217 before finally settling at ₹ 210 against the previous closing of ₹ 192.

REPORTS FROM STATISTICAL DATA

Statistical methods can be used to summarize or describe a collection of data. Statistical reports are created based on aggregates of this data.

Advantages of Reports Prepared from Statistical Data

Any vague or common-sense analysis of market trend will not lead a business man anywhere; it may even mislead him. But if reports are prepared from statistical data, he is sure to derive immense benefits.

Revealing the truth: Since reports are based on statistics, they reveal the facts.

Taking the right step: Right steps can be initiated for arresting inhibitive factors and promoting achievement of pre-determined goals.

Analyzing the trend: Trend can be analyzed in various directions. For example, a business man can analyze growth in sales volume for the different years. He can analyze how different products have fared in the same year too.

Decision-making: Statistical reports assist in decisioin-making. They supply the premises needed for a logical analysis of events. For instance, a departmental store can know the profit-making departments and also the loss-causing ones. Such statistical data provided in a tabular form helps to decide on the closure of a department or its continuance.

Judgement free from bias: A report devoid of relevant statistical data may have the danger of incorporating the report-writer's personal bias. Any prejudiced opinion will impair fair judgement of events. But reports prepared from statistical data are free from prejudice or passion, because statistics does not lie. Whether bitter or pleasant, they point to the correct direction only.

Invaluable aid to the government: All planning essential for economic development and review of schemes which are to be implemented are based on reports prepared from statistical data.

A maze of data will not be of much assistance. A clear report containing the list of points emerging from such statistics will make reading interesting, besides being of real value to the authorities for taking appropriate action.

For example, a report based on statistical data regarding branch expansion of banks will disclose whether banking facilities have been extended to even far-flung areas and whether any further expansion is to be encouraged. Thus, this facilitates policy formulation on correct lines.

Points to be Borne in Mind While Preparing Reports Based on Statistical Data

1. The report should point to the source from where the report-writer has collected the data, if the data is from secondary source.
2. If they are collected by him (primary data), he should explain the limitation of data.
3. The body of the report should not contain a maze of data collected by him. It will not only make the report dull and uninteresting, but also makes it confusing.
4. The data relevant for the point to be stressed alone must be used in the body of the report.
5. Detailed data should not be incorporated in the body of the report. They can be classified, tabulated and presented as annexure or tables at the end of the report. Analysis discussed should take only the percentage or the main item pointing to the detailed figures given in the particular table. For example 'As Table No.10 indicates, the priority sector advance by all commercial banks for the year 2010-11 forms......percentage of the total advances.'
6. The language used should not be too technical or bombastic. It should be simple. A lucid style is most welcome.
7. Points should be arranged in logical sequence and presentation of data intelligible even to the layman.
8. The report should end with a summary and a conclusion together with his recommendation. Recommendations should not be definite and clear cut.
9. Since reports based on statistical data have definite aims, such a report should contain correct interpretation of figures.
10. Any wrong interpretation will defeat the very purpose, and the report itself will lose its

utilitarian value.

Sample 15: Specimen statistical report

Distribution of new Bank Offices

(During July 1969 to April 2000)

Increase in number

Category of Banks	Total	Banked areas	Unbanked centres	% of new offices at unbanked areas to total new offices opened by each category
State Bank of India	1209	493	716	59.2
Associates of SBI	658	246	412	62.7
14 Nationalized Banks	3854	1568	2286	59.3
Public Sector Banks	5721	2307	3414	59.7
Private Sector Banks	1171	561	610	52.1
All Commercial Banks	6892	2968	4024	58.4

Report on Branch Expansion Based on Statistical Data

The statistical data furnish important information relating to branch expansion, and they help us to conclude whether one of the basic objectives of nationalized banks, namely extension of banking facilities to rural and semi-urban areas particularly to unbanked areas, has been fulfilled.

General branch expansion

The total number of bank offices opened during the four year period is 6,892. Of this, SBI alone has opened 1,209 offices. This works out to 17.5% while the 14 nationalized commercial banks have opened 3,854 branches, constituting 55.9% of the total new offices .

Branch expansion in unbanked areas

The total number of branches opened in unbanked areas is 4,024. The share of the SBI in this is 17.5% while that of the nationalized banks is 55.9%

On the whole, the public sector banks have opened a total of 5721 new offices (which works out to 83%).

Concentrating 33.5% of new offices in banked areas and 49.5% in totally unbanked areas is quite welcome.

Contribution of private sector banks

The total number of branches opened during the period under review by the private sector banks is 1,171. Of this, 561 branches (48%) have been opened in banked areas and 610 (52%) in unbanked areas.

In terms of percentage, private sector banks have contributed to the extent of 17% of the newly opened offices. Their contribution to banked areas is 8% and unbanked area is 9%.

Unbanked areas receive top priority

Another revealing feature of branch expansion of commercial banks is that all categories of banks, including private sector banks, have attached greater importance to unbanked areas. The highest proportion of new offices at unbanked areas is that of the associates of the State Bank of India

(62.7%) while the next is that of the nationalized banks with 59.3%.

Contribution to unbanked areas by each category

Of the total of 4,024 new offices opened in unbanked areas, the contribution of each sector of banks is as follows:

State Bank of India	17.8%
Its Associates	10.2%
14 Nationalised Banks	56.84%
Public Sector Banks	84.84%
Private Sector Banks	15.16%
	100%

Per day expansion

For the period under review consisting roughly of 1,395 days, the banks have opened new offices at the rate of 5 branches a day, 3 in unbanked areas and 2 in banked areas.

SUMMARY

Uses of report are facilitating the performance of planning and controlling function, intimating the progress, arguing a course of action, disclosing performance gap, helps in decision- making.

Types of reports include routine report (progress report, inspection report, appraisal report, periodical report), special report (investigation report, feasibility report, project report).

Planning the report includes collection of information, organizing, dividing and writing the report.

Organizing the report can be done in a simple letter form, memorandum and letter-cum-text form.

Layout or structure of a report has title, terms of reference, procedure, findings, recommendation and other parts of the report like table of contents, acknowledgement, appendix and bibliography.

Characteristics of a good report are objectivity, focus, conciseness, clarity, completeness, time line and disinterestedness.

Reports can be classified into Legal (formal, informal), persons-in-charge of preparation (individual, committee), length (long, short), content (informational, analytical, technical, project report) and periodicity (Routine, Annual).

Characteristics of a press report are accuracy, faithful reproduction, lucidity, comprehensiveness, fearlessness, attractiveness and mobilising public opinion.

Structure of press report includes caption or title, lead, narration and a concluding paragraph.

Structure of a market report includes introduction, opener, the body containing the particulars of business and closer.

Advantages of a market report are furnishing up-to-date information, index to future price movement, providing data for speculation, arbitrage benefit and enlightening the readers.

Reports from statistical data are useful for revealing the truth, initiating right steps from the insight there, analyzing the trend, aids in decision-making, invaluable aid to government and unbiased information.

Points to be borne in mind while preparing a statistical report are highlighting the source of data, statement of limitations, using the relevant data, providing detailed data in the body of the reports, ordinary language in place of jargon, presenting points in a logical sequence, presenting in a layman style, correct interpretation and ending the report with a summary and a conclusion.

REVIEW QUESTIONS

Part A: Short Questions

1. What is meant by a report?
2. What is a feasibility report?
3. What is a periodic report?
4. What is F.I.R?
5. What is a project report?
6. What is a technical report?
7. What is a long report?
8. What is a short report?
9. What is a statutory report?
10. What is a market report?
11. What is a press report?
12. What is commodity market?

Part B: Paragraph Questions

1. Highlight the importance of a report.
2. How would you plan the business report?
3. State the three methods of presenting the report.
4. Enumerate the advantages of a market report.
5. What are the advantages of a report prepared from statistical data?
6. What points are to be borne in mind while preparing reports based on statistical data?
7. Draft a brief commodity market report for (a) groundnut oil (b) cotton (c) jute
8. State the structure of a press report.
9. State the characteristics of a press report.

10. State the purpose of a report.

Part C: Essay Questions

1. Highlight the features of a good report.
2. Explain the body of the report or layout/structure of a report.
3. How would you organise the report?
4. What are the various types of reports?
5. How would you classify reports

Part D: Objective Type Questions

Choose the correct answer

1. Which one of the following is a routine report?

   a. Confidential b. Technical report c. Statutory report

   (Ans: a)

2. Which one of the following is a technical report?

   a. Press report b. Report by an engineer on machinery installation
   c. Confidential report

   (Ans: b)

3. Report on investigation of fraud committed by the cashier which is submitted by HR manager is

   a. Committee report b. Individual report c. Confidential report

   (Ans: b)

4. Which one of the following is a statutory report?

   a. Auditor's report b. Director's report c. Both

   (Ans: c)

5. Report submitted after a thorough investigation is

   a. Informative report b. Analytical report c. Confidential report

   (Ans: b)

6. Report submitted by a group of people appointed to investigate a problem is

   a. Individual report b. Committee report c. Special report

   (Ans: b)

7. Report prepared after analysing the figures presented is

   a. Investigative report b. Statistical report c. Commodity report

(Ans: b)

Fill in the blanks

1. Orderly presentation of factual information, data, records or events about a specific business incident, activity, programme is ______. (Business report)
2. Report disclosing the progress at different stages is ______. (Progress report)
3. Report made after inspection of a site or task assigned is ______. (Inspection report)
4. Report evaluating the work performance of employees is ______. (Appraisal report)
5. Report prepared with available information after an accident or disaster, or an event is ______. (F.I.R.)
6. Report revealing the workability of a project envisaged is ______. (Feasibility report)
7. Report prepared by a correspondent or reporter is ______. (Press report)
8. Report indicating the state of commodity market is ______. (Market report)
9. Auditors, directors and annual reports are examples of ______. (Statutory report)
10. Reports prepared by an expert or technical person is ______. (Technical report)
11. Report submitted after the conclusion of an arranged is training ______. (Informational report)
12. Confidential report comes under the ______ category. (Routine report)

Exercises

1. Give the meaning of the following market report.

The market was dull and easier owing to lack of demand.

Answer: Very little business was done and prices were showing a downward trend because there were no buyers.

2. Give the meaning of the following report in the wheat market. The sentiment has been extremely dull; the offtake has been poor.

Answer: There has been very little purchase and no business activities in the wheat market.

3. Explain the following passage in simple English.

There has been a quietier feeling in the local piece goods market, as the upcountry centres have displayed even less interest during the period.

Answer: During the period under review, not much business was done in the local piece goods market because there was almost no demand in the consuming centres.

4. Rewrite the following market report in simple English.

The cotton market opened steady around previous levels, but soon developed a sagging tendency on profit realising and fresh speculative sales, following subdued demand in the ready section

(exportable varieties faced liquidation at higher rates registered previously). Bengal broke by more than 10 points.

Answer: The cotton market opened at prices slightly higher than the closing rates of the previous day. But with reduced demand for ready cotton, prices began to fall soon because of profit-making sales by bulls and speculative sales by bears. However, exportable varieties were sold at a higher rate. The price of Bengal variety of cotton fell by more than Rs.10.

5. Rewrite the following stock exchange report in simple English, explaining the words in italics.

Although the *undertone* in the *industrial market* was fairly satisfactory, conditions became dull after a *fairly firm start* on Monday and the volume of business remained small.

Undertone	: The future tendency of the prices.
Industrial market	: Section of the Stock Exchange which deals in shares of industrial companies.
Fairly firm start	: The opening price was fairly high.

Explanation

The future tendency of the price of shares and securities of industrial concerns was satisfactory. On Monday, the opening rates were fairly high but they soon began to decline and the volume of business transacted was small.

6. Rewrite the following stock exchange report.

Steel shares recorded a new high level, following firm advice from Delhi and bear-covering by Madras operators.

Answer: The price of the shares of steel companies reached new heights because of the purchases by Delhi operators and Madras bear speculators.

7. Rewrite the following report:

Some parties in Kolkata are long in Indian Iron by 10,000 shares while a few in Mumbai are short in by 2,000 shares.

Answer: Some bulls in Kolkata have bought 10,000 shares of the Indian Iron company, while a few bears in Mumbai have sold 2,000 shares (This is an over-bought position).

23 CHAPTER

PROPOSAL DOCUMENTATION

INTRODUCTION

A proposal can be defined as an offer document presented to undertake works, affecting the future of an organization. Proposals are tools of communication. It does not limit itself to expressing facts but also probable solutions to a particular problem. They can be written to people inside or outside the organization.

A proposal invited by the management is called a invited proposal. Proposal submitted voluntarily is called an uninvited proposal.

MECHANICS OF WRITING A PROPOSAL

Proposal has to be prepared like a report. So all the rules relating to making a report apply to preparation of a proposal. It is to be written on the basis of AIDA (Attention, Interest, Desire and Action). The very beginning of the proposal should attract the attention of the reader and retain it throughout.

- It has to start with a clear objective.
- Proposal-maker has to gather all the relevant information to put forward an idea.
- He has to put forth arguments in favour of the proposal.
- The proposal has to be worded so that it evokes a positive response from the reader.
- The structure of the proposal may be based on the 4 P's:

  Position: This shows current status.

  Problem: This shows the negative side of the current position and underscores the need to change.

  Possibilities: This gives the options for the changes to be brought about.

  Proposal: This part lists out the actual proposal, the plan for bringing about the change and the requirement for implementing it.

- The structure of the proposal can be divided into introduction, body of the proposal highlighting the problem, need for change, scope, limitations, cost estimate and conclusion.

SAMPLE PROPOSALS

Sample 1: A voluntary proposal for automation in a printing press.

KPT printers
Nehru Street,
Chidambaram – 608 002

Dear Sir,

It is a great pleasure to introduce ourselves as people who have been bringing about revolution in printing technology.

Please, have a look at the specimen enclosed, four colour pictures. You can discern the difference between pictures printed using conventional technique and the one printed with automatic dust-proofing technology.

Surprisingly, the new device we have innovated is not expensive as you might think. We request you to pay a visit to our outlet to see the device in action. With your consent, we would like to arrange a visit to a few printing facilities in the neighbourhood which have installed our new device and are experiencing the benefits.

Please calls us on 9494171771. Also, you can visit our website *www.printinginnovation.com*

Yours faithfully,
Marketing Development Officer

Sample 2: Proposal for relocating our godown to a new place.

The General Manager
Tai Nadu stationery – A stationary chain,
Pondicherry – 605 001

Dear Sir,

This is about relocating our godown which is three streets away from the stores. The proposal put forwards two propositions:

- Renting an accommodation at present available in the same street
- Redesigning our present sales outlet so as to house our godown

Currently, we have been stocking in a godown in Singer street which is three streets away from our sales outlet. It is very difficult to move the stock through the crowded streets during the day time. At present, stocks need to be moved to sales outlet after 9 p.m. Our sales crew is forced to stay back to receive delivery, which means paying overtime charges. Further, the physical movement of stock from Singer street to our sales outlet involves transportation charges and transit insurance.

In this context, there is an accommodation available in the same street on rental basis which is less than the rent paid for the house used at present as godown. Shifting the godown would helps save the overhead charges.

The other alternative involves a capital cost. If permission can be secured from local authorities, we can add one more floor in our present building to house our godown.

I am putting forward these two propositions for your kind consideration and to provide a solution to our physical distribution hitches.

Yours faithfully,
Aubrabindo
Branch Manager

To: The General Manager
From: The Manager (Administration)

SUMMARY

Proposal is an offer document affecting the future of an organization. It can be invited or uninvited

The mechanics of writing a proposal are rules of report writing, follows AIDA, objectivity, gathering relevant information, favourable argument, should evoke positive response, based on 4P's — Position, Problem, Possibilities, Proposal.

The structure a proposal includes introduction, body highlighting the problem, need for change, scope, limitations, cost and conclusion.

REVIEW QUESTIONS

Part A: Short Questions

1. What is a proposal?

Part B: Paragraph Questions

1. Write the mechanics of preparing a proposal.

Part c: Objective Type Questions

Choose the Correct Answer

1. Proposal submitted by an officer containing solutions to the problem faced by an institution is

   a. Solicited proposal b. Unsolicited proposal c. A good-intention letter

   (Ans: b)

Fill in the blanks

1. A document presenting probable solutions to a problem faced is _______. (Proposal)
2. Proposal invited by the management is _______. (Invited proposal)
3. Proposal voluntarily submitted is _________. (Unsolicited proposal)

PART 5

GROUP COMMUNICATION

24

CHAPTER

GROUP AND TEAM INTERACTIONS

GROUP DEFINITIONS

Group can be defined as the coming together of two or more people with a common purpose who stay joined over a period of time.

Group is a cluster of two or more individuals who interact with each other on an enduring basis, identify themselves as a part of a distinctive unit and share certain common interests, values, goals and activities.

TYPES OF GROUPS

Groups can be sub-divided into:

Small group/primary group: It is cluster of a few individuals.

Large group/secondary group: It is a collection of few small groups.

Formal group: Work unit established as a part of an organisation and its structure.

Informal group: It is a voluntary and unofficial formation of people of an organisation.

CHARACTERISTICS OF A GROUP

The characteristics of a group are:

- Group consists of two or more individuals.
- There is some level of stability of tenure and function.
- It is associated with a common goal or interest.
- Members should identify themselves as they are all part of the group.
- Group represents collective power. In other words, there is a strong binding force which translates into pressure to get things done or problems solved.
- Groups have their own prejudice as an individual does.

GROUP DYNAMICS

It is a separate field of study concerned with research and analysis of various forces and patterns of formation of small groups in organizations. It covers formation of a group, structure of a group, composition of a group, growth of group decision-making, adaption to changes, motivation and achieving member satisfaction.

Merits of Group Decision-making

1. The sum total of information of all members is far greater than that of an individual. Information is a vital raw material for correct decisions.
2. Since each individual thinks differently from different perspectives, varieties of approaches are available for decision-making.
3. Decisions at group meetings are taken mostly on consensus basis, after deliberating and debating diverse viewpoints. Thus, decisions arrived at through democratic process carry weight.
4. Most of the members comprising the group are usually experts. Therefore, decisions made using expert opinions command greater acceptability.
5. The meeting of experts infuse in all of them a sense of involvement. There is less scope for resistance.
6. It encourages internal democracy. Since no member is individually accountable for failure of decisions arrived collectively, each member feels free to offer views and suggestions for reaching better decisions. Thus, group decision-making fosters a sprit of democracy.

Demerits of Group Decision-making

1. Arriving at a consensus is time-consuming. Immediate and emergency decisions cannot be made through this forum.
2. In the event of failure of group decision, accountability cannot be fixed on any particular individual.
3. It is expensive in terms of time, money, energy, resources, physical facilities, etc.
4. Owing to pressure from several quarters, members may tend to reach a compromise instead of debating the issues concerned threadbare. In such a case, the quality of the compromised decision is questionable.
5. Though group decision-making appears to be democratic, when groups are headed by dominating members enjoying the support of powerful external and internal groups, they muffle the voice of other members. Thus, the very purpose of group decision is defeated.
6. The formation of such groups on the basis of caste, community, religion, region, field of specialization etc., tends to mar the effective functioning of a group, thereby affecting group decision.
7. The time required for assembling the group members, arranging facilities, co-ordinating their meetings, defining and explaining the purpose of meeting is more. A lot of bureaucracy is involved in organizing group meetings, especially in public sector environment.

TECHNIQUES OR FORMATS OF GROUP DECISION-MAKING

Group decision-making is sub-divided into:

Committee Meetings

Committee is a forum where a group of people representing different interests meet together to address the problem referred to it.

Types of committees

Standing committee: It is a permanent committee formed to run the organisation smoothly.

Advisory committee: It is a committee of experts which is consulted for expert opinion. The members are usually nominated at regular intervals by the constitution. Even persons from outside can be made member of this committee.

Ad hoc committee: It is a committee formed to address a specific issue. It is disbanded after the purpose is over.

Any committee has to do the functions like collecting data, enquiring attitude and opinions of members, arriving at a decision and keeping an accurate record of decisions arrived at.

Command Meetings

It is a committee headed by a manager, who issues instruction to his subordinates. Such meetings are held specifically to allow a manager to share information with his subordinates. There is no collective responsibility assumed by all the members. The onus of decision taken rests with the manager.

Table 24.1 Differences between command meeting and committee meeting

Command Meetings	Committee Meetings
It is a meeting between manager and his subordinates.	Group appointed by parent organization comprising experts.
The objective of the manager is to share information, state policies and give direction.	Objective is to advise the appointing authority on the issues, to address a specific problem and to address recurring issues.
Manager is solely accountable for decisions arrived at.	All members one collectively accountable.

Brainstorming Sessions

It is a session dedicated to generate as much ideas as possible for an issue. It was first developed by an advertising agency in 1939 in the US. The main aim of the session is to let the brain of members attending the session think. There is no criticism of ideas contributed. All ideas are welcome and recorded. After mobilising all ideas, each one is critically reviewed and assessed for its potential to address the problem. Thus, the collective decision is arrived at to address a specific problem.

Nominal Group Technique

People meet as a group but inter-personal communication is restricted. Even if they meet as a group, they function individually. Each member is required to write down his idea on the issue concerned. All ideas of the members are collected and recorded. The group then deliberates each and every idea from various angles. Finally, all the members are asked to rank the ideas deliberated. The idea which scores maximum points is adopted.

Delphi Technique

This is similar to a brainstorming session with the difference that it does not warrant physical presence of members. Members can arrive at a consensus sitting at different locations. In this method, a questionnaire is sent to members at various places; each member gives his own idea, perception and attitude to the questions in the questionnaire. The responses are collected and compiled. Each member is given feedback on his earlier response. The questions are churned or rechurned and sent to the persons whose opinions are divergent from others. This process will go on till the consensus is reached on vital issues discussed. This technique has advantages. There is no question of one member influencing the response of the other members. Each member gives his independent view. There is no fear of his opinion being criticized or ridiculed. However, it is time-consuming. The repeated sending of the questionnaire, getting replies and redrafting questions are all time-consuming. Also, it calls for great intelligence in framing of the questions.

Group Discussion (GD)

It is a discussion among participants on an agreed topic. In the workplace, discussions trigger new ideas and new expertise. Each member contributes ideas in the presence of others. The moderator allows the groups to deliberate on the ideas and helps arrive at a consensus. Thus, each member's ego needs are satisfied and each one's knowledge is increased.

Guidelines for GDs

Setting up the group: The leader has to put together a group at a time and place convenient for all people. The leader should have a clarity of purpose of the GD and also an agenda. The leader should have an idea as to how to structure the discussion.

Role of a facilitator: Facilitator has to explain his role to the members. He should pay attention to the process and time, and work to keep the discussion on the agenda whenever discussion digresses. He should make sure that group rules are observed by all members.

The facilitator has to conduct himself in an informal manner for better results. He has to frame group rules relating to respecting the opinion/perception, respecting timelines allowed, ensuring address of rules for discussion, etc.

Role functions in GDs

The following are the roles involved in a GD:

Initiating: The first role involves introducing the theme or suggesting an idea or defining a problem.

Supplying information: It involves offering facts and soliciting input from the participants.

Inviting reaction: The facilitator himself shares his inputs and encourages others to react and seek clarifications from the discussions.

Clarification: The facilitator has to restate or clarify the original idea; aiding in understanding and providing examples and illustrations.

Confronting and reality testing: This includes challenging ideas and information, seeking to activate the discussion as to the implications of carrying out the idea and showing how it can or cannot work in reality.

Synthesizing and summarizing: This includes clarifying the idea and pulling together related ideas or suggestions after the group discussion is over.

Other role functions

Group building and maintenance: Facilitator has to encourage every member to contribute; he has to be friendly, warm, responsive to others, accepting the contributions of others, praising others for their ideas, supporting the idea, etc.

Time keeping: Suggest limited time to everyone and oversee that everyone talks and contributes.

Types of GDs

Structured GD: In this type of GD, the topic is pre-fixed. No leader is chosen or consensus expected. This is easier to handle. It does not require any technical knowledge.

Unstructured GD: A leader is chosen. Group has to arrive at a consensus. The leader has to direct the group, set the tone for discussion and controls group dynamics.

Specialised GD: It includes role-plays. Candidates are given roles to play. For example, assuming that two companies are negotiating, candidates are given profiles of CEOs, marketing managers, HR, advisors, consultants, etc., and they are required to play a role in a simulated environment.

Success factors in GDs

- Ability to have an entirely different perspective
- Level of preparedness
- Ability to reason, think and debate
- One needs to be assertive and not aggressive
- Clarity of thought
- Demonstrating leadership quality at every stage
- Ability to switch over to various roles

Team Presentation

Team is a group of more than two people who work interdependently towards a common goal.

It represents a co-ordinated effort by its members who plan, organize and deliver a unified message aimed at achieving a common purpose with respect to an audience of one or more listeners.

Benefits of team presentation

1. It is used to get approval from top management to begin work on a new product or service that requires commitment of human or capital resources.
2. To report the progress made by the unit and have the management apprised of the progress.
3. To instruct newcomers on the do's and don'ts.
4. To orient the freshers towards company's policies, procedures, strategies and other practices.
5. To secure adequate financial backing from funding agencies by justifying its fund requirement.
6. To secure business contract from other agencies by making a case showcasing the capabilities of the firm to execute the contract.
7. To win tax break or exemption from a public agency or regulatory authority.

Mechanics of team presentation

- Team leader should know the purpose of the presentation. It may be informative or persuasive. Informing the progress to the authority concerned through team presentation is informative, and informing the top echelons of the management to get approval or sanction is persuasive.
- Team leader should know who the target audience is. The latter may be colleagues, prospective clients or higher authorities. He should design the presentation accordingly.
- He should analyze the audience. He has to find out the demography of audience and assess the familiarity of the audience about the subject matter. He has to focus on its needs and expectation. The success of a presentation depends on meeting these needs and aspirations.
- He has to gather information about the audience through interviewing the executive or person in charge of an event, by interviewing a sample of the audience, by reviewing the literature of the organization, by searching information via internet, newspapers and by contacting the research associates.
- He has to know other logistics about the occasion i.e., he should know the place and time of the presentation, members of the panel presenting the information, room size, physical facilities, etc.
- Team members have to choose the team leader for presentation. The leader should be a person knowledgeable about the various aspects of the functioning of the team.
- If needed, the team leader can delegate different segments of a presentation to different team members.
- Team leader has to allocate time, decide on speakers, order of presentation and content of the presentation. He has to prepare and execute the summary and sequence of other activities.
- Since it is a special occasion, all the members have to wear formal attire.

- Team leader has to synchronise the visuals by standardizing the format of slide presentation. He has to check the grammar, use of jargon and level of formality in the slides. Every presenter has to use the same vocabulary, for example, one presenter uses the word *slides* while other use the word *overheads*.
- It is better to rehearse the presentation before a group of non-presenters to find out errors in slides, clumsy transitions, moments of uncertainty, spelling mistakes, etc.
- On the day of the presentation
  - Presenters have to reach the room well in advance of the session and check the functioning of the different equipment.
  - Fix the positions which the presenters have to take during the presentation.
  - Fix who has to handle the visuals.
  - Team leader introduces the theme, topic, agenda and the presenters.
  - When one presents, all presenters have to give close and serious attention to him.
  - Fix one or two members to monitor the time and see that each presentation ends on time scheduled.
  - All the team members have to be present on the stage to handle the questions. Suppose a person is designated, he/she would handle the questions.

SUMMARY

Types of groups are small, large, formal and informal.

Characteristics of groups are plurality of individuals, stability of tenure, associated with a common interest, members' identifying themselves, act as a binding force and has prejudice.

Merits of group decision-making are different shades of opinion, consensus-based decision-making, expert advice and internal democracy.

Negatives of group decision-making are time-consuming, no accountability, expensive, pressure from different quarters, domination of vested interest, different divisions in a group and time for assembling a group is high.

Types of committee includes standing committee, advisory committee and ad hoc committee.

Command meetings are headed by a manager who issues instructions to subordinates. Decisions are taken only by the manager.

Guidelines for organizing GD are the role of a facilitator which comprises of setting up the group, informal conduct and framing group rules.

Role functions in GD are initiating, supplying information, inviting reactions, clarification, confronting and reality testing, synthesizing and Summarizing, group building and time keeping.

Types of GDs are structured, unstructured and specialised.

Success factors in GD includes different perspectives, level of preparedness, reasoning ability, assertiveness, clarity of thought, demonstration of leadership qualities and ability to switch over to various roles.

The benefits of team presentation are getting approval from top management, reporting progress made, instructing newcomers, orienting freshers, convincing funding agencies, securing business contracts and getting privileges from public agencies.

Organizing a presentation can be done with knowledge of purpose, knowing the audience, collection of information about the audience, knowledge about logistics required for the presentation, selection of a team leader, delegating different segments of the presentation, wearing formal attire, synchronizing visual, rehersal and things to be checked on the date of presentation.

Things to make the presentation effective are investing time on building a good team, getting to know the members, cohesive functioning, appointing a leader, analyzing the audience, understanding the importance of listening and appointing a person to co-ordinate the written and visual materials.

REVIEW QUESTIONS

Part A: Short Questions

1. What is a group?
2. What is a small group?
3. What is a large group?
4. What is a formal group?
5. What is group dynamics?
6. What is a standing committee?
7. What is an ad hoc committee?
8. What is a command meeting?
9. What is brainstorming?
10. What is Delphi technique?
11. What is a group discussion?
12. What is team briefing?
13. What is team presentation?

Part B: Paragraph Questions

1. Highlight the characteristics of a group.
2. Point out the merits of group decision-making.
3. State the types of committees.
4. State the guidelines for GD.
5. What are the role functions in GD?
6. What are the different types of GDs?
7. How can a GD be successful?
8. Enumerate the benefits of team presentation.
9. How would you make team presentation effective?

Part C: Essay Questions

1. Discuss the negative aspects of group decision-making.
2. Bring out the mechanics of team presentation.

Part D: Objective Type Questions

Choose the best answer

1. Work unit established as a part of business is

a. Formal group b. Informal group c. Ad hoc group

(Ans: a)

2. Permanent committee formed to address standing issues

a. Ad hoc committee b. Informal committee c. Standing committee

(Ans: c)

3. Which one of the following is used for idea generation

a. Group discussion b. Team presentation c. Brainstorming

(Ans: c)

4. Meeting between a manager and the subordinates is

a. Command meeting b. Committee meeting c. Delphi technique

(Ans: a)

5. Discussion among participants on an agreed topic

a. Team presentation b. Group discussion c. Delphi Technique

(Ans: b)

Fill in the blanks

1. Group of more than two persons work interdependently towards a common goal is ________. (Team)
2. Co-ordinated efforts by a member who plans, organizes and delivers a unified message is ____________. (Team presentation)
3. Discussion among participants who agree on a topic is ________. (Group discussion)
4. Consensus is reached by consulting experts in different physical locations under ________. (Delphi technique)
5. Though people move in group, inter-personal communication is restricted under ___________. (Nominal group technique)
6. Committee set up for a particular issue is __________. (Ad hoc committee)
7. A specialized field of study concerned with studying pattern of behaviour of a group is _________. (Group dynamics)
8. Coming together of two or more persons for a common purpose is __________. (Group)

25

CHAPTER

TEAM BRIEFING

INTRODUCTION

Briefing can be defined as a short talk that informs a generally knowledgeable audience about a subject on which they would like to acquire new or additional information. For example, in a pre-placement campus interview, a company gives briefing about the profile of the company, progress, achievements, ongoing projects, job prospects, career advancement, etc.

Features of Team Briefing

It involves the following:

- Face-to-face group meeting in teams
- Lasting for around 30 minutes
- Given by team leaders
- Held at least once a month or a pre-set date with prior notification.

PROCESS OF TEAM BRIEFING

The process of team briefing is managed by records and managers attending the briefing.

- Every month the CEO or the board of directors agree on the core brief.
- Core brief covers subjects like financial performance, organizational policy, strategy, business direction, market condition, success and failures, changes in senior people's roles.
- Line managers in the level of board of directors and below, give interpretation or explanation to the core brief.
- Line managers prepare their own brief.
- Briefings cascade down the organization. Immediately after the briefers attend a briefing, they revise and get approval from their bosses for their own local brief.

SAMPLE TEAM BRIEFINGS

Sample 1:

Team Briefing – Core Management Brief	Lakshmi Textiles Company
Originator: Deepak Gupta (MD)	Date: 4th December 2004
Standing Instructions to Team Briefer	
	This is the core brief of the MD concerning corporate goals and objectives which the Heads of Departments can expand on. Please express these points in whichever way you feel best to help your staff understand. Make notes, action points, target dates. Please raise queries and get feedback.
Core Brief – important points below:	Briefer's notes (supplement with your own points below to use in your local brief):
Results – A large contract for the export of garments has been received from the USA worth $10 million. Target date of execution: March 2005. Sales to date are up 20%. Profits are up 30% for corresponding period. This is very good news. Costs are lower than the budget. Results are better than targets and are expected to improve as a consequence of the US order.	In-house capacities not adequate to execute the order. Outsourcing activities to commence.
Organization – The multi-fiber agreement removes quota controls from April 2005. To exploit the business potential, the marketing department needs strengthening.	The current marketing team cannot focus on all territories. Territory-based marketing executives to be appointed. Logistics department to be strengthened for timely order executions.
Policy — All departments to prepare balanced score card performance appraisal system to evaluate employee job performance. Mobile phones with cameras brought in by staff/visitors could pose security problems. Employees should be discouraged to use them. Visitors' car-park spaces should be kept for visitors' use only.	Evaluation should determine training needs and appropriate job allocation based on competencies. Make arrangements with security to store mobile phones submitted by employees/ visitors. Staff on night shift can use visitors and directors' parking slots, as the ongoing drain repair work prevents access to the main car park.
Team Briefing – Core Management Brief	**Lakshmi Textiles company**

People Ajay Srinivasan is joining the company as CIO. Sanjar Mathur has resigned and his assistant Rakesh Dua assumes his responsibility. Jayashree Mani joins the HR department as Head Trainer.	The company is going to implement an ERP system; hence, there is a need to appoint a Chief Information Officer. Jayashree Mani will require a secretary. Hopefully, someone from the company will be recruited. Applicants should have some prior experience in HR.

Sample 2: A typical team briefing

Team Briefing – Local Brief Originator – Dilip Rao of logistics department	Date and Time: 5th December 2004, 3 pm
Attendees and Absentees:	
Local Brief – Main points below:	**Briefer's notes with examples and answers to possible questions:**
Progress A new packing machine installed which will double the packing capacity of the department. Productivity should improve to keep pace with the demand.	Trained machine operators should ramp up productivity in the new machine to optimum capacity. Winners of cost reduction projects and productivity projects will be sent on an overseas training programme-cum-holiday.
Policy Mobile phones with cameras not to be allowed into the factory for both employees and visitors.	Mobile phones with cameras to be deposited at the security gate by visitors.
People Rajesh Pilot joins the logistics cell as Efficiency Manager.	He will set up teams to be trained, identify areas of idle time and non-productive activities, and thus increase productivity.
Points of Action To develop low weight, compact and strong cartons. Objective: Reduce freight and insurance costs. Please give suggestions for the venue of the annual staff picnic.	Identify cross-functional team to work on the project. Maybe a day trip to one of the local resorts? Check on transport options.

BENEFITS OF TEAM BRIEFING

The benefits of team briefing are many. A few of them are mentioned below:

1. Communication process is strengthened. After attending a briefing, people understand what is happening and how one's contribution is important. The whole organization will be positively charged and united behind a shared vision. Thus, it improves the communication process.

2. It can act as an important tool in facilitating lateral communication among various departments of an organization.

3. It improves interpersonal relations.

4. It provides a consistent and measurable process for conveying strategic and operational information and answering feedback questions throughout an organization.

5. Team leaders in charge of implementing a given task find it most convenient to communicate with their members, as they can brief each and every member individually.

6. It is used increasingly in pre-placement talk. This is given in the form of team briefing. Company representatives brief the young aspirants in the campus about various aspects of functioning of a company and answer the queries of the job aspirants. Thus, it lays a foundation for development of employee's involvement at work.

7. It provides junior executives an opportunity to act as leaders. Briefings by them to their juniors infuses in the former a sense of responsibility.

PRE-REQUISITES FOR SUCCESSFUL BRIEFING

There are a few pre-requisites which have to be followed for a team briefing to be successful. They are as follows:

1. Briefer has to be committed to the idea or subject of briefing and should be prepared to be involved in its implementation.

2. Briefer should have a clarity of purpose. Only when the team leader is clear about the purpose of the brief, he can accordingly decide the contents of briefing. For example, a team leader wants to brief about internet-based training, he has to collect information about what it is, how to use it and where it can be used.

3. Briefing is effective when the size of the audience is small.

4. Briefing has to be given to a selective audience. For example, briefing in a campus interview is given only for those who have applied for the job and not for all students. Similarly, when briefing is given about a newly developed product, only the audience who can critically review and give suggestions for its betterment need to be invited.

5. Briefer has to do homework like deciding the content, collecting necessary information about the content, deciding the structure and format of the briefing, audio visuals to be used, etc., for making the briefing effective.

6. Briefing has to be used for informing the listener of the facts and not the conclusion or recommendations. It can be used for presenting high priority information requiring immediate attention. For example, complex information involving complicated plans, system and statistics; controversial information requiring immediate attention.

FORMAT OF TEAM BRIEFING

Team briefing has to be prepared in a particular format which is given below:

Introduction

Greeting	: Address the people receiving the briefing
Purpose	: Briefer has to state the purpose of the briefing
Procedure	: Explain the procedure involved
Co-ordination	: Indicate the coordination achieved in this regard
Classification	: State the classification of the briefing

Body

Assumptions	: These must be valid, relevant and necessary
Facts bearing on the problem	: These must be supportable, relevant and necessary.
Discussion	: Analyze the course of action
Conclusion	: Degree of acceptance or the order of merit of each course of action
Recommendation	: State the actions recommended

Close

Ask for questions.

Request a decision.

Follow-up

Inform the outcome of the briefing to the secretary of officers who did not attend the briefing.

SUMMARY

Features of team briefing are face-to-face meeting, lasting for 30 minutes, given my a team leader and held at periodical intervals.

Process of team briefing: proceedings are recorded, deciding the core brief and coverage of subjects in the core brief, interpretation of core brief and flow of the briefing.

Benefits of team briefing include strengthening communication process, facilitating lateral communication, improving inter-personal relations, medium to convey strategic information and convenience of communication, being used increasingly in pre-placement briefing, infusing confidence in prospects and providing opportunity to junior executives to act as leaders.

Pre-requisites for successful briefing are briefer's commitment to the idea; clarity of purpose; effective only when the size of audience is small; Briefing to be given to a selective audience; homework by briefer essential for successful briefing; Briefing should present only facts.

Format of briefing includes introduction, body, close and follow-up.

REVIEW QUESTIONS

Part A: Short Questions

1. What is team briefing?

Part B: Paragraph Questions

1. Highlight the features of team briefing.
2. State the process of team briefing.
3. What are the benefits of team briefing?
4. Point out the pre-requisites of team briefing.
5. Give the format of team briefing.

Part C: Objective Type Questions

Choose the Correct Answer

1. Team briefing is

   a. Face to face meeting   b. Review meeting   c. Brain storming meeting

   (Ans: a)

2. Team briefing is led by

   a. Director   b. Company secretary   c. Depends on the person who leads the team

   (Ans: c)

3. Team briefing is

   a. Horizontal communication   b. Vertical communication   c. Lateral communication

   (Ans: b)

Fill in the Blanks

1. Short talk that informs enlightened audience on a topic is ________. (Team briefing)
2. In recruitment, the persons giving the profile of company to job aspirants is an example of _______. (Team briefing)
3. Providing career advice to promotion aspirants comes under ________. (Team briefing)

PART 6

SPOKEN COMMUNICATION

26

CHAPTER

ESSENTIAL CONVERSATIONAL ABILITY

INTRODUCTION

Visualise a scenario wherein you convey to your friend, the news of your selection in U.P.S.C exam as an I.A.S officer. If your friend does not reciprocate your excitement, your spirits would be dampened, as you expect him to congratulate you on your strenuous and sustained efforts to win such a coveted post. On the other hand, if the other person prolongs the conversation allowing you to express your efforts that has gone into this achievement, you would be delighted.

All of us have the power of transmitting our thoughts in one way or the other. What discriminates a simple talking from a conversation is the way the thought is transmitted, not in isolation but in the company of others. Mere talking is not a conversation. A person may talk for hours together, yet he may not have conveyed anything worthwhile. A conversation is a mental occupation and not a simple dribbing into words of casual thought.

Talks of lawyer, teachers, public speakers, actors, debaters, etc., cannot be taken as conversation *per se.* A person who keeps the audience spellbound cannot be termed as a conversationist. Therefore, it is clear that a good conversationalist is neither a person who monopolises the conversation nor the one who keeps silent all the while. The conversation is a glow that warms without scalding. Thus the conversation is a two way communication process wherein the speaker and the listener interchange the role several times during the conversation. Both the parties i.e. the speaker and the listener should take part in the talk. The conversation facilitates winning new contacts and sustaining existing ones. One may be intellectually sound. Yet, in the absence of conversational ability, he may not share his ideas with others. A person who has conversational ability has an edge over others who lack this skill.

TYPES OF CONVERSATIONS

Following are the types of conversations:

Chat: It is the least formal type of conversation. For example, a mother sharing her school experience with her son.

Tête-á-Tête: It means head-to-head. For example, The conversation in an interview or an employee sharing his grievance with the grievance officer.

Dialogue: A two-way conversation that involves opposing points of view is a dialogue. For example, the discussion between two rival leaders on a particular matter.

Parley: It refers to a formal discussion between people. For example, the discussion between representatives of two countries.

Colloquy: It is the most formal conversation.

Communion: It is a form of conversation taking place at such a profound level that no words are necessary. For example, communication with nature.

STRATEGIES FOR EFFECTIVE CONVERSATION

The strategies discussed below enable conversation to take a new shape:

Involve Everyone

Every member in the group should have a sense of participation and feel that they have contributed their bit. Everyone should have a chance to speak. A good conservation is one which involves everyone in the conversation.

Arousing and Sustaining Interest

Conversations become successful only when all the participants evince interest in the talk and show respect and interest in the others present in the group. To make the conversation interesting, every member should exchange questions, views, expressions, statements and information.

Listening Keenly

Listening actively means receiving the meaning and paraphrasing the sender's message so as to comprehend it. Therefore, listening is as tiring as speaking. Only when we listen to others, we will be able to react, respond and regale them. Thus, active listening is an essential ingredient of an effective conversation.

Idea Development

To be a good conservationist, we have to equip ourselves with facts, figures, anecdotes, own experiences, incidents shared by others, stories, recent advances sourced from newspapers, journals, magazines, speeches, websites, television, radios, etc. If a member is able to cite from various sources, he can easily win the attention of others. It may impel others to accept or challenge the views expressed. Many new ideas may emanate from a serious debate.

Paraphrasing the Message

It means that the listener restates the sender's message in different words so as to make the sender confirm that the listener has understood the message. For example,

Original message

> I am sure that the children would go and play somewhere else. I get along very well with them. They are very nice kids. I used to give cookies in the afternoon. Today, I do not have strength to go outside and tell them. They do not know that I am ill.

Paraphrased message

> It sounds like you are very much fond of children. Because you are ill, you wish they would go somewhere else. You are too weak to tell the children this message.

Benefits of paraphrasing

1. Paraphrasing encourages your partner to continue.
2. It prevents your partner from repeating the same statement.
3. Encourages your partner to explore and clarify. The tone of your voice will also convey to your partner whether you want them to continue to explore further or to move on to a different point of discussion.

Reflecting Feelings and Emotions

It means giving feedback to the feelings of the partner. Reflection of feelings provides an opportunity to show your empathy with the partner. Reflecting the underlying feelings in a conversation turns out to be effective not only in negative emotions but also in positive emotions. For example,

Paraphrased message

> Since you are sick, noise made by kids is bothering you. But you do not sound angry.

When your partner shows excitement about his achievement, you need to reflect his underlying feeling of excitement and enthusiasm. Given below are some statement that mirror the inner feelings of your partner:

- Fantastic! How do you get such ideas?
- What a memory!
- You learn fast.
- Had it happened to me, I would have been upset.
- I guess that must make you anxious.

Reflecting Implications

To make your conversation lively and interesting, you need to go beyond manifesting what your partner expresses. You need to bring out the implied message of your partner. In other words, you need to read between the lines to understand and complete the message. For example,

Original message

I am sure that children would go and play elsewhere. I get along with them very well. You know, they are very nice kids. I used to provide cookies in the afternoon. I have no strength to go outside and tell them. They do not know I am sick.

Your response reflecting the implication

That means, if the kids know that you are sick, they would avoid playing here.

Given below are some of the expressions that reflect implications of your partner's original message.

- It would then lead to a situation...
- Would it not help solve the problem if...
- I suppose if you did that, you would be in a position to...

Inviting Further Contribution

When a person has not understood enough to follow with the indications of understanding, empathy and acceptance, he can communicate his interest in hearing more about what is being said by the partner. This motivates the partner to contribute more so that you can understand better. For example,

Original message

I am sure that children would go and play somewhere else. I get along with them very well. You know, they are very nice kids. I used to provide cookies in the afternoon. I have no strength to go outside and tell them. They do not know I am sick.

Message inviting further contribution

- How do you feel about asking the kids to play elsewhere?
- Could you tell me a bit more about your sickness?
- How did you feel when you learnt of your promotion?
- What happened then?

Exhibition of Appropriate Non-Verbal Signals

Non-verbal signals like eye contact, body posture, nodding the head, etc., reveal interest and understanding. *How* you say something is more important than *what* you say.

When the partner expects emotional reaction from you, his tone of the voice changes accordingly. Non-verbal behaviour reinforces the words spoken and implies the intended message. For example, by making eye contact and facing the person with whom you are conversing with, the intent of your spoken message can be confirmed and enhanced by your corresponding body language. Thus, appropriate body language not only helps your partner in delivering effectively but also the listener in interpreting the message effectively. For example, an affirmative nod can validate your feeling and show that you have heard and understood your partner's opinion. Similarly, a purposeful blink may also serve the purpose. Leaning the body towards your partner tells him that you are interested in listening.

Using Voice Effectively

A person needs to use his voice to convey his emotions. If he is gruff, he is miffed. If he talks too softly, he is shy. It he is loud, he is confident or an extrovert. Talk softly when what you are saying is less important. Inflections and volume convey a meaning. Thus, voice is an effective tool to reflect implications and underlying feelings during a conversation. Equal attention should also be paid to pronunciation, articulation, pitch, rate and volume of your voice. A person needs to provide a pause at the appropriate place to drive the right meaning of his utterances.

TELEPHONE CONVERSATIONS

Telephone conversations play an important role in an organizational setup. It has to be professional and polite. There has to be a consistent standard of handling calls to make a good impression on the callers.

Telephone Etiquette for Secretaries and Receptionists

Presenting a professional image, both in person and on the telephone, is very important in the office skills profession. Taking care of your customers over the telephone and making them feel well informed and appreciated is essential. Whether you are a front office receptionist or an executive secretary, the following phone tips should always be followed:

1. Speak clearly. The caller on the other end of the phone can only hear you. They cannot see your face or body language. Therefore, taking the time to speak clearly, slowly and in a cheerful, professional voice is very important.
2. Use your normal tone of voice when answering a call. If you have a tendency to speak loudly or shout, avoid doing so over the telephone.
3. Do not eat or drink while you are working. Eat or drink only during your coffee break or lunch break.
4. Do not use slang words or poor language. Respond clearly with *yes* or *no* while speaking. Never use swear words.
5. Address the caller properly by his or her title (Good morning Mr. Brown, Good afternoon Ms. Sanders). Never address an unfamiliar caller by his or her first name.
6. Listen to what the caller has to say. The ability to listen is a problem in general, but it is very important to listen. It is always a good habit to repeat the information to the client when you are taking a message. Verify that you have heard and transcribed the message accurately.
7. Be patient and helpful. If a caller is irate or upset, listen to what they have to say and then refer them to the appropriate resource. Never snap back or act rude to the caller.
8. Always ask if you can put the caller on hold. If you are responsible for answering multiple calls at once, always ask the caller politely if you may put them on hold. Remember that

the caller could have already waited several minutes before getting connected to you and may not take it lightly to being put on hold again. Never leave the person on hold for more than a few seconds as they may become upset and hang up.

9. Always focus on the call. Try not to get distracted by people around you. If someone tries to interrupt you while you are on a call, politely remind them that you are on a customer call and that you will be with them as soon as you are finished.

Telephone Etiquette While Making Calls

Always identify yourself properly: While speaking to a client or customer or while leaving a message, always identify yourself properly by providing your name, company name and contact telephone number. For example, 'Good afternoon Mr. Joseph. This is Ms. Mary from Officeskills.org. My telephone number is 2486 5670.' Always be aware of confidential information while leaving a message. Also, be aware of people around you while talking on the phone. Be discreet. Someone next to you might overhear confidential information that could negatively affect your business.

Avoid long messages: Avoid leaving long messages. Remember that someone has to listen to your message. Your message may be just one of many messages that need to be handled. It is a good habit to write down or type out the message in advance. Keep it brief and to the point.

Avoid being loud: The person at the other end of the phone cannot see the facial expressions or gestures, and the impression he receives depends on what he hears. The telephone carries your voice at its natural volume and pitch. Try not to shout but speak clearly and distinctly.

Telephone Etiquette While Answering the Phone

- The correct way to answer a telephone is by saying '*hello.*' '*Yes*' is abrupt and a bit harsh. '*This is the Aruvi's house*', '*Mrs. Aruvi speaking*' are vague.
- When the telephone is answered by someone other than the head of the house and the caller asks for them, he or she should say, '*just a moment, please.*' If that person is unable to come to the phone, the correct reply would be: '*Mrs. Radha is unable to attend the phone now. May I have your name and number and she will call you back as soon as possible*?'
- If you must put the telephone down during the conversation or when you hang up, do it gently. Do not slam down the receiver. The person on the other end may still have the phone close to his ear and a sudden sharp bang can be hurtful as well as rude.

Common Telephone Courtesy

- Make sure that the number is correct so that strangers are not disturbed.
- Make sure that your conversations with busy people are as brief as possible.
- When calling friends who do not recognize your voice, announce yourself right away.
- Time your calls so as not to interfere with the receiver's work schedule.

- Make business calls well before the close of office hours.
- If you dial a wrong number by mistake, simply say, '*Sorry, wrong number.*'
- When the call is not answered quickly, wait long enough for the receiver to put aside what they are doing to answer the call. It is very annoying to find that the caller has hung up just as you answer it.

Tips for Effective Telephone Conversation

Choose an appropriate time: Put off making business calls when you're too distracted or tired. You will not make a great first impression if you are prepared. You need to be full of positive energy, otherwise your voice will sound dull with no power to persuade or move the listener into action. Smile when you talk to people on the phone; it will show in your voice. Remember that enthusiasm is infectious. Let your voice be natural, calm, relaxed and easy-going.

Try not to keep the other person on hold for a long time. If possible avoid it altogether. If you are making the call, you should have all the information readily available. If you can't help him right away, tell him that you'll call back and remember to do so.

Call opening: Begin the call with a standard professional greeting, depending on the time of the day. Eliminate any disturbing background noise, if possible. Mention your first name, organization and purpose of the call clearly and be as direct as possible. Don't beat around the bush; it can be very irritating. It's a good idea to rehearse saying the person's name several times before the phone call. This will help with any pronunciation problems and also personalize the call. Remember to get his/her title right.

Ask if this is a good time for you to be calling. If not, ask when you can reach them again. Do not keep repeating their name during the conversation, but stick to the rule of saying the listener's name three times during an 8 to 10 minute conversation. Leave brief, clear messages on answering systems, giving your name, reason for the call and contact information. Don't forget to leave your phone number, even if the person has it, so that he doesn't have to look it up.

Display genuine interest: Allow the other party plenty of time to speak, and use prompt words such as '*I see*' and '*really*' in a sincere tone. This shows them that you are truly interested in what they have to say. Avoid acting rushed, even if you are. If you're so stressed that you can't handle the call well, let the voice mail pick it up until you collect yourself.

Response options: If the person you have called needs to get back to you with information, give him a variety of options like e-mail, fax, voicemail, etc. The objective is to make it easy for them to get back to you.

Follow-up: Make sure you call back whenever you promise you would. But don't be persistent to the point of sounding desperate. Timely follow-ups will show that you are sincere and committed to the task. Learning good telephone etiquette is extremely important and those who master it stand a better chance of succeeding.

SUMMARY

Conversation types are chat, têtê-á-têtê, dialogue, parley, colloquy, communion.

Strategies for effective conversation includes involving everyone, arousing and sustaining interest, listening keenly, idea development, paraphrasing the message, reflecting feelings and emotions, reflecting implications, inviting further contribution, exhibition of non-verbal communication, using voice effectively.

Telephone etiquette while making calls includes identifying oneself and avoiding long messages. Care should be taken while answering a caller and placing the receiver.

Tips for telephone conversation includes choice of time, opening the call, displaying genuine interest, response options and follow-up.

Telephone manner for a secretary includes speaking clearly, using normal tone, not drinking while attending the phone, not using slangs, listening to the caller patiently, not putting the call on hold for a long time and focusing on the call.

REVIEW QUESTIONS

Part A: Short Questions

1. What is a conversation?
2. What is a dialogue?
3. What is a parley?
4. What is a colloquy?
5. What is a communion?
6. What is a chat?

Part B: Paragraph Questions

1. What etiquette you would observe while making a telephone call?
2. State the telephone etiquette for answering a phone call.
3. List the common telephone courtesy.
4. What are the different types of conversations?

Part C: Essay Questions

1. How would you conduct an effective telephone conversation?
2. What are the telephone manners observed by a secretary?
3. Suggest strategies for an effective conversation.

Part D: Objective Type Questions

Choose the Correct Answer

1. Formal discussion between people

   a. Parley　　b. Conversation　　c. Communication

   (Ans: a)

2. Least formal type of conversation

   a. Communion　　b. Tete-a-tete　　c. Chat

   (Ans: c)

3. Communication with nature in

   a. Conversation　　b. Parley　　c. Communication

   (Ans: c)

4. Discussion between two rival parties is

   a. Dialogue　　b. Parley　　c. Communication

   (Ans: a)

Fill in the blanks

1. Casually conversing with others is ________. (Chat)
2. Very formal conversation in an interview is __________. (Têtê-á-têtê)
3. Discussion between the representatives of two different countries is __________ (Parley)
4. Deep conversation with something unknowable is __________.(Communion)
5. Restating the speaker's words as understood by the listener is __________. (Paraphrasing)

27

CHAPTER

PUBLIC SPEAKING

INTRODUCTION

While some people find it easier to address even a large gathering, there are many who are scared in front of an audience. The difference in the two categories of people lies not in the knowledge but in their attitude.

Giving a presentation to a large gathering on a light content is easier than to a small gathering of educated, elite and erudite scholars at a conference, seminar or business meet. Speaking before an audience is a privilege for a speaker to express his point of view. It is a person's fear and nervousness that is holding back him from giving a speech. Therefore, speaking is an art. If right training is provided, one can become a good speaker.

OCCASIONS WARRANTING A PRESENTATION IN BUSINESS

Presentation of annual reports, launching a new product, inaugurating a training session, presenting a new business proposition, uncovering a marketing plan, presenting one's views and experiences on a conference attended, business diversification, equipment or machinery demonstration, presentation before an interviewer for appointment and promotion are some of the occasions necessitating a speech.

COMPONENTS OF A PRESENTATION

The components of a presentation are as follows:

- **Presenter:** Person who is going to deliver the speech or presentation.
- **Audience:** The people for whom the presentation is meant. The audience may belong to the same age group, profession or different sections.
- **Content:** The theme of the talk is formulated and it is delivered as the speech or presentation.

STEPS FOR A SUCCESSFUL PRESENTATION

The following should be kept in mind while preparing for a presentation:

Considering the Occasion

The presenter or speaker has to be clear about what he intends to achieve through his presentation. He should not stray away from the focal point. The more he centres around the thrust area, the greater the chances of success.

Audience Analysis

The speaker has to understand the target audience well in advance of his speech. The age, sex, nationality, educational status and experience of the audience have a great relevance to the presentation. The taste and presence of different groups vary. For example, children like stories, teenagers love to hear new ideas, middle-aged people are conservative who may not like new ideas and senior citizens may like to be reminded of the good old days. Therefore, the speech has to be tailored to meet the varying needs of the audience.

Familiarising Oneself with the Environment

The speaker, before giving a speech, has to visit the venue to know the size of the room, seating accommodation, speaker's position, podium, mike, lighting, ventilation, position of visual equipment, etc.

Mode of Presentation

There are three different ways of presentation, namely reading, memorized presentation and extemporaneous presentation. The speaker has to decide the mode of presentation depending on the profile of the audience. Further, he has to decide where the visuals need to be shown, emphasis need to be given, gist of points to be covered in an extempore speech, etc.

Preparation of Scripts

The speaker or the presenter has to decide the length of the script. Style of presentation and humour, if possible, would make the speech more enjoyable. The format of a script may be made as follows:

Opening

1. Introductory remarks
2. Statement of objectives
3. Cultivating a rapport with the audience
4. Giving an outline of the presentation

Middle

1. Main body of the presentation
2. Examples and visual aids
3. Explanation of key points in order of importance

Closing

1. Giving the message of the whole presentation
2. Summary of presentation
3. Inviting queries
4. Answering the questions raised
5. Thanking the audience

Some presenters observe processes.

Table 27.1 Breakup of a Presentation

SI. No	Stages	Purpose
1.	Ice-breaking	Warming up the audience
2.	Introduction	Topic introduction
3.	Need for new idea	Soliciting willingness and co-operation
4.	Main idea	Thrust area
5.	Discussion of results	Importance and significance of the idea
6.	Summary and conclusion	Improving recall measures

Mere lecture would bore the audience. Hence, it is better to use visuals to achieve better results.

Preparation of Visuals

The speaker has to ready the visuals in advance for a presentation. The visuals may include transparent sheets, charts, diagrams, maps, pictures, slides, etc. The following guidelines aid the effective presentation of visuals:

- All the slides should be numbered and kept in order.
- No overwriting or spelling mistakes should be present on the slides.
- Materials should be spaced properly and written in capital or block letters.
- Speaker has to explain the visual and not read from it.
- Speaker with the help of a pointer light should bring the attention of the audience to the place where emphasis has to be laid.
- Speaker should look at the audience.
- Slides should be kept to a minimum.
- Speaker can use picture, colours, drawings for invoking interest.
- Only the essence of the speech should be on the slides. The entire speech material should not be given in slides.

Preparation of Handouts

Handouts should be handed over to the participants prior to the commencement of the session. This would enable the audience to pose pointed questions at the end of the speech.

Feedback Forms

The speaker has to prepare feedback forms which are handed to the participants at the end of the presentation. This would shed light on the strength and weakness of the presentation. The points like information about the audience, level of acceptance of the speaker, scope for improvements, inadequacies, expectations from the participants, expectations met, benefits derived from the session, suggestions, etc., should be included in the feedback form.

Rehearsal of the Presentation

Rehearsal improves the quality of presentation. The more a person rehearses, the better the performance is. It helps in eliminating fear and builds up confidence. Management of the available time, exposing the weakness in the presentation, unnecessary body movements, absence of eye -contact, too much focus on slides, omission of vital points, unnecessary explanation of trival points, problems in recalling the core points—all these negativities can be addressed through rehearsal.

Personal Aspects of the Presenter

The speaker has to choose an outfit appropriate for the occasion. Formal clothes, proper hairstyle, confident voice, right posture, eye-contact, meaningful gestures, makeup, good body language are some of the important aspects the presenter has to pay attention. Some of the negative repercussions which mar the speech are nervous pacing, shabby dress, abrupt movements, covering the mouth while speaking, lack of eye-contact, fidgeting, etc., which distract the attention of the audience.

Overcoming Nervousness

Even experienced speakers experience initial nervousness, butterflies in the stomach, palpitations, shaking legs and forgetfulness. The following tips help overcome nervousness:

- Taking few deep breaths
- Proper rehearsal
- Giving pauses in between for relaxation
- Moving amongst audience
- Using visual aids
- Taking sips of water

Making Effective Presentation

The following points have to be practised to make an effective presentation:

- The speaker has to face the audience, carefully introduce the subject and cautiously conclude it.
- The speaker has to use a variety of strategies to strike a chord with the audience.

- Use ice-breakers like music and games which would help the participants do away with the initial hesitation.
- Use anecdotes to pep up the talk.
- Share personal experience.
- Use proverbs, quotations and sayings wherever necessary.
- Give statistical support to emphasize the point.
- Pose questions to get the participation of the audience.
- The speaker should be time-conscious as to when to start, pause, continue and end the session.
- Before concluding, it is better to summarize the talk.
- End with a positive note.

SUMMARY

A presentation is a live mode of sharing information with a select audience. It is a form of oral communication, in which a person shares factual information with a particular audience.

There may be **several occasions for a presentation** in a business such as annual presentation of reports, launching a new product or service or starting a training course/ session.

Presentations have three major elements — speaker, audience and specific content — depending on the objective of the presentation.

The steps for a successful presentation are considering the occasion and objective, making audience analysis, knowing about the location and getting acquainted with the venue, organizers, etc., deciding on the mode and manner of presentation, whether it is to be memorized, read out or extemporaneous, preparing the script, preparing visual aids like charts, transparencies, etc., handouts and feedback forms to assess, rehearsing the presentation to bring perfection and instill confidence, considering personal aspects like taking care of appearance, body language, overcoming nervousness and to be fearless and effective, and making a effective presentation by sharing ideas, information and knowledge.

REVIEW QUESTIONS

Part A: Short Questions

1. What is a presentation?
2. State the elements of a presentation.
3. What is an audience analysis?
4. State the modes of a presentation.

Part B: Paragraph Questions

1. Point out the occasions for a presentation.
2. Write the format of a presentation.

3. How would you make your visuals effective in your presentation?
4. Stress the importance of rehearsal in a presentation.
5. How would you overcome nervousness during a presentation?

Part C: Essay Questions

1. Explain the process of a presentation or different stages involved in a speech.

Part D: Objective Type Questions

Choose the Correct Answer

1. Which one of the following is to be presented before the commencement of a session?

   a. Feedback b. Handout c. Tips

   (Ans: b)

2. Which is given after a presentation?

   a. Handout b. Feedback c. Summary of the task

   (Ans: b)

3. Which is not an element of presentation

   a. Presenter b. Content c. Physical environment

   (Ans: c)

4. Which form enables the speaker to assess his strength and weakness of the presentation

   a. Handout b. Brochure c. Feedback

   (Ans: c)

5. Which one of the following introduces the topic and quintessence of one's speech

   a. Booklet b. Handout c. Feedback form

   (Ans: b)

Fill in the Blanks

1. Breaking the silence of the audience is ________. (Ice breaking)
2. What are the three modes of presentation ________, ________ and ________. (Reading, memorized presentation, extempore presentation)
3. Practising the presentation is ________. (Rehearsal)
4. ________, ________ and ________ are the components of a presentation. (Presenter, audience, content)

PART 7

TECHNOLOGY-AIDED BUSINESS COMMUNICATION

28

CHAPTER

INTERNET / E-MAIL / WEB-BASED COMMUNICATION

INTRODUCTION TO ELECTRONIC MAIL (E-MAIL)

The Contemporary executives employ a variety of channels in their workplace to communicate with insiders and outsiders. E-mail is one of the channels in this digital age. While snail mail sent through post or courier takes days to reach the address, e-mail reaches the addressee in no time. It is cheaper to send messages through e-mail. A letter or document sent through post passes through different locations, but e-mail passes from one computer to another as it travels along the network. In this process, each computer reads the e-mail address and routes it to another computer until it reaches the mail box of the addressee. One can send e-mail on the internet to anyone with an e-mail address with the advent of Multipurpose Internet Mail Extension (MIME). One can send not only messages but also graphics and documents electronically. According to Radicati (www.radicati.com) group study, there are about 1.3 billion e-mail users worldwide.

E-MAIL – NAME AND ADDRESS

E-mail allows information to be sent between computers and people on the internet. It can be sent to different recipients. E-mail address identifies the person and the computer for the purpose of exchanging electronic message. The basic structure of an e-mail address is:

Username@host.subdomain.second-level-domain.first level domain

For example, *kumararaj@gmail.com*

'kumararaj' is the name of the person receiving or giving the message; this is username.

'gmail' is part of the domain name of the organization.

'com' is part of the domain name and indicates that gmail is a commercial organization.

MECHANICS OF AN E-MAIL

To compose an e-mail message, one has to click the 'compose new message' button on the tool bar. You will get an empty mail form which will accommodate the following:

To – enter the e-mail address of the addressee.

Cc – persons to whom the copies need to be sent are entered.

Subject – give a brief description of what the message is about.

Body – type the actual message.

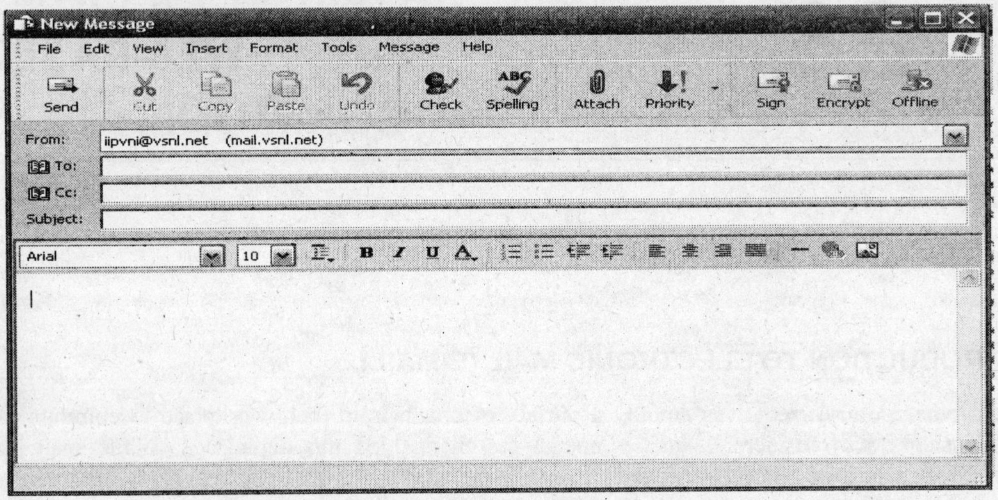

Address Book

It is a place where a person stores information about the people with whom he corresponds. The main benefit of an address book is that you need not type the e-mail address of a person each and every time you send a message. You can just select the person's name, and the e-mail address automatically gets inserted.

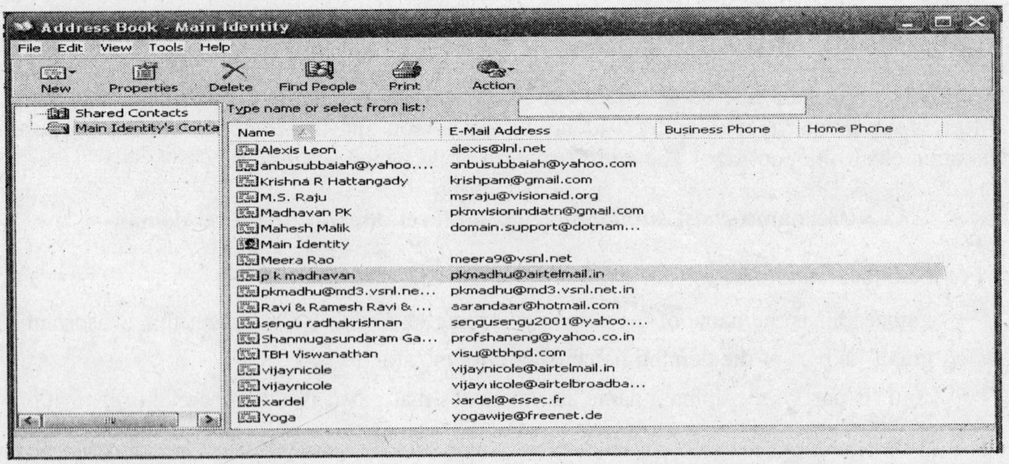

Adding a New Address

You can add a new address and create groups so that you can send mails to all the members of the group. Instead of selecting each person's e-mail ID, the sender can just select the group. If you want to add an e-mail ID of a person, press the small icon by the side of 'To' or 'CC' columns. Address book will pop up from which you can select the names and it will appear in the respective columns.

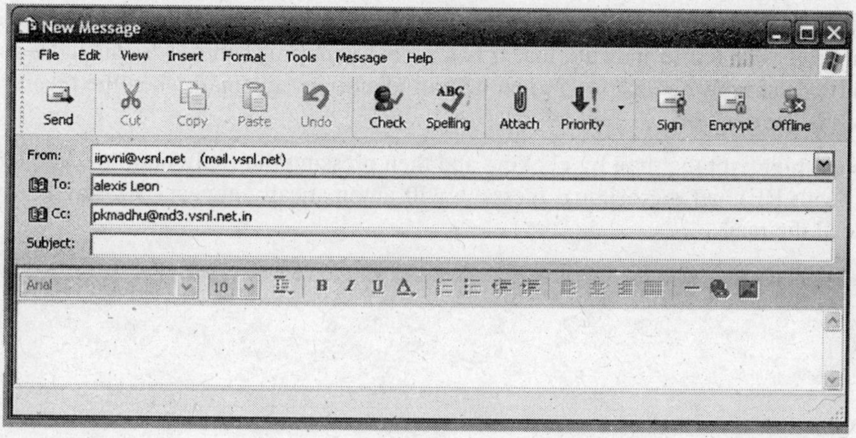

File Attachment

One major downside of e-mail is that we cannot send a formatted text. If you send a word document containing pictures, bulleted lists, etc., all the formattings will be lost. This problem is addressed by *attachment*. You can attach any file to a mail. It is advisable to compress the file you are attaching, using options like *pkzip* which will reduce the file size and save time and money during the transmission.

- Press the icon with the picture of a clip. A dial box appears asking you to specify the name and location of your file for attachment. Once this input is given, the file will be attached to the mail.
- A mail with an attachment will have a paper clip icon, indicating that the mail has been attached with a file.

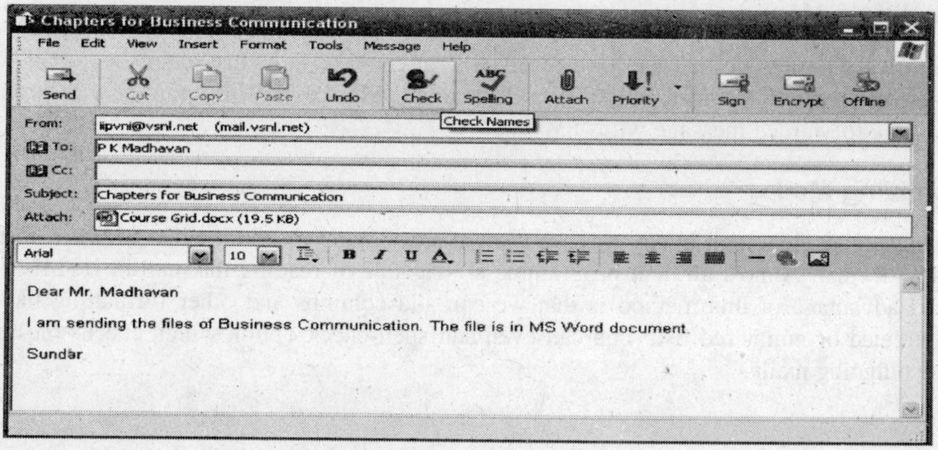

Signature

We tend to get tired of typing in our name and address at the end of the every message we send. We can opt for the signature option. By configuring the system suitably and pressing the signature icon with the picture of a pen, our signature will be appended to the message.

Replying E-mail Message

While replying to a mail, we need not type the e-mail address of the sender again. It is enough to prefix the subject with RE to indicate that it is a reply. This programme also includes the original mail as a part of the reply, which is of great help in identifying the mail when the receiver receives hundreds of mails every day.

We should highlight the mail by clicking and then pressing the reply button. The 'To' address, the subject (with RE) and the original message will automatically appear. We have to type in the reply and send the mail.

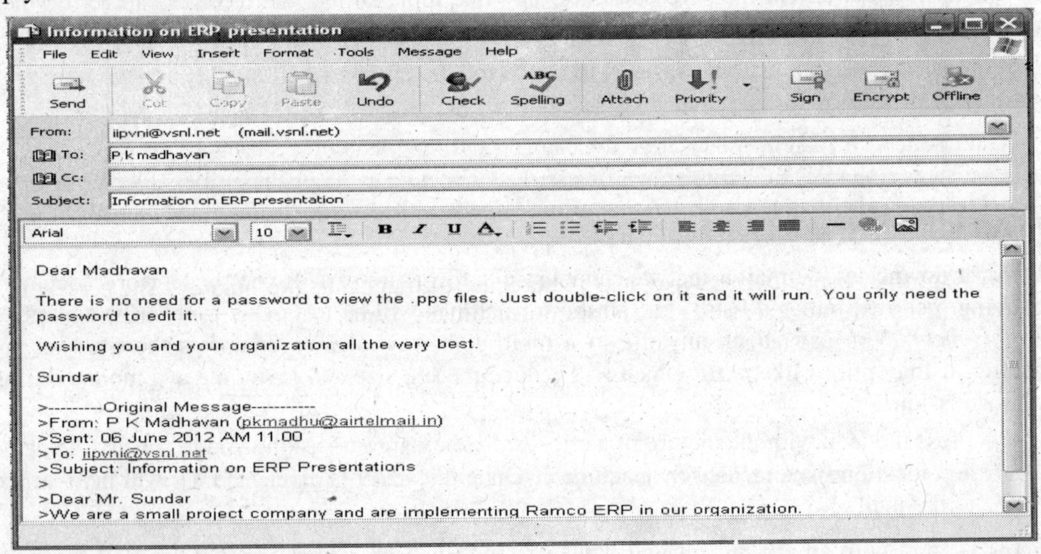

Forwarding a Message

We can forward a message that we have received to anyone we like. Just enter the e-mail address of the person to whom the message is to be forwarded. Most e-mail programme will profile the subject of the forwarded message with 'FW'.

Customizing Mail

We can customize the e-mail in any way we want to send. We can send it either in '*Text*' format or in '*HTML*' format. Almost all mail programme are capable of reading the mail in HTML format. The chief advantage of this method is that we can add columns and other formatting like bold, italics, bulleted or numbered list. You can even add spell-check option which checks the spelling of all the outgoing mails.

Spam

To have an e-mail account is sometimes frustrating as our mail boxes are filled with unwanted advertisements, forwarded messages, product details, business offers, Separating the messages we really want from the unwanted ones is a daunting task. But we can prevent these unwanted mails by having special filters designed to block the spam. Microsoft 2007 has a junk e-mail folder to which the suspected e-mails are moved. If the e-mail client does not have a spam filter, we can use products like CA anti-spam, spam eater, spam fighter, spam buster and entice mail. Another option to prevent junk mail is by giving message to our ISP or online service and telling them that we are receiving unwanted mails and requesting them to provide the originating address.

CHARACTERISTICS OF AN E-MAIL MESSAGE

E-mail messages share certain characteristics:

Topic: A good e-mail message discusses only one topic so that the receiver can act on the subject and file it appropriately.

Tone: The tone of e-mail messages is expected to be conversational as the communicators are usually familiar with one another.

Conciseness: E-mail messages need to be concise as they require less background explanation. One should be alert to eliminate wordiness. It is better to avoid opening fillers like '*there is*', '*It is*', etc., and long leads like '*I am writing this memo to inform you that*' and wordy phrases like '*because of the fact that*'.

Highlighting: E-mail writers may make liberal use of highlighting techniques. The content of many printed memos is enhanced by numbered or bulleted items, headings, tables, paragraphing, asterisk points, side-headings, etc.

Writing the message: The following points aid the e-mail writer in composing the message.

i. Logical arrangement of messages, in terms of paragraphs bullets etc.

ii. Enhance readability using short sentences, short paragraphs, tables, graphs etc.,

iii. Avoid technical jargons

Necessity: E-mail writer has to decide whether the e-mail message is necessary or not. If he is able to achieve the purpose by a phone call or visiting his co-worker, he can save time and the expense the of a written message.

Clarity of the message: We have to know what we are going to write, so we should be clear of what we intend to achieve.

Assessing the impact on the reader: Visualize the readers and the effect the message will create.

Outline of points to be covered: Make an outline of points you intend to cover. You can jot down notes on the documents you would be answering.

Message revision: It is always better to revise the message and proofread the final copy.

Checking the message through a third person: Ask a third person to read it so as to ensure that the message is clear and adequate.

Checking the grammatical aspect: One has to see whether sentences are complete and punctuated properly. It is better to use a spell checker and grammar checker to proofread the message.

LAYOUT OF E-MAIL MESSAGES

It contains the following parts:

Subject Line

It summarise the central idea. It provides a quick indentification of the reader and the filing. It is written in an abbreviated style without articles. It need not be a complete sentence. It need not end with a period. For example,

Subject: Three promotional items to showcase at our Next Trade show
(rather than 'trade show').

Subject: Beefing up our messaging capabilities
(rather than 'new software')

Subject: Staff meeting to discuss summer vacation schedules
(rather than 'meeting')

Opening

It reveals the idea immediately. Even though the purpose of an e-mail is stated in the subject line, it is restated or amplified in the opening segment. Some readers skip the subject line and jump to the first sentence. There are two types of opening, namely indirect opening and direct opening. For example,

Table 28.1 Types of opening

Indirect opening	Direct opening
For the past six months the human resources department has been considering changes in our employees' benefit plan.	Please review the following proposal regarding employees' benefits, and let me know by May 20th if you approve these changes.
As you may know, employees in the document production have been complaining about eye fatigue as a result of the overhead fluorescent lighting in their center.	If you agree, I'II order six high-intensity task desk lamps at Rs.1890 each for use in the document production center.

Body

It explains and justifies the main idea. It discusses the subject logically. It is better to design the data for easy comprehension by using bullets, numbers, tables, graphics and, highlighting techniques. For example,

Hard-to-read paragraph version

Effective immediately are the following air travel guidelines. Between now and December 31, only account executives may take company approved trips. These individuals will be allowed to take a maximum of two trips, and they are to travel economy or budget class only.

Improved version with graphic highlighting

Who may travel:	Account executives only
How many trips:	A maximum of two trips
By when:	Between now and December 31
Air class:	Economy or budget class only

Closing

Closing ends with information like dates or deadline, summary of the messages and a closing thought. For example,

Please submit your report by July 30th so that we can have your data before August.

I am glad to answer your question.

Closing may show a gratitude or may encourage a feedback. For example,

I sincerely appreciate your co-operation.

What are your idea on these proposals.

Sometimes closing may be asking for directions to go forward. For example,

How would you like to proceed.

It is better to avoid overused endings. For example,

Please let me know if I may be of further assistance.

Sample :1

Date: May 2, 2000 To: Andrea Kanarek, operations manager From: Steven W. Timms Mail, services supervisor Subject: Your April 30th memo about reducing mail costs	**Subject line identifies previous memos and summarizes purpose**
Dear Ms. Kanarek, As you requested, here is a summary of the three measures that mail services is taking to reduce the overall mailing costs.	**Opening states purpose concisely**
• Eliminating duplicate addresses: For mass mailings, we're redoubling our efforts to locate duplicate entries, particularly when we merge multiple mailing lists. • Limiting envelope size: We're asking all departments to use envelopes no larger than 61/8 by 111/2 inches. Larger envelopes cost more. • Using presorting discounts: To take advantage of the first and the third class discounts, we're considering presorting large mailings by zip code and by carrier route.	**Body organize main points for readability**
These are the cost reduction steps we've taken thus far. If you'd like more detailed information, I'd be happy to talk with you about our efforts or to prepare a more formal report. Regards,Stevens	**Closing summarizes and looks forward to next action**

FORMATTING E-MAIL MESSAGES

E-mail is undoubtedly a developing communication channel. But its formatting and usage convention are still fluid and differ in its formatting. The following guidelines may be of use:

Guide Words

It refers to 'To' in the e-mail layout. Some writers write the recipient's electronic address eg: commercesundar@gmail.com. Some prefer to write the recipient's full name plus electronic address eg: K.sundar,commercesundar@gmail.com

Most e-mail programmes automatically add the current date. In the 'CC' line, one can type the address of anyone who is to receive a copy of the message. Most e-mail programmes have a line for 'Bcc' (Blind carbon copy). This line sends a copy to people, without the addressee's knowledge. Subject line helps in identifying the subject of the memo.

Salutation

It is always good to include salutation like '*Dear*', '*Hi*', '*Greetings*' or just a name. Omission of salutation hurts the feeling of the recipient.

Body

The body of the e-mail should be typed with upper and lower case characters. Many e-mail programmes have basic text editing features like cut, copy, paste and word wrap. However, it is better to avoid boldface and italics, as they create a string of control characters that cause chaos on the recipients' computer.

Closing line

One needs to conclude the message with a closing like *cheers* or *all the best* followed by your name and mail address. If the recipient is not aware of your identity, it is a good idea to include your title and organisation. Some e-mail writers use signature file. It is better to omit closing, in the case of e-mails sent to people within the organisation as the recipients can recognize the writer from the opening line itself.

MEMOS VIA E-MAIL MESSAGES

Many organizations prepare different kinds of memos and e-mails to carry on its operations. Memos are of 3 types, namely procedure and information memo, request and reply memo, and confirmation memo.

Tips for E-mailing Procedure Memo

a. Purpose of memo

Memo writer has to mention the purpose of the memo and offer brief explanation.

b. Language

He has to use conventional language to justify the reasons for change in procedures.

c. Steps in implementation

Give the steps in chronological order to implement the procedure. Begin each numbered items with a verb. It enhances the readalilily and comprehension.

Sample 2:

Memo to: Staff

Opening reveals purpose and offers brief explanation→	To improve budget planning and to control costs, please follow the new procedures listed below while submitting the future requests for outside printing jobs.
Body uses conversational language in justifying reasons for change in procedures→	In our business, of course, printing is a necessary expenditure. However, our bills seem very high lately, particularly those from Print Masters. The following procedures should help protect us from being overcharged.
Listing of steps in chronological order tells readers exactly how to implement the new procedure. Beginning each numbered item with a verb improves readability and comprehension→	1. Determine your exact printing specifications for a particular job. 2. Secure two estimates for the job. 3. Submit the written estimates to Kelly. 4. Place the order after receiving approval.

Following these new procedures will result in more competitive pricing and perhaps may even provide you with new creative printing options.

The preceding procedure memo applies a direct strategy in telling how to complete a task. Information memos also use the straightforward approach in supplying details about organization activities, services and actions.

Tips for E-mailing the Request and Reply

Direct approach is far better in requesting routine information or in requesting action within the organization. Tips for writing request review:

a. Open the message with a polite command.

b. Explain the purpose concisely.

c. List parallel questions for easy reading and comprehension.

d. Include the end date and the benefits the reader will get.

Sample 3:

Memo to: Staff

Please answer the questions listed below about the use of temporary help in your department.	**←Opens with a polite command.**
With your ideas, we plan to develop a policy that will help us improve the process of budgeting, selecting, and hiring temporaries.	**←Explains the purpose concisely.**
1. What is the average number of temporary office workers you employ each month?	
2. What is the average length of a temporary worker's assignment in your department?	**←Lists parallel questions for easy reading and comprehension.**
3. What specific job skills are you generally seeking in your temporaries?	
4. What temporary agencies are you using now?	
By replying before January 20, you will have direct input into the new policy, which we will be developing at the end of the month. This improved policy will help us fill your temporary employment needs more quickly and more efficiently.	**←Includes end date, along with reasons and reader benefit.**

Tips for E-mailing Confirmation Memo

When a person wants to confirm an oral agreement, the following tips would be of much use in writing a confirmation memo.

a. Include names and titles of the individuals involved. In other words, use the receiver's name in the salutation.

b. Create record of telephone conversation.

c. State the purpose of the message precisely.

d. Itemise the major issues.

e. Request feedback regarding unclear or inaccurate points.

Sample 4:

Hints at	Samples	Hints at
Uses receiver's name in the first sentence/salutation→	Thanks, Lincoin,	
Creates record of telephone conversation→	for talking with me on Friday, August 1, about how your unit would market our software products at national trade shows. This e-mail message confirms our conversation and the four specific points on which we agreed:	**←States the purpose of the message precisely and concisely.**
	1. David Williams, the chief product manager for my unit, will supply you with product descriptions, ad mats, catalog tear sheets and current price lists.	
Enumerates major points, including names, dates, and figures→	2. You will receive a 15 per cent commission on all orders you generate from trade shows.	**←Lists parallel questions for easy reading and comprehension.**
	3. You will allow us three hours to demonstrate our new products at your September field staff meeting in Orlando.	
	4. This new arrangement is a six-month test to determine how much additional sales revenue your staff can generate for our software products.	
Requests immediate feedback→	We are confident that this new arrangement will be profitable for both of our divisions and we look forward to using this new sales arrangement. If you agree that this message accurately reflects our conversation, please reply immediately with your agreement.	**←Closes with a forward-looking statement**

Checklist for Writing Routine Memos and e-mail Messages

The following has to be incorporated while writing messages and memos through e-mail.

Subject Line

Summarize the central idea: Let the subject line read like a newspaper headline brief but more clearly.

Use an abbreviated style: Omit articles (a, an, the) and do not try to make the subject line a complete sentence. Omit an ending period.

Opening

State the purpose of writing: Include the same information that is in the subject line, but expand it a little.

Ask questions immediately: If you are requesting information, begin with the most important question or use a polite command (Please answer the following questions about...).

Supply information directly: If responding to a request, give the reader the requested information immediately in the opening. Explain it in detail later.

Body

Explain details: Arrange information logically. For complex topics, use separate paragraphs developed coherently.

Enhance readability: Use short sentences, short paragraphs and paralled construction for similar ideas.

Supply graphic highlighting: Provide bulleted and/or numbered lists, tables or other graphic devices to improve readability and comprehension.

Be cautious: Remember that memos and e-mail messages often travel beyond their intended audiences.

Closing

Request action: If it is appropriate, state specifically what you want the reader to do. Include a deadline, with reasons, if possible.

Summarize the memo or provide a closing thought: For long memos, provide a summary of the important points. If neither an action request nor a summary is necessary, end with a closing thought.

Avoid clichéd endings: Use fresh remarks rather than overused expressions such as 'if you have additional questions', 'please do not hesitate to call' or 'thank you for your cooperation'.

SMART E-MAIL PRACTICES

E-mail is best suited for simple communication. Since it is also easy to misinterpret, it is not suitable for emotive or complicated issues and criticism. The following are some smart e-mail practices to be followed:

Get the Correct Address

E-mail writer has to type the correct address. Omission of comma, character or use of capital letter will cause your message to bounce. It is a better practice to use electronic address book for sending messages to people to whom you write frequently.

Avoid Misleading Subject Lines

Subject line should be relevant and helpful. Generic tags like 'hello' and 'great deal' may cause your message to be deleted before it is opened.

Be Concise

Don't burden the reader with abundance of information. It is always better to organize your ideas tightly in view of the smallness of screen of the monitor and difficulty experienced in reading the typefaces. Therefore, messages given need to attract the reader's interest.

Don't Include Anything You Don't Want

E-mail creates a permanent record. Any message or corporate communication can be used against you and your employees. Therefore, it is advisable not to include anything that you do not want anyone to read.

Don't Use Mail to Avoid Contact

E-mail is an inappropriate channel for breaking bad news or for revolving argument. For example, it is improper to use e-mail for terminating the services of an employee. It is not a good channel for resolving conflict with supervisors, subordinates or others. Personal visit or telephone is the right medium.

Never Respond in an Angry Mood

When one is in the grip of anger, it is better not to send a mail. Allow your anger to cool off, before sending a response to an upsetting message. It is always wise to iron out differences in person.

Care About Correctness

Initially senders and receivers were casual about spelling, grammar and punctuation. Since e-mail is becoming a mainstream channel of communication, one has to observe utmost care in spelling, grammar and punctuation. Any lapse in this regard is likely to lower the image of the mail writer.

Avoid Humour

It is good to avoid humour and tongue-in-cheeck comments which can be easily misunderstood.

Limit the Tendency to Send Blanket Copies

It is a better practice to send mails to only the recipients intended.

Use Design to Heighten the Readability of the Message

It is better to add value to the message by using bullets, numbers, headings and side headings. All these things shorten the reading time.

Use the Correct Language in View of Cultural Differences

A person has to be very alert in using clichés like 'pull up stakes', 'playing second fiddle; slangs like 'cool stoked'; sports references like 'hit a home run', 'play by rules, etc. It is always better to use formal language.

E-MAIL ETHICS

The following guidelines would help in communicating through e-mail. It reflects a lot about values, seriousness of one's attention and reputation of the organization a person represents. Simplicity, brevity and directness are the hallmarks of a good e-mail.

- Message may have a personal touch.
- Be friendly and use humour to break up the tension of what you have to say.
- E-mail message works best when messages are short and to the point.
- Avoid sarcasm in mail.
- Be brief, as it saves bandwidth and cuts down eye-strain.
- Make the subject line precise, given the receipent's time and online charges.
- Don't copy the full text of a lengthy message into your response. Select the parts you need to send.
- Use technology to have the spelling mistakes corrected.
- Compose your message offline. A regular word processor is much more powerful than the text editor used on most e-mail systems.
- Read the message before it is sent.
- Configure your e-mail to check all your accounts in one go.
- If security is not a concern, configure your e-mail client to remember your password.
- While sending large files, use compression facility like *pkzip*.
- Briefly introduce yourself, when the recipient does not know you.
- Avoid using capital letters.
- Cultivate the habit of checking mails regularly.
- Avoid 'urgent' or 'priority' unless it really is.
- Be aware that e-mails can be archived. However, it may not be secure.
- Online service and public e-mail providers provide confidentiality for the subscribers' e-mail, while some companies consider the e-mails sent through the office network to be company property and subject them to scrutiny.
- Write in paragraphs and avoid lengthy sentences.
- Get a free e-mail account for personal e-mails or mailing list.
- Stay on the topic if you are posting to a public board, forum or news groups, as digression from the topic annoys the receiver.

TIPS FOR EFFECTIVE E-MAIL USAGE

Following points help in effectively using e-mail as a channel of communication:

1. Organise the mails in different folders so that it can be tracked easily.
2. Compose your mail offline. This will save you online time and enables you to review the mail.

3. Keep the e-mail IDs of people you want to correspond with in the address book so that you need not key in their e-mail IDs each time. This will reduce the chances of error and also saves time.
4. Proofread the message.
5. Inform your friends and colleagues of the type of document you want to receive.
6. If the mail is automatically delivered to your mail box, shut off your computer beep that alerts an incoming message.
7. If you do not get your mail in your inbox, check your mails by connecting to the mail server.

SUMMARY

Characteristics of e-mail messages are single topic, conversational tone, conciseness, graphic highlighting.
While writing a message, the points to be considered are: necessity for e-mailing, clarity about message, assessing the impact of the message on the reader, outline of points be covered in the message, revision of message, checking through a third person and checking grammatical aspects.
Layout of the e-mail includes subject line, opening, body and closing.
Message formatting includes guide words, saluation, body and closing line.
Memos via e-mail includes purpose of the memo, language, steps in implementation.
Tips for e-mailing the request and reply include direct approach, opening the message politely, explaining the purpose, listing questions and including deadlines.
Tips for e-mailing confirmation memo include inclusion of name and title of the person, salutation, creation of record of telephone conversation, itemizing the issues and requesting feedback.

Smart e-mail practices include correct address, avoidance of misleading subject, conciseness, exclusion of unwanted messages, not to use mail to avoid conflict, not responding in an angry mood, care about correctness, avoiding humour, limiting blanket copying practice, increasing readability and using correct language.

REVIEW QUESTIONS

Part A: Short Questions

1. What is an e-mail?
2. What is a spam?
3. What is message forwarding?
4. What is a junk mail?

Part B: Paragraph Questions

1. Highlight the characteristics of an e-mail message.
2. Write down the tips for e-mailing a procedure.
3. Write down the tips for e-mailing the request and reply.
4. How would you confirm an oral message by e-mail?

5. How would you compose an e-mail?
6. How would you attach a file?
7. How would you add a new address in your mail?
8. What is the protocol for replying to an e-mail?
9. How would you forward a message?
10. Give tips for effective usage of E-mails.

Part C: Essay Questions

1. Elucidate the mechanics of e-mail.
2. How would you compose a message?
3. Explain the layout of e-mail messaging.
4. State the procedure of formatting an e-mail message.
5. Bring out the smart e-mail practices.
6. Write down the ethics followed in sending messages by e-mail.

Part D: Objective Type Questions

Choose the Correct Answer

1. Which accomodates the main menase
   a. Body b. Subject line c. Closing of email
   (Ans: a)
2. Which gives central idea about the manage sent
   a. Opening b. Subject line c. cc
   (Ans: b)
3. Dear, hai, greetings etc. Represent
   a. Body of email b. cc c. Salutation
   (Ans: c)
4. Guidelines observed in writing e-mail are accomodated in
   a. E-mail adiquettee b. E-mail ethics c. E-mail practices
   (Ans: b)

Fill in the Blanks

1. Unwanted messages are stored in ____________. (spam)
2. ____________ allows information to be sent between computer and people on the net. (e-mail)
3. _________ is a place where a person stores information about people with whom he corresponds. (address book)
4. _________ gives a brief description of what the message is about. (subject)
5. _________ represents the persons to whom copies are sent . (cc)
6. _________ line summarises the centeral idea about the message .(subject)
7. _______ accomodates the main message. (body)

29 CHAPTER IT TRENDS IN COMMUNICATION

INTRODUCTION

Globalization, revolution in communication technology, hectic competition and the consequent need to take decisions to survive in the competitive environment, realisation of the value of time, etc., are some of the factors that have been transforming the face of communication technology. Business operations are carried on in large volumes and over long distances. Foreign trade has developed to a greater extent. Technology has changed the world into a global village. It has increased the speed, accuracy, efficiency and effectiveness of communication. Modern business enterprises are conducting business in a paperless and cashless manner due to the sophisticated technical devices. Enquires, offers, quotations, orders, complaints and adjustments, and claims are carried out by business managers with just a laptop and scanner fitted with a web camera. Business meetings are held through video conferencing and web camera conferencing, eliminating the need to travel to a central place at the cost of time, energy and money. Supply chain management, just-in-time management facilitated by modern communication devices reduce the need for inventorising and save the attendant cost. The capacity to store and transfer of data, saves space. The instant transmission of data through sophisticated tools in the required form, facilitates deep analysis of facts and figures, and quality decisions. With this backdrop, let us analyse the implications of technology on modern business.

IMPLICATIONS OF TECHNOLOGY ON MODERN BUSINESS

Though revolution in technology has ushered in a lot of benefits, it is not without certain implications. They are as follows:

- Modern business enterprises can function with less manpower.
- Files, cabins, tables containing files are replaced by data storage devices, thereby saving storage space.
- Lengthy paper-based and time-consuming communication is getting displaced.
- Errors in the letter and documents are corrected by spellcheck option with less effort.

- Speed and reduction in cost are achieved.
- Teleconferencing and e-mail obviate the need for travel of executives, thereby saving their precious time, energy and other resources.
- Decisions are taken in an enlightened business environment spruced up by sophisticated technical devices.

IMPACTS OF TECHNOLOGY-AIDED COMMUNICATION ON BUSINESS ENTERPRISES

We live in an inter-connected global village. Our technology has increased our data mobility and reduced our need for physical mobility. Data is routed from shop floor level to board room in no time. A technician can oversee the production processes in distant locations through wireless sensor. It enables the business enterprises to communicate with one another more frequently and closely. Most of those enterprises which do not embrace technology may not be able to survive. Organizations need to have resources to embrace the technology. Those who cannot afford such resources lag behind in the race.

Positive Impacts

1. Communication across the globe has become easier. Distance is no longer a barrier.
2. Speed of information flow has increased tremendously.
3. Accuracy of the message transmitted through sophisticated devices is higher than the traditional ones.
4. Time, energy and resources of manpower are saved.
5. Organization structure has become flat from the previous vertical structure due to the manager's ability to contact the subordinates facilitated by the technological devices.
6. Time required to make decisions has decreased, because managers can have access to increased information resources.
7. The manager is no longer rewarded as a primary source of information, as all the people in the organization have access to more information.
8. Market research has received more impetus due to copious availability of data.
9. Supply chain gets shortened due to direct link between the producer and the customer.
10. Recurring costs like wage, storage, stationery, etc., can be cut down.
11. Managers across the levels are forced to learn the modern communication process.
12. Works are done in teams. Organisation charts are designed around the computer.

Negative Impact

Information technology has enhanced the way organizations conduct business. Though it has a lot of positive impact, there are a few disadvantages which are as follows:

1. Conventional managers shy away from new advancement in technology.

2. Opposition from unions is stiff due to the fear of retrenchment and reduction of employment opportunity.
3. Unwillingness to make an investment in an area that becomes obsolete due to faster pace of technological change.
4. Constant need to keep oneself updated due to the fast-changing technology, stresses the employees.
5. Technology-enabled communication invades the privacy of employees at home. Increased use of mobiles and laptop at home in connection with work-related matters eat into one's quality time with family members.

MODERN COMMUNICATION DEVICES

Communication devices are devices that can be used for communication. These are generally hardware components used alone or in association with a computer to send and receive data, instructions and information to one another.

FAX & Scanner

- Facsimile xerox is the abbreviation of FAX.
- These machines scan the documents and transmit signals though telephone modem. The fax machine at the other end reproduces the exact copy of the documents. The scanned documents are received via e-mail.
- It is the best method of transmitting charts, graphs, designs, contracts and testimonials.
- Modern fax machine is attached to e-mail through a computer. As a result one need not be near the fax machine. The copy taken is e-mailed by the machine.

Computers

The uses of computer in business are beyond question. The various modes of computer are:

Desktop

This one is kept on the desk. It consists of central processing unit (CPU), flat monitor, modern ethernet card, CD/DVD drive, USB port, printer, keyboard and mouse.

Laptop

It is portable. A single unit contains a combination of the hardware mentioned for the desktop.

Docking station allows you to plug your laptop into a unit at your office, enabling you to use your laptop as the basic processing unit while enjoying the ease of larger monitor.

- It is quite suitable for people who travel frequently and who need computing facility.
- We can access the internet in most of the areas using data card.
- Upgradion of laptops is not as easy as desktop computers due to the very nature of construction.

Personal Digital Assistant

- It is a hand-held computer. It is also called palmtop.
- There are two versions in it. One has palm pilot operating system and other one has microsoft pocket PG operating system.
- These units allow you to synchronise your key organizational elements with your computer.
- It allows you to receive and send e-mails via wireless or modem transmission. We can have contact lists, calendar, diary, etc.

Other products that can be added to a computer

There are many products that can be used in conjunction with your computer to increase the functionality and image of your business. All one needs to do is to load suitable packages into the computer.

Digital camera: Pictures taken by the camera can be directly loaded into your computer for a variety of uses.

Scanner: Scanner creates a digital image of printed material and it can be stored in one's computer.

Wireless transmission: This feature allows one to communicate with other devices equipped with the same feature.

Local area network (LAN): The benefit of data stored in two or more isolated computers can be synergistically exchanged by interconnecting them.

A network is a connection of two or more computers through a cable, so that they can exchange information and communicate with one another. Networks which serve small areas are called local area networks.

Two or more computers can be connected together by fiber optics cable (small bundles of cable that carry millions of bits of information) or through satellites. With this, the user can exchange files and share printers. This benefits all users, saving considerable time and money, and increases the ease and speed of communication. When more than one terminal is connected to a host computer, several people can use the same data for their different purposes.

It refers to a set of computers connected and stationed at one spot, sharing hardware, software and the data.

LAN can do the following functions:

1. It enables many users to share a single copy of file stored centrally.
2. A LAN facilitates quick transfer of files from one computer to other without having an exchange of floppy disk.
3. Because of LAN, different computer operators can share one or more expensive laser printers.
4. LAN can be used as a post office to send memos, reports, office circulars, etc., to people located either near the computer or in other parts of the building.

5. With LAN, two people can use the same document simultaneously.
6. With LAN, programs can be shared among two or more computers.

Because of the above functions, LAN provides the following advantages to the company:

1. It eliminates the need for employees to pass papers and copies, and consequently reduces the risk of damage or loss of files.
2. It speeds up communication and work flow by providing each employee e-mail and phone messages.
3. It acquaints every employee with automatic notice of meetings, appointments, agendas, directions and so on.
4. It helps to store and sort the data in central filing system.
5. It facilitates employees to work at remote sites or at home without the need of coming every day to the office to submit their work.

Wide area network (WAN): LAN is restricted to local areas and cannot be used over a long distance. For connecting computers on separates sites, separate cities or even separate countries, wide area network (WAN) is used.

LAN and WAN can be connected together by devices called *gateways*.

In contrast to LANs, which only have a few computers, WANs involve a large number of devices between the source and destination of data. As data is transmitted over a distance, it is essential to use a modem. Even communication controllers are to be introduced to check and correct the errors in transmission of data. Whereas LAN is limited in its application, WAN is a complex and multi-faceted system. Big corporations often use WAN for communicating with executives and employees. With the use of WAN, they make less long distance phone calls, reduce the use of written documents and overcome time lags in overseas communication.

More than two LANs connected across a wide area make a wide area network, which includes connection of computers scattered over a wide area through dedicated telephone lines, fiber optical cables or satellite lines.

Internet

It is a large network of computers spanning the globe connecting a number of countries.

The uses of internet to business

1. It ensures speedy communication and also increases the quality of communication. Information can be sent in any format.
2. It connects buyers and sellers scattered across the globe.
3. It helps provide after-sales service.
4. It enhances the quality of negotiating business deals.
5. It displays information about whether the market is upbeat or sluggish.
6. It facilitates business chat at one-to-one level. Video conference can also be done. The consultation with experts is also possible.

7. We can publicise goods and services.
8. Business enterprises can post and update information so that stakeholders can access it without physically visiting the enterprise.
9. It can share business and research data.
10. We can join group discussion on any subject.
11. We can access multimedia information which includes photographic images, audio and video.
12. We can gather valuable feedback and suggestion from customers and business partners.
13. Business enterprises can request and provide help with problems and questions.
14. We can exchange electronic mail with friends, customers, suppliers and also attach files.
15. We can find suitable manpower through the net.
16. Business enterprises can pay all utility bills through the net; make travel booking for executives for various modes of transport.
17. Settle inter-company owings via net banking; make money transfer; make collections from customer etc.
18. It allows business enterprises to access a variety of services like:
    - E-mail
    - Internet relay chat for sending private and public messages to other users in real time.
    - USENET news groups for posting and answering messages on public bulletin board.
    - A video conferencing system allows the users to send and receive sound and picture simultaneously over the internet.

Teleconferencing

Individuals and groups in various locations can make use of this facility. The telephone/computer and the television/net camera combined can create a variety of teleconferencing networks.

Advantages of teleconferencing

1. It is cost-effective. It obviates the physical movement of participants to assemble at one place.
2. It is time-saving. People can be contacted immediately.
3. It is a speedy way of addressing a problem.
4. It eliminates the hassles of travel.
5. It is productive as it facilitates the free flow of ideas among the participants.

Audio or Voice Conferencing

It enables five to six people at different locations get on to a network and hold a conference using the conventional analogue telephone. It is mostly used in stock market. It requires re-establishment of the network every time you want to resume a conference. Telephone companies can provide exclusive lines to enable us to have 24-hour conferencing facility. It has the facility of storing and forwarding the message, if a person is not present.

Teleconferencing can bring people together without anyone having to spend time and money on travel. There are two types of teleconferencing, namely audio teleconferencing and audio graphics teleconferencing.

Audio teleconferencing is a conference using telephones. It is the most frequently used, most productive and inexpensive medium. It is also called *phone meeting*; it does not need any special equipment other than the ordinary telephone.

The main factors for its wide spread acceptance are:

- Easy to use — everyone can use a telephone.
- Easily available — telephones are available anywhere.
- Easy to participate — from any telephone line in the world.
- Takes only a few minutes to set up a conference call.
- Costs less.
- Many people can share information.

Audio graphics teleconferencing provides the facility to move texts, computer-generated images, photographs and large files over ordinary telephone lines (like the internet). It is not as expensive as video conferencing but still requires going to the location that has the equipment or investing in the equipment.

Video Conferencing

Video conference is a network of studios in different locations. Each studio is equipped with cameras, microphones and speakers, different kinds of network like one-way, two-way, ad hoc/ fixed network.

The connections can be operated like the ones in a telecast. The anchoring person connects a number of reporters stationed at different locations. This is two-way ad hoc network. In one-way, communication can be sent in any one way only.

Computer Conferencing (CC)

Computer conferencing refers to those systems that allow numerous users to connect via a network, send e-mail messages to the conference address and receive posting of others.

Interactive communication takes place among networked computers in which data is shared. Data may take the form of audio, text, e-mail, video conferencing, etc. This type of conference happens in real time. In other words, messages appear as they are being typed or they can happen asynchronously with the message being stored for later use.

Varieties of CC include groups organized by topics (within a discipline), for specific project (research, editing a book) or for the purpose of meeting (information sharing). These run on many platforms from PC to mainframes and traverse the network within four walls or extend beyond those boundaries.

Types of computer conferencing

- Bulletin board/message and board/online forum (web forum): These are used to distribute information or have an online discussion on various topics. Messages are arranged by the thread and remain available as long as desired in Microsoft outlook public folder.
- E-mail discussion lists: These are used for similar purposes but messages are sent by e-mails to all participants. There may be an archieve of messages that can be viewed in various ways such as by data, by author or by thread.

Uses of computer conferencing

It is used for sales presentation, product demonstration, training, meetings among geographically dispersed team members and brainstorming sessions.

Through web conference, virtual teams can be set up. It can keep the members linked. It can be used for showing product demonstration. Prospects can watch the demonstration and ask questions. This convenience enables the sales team to address concerns and book sales quickly. It is less expensive than travelling for face-to-face meetings. Further, it allows users to collaborate data while viewing and sharing documents electronically.

As more attention is focused on ideas than on the people who communicate, this channel offers democracy.

Website

Website is an excellent medium for assessing all segments of customers. Business enterprises, through a website, can display its size, nature, line, catalogue, ethical values, branch network, method of placing orders, grievance redressal, mode of payment and other information useful to customers.

Public notices, press releases, bulletins and other company publications can be listed on a website. A company can include information about its organization structure and branch networks.

Benefits of website

1. Company can enhance its turnover.
2. It can build a good image.
3. Advertising becomes easier.
4. Information reaches to potential customers.
5. Orders can be secured without physical exertion.
6. Tele-shopping is facilitated.
7. It provides transparency.
8. Market research and market survey are easier.
9. The outreach of website is wider and deeper than the sales personnel.

Mobile Phone

Benefits of mobile phone

1. We can contact anyone, anywhere, any time using a mobile phone. In short, accessibility is the chief advantage of mobile phones.
2. It provides more time to communicate. While using a landline, one cannot be contacted during travel. But mobile phones places no restriction on time.
3. One can surf the net and check e-mails in mobiles using WAP and GPRS.
4. Calls coming through landlines can be redirected or forwarded to mobiles.
5. Mobiles can be used in foreign location when one has to travel out of the country.
6. Mobiles are used as one of the advertisement media. The advertisements are routed through messages.

E-mail

Today e-mail has emerged as one of the popular forms of business communication surpassing the telephone, conventional mail and fax. E-mail conveys the information from one destination to another in a fraction of seconds. Messages can contain simple text or character formatting similar to word processing. We can send documents, pictures, movies, worksheets or any other important information. Thus, the attachment is the important component of an e-mail.

Benefits of e-mail

1. Accuracy and speed are the merits of e-mail business communication.
2. Message can be digitally signed by the sender to show authenticity.
3. Messages can be encrypted to ensure that only intended recipient can get the message.
4. It can be stored in internet service provider's mail server.
5. We can download the message and read it leisurely.
6. We can attach files to the message.
7. It is an inexpensive mode of communication.
8. Messages can be sent anytime from anywhere.

Voice Mail

Voice mail is a communication service on a telephone line. The simple answering machine which can be attached to a telephone is a form of voice mail; it allows a caller to leave a name/number and message if we do not answer the phone. The message can be retrieved and answered later at a more convenient time.

Cellular phone companies offer voice mail service as a part of their network offerings. The service is inexpensive and available 24 hours a day. A voice mail device can be attached to a telephone directly or though a computer. Fax machines have voice mail facility.

Some voice mail services add the date and time to each message so that you know exactly when the call was recorded.

Voice mail has many advantages. For the organization, it helps to make better use of time. It can help to prevent interruptions in office work.

Sometimes just trying to communicate a simple message can entail a series of phone calls back and forth, because the other person is not available when you called. The result is wasted time and productivity. Voice mail systems are meant to address this problem. It acts as a corporate answering machine, replaying messages from people both inside and outside the company. It reduces paperwork since messages to be passed do not have to be taken down.

Callers can leave a detailed message up to three minutes long, even when he is talking on another call. As each message is in the voice of the caller, it avoids miscommunication and misunderstanding which can occur if the message is conveyed by a telephone operator or an attendant. It increases communication capability of the organization.

For individuals, voice mail avoids the constraints of answering a telephone call on the spot. The call can be retrieved and answered at a convenient time. It allows us to avoid taking an unnecessary call, and also relieves us from the anxiety of losing a call. Since a person can hear the caller speak, he can pick up the receiver and answer if he wants to talk to the person.

A person needs to develop the skill to use the voice mail. Make a clear statement of purpose after you have identified yourself. The voice mail carries the tonal quality of your voice and your feelings. Speak as if the other person is present at the other end of the line. You may feel uncomfortable delivering a monologue, but you have the advantage of not being interrupted.

Groupware

It allows several people to use the software at the same time to create documents, keep track of the project, route messages and manage deadlines. Supervisiors can manage the workflow through individual computers without physically moving to the work site for face- to-face meetings. It is nowadays used in team-based organizations. It allows members to work from home. Microsoft Project is the leading product in this connection.

CD - ROM Databases

Compact Disc Read only (CD-Rom) has been available for several years and is becoming more popular. The information stored in CD-Rom's are encyclopedias, dictionaries, telephone directories, articles and abstracts on various subjects. Thus, mass information can be stored in CDs.

Instant Messaging (IM)

It is a new dimension tool for enhancing employee productivity, fostering team-building efforts and enabling cost-effective speedy communication. Instant messaging facilitates interacting with project team members, discussing project details, taking project approvals and seeking clarifications. MSN and Yahoo messengers are increasingly used in IM. Infosys uses Microsoft exchange 2000 server for communication within the organization to exchange short informal messages.

Uses of IM

1. Organizations operating in multiple locations use IM to keep disparate team together. It is a real-time communication which is simple and user-friendly. It is easy and helps in multi-tasking. Many people can chat at the same time with one another.

2. Constant communication through IM strengthens the inter-personal relations among employees. Informal communication encourages free flow of ideas.
3. It is used on knowledge management process for instant knowledge sharing and collaboration.
4. As it is instant, sender can get acknowledgement from the recipient instantaneously.
5. Files can be transferred online in real time without waiting to receive an e-mail.
6. Addressal of queries in real time does not keep the matter pending, thus saving precious time and increasing productivity.
7. People can see who is online so that they do not waste time swapping e-mail or voice mail with people who are not available.
8. We can multitask. In other words, even if while speaking on the telephone, we can send or respond to a message.

Despite the enormous advantages associated with technology-enabled business communication, there are threats of cyber crime, hacking, floating computer virus, etc. Strict and stringent laws need to be put in place to deal with criminals indulging in cyber crimes.

Short Message Service (SMS)

The short message service (SMS) is the ability to send and receive text messages to and from mobile telephones. This text may be in the form of words or numbers or an alphanumeric combination. The other features of SMS include:

- SMS supports several input mechanisms that allow interconnection with different sources and destinations of message.
- With SMS, an active mobile handset is able to receive or submit a short message at any time, independent of whether a voice or data call is in progress.
- SMS guarantees delivery of the message by the network. The temporary failures due to unavailable receiving stations are identified, and the short message is stored in short messaging service centre (SMSC) until the destination device becomes available.
- Its out-of-band packet delivery and low bandwidth message transfer are highly efficient means for transmitting short bursts of data.
- Additional services like e-mail, fax, paging integration, interactive banking, etc., are available.
- Additional facilities like instant messaging, gaming and chatting are also available.

Benefits to subscribers

The benefits of SMS to the subscribers include:

1. Guaranteed message delivery.
2. Delivery of message to multiple subscribers at a time.
3. Ability to receive diverse information.
4. Convenient to use.
5. Seamless integration with other data and internet-based applications.

Benefits to the service provider

The benefits of SMS to the service provider include:

1. Increase in incremental revenues due to increased number of calls on wireless network.
2. Wireless data access for corporate users.
3. Additional value-added services like e-mail, voice mail, fax, stock and currency quotes, airline schedules, etc., providing new revenues.

Enhanced messaging service (EMS): EMS is a direct descendent of SMS. EMS text messages use words, pictures, melodies, animations and formatted texts to bring personal communiques to life. EMS can be used on GSM networks.

Multimedia messaging service (MMS): MMS has the ability to send messages comprising a combination of texts, sounds, images and videos to MMS capable handsets.

RECENT TRENDS IN COMMUNICATION TECHNOLOGY

Recent trends in communication technology have made the need for a common platform to share ideas, update knowledge and work with frontier areas of communication. They consist of the following:

Multimedia Applications

Multimedia application uses technology for business, education and entertainment. This includes:

Computer-based training (CBT): It enables a person to learn things in a simulated environment. We can learn and complete the exercises with instruction softwares such as skill assessment manager (SAM) or training online manager. With SAM, we can know how well we understand and perform in end-user applications.

Corporates set up training labs. Employees can update their skills in such trainings. CBT software loaded on the employee's computer or on the company's network enables the employee's to update their knowledge at their desk, at their homes or even while travelling. Learners receive instant feedback on their performance in the form of correct answer and additional information, or incorrect answer, scoring, etc. Instructors can assess the performance of the learners.

Computer-aided instruction (CAI): Computer-aided instruction is popular in business, industry and schools to teach new skills or to upgrade the existing skills of employees, teachers and students. Schools use it to train teachers and to teach student mathematics, language and software skills. Learners receive instant feedback. Interactive CBT software is available on CDs, DVDs or shared over a network.

Web-based distance education: Many colleges and universities offer numerous distance learning courses in the form of web-based or web-enhanced courses. It allows students living far away from the institution to complete the course-work from home or at any time that fits their schedules. Many companies encourage their employees to study while on the job.

Classroom education: It is an effective tool for delivering educational material to potential learners. It makes learning exciting and interesting. Students perform an experiment in a risk-free environment. For example, one can dissect a frog in a virtual environment. Student could listen to a speaker reciting French vocabulary to help with pronunciation of difficult words. It is also useful for physically impaired and learning disabled students. It is cost-saving.

Electronic books (e-books): It is a handheld computer which can hold up to 4000 pages or about 10 books. By clicking a button, user can move forward or backward, add notes, and highlight text stored in e-books.

Electronic reference books: It is a digital version of a reference book that uses text, graphics, sound, animation and videos to explain a topic or to provide additional information. Health and medicine are the two areas where multimedia reference texts play an important role. Instead of using volumes of books, health professionals and students rely on reference CDs and DVDs for information, illustration and animations on hundreds of health and first-aid topics.

Newspapers and magazines: It is nothing but the digital version of a newspaper or magazine distributed on CDs, DVDs or through the web. It has all sections contained in a physical newspaper. Besides, it has audio and video clips. It can show recent albums, movie releases and animations. It can depict weather patterns or election results.

Multimedia in marketing: Many business enterprises use multimedia to create marketing presentations that advertise and sell products. Advertisers use this software to produce television commercials with unique media effects. Sales representatives use multimedia in presenting the products to potential customers who are shown the usage of the products graphically. Interactive kiosks with multimedia delivery platform that draws information stored on a CD or videodisk is being used to promote products, provide information and customer service. Kiosks with touch screen help customers in getting direction to places like airport, museum, libraries, police station, hospital, etc.

Hypermedia

It is a term derieved from hypertext. It includes a set of multimedia objects, sound, video and virtual realities. It is used for inter-group communication, structuring thoughts and ideas, interactive instruction system, publishing, etc.

Artificial Intelligence (AI)

AI is an area of computer science, focusing on creating machines that can engage on behaviours that humans consider intelligent. The various areas where AI is used include games, speech recognition, neural networks, robotics, computer vision, natural language, etc. AI is used in some of the business functions like finance, manufacturing, telecommunication, civil aviation, etc.

Business Intelligence (BI)

It is a broad category of allocations and technologies for gathering, providing access to and analysing data for helping the enterprise user make better decisions. It can eliminate a lot of the guess works within the organization, enhance communication among departments while co-ordinating the activities and enabling companies to respond quickly to the changes in financial conditions.

Knowledge Discovery Database (KDD)

KDD is a new field that combines several techniques from computer science and artificial intelligence. It seeks to establish relationship and global pattern in a large database. KDD is capable of handling a large volume of data. It discovers new information by using the existing information. New patterns or trends in mass data can be discovered using this technique.

Data Warehousing

Data warehouse is a collection of data designed to support management decision-making. It provides access to the data of an organization, data consistency, capacity to separate and combine data. It has a set of tools to query, analyse and present information. It allows the business enterprises to function with less manpower. It provides reliable and accurate results. An enterprise can provide better customer service using warehousing architecture. It facilitates business re-engineering.

Data Mining

It means extraction of hidden and predictive information from large databases. It enables an enterprise to focus on the most important information in their data warehouses. Data mining tools predict future trends, and behaviour which allows the business to make proactive and knowledge-driven decisions.

Online Analytical Processing (OLAP)

This application allows a user to interactively analyze data. It makes multiple dimensional analysis of business data possible. It is used in a variety of business areas like sales, marketing analysis, financial reporting, consolidation, budgeting, planning product profitability, tracking, pricing analysis, activity-based costing, manpower planning, quality analysis, etc.

Enterprise Resource Planning (ERP)

It refers to the means, techniques and concepts for integrated management of businesses as a whole from the viewpoint of effective use of management resources to improve the efficiency of enterprise management. ERP software automates most of the business processes. The main benefits of ERP include improved efficiency, information integration for better decision-making, faster and quicker response to customer queries, etc.

Supply Chain Management (SCM)

SCM oversees the flow of material, information and finance, as they move in a process from the supplier to the manufacturer, to the wholesaler, to the retailer and to the consumer. It coordinates and integrates these flows within and among companies. In other words, there are three flows involved in SCM. Product flow involves movement of goods from suppliers to customers. Information flow involves transmitting orders and updating the status of delivery. Financial flow consists of credit terms, payment schedules, consignment and title ownership arrangements. SCM uses advanced algorithms to determine the best way to fill the order. Execution application tracks the physical status of goods, management of materials and financial information involving all parties.

Customer Relationship Management (CRM)

It consists of the processes a company uses to track and organize its contact with its current and prospective customers. CRM software is used to support these processes. The software can be accessed and information about customers and customer interactions can be entered, stored and accessed by employees in different departments of the company. The goal of CRM is to improve the service provided to customers, and use customer contact information for targeted marketing.

It provides online access to product information and technical assistance, identifies what customers value and devise appropriate strategies for each customer, tracks all contacts with the customer, identifies potential customers, provides a mechanism for registering customer complaints and remedying the grievances, stores customer interest to target customers selectively and provides a mechanism for managing and scheduling maintenance, repair and ongoing support.

Geographic Information System (GIS)

GIS is a computer-based tool for mapping and analyzing things that exist and events that happen on earth. GIS gives us the power to create maps, integrate information, visualize scenarios, solve complicated problems, present powerful ideas, develop effective solution, etc. GIS is a tool used by individuals, organizations, schools, governments and business enterprises seeking innovative ways to address their problems. Its applications in the areas like vegetation mapping, ground water modelling, policy assessment, natural resources management, environmental impact assessment, waste management and site remediation deserve special mention.

Global Positioning System (GPS)

GPS is a U.S-owned utility that provides users with positioning, navigation and timing services. GPS provides accurate information and time-related information for an unlimited number of people in all kinds of weather, day and night, anywhere in the world. GPS consists of three aspects — the space aspect, the control aspect and the user aspect. The U.S. military operates this system. Individuals can buy GPS. They can locate accurately where they are currently and where they want to go. GPS is playing an important role in all means of transportation. Disaster and emergency services are rendered with the help of GPS. Day-to-day activities like banking, mobile phone operations and control of power grids are facilitated by accurate timing provided by GPS. Farmers, surveyors, geologists and others perform their works more effectively due to GPS.

SUMMARY

The implications of technology are functioning with less manpower, saving space, displacing paper-based work, easier location of error, speed and cost reduction, decisions taken in an enlightened environment.

The positive impact of technology are communication throughout the world quicker and easier; accuracy; saves time, energy and resources; changing the organization structure; decision-making time shortened; cutting down recurring cost; team work encouraged; supply chain shortened.

The negative impact of technology are opposition from unions, lack of willingness to learn communication technology by officers, reluctance to make investment, need to keep oneself updated, invasion of privacy.

Modern communication devices include fax, computer desktop, laptop, personal digital assistant, digital camera, scanner, LAN and WAN, internet, teleconferencing, audio or video conference, computer conference, websites, mobile phones, e-mail, voice mail, groupware, CD-Rom, instant messaging and short messaging service.

Uses of internet are fast communication, worldwide connectivity, after-sales service, enhancing quality of business deals, business chat, publicizing goods and services, posting updated information, sharing business data, group discussion, gathering feedback, finding suitable manpower, setting inter-company owings and paying utility bills.

Types of conferences include teleconference, video conference and computer conference.

Advantages of teleconferencing are cost effectiveness, saving time, speedy addressal of problems, eliminating hassles of travel and higher productivity.

Uses of website are image building, easy to advertise, reaching the potential customer, winning orders without physical exertion, tele-shopping, transparency, market survey easier and wider outreach.

Uses of mobile phone are accessibility; more time to communicate; surfing the net is possible; redirection of call from landline to mobile is possible; can be used in foreign locations; used as an advertisement media.

Uses of e-mail are accuracy, speed, cost-saving, authentication ensured, encryption of message, storability, attachment facility, anytime and anywhere advantage.

Instant messaging is advantageous to units operating in multiple location, strengthens inter-personal relations, knowledge management process, transferring files online, immediate acknowledgement for documents sent, instant addressal of queries, facility to see the availability of the person online, ability to multitask.

Recent trends in communication technology include multi media applications, hypermedia, artificial intelligence, business intelligence, knowledge discovery database, data warehousing, data mining, online analytical processing, enterprise resource planning, online analytical processing, enterprise resource planning, supply chain management, customer relationship management, geographic information system and global positioning system.

REVIEW QUESTIONS

Part A: Short Questions

1. What is an e-mail?
2. What is video conferencing?
3. What is Fax?
4. What is LAN?
5. What is WAN?

6. What is internet?
7. What is teleconferencing?
8. What is computer conferencing?
9. What is website?
10. What is groupware?
11. What is CD-Rom?
12. What is instant messaging?
13. What is SMS?
14. What is an electronic book?
15. What is hypermedia?
16. What is artificial intelligence?
17. What is business intelligence?
18. What is data warehousing?
19. What is data mining?
20. What is geographic information system?
21. What is global positioning system?

Part B: Paragraph Questions

1. What is personal digital assistant?
2. Specify the other products that can be added to a computer.
3. State the types of computer conference.
4. Mention the advantages of teleconferencing.
5. What are the uses of computer conferencing?
6. Specify the benefits of website to a business.
7. Point out the uses of mobile phones to business enterprises.
8. List out the benefits of e-mail to business.
9. Enumerate the advantages of instant messaging.
10. State the features of SMS.
11. Write a note on enterprise resource planning.
12. Write a note on knowledge discovery database.
13. Write a note on customer relationship management.
14. Write a note on supply chain management.

Part C: Essay Questions

1. Discuss the implications of modern communication technology to the business world.
2. Briefly state the uses of internet to business world.
3. Elaborate on the various types of conferences.
4. Examine the advantages of SMS.
5. What is LAN? What are its features and advantages?
6. Elucidate the recent trends in communication technology.
7. How would you use multimedia for business, education and entertainment?

Part D: Objective Type Questions

Choose the correct answer

1. Which one of the following helps organizations functioning in multiple locations keep disparate teams together?

   a. Instant messaging b. CD-Rom c. Laptop

   (Ans: a)

2. A mass of information can be stored in

   a. Cell phone b. Zocker c. CD-Rom

   (Ans: c)

3. Workflow at different locations is monitored through

   a. Website b. Video conferencing c. Groupware

   (Ans: c)

4. Mass of information can be passed in a fraction of second through

   a. E-mail b. Telephone c. Fax

   (Ans: a)

5. A large number of computers spanning the globe connecting a number of computers is

   a. Voice net b. Internet c. Cell phone

   (Ans: b)

6. The instrument that creates a digital image which can be stored in a computer is

   a. LAN b. WAN c. Scanner

   (Ans: c)

7. Network of studios in different locating is

   a. Teleconference b. Video conference c. Audio conference

   (Ans: b)

8. The system which allow numerous users to connect via a network is

a. Audio conference b. Del net c. Computer conference

(Ans: c)

9. Chief advantage of a mobile is

a. Used as advertisement media b. Cheaper call charges c. Accessibility

(Ans: c)

10. Which of the following helps in locating of an item on earth?

a. Global information system b. Global positioning system c. CRM

(Ans: b)

11. Which keeps track of the movement of materials, money and information in the process of supply of goods from suppliers to manufactures?

a. CRM b. Supply chain management

c. Geographic positioning system

(Ans: b)

12. Which is useful as an integrated management of business as a whole?

a. Enterprise resource planning b. Data warehousing

c. Global positioning system

(Ans: a)

13. Name the application that allows interactive analysis of data

a. Online analytical processing b. Data mining

c. Data warehousing

(Ans: a)

14. Which software facilitates deep research of client behaviour?

a. Supply chain management b. Enterprise resource planning

c. Customer relationship management

(Ans: c)

Fill in the blanks

1. Computer kept on a desk is called ________. (Desktop)
2. Machine which sends photocopy to distant places via telephone line is ________. (Fax)
3. Portable computer is ___________. (Laptop)
4. Equipment which takes a digital image that can be stored in a computer is _________. (Scanner)
5. Set of computers connected and stationed at one spot sharing hardware and software is _________. (LAN)
6. More than two LANs connected across a wide area make ________ network. (WAN)

7. Network of computers spanning the globe connecting number of computers is ________. (Internet)

8. ________ is a network of studios in different locations. (Video conference)

9. ________ is a medium for accessing all segments of customers. (Website)

10. Messages sent electronically via computer network is ________. (E-mail)

11. ________ allows several people to use a software to create documents, keep track of projects, routine messages, etc. (Groupware)

12. Encyclopedia, dictionaries, directories, etc., can be stored without occupying any physical space in ________. (CD-Rom)

13. Organizations functioning in multiple location use ________ to keep disparate team together. (Video conferencing)

14. ________ enables a student to learn in a simulated environment. (Computer based training)

15. ________ facilitates distant learners. (Web-based distance education)

16. ________ is an area of computer science focusing on creating machines doing the functions of human. (Artificial intelligence)

17. ________ is a collection of data designed to support management decision-making. (Data warehousing)

18. Extraction of hidden and predictive information from a large database is ________. (Data mining)

19. ________ is helpful in mapping and analysing things or events happening on earth. (Geographic information system)

20. ________ facilitates the identification of the location of an object in earth. (Global positioning system)

PART 8

INTERNAL COMMUNICATION

30

CHAPTER

MEMOS / CIRCULARS / NOTES

INTRODUCTION

Communication is the lifeblood of any business. Communication in the small and medium enterprises is easier than that in the large-scale industries.

Since the external communication has been elaborately discussed in a separate chapter, this chapter deals with internal communication in large enterprises.

Depending on the number of employees of the organization, face-to-face communication, faster communication, and need for lesser channels for internal communication are possible. The workforce size influences the pattern of communication in big enterprises.

The common documents used in internal communication are:

- Memorandum
- Office order
- Office circular
- Office note

MEMORANDUM

A memorandum is widely known by its abbreviated form, *memo*. It serves as a warning to the person to whom it is issued, inviting his attention to the acts of omission or commission. It is used internally. It is a short statement of an instruction to be done or acted upon.

Characteristics of Memorandum

a. A short written communication sent to members within an organization.
b. It may be used for recording and confirming an oral agreement, to communicate policy or procedure to one or many people and place information on record.
c. It is written in a formal style.

d. Used for routine day-to-day exchange of information.
e. It has the organization's name printed on the top.
f. Helps in fixing accountabilities of the sender and the receiver.
g. Provides the receiver time to think and act.
h. It may be for the attention of a single person or all, in the form of a circular.

Table 30.1 Differences between Memos and Letters

Letters	Memos
1. Letters are long.	Memos are short.
2. Letters have several parts.	These are designed according to convenience. They do not have a set part.
3. Mostly used for external communication.	Used for internal communication.
4. It has to conform to the rules of letter writing.	Though memos are formal, they do not follow the rules a letter has to observe.

Dr. Joan Minniger gives the following method of drafting a memo:

Stage - 1

Exploratory phase

- Write down clearly about the subject.
- Use personal pronouns.
- Don't judge or analyze the written matter.

Stage - 2

- Underline every item useful to the reader.
- Jot down the purpose of the memo at the top of the page.
- Distribute your underlined items into separate categories.
- Title the memorandum.

Start writing

- Begin with the body of the memo.
- Title the headings of grouped information.
- Give subtitle wherever necessary.
- Add additional points, if necessary.
- Rearrange and edit.
- Finalise the draft.

Sample 1: An office memorandum warning an employee against his habit of reading newspapers and magazines during office hours.

Office Memorandum

ABC Limited

22nd January 2011

To : Mr. P.K. Nirma, senior clerk, purchase department

From : General manager

Ref : 109/PD/2005

It has been reported that you were often found reading dailies and film magazines during office hours, in spite of clear direction against this practice by your immediate superior. Reading newspapers, etc., during working hours is against Service Conduct Rules.

You are hereby advised to resist from such activities and to strictly follow the directions given by the superiors. Any violation of these instructions in future would be viewed seriously.

Sd/-
General Manager

Sample 2: A memorandum warning an employee on account of being habitually late (different format).

Office Memorandum

Annamalai and Sons Limited

To : Mr. Grace Ratnam, data entry operator, sales division
From : HR manager

Ref : 119/SD/2005

It is noticed that for the last four days you have been reporting very late to duty without prior permission. You are hereby advised to attend office on time and maintain office punctuality. Failure to maintain office discipline would invite disciplinary action against you.

Sd/-
HR Manager

Sample 3: A memo to the customer relations officer reporting a customer complaint.

All India Corporation

From the desk of: The managing director
To: The customer relations officer

1st June 2011

Ref: MD-106

Subject: Complaint from Nixon Ltd.

The chief manager of Nixon Ltd has just telephoned to me that his written complaint dated 28th May 2011 about the colour printers in their store remain unattended by us. You must be aware that they are our valued customer and that their promotional work is hampered due to this. When we are on a business drive, you will surely appreciate that good after-sales service and satisfied customers form a major boost to this drive. I trust you will resolve the complaint without further loss of time and keep me informed.

Sd/-
Managing Director

OFFICE ORDER

It is an order containing directions or instructions to be complied by the recipient. The purpose for which it is used are:

i. Officer order may be used for transfer, extension of probation, refusing leave of absence to an employee, performing overtime to complete work, work allotment, service termination, deputation, granting promotion, declaring benefits, etc.

ii. Officer order should be drafted carefully, typed and signed by the authority concerned. It has to be acknowledged by the person who has to comply with it.

Points to be Kept in Mind on Drafting an Office Order

1. It should be short and to the point.
2. Should draw the attention of the person who have to comply with it.
3. Should contain specific instruction/direction for compliance.
4. Should be authentic, duly signed by a competent authority.

Sample 4: An office order banning smoking in the office premises, except in the canteen.

It has been decided that all the offices of the company shall be made a non -smoking zone with effect from 1st January 2011 in view of their centralised air-conditioning. However, smoking within the canteen premises would not be prohibited. This decision has been taken to protect the general health of the employees and also the members of the public visiting the company's offices. All employees are requested to co-operate and adhere to the decision strictly.

Sd/-
Office Manager

Sample 5: An office order asking an employee to show reasons for why disciplinary action should not be taken against him for being disobedient to his superior.

> **XYZ Limited**
> **Delhi**
> **Office Order**
>
> 1st June 2011
>
> Re: 108/PER/05
>
> Mr. S.K. Belson, junior assistant, is hereby required to show reasons in writing by June 15, 2011 as to why disciplinary action should not be taken against him for his persistent refusal to carry out faithfully the instructions issued by his section officer.
>
> Mr. Belson is hereby informed that on his failure to give satisfactory explanation about his conduct, disciplinary action will be taken as per the company's rules.
>
> Sd/-
> Personnel Manager

OFFICE CIRCULAR

Circular is a letter addressed to all officers, branches or departments of a company. The purpose is to circulate information contained therein among persons intended.

A circular letter is different from office circular.

Table 30.2 Differences between Office Circular and Circular Letter

Office Circular	Circular Letter
It is a letter or memorandum addressed to a number of employees, and is intended for general circulation.	Letter conveying some information from business enterprises to a large number of customers and suppliers.
It is an intra-office communication and it seeks to bring the important matters to the notice of the organization.	It is an unsolicited communication sent to customers/suppliers.
It is usually brief.	It is elaborative compared to office circular.

Features of Office Circular

- It is written in a simple language free from technical jargon, as it is intended for employees across the organization.
- It is a letter addressed by the head office to all branches and departments.
- It is a medium to carry information over to a large number of people.
- Since management issues a number of circulars on many occasions, each circular has to carry a reference number which is self-explanatory. For example, HR/07/2010/5. means that the circular is from the HR department, issued in the 7th month of 2010 and it is the fifth circular of the year.

Sample 6: Circular regarding computer training programme.

Omega Limited
New Delhi

Feb 1, 2005

Circular No. HR/07/2010/5

To all employees

A four hour computer training programme has been arranged for all employees on Sunday, 10th August, 2010, in the office premises. The programme will commence at 10. a.m. All employees are required to attend the programme.

Signature
Israel
HR Manager

OFFICE NOTE

It is a very short memorandum. It is exchanged between persons who work on the same task and need to exchange items of information frequently.

Characteristics of Office Note

- The note should be concise and clear.
- Should convey the decision of the note-maker.
- Should be written in a courteous fashion.
- Lengthy information, if any, needs to be given in appendix.
- It should be signed by the note-maker with his/her designation and department for further action.
- It must be clearly marked to the person/department concerned for further action.

Sample 7: Specimen office note.

Spectacular India Limited
Office Note

From

Company secretary, secretarial department.

To

Mr. S. Somasundaram, HR department
23rd July/CS/2011

Please make sure that all arrangements for the reception of the delegation from China are perfect. There should not be any confusion or chaos after they have arrived. Everything and everyone should be in place by 9.00 a.m. tomorrow.

Please report the completion of arrangement to me by 7 p.m. today.

Paari
Company Secretary

SUMMARY

Features of a memorandum are a short written communication, used for confirming oral agreement, written in a formal style, used for routine day-to-day exchange, organization name printed on the top, fixing accountability by the sender to the receiver, providing receiver time to think and act.

Features of an office order are short and brief, draws the attention of people for whom it is meant, contains instructions, authenticated by the issuing authority.

Features of an office note are brief, conveys the decision of the note-maker, to be written in a courteous style, lengthy information, if any, to be appended, to be marked to persons/ departments for whom it is meant.

Features of an office circular are to be made in a simple language, addressed by an office to all branches, medium to carry information to many persons, contains a reference number.

REVIEW QUESTIONS

Part A: Short Questions

1. What is a memorandum?
2. What is an office order?
3. What is an office circular?
4. What is an office note?

Part B: Paragraph Questions

1. State the characteristics of an office memorandum.
2. Highlight the features of an office order.
3. What are the characteristics of an office circular.
4. Distinguish between office circular and circular letter.
5. What are the features of an office note.

Part C: Essay Questions

1. Draft an office note revealing the suspension of transactions for two days due to stock taking.
2. Draft an office order requiring employees to sign the attendance register at the specified time in both sessions.
3. Write a circular informing the employees about withdrawal of free transport service provided to them.
4. Write an office memorandum warning an employee against his smoking inside the office premises.

Part D: Objective Type Questions

Choose the correct answer

1. Office order indicates

   a. Upward communication b. Downward communication

   c. Lateral communication.

   (Ans: b)

2. Document through which information is conveyed to employees across an organization.

   a. Memo b. Office circular c. Circular letter

   (Ans: b)

3. Document issued warning an employee

   a. Circular letter b. Office note c. Memorandum

   (Ans: c)

4. Document through which an employee makes a proposal or suggestion

   a. Memorandum b. Office circular c. Office note

   (Ans: c)

5. Document issued when an employee is intimated of his deputation

   a. Circular b. Memo c. Office order

   (Ans: b)

6. Document through which all employees are intimated of withdrawal of privilege

   a. Memorandum b. Office circular c. Office note

   (Ans: b)

7. Letter informing change in the location of office premises to customers.

   a. Office memorandum b. Office circular c. Circular letter

   (Ans: c)

Fill in the blanks

1. A method of internal communication warning an employee against his late-coming is made through ________. (Office memorandum)
2. A method of communication meant to inform the employees across the organization is through ____________. (Office circular)
3. A method of communication informing transfer, promotion, deputation, etc., is through __________. (Office order)
4. A method of communication through which suggestion made is passed through is _________. (Office note)

31

CHAPTER

COMPANY MEETINGS, AGENDA AND MINUTES

MEETINGS

The meetings in companies have to be convened as per the rules framed in the Companies Act of 1956. To be a validly convened meeting, the requirements of the Companies Act must be completely complied with. A meeting is proper and valid only if it is convened by the proper authority, namely board of directors, share holders or company law board. Proper notice must be given to all those entitled to attend, prior to the meeting. There must be a quorum and there should be a chairperson.

Types of Meetings

The meetings play an important role in the management of a company. It is where all decisions are made; members express their will and exercise their rights through annual general meeting. Board of directors exercise their powers and make decisions through board meetings.

Classification of company meetings

Shareholders' meetings

The following meetings are to be convened as per the statute:

- i. Statutory meeting
- ii. Annual general meeting
- iii. Extraordinary general meeting
- iv. Meetings convened by class of members.

Directors' meetings

- i. Meetings of the board of directors
- ii. Meetings of the committee of board of directors

Creditors' meetings

i. Debenture holders' meetings

ii. Other creditors' meetings

Drafting Notice for Meetings

A notice is a formal communication of certain facts to the people concerned, so that the latter are able to come prepared to attend the proposed meeting. It contains the venue, date, time and agenda of the meeting.

The key requirements of a notice inviting a meeting are:

- It is to be given to every person entitled to receive it.
- It is to be given at the proper time.
- It should disclose the purpose of the meeting.

Contents of a notice

A notice should contain:

- Company's full name and address of the registered office.
- Date, day, place and time of the meeting.
- Statement of business to be transacted.
- Statutory reminder with regards to proxies.
- Signature of a director, secretary or some authority authorised by the company.
- Agenda of the meeting.
- Explanatory statement in respect of special business to be transacted, if any, at the meeting.

Nuances of writing a notice

- Person authorized to draft a notice should issue a notice on the authority of the person empowered to convene the meeting. It is usually one of the board of directors in the case of a company.
- It should ensure strict adherence to statutory requirements and articles of the association.
- It should be signed and dated, and should indicate under whose authority it is issued.
- The length a of notice is governed by the law or articles of the association.
- Statement of business to be transacted should be enclosed.
- Special business, if any, to be transacted u/s 173 (2) must be enclosed.
- It should be sent to all those entitled to receive it.

Sample 1: Specimen notice of Annual General Meeting.

Bombay Mills Ltd.
Notice of Meeting

Nagini House
20, Stephen Street,
Navi Mumbai,
Mumbai – 400 020

April 2, 2011

To

All members

A notice is hereby given that the annual meeting of members of the Bombay Mills Ltd., will be held on 28th April 2011, at 4.00 p.m. at the Taj Mahal Hotel, Mumbai – 400 039, to transact the following business:

To adopt the income and expenditure account, the balance sheet, the report of the auditors and the report of the committees for the year ended 31st March 2011;

To declare the results of the election of the president, vice-president, honorary secretary, honorary treasurer and four ordinary members of the executive committee for the years 2009-2010 and 2010-2011, in accordance with Rule 34 (iii) of the rules and regulations of the association;

To appoint auditors for the year 2011-2012 and fix their remuneration;

To consider any other matter that may be brought forward for which written notice of at least seven days has been given.

By order of the Executive Committee
Kalaimahal
Honorary Secretary

Mumbai
April 2, 2011

Sample 2: Specimen notice of board meeting.

Paari Engineering and Locomotive Co. Ltd.
Jafer House, 24, Thomas Street, Parrys Corner,
Chennai – 600 001

Ref. No. 123/MJ/92 16th July 2011

Pallavan
A-3/15, Mahesh Nagar,
S.V. Road,
Pudupet,
Trichy.

Dear Sir,

A meeting of the board of directors will be held on 5th September 2011, at the registered office of the company at 2 p.m. The agenda for the meeting is enclosed. Please be present at the meeting.

Yours sincerely,
P.A. Annamalai
Secretary

Encl: Agenda

AGENDA

An agenda refers to a list of items of business to be transacted in a meeting. It is prepared in advance for any type of meeting, in order to ensure an effective and systematic conduct of the meeting. The items included depend on the type of meeting. A good agenda would contain not only a list of items but also a brief explanation to the various items, so that a better deliberation takes place, helping to arrive at quality decisions. The items listed are taken up for deliberation in the order in which it is listed.

- The first item in the agenda is the approval of the minutes of the previous meeting. Current items in the agenda cannot be taken for discussion without the approval of the previous meeting.
- Then, items to be dealt with should be mentioned.
- When all the items have been dealt with, the chairperson of the meeting may permit members to raise any issue that is not mentioned in the agenda. Therefore, an item reading 'any other business with the permission of the chair' should be given as the penultimate item.
- It is a usual practice to fix the date of the next meeting during the current meeting itself. It should be the last item in the agenda.

In the case of Annual General Meeting (AGM), items in the agenda are split into two, namely ordinary business items and special business items.

Ordinary business items include

- Consideration of final accounts, balance sheets, reports of directors and auditors.
- Declaration of dividend.
- Appointment of directors in place of those retiring.
- Appointment of auditors and fixing remuneration for them.

Special business items include

According to the companies Act 173 (2) all businesses other than the ordinary business items are called *special business*. Special items need to be annexed as an explanatory statement to the notice calling the meeting.

The agenda may be written either in the noun form or the infinitive verb form.

Noun Form

- Appointment of subcommittee to look into losses
- Fund collection

Infinitive Form

It starts with the word 'To'.

- To appoint a subcommittee
- To consider a proposal to open a branch
- To collect funds

Sample 3: Specimen

AGENDA

Item No	Particulars
1.	To confirm the minutes of the last meeting.
2.	To grant leave of absence to Mr. Vaidya and Mrs. Vincent.
3.	To approve transfer and transmission of shares.
4.	To propose the appointment of Messrs. Amanulla and Sons as agents for the State of Maharastra.
5.	To fix the date of the next meeting.

MINUTES

The minutes may be defined as a written record of the proceedings, business transacted and the decisions arrived at in the meeting of the directors or shareholders of a company.

Hallmarks of a Good Minutes Writing

The minutes writing should contain the following:

Accuracy: It should be written as accurately as possible since it serves as a documentary evidence in any court of law. Inaccuracy is fatal to the business transacted.

Clarity: The minutes should be free from confusion. The items like date, amount, quantities, etc., should be stated clearly. If the meeting gives any special direction to be carried out, the officials receiving such directions should be named or otherwise described.

Preciseness and pointedness: While it is required to be precise, it should also be comprehensive. In other words, the essential facts should not be omitted in the name of preciseness. It should set out what exactly had been done, so that even an absentee member can understand what transpired in the meeting. At the same time, it should not be loaded with unnecessary statements.

Completeness: The minutes should be complete, so that one may assume that items not stated in the minutes were not dealt with.

Indexation: It is better to index the items for ready reference. It is prudent to give a title to each and every item and number all the items. For example, finance, appointment, borrowal, etc.

Language aspect: The minutes writer needs to use past tense and passive voice.

Past tense

The secretary read out ...

The chairman informed ...

The meeting ended ...

Passive voice

The minutes were taken as read, confirmed and signed.

Progress report for December was presented...

Secretary was authorised ...

It is advisable to use impersonal passive voice for recording decisions and resolutions. For example,

It was decided that a committee be appointed. It was resolved that meeting be adjourned. Resolved that a special fund be created for ...

When an action is proposed, intended, planned or thought but not yet completed, it is usual to use verbs of command and desire. For example,

I move that Zaviour be appointed.

I propose that the secretary be authorized.

When a suggestion is adopted by the meeting, common decision is recorded as follows:

- Resolved that secretary be authorized.
- To indicate the appointment of the official.
- It was resolved that Anna be and is hereby appointed.
- Resolved that a committee consisting of Akbar, Baba and Ibrahim be and is hereby appointed.
- It was decided that the secretary be and is hereby authorized to ...

To indicate that decision has been taken and further action has to be started. For example,

Resolved that a new building is to be constructed for staff welfare centre. It was further resolved that the secretary be and is hereby authorized to invite tenders for the construction.

Let each resolution be headed or titled. For example,

Appointment of secretary

Appointment of bankers

Sample 4: Specimen minutes of Annual General Meeting.

The minutes of the proceedings of the second Annual General Meeting of Cherran Limited was held on Tuesday, 24th September 2011, at 3:30 p.m. at 123, Central Avenue, Nagpur.

The following were present:

Mr. Yazhini (Chairman)

Mr. Pozhil (Director)

Mr. Mathi (Director)

Ms. Kala (Director)

Mr. Mullai (Director, Chairman of Audit Committee)

Mr. Padi (Company Secretary)

Members present in person (120)

Members present by proxy (11)

Mr. Ezhil, Partner of M/s AB & Co. Chartered Accountants, Auditors of the Company, was present.

Mr. Pothigai, Practising Company Secretary, was also present.

1. **Chairman:** In accordance with Article 30 of the articles of association, Mr. Yazhini, Chairman of the board of directors, took the chair.

2. **Welcome:** The chairman welcomed the members and introduced the directors seated on the dias.

3. **Quorum:** The chairman declared that the requisite quorum was present and called the meeting to order.

4. **Register of directors' shareholding:** The chairman informed the members that in accordance with section 307 of the Companies Act, register of directors' shareholding is available at the meeting for inspection.

5. **Notice of meeting:** With the consent of the members present, the notice convening the Annual General Meeting of the company was taken as read.

6. **Auditors' report:** The chairman requested the company secretary to read the auditors' report. After the auditors' report had been read, the chairman delivered his speech.

   The business of the meeting as per the notice thereof was thereafter taken up itemwise.

7. **Adoption of accounts:** The chairman requested Mr. Battliboe to read the Ordinary Resolution for the adoption of the Accounts for the year ended 31st March 2011 and Mr. Battliboi read out the Ordinary Resolution as follows:

   "Resolved that the audited balance sheet of the company as at 31st March 2011 and the profit and loss account of the company for the financial year ended on that date, together with the schedules and notes attached thereto, along with the reports thereon of the directors and the auditors, as circulated to the members and laid before the meeting, be and are hereby approved and adopted."

   After the above resolution was proposed and seconded, but before it was put to the vote, the chairman invited members (other than those present by proxy) to make, if any, on the reports and accounts, observations and comments as well as on the other resolutions set out in the notice convening the meeting. Some members raised queries on the annual report, accounts and other items set out in the notice and the chairman answered their queries.

   On a show of hands, the chairman declared the aforesaid Ordinary Resolution carried by the requisite majority.

8. **Declaration of dividend:** Mr. A read the following resolution as an Ordinary Resolution: "Resolved that the dividend @ ₹ 2 on the equity shares of ₹ 10 each, fully paid-up, be and is hereby for payment, after deduction of tax at source, if any, to those members whose names appear on the company's register of members on Tuesday, 24th Oct 2011."

   The resolution was proposed by Mr. Pozhil and seconded by Mr. Mathi, and was put to the vote as an Ordinary Resolution.

On a show of hands, the chairman declared the aforesaid Ordinary Resolution carried unanimously.

9. Appointment of directors

Proposed by: Mr. Pozhil

Seconded by: Mr. Mathi

The following resolution having been proposed and seconded by the aforementioned two members, was put to the vote as an Ordinary Resolution:

"Resolved that, pursuant to section 256 of the Companies Act, 1956, Mr. Mahilendi who retires by rotation and, being eligible for re-appointment, offers himself for re-appointment, be and is hereby re-appointed as a director of the company and that his period of office be liable to determination by retirement of directors by rotation."

On a show of hands, the chairman declared the aforesaid Ordinary Resolution carried unanimously.

10. Appointment of auditors

Proposed by: Mr. Pozhil

Seconded by: Mr. Mathi.

The following resolution having been proposed and seconded by the aforementioned two members, was put to the vote as an Ordinary Resolution:

"Resolved that AB & Co., Chartered Accountants, Nagpur, be and are hereby re-appointed as auditors of the company to hold office from the conclusion of this meeting until the conclusion of the next Annual General Meeting of the company on a remuneration of ₹ 50,000, plus applicable service tax and other out of pocket expenses incurred for the purposes of the audit."

On a show of hands, the chairman declared the aforesaid Ordinary Resolution carried unanimously.

11. Termination of meeting

The meeting ended with a vote of thanks to the chairman.

Chairman
Yazhini

SUMMARY

Key requirements of a notice are it has to be sent to every person entitled to attend and within a stipulated time.

The contents of a notice are Full name and address of company, date, time and venue of the meeting, signature of the person conducting the meeting, statement of business to be transacted, annexing explanatory statements, if necessary.

The nuances of notice writing are: It has to be made by a person authorized in this regard, strict adherence to the provisions of company law regarding conduct of meeting, dated and signed by a designated officer, statement of business to be transacted to be enclosed, enclosure of statements revealing special business to be transacted.

The hallmarks of minutes are accuracy, clarity, preciseness, completeness, indexation and language aspect.

REVIEW QUESTIONS

Part A: Short Questions

1. What is an agenda of a meeting?
2. What are minutes?

Part B: Paragraph Questions

1. What are the different types of meetings conducted in a company?
2. State the contents of a notice.
3. State the mechanics of writing a notice.
4. How would you draft a notice and for what?

Part C: Essay Questions

1. Enumerate the hallmarks of good minutes.

Part D: Objective Type Questions

Choose the correct answer

1. A list of items to be transacted at a meeting is

   a. Memorandum b. Articles c. Agenda

   (Ans: c)

2. Written record of the proceedings of a meeting is

   a. Agenda b. Minutes c. Information booklet

   (Ans: b)

Fill in the Blanks

1. Formal communication of facts relating to any aspect of functioning of a concern is ________. (Notice)
2. A list of items to be transacted at a meeting is called ________________. (Agenda)
3. Written record of the proceedings of a meeting is ______________. (Minutes)

PART 9

CORPORATE COMMUNICATION

32

CHAPTER

INTERNAL COMMUNICATION

INTRODUCTION

The term *corporate communication* refers to the official channels through which a message is delivered horizontally, vertically and diagonally in an organization.

FORMS OF CORPORATE COMMUNICATION

It takes many forms. Information is sent internally through in-house magazines and conducting programmes to improve managers' speaking, writing skills and personality traits. External communication goes through corporate brochures, information booklets, press release, press conferences advertisements, etc. Big companies have public relations department, which connects external and internal people and seeks to maintain a corporate image.

INTERNAL CORPORATE COMMUNICATION

Good internal corporate communication serves many purposes like attracting good employees, ensuring the satisfaction of existing employees, attracting good clients and suppliers, getting recognition from government and expanding the market for the corporate.

In-House Journal

It is the company's own journal meant for internal circulation. It may be bulletins and newsletters. It reflects the company's pride in itself. The contents of the magazine are:

- Latest development in the top echelons of management.
- Outcomes of meetings with leaders and dignitaries.
- Opening of a new branch office.
- Major postings and reshuffles.
- Achievements of employees in different spheres like sports, academics, public service, fine arts, etc.

- Scholarly writings on any field of activity.
- Creative writing like poems, short stories, satires.
- Photographs of general interests.
- Paintings by employees.
- News on birth, marriage and promotion of employees.
- Charitable activities like donation to various bodies, philanthropies, etc.
- Social activities like awarding scholarship, doing tree plantation, running blood bank and rendering community service.

Purposes served by the in-house magazine

- Highlighting all positives about the company, its growth and prospects.
- Sharing the breakthrough with internal stakeholders, thereby creating a transparent environment.
- Giving an outlet to employees to demonstrate their creative talents.
- Keeping a harmonious relation with employees by providing them a channel to display their latent talents.
- Familiarizing the top echelons of management with middle and lower level functionaries.
- Spreading an image of being a responsible corporate citizen by demonstrating the company's concern towards its various stakeholders.
- Creating a feeling of bond among the employees.

Corporate Brochure

Brochures are printed in the form of handouts, leaflets or folders in a glossy paper. It explains the various aspects of a company. It is usually drafted by professional copywriters, graphic artists and publicity personnel. It is distributed to clients or prospective dealers and distributors connected with the company. A colourful and glossy brochure reflects the company's image and pride.

Points to be noted while preparing a brochure

- It should be compact and impressive.
- Writing should be minimal.
- Pictures, diagrams, charts and tables should be arranged in order.
- Pictures of company's plant, office, branch office, machinery, testimonials of satisfied users, etc., need to be included to impress the reader.
- A sample of the product can be included like in the case of fabrics, perfumes, etc.
- Catchy headlines, factual statements about the company's product may be included.
- Technical process may be included to appeal to the tech-savvy readers. It should be prepared in a language easily understandable by its target audience.
- It should be printed to the exact number required.
- It should be updated.

Usefulness of a brochure

- It enlightens the company about its operations, product, process, etc.
- Pictorial presentation adds to the appeal value.

- Tables, charts and comparative statements show how the company is distinct from others.
- It reaches even the person unapproached by the company.
- It supplements the marketing endeavours of the company.

Information Booklet

Varied information concerning the company covering numerous aspects like name, address, schemes, branch office, regulations, etc., is published in a handy, readable form for ready reference by different categories of people dealing with the company. This is called a *booklet*. Financial service providers may bring out booklets detailing various schemes, rate of interest, payment mode, encashment, tax concession, etc. Information booklet should be simple enough to be understood by all. It by itself serves as an advertisement. Another variant of booklet is 'manual'. It usually contains instructions. For example, office manuals contain all the rules, regulations, process of work, organization structure, etc. Whenever technically superior products are unveiled, the company concerned issues a manual explaining the process of operation, maintenance, do's and don'ts, etc.

Press Release

Press release keeps the general public informed of a company's activities. Media reporters are given the company's version of the activities and developments. These releases are mailed or may be delivered directly to the media office. Companies use different methods to induce the media to print their versions.

Nature of a press release

- It is given on a company's letterhead signed by a responsible officer.
- It should contain accurate information with names, places, figures and endorsements.
- Services of skilled writers need to be used for drafting it.
- It should be supported by a signed document and statement to convince the media about the veracity of the release.
- Company should share good relations with the press to get good coverage.
- PR department has to follow it up and ensure that it is reported accurately.

Functions of a press release

1. It conveys vital news about the company to the general public. For example, a company may inform the general public about its new product, new branch, expansion, diversification, merger, amalgamation, relocation, new appointment, new issue, etc.
2. It can be used to remove misinformation. Suppose the public get panicked about drinking a particular brand of cool drinks, the company can remove such apprehension through a press release.
3. Since press release is presented through a third party i.e. media, it has more convincing value.
4. Frequent press releases keep the company in the limelight.
5. It is the right medium to convey the message to the different stakeholders of the company.
6. Company can present lengthy information through press releases, while it is expensive if it is by way of advertisement.

Sample 1: Specimen of a press release.

Safe chickens, disease-free and safe food

Chicken consumers would be glad to know that our chicks are grown in the bird-flu-free state of Tamil Nadu. Our birds are moved from the farm to the various shopping outlets in hygienic conditions. All our chicken farms are maintained according to international standards. There is a centralized system monitoring every stage of production. Thus, we maintain product quality at every stage.

We also would like to inform that the bird flu virus cannot survive beyond a temperature of 70°C. Therefore, we ensure that our chickens are 100% free from bird flu. Please visit our website for detailed information.

Covering letter for publishing the aforesaid press release in a daily.

Sample 2: Press release for informing the public about the safety of eating chickens.

The Editor
Dravida Nadu,
New Delhi – 110 011

Dear Sir,

We would like to inform the public correctly about the safe food value of our chickens. We enclose a write-up giving the facts. We request you to publish it in your daily at the earliest, as the matter affects thousands of workers, dealers and chicken consumers.

We trust you will, as always, support the cause of truth.

Thanking you,

Yours faithfully,
Public Relations Officer

Press Conference

Press conference is a meeting arranged by the company with the media. It is a two-way communication.

Purpose of a press conference

It is helpful to:

- Launch a new product, or new model.
- Declare the opening of a new branch or new establishment.
- Announce merger or amalgamation.
- Clarify one's version in case of misinformation.
- Announce breakthroughs.
- Announce new schemes.

Organising press conference (mechanics):

Prior to the conference

An organizer has to think about the venue, time, spokesperson, the message and attendees to be Induced to participate through glossy invitation, intellectual bait and other incentives like presents or gifts.

During the conference

- Audio-visual aids need to be kept in readiness.
- Greet the participants.
- The conference plan has to be communicated in 30 seconds.
- Spokesperson has to deliver the quintessence of the conference by handouts or press release with refreshments.
- Detailed briefing about the conference has to be presented together by one male and one female alternatively to hold the attention of the audience. Graphic aids can be used to relieve the monotony.
- Give a summary of the talk.
- Organizers have to face questions from the media people. The latter should be encouraged by answering as many questions as possible convincingly. There should be a two-way communication. The participants who would like to raise questions have to introduce themselves and then pose the questions unequivocally. The organisers have to decide who would handle the questions posed and respond according to the role assigned to the members of the organizing team.
- Give a summary of the conference and thank the participants and invite them for refreshments.

SUMMARY

Corporate communication refers to the channels through which a message is delivered officially in an organization.

Forms of corporate communication includes in-house magazines, PR meetings, press release, corporate brochure, information booklet, press meet and video conference.

Nature of a press release – It is given by the company, signed by a responsible officer, drafted by a skilled person, accompanied by supporting documents to convince the press to get wide coverage. Proper follow-up is needed for an effective outreach.

Functions of a press release are conveying vital information about the company, eliminating rumours and misinformation presented through a third party, acting, as a medium to convey information to different stakeholders and being useful to present lengthy information.

Organizing a press conference requires arrangement of audio-visual aids, greeting participants, communication of the purpose of the conference, presenting a detailed briefing by one of the organizers, giving a summary of the talk, facing questions and finally thanking the participants.

REVIEW QUESTIONS

Part A: Short Questions

1. What is corporate communication?
2. What is an in-house journal?
3. What is a corporate brochure?

4. What is an information booklet?
5. What is a press release?
6. What is a press conference?

Part B: Paragraph Questions

1. State the forms of corporate communication.
2. Point out the purposes served by an in-house journal.
3. Highlight the usefulness of a corporate brochure.
4. Write a note on information booklet.
5. Point out the features of a press release.

Part C: Essay Questions

1. State the contents of an in-house journal.
2. Write down the points to be noted while preparing a brochure.
3. Bring out the functions of a press release.
4. How would you organize a press conference?

Part D: Objective Type Questions

Choose the correct answer

1. Meeting arranged by the company with the media

   a. Conference b. Press conference c. Meeting

   (Ans: b)

2. Medium through which the public is kept informed of a company's activities or point of view

   a. Minutes b. Press release c. Agenda

   (Ans: b)

3. Medium through which the internal public is informed of the company's activities

   a. Advertisement b. In-house journal c. Brochure

   (Ans: b)

Fill in the blanks

1. The channel through which a message is transmitted officially, vertically, horizontally and diagonally is ____________. (Corporate communication)
2. Bulletins and newsletters come under ____________ category. (In-house journal)
3. Profile of a company prepared in a handy and readable form is _______. (Information booklet)
4. _________ is one which is used to keep the general public informed of a company's activities. (Press release)
5. Meeting arranged by the company with the media is ____________. (Press conference)

33

CHAPTER

PUBLIC RELATIONS (PR)

INTRODUCTION

Public relations is the company's organized effort to understand the public (both internal and external) and make it understood for the sake of its self-interest.

It is defined as an organized effort by the company to build its own image among those who count.

OBJECTIVES OF PR

Public relations means the way by which the company relates within and to generate goodwill for it to pursue its business and other ideals. The objectives of PR are:

- Creating awareness about the company's goals, products and services.
- Sustaining awareness on an ongoing basis about what the competitors are up to.
- To get accepted by the public.
- Creating a bond of trust so as to counter the threat of misinformation and disinformation.
- Winning co-operation from various constituencies.
- Earning recognition so that the company is popular for its credentials in social service, pollution control, grievance redressal, employee care, customer care, etc.

CONSTITUENCIES OR STAKEHOLDERS OF A COMPANY

The following constituencies have a stake in the functioning of a company:

Customers, suppliers, employees, potential customers, tax authorities, utility service providers, media, regulatory authorities, financing agencies, professionals, channel members, local residents, logistic service providers, etc.

MEANS OF COMMUNICATING WITH INTERNAL PUBLIC

The term *internal public* refers to employees, management and unions. The various means of communicating with them are through:

Counselling

Companies appoint counsellors to help the employees get used to the jobs.

Suggestion Scheme

Employees who have good ideas may contribute them in the suggestion box. Companies reward good and workable suggestions.

Publications

In-house journals and magazine keep the employees informed of changes, of people occupying the various positions in the hierarcy, progress made by the company, challenges faced and to be faced, achievements of employees, events conducted, social services rendered, etc.

Entertainment

Screening films, conducting magic shows, gymnastic shows, hypnotism shows, etc., conducting special lectures on stress management, diet system, yoga and meditation, conducting literary competition and sports events are some of the means of solidifying the bond with the employees.

Felicitations

Employees and their families can be felicitated for their meritorious performance, special adventure and scholarship.

Inviting Family Members

Inviting family members on occasions like festivals, New Year's Day, Independence Day etc., would strengthen the bond between the company and its employees.

MEANS OF COMMUNICATING WITH EXTERNAL PUBLIC

The term *external public* includes customers, financiers, channel members, general public, institutions, etc. The means of communicating with them are:

Organizing Various Mechanisms

Constituting grievance cells, call centres, organizing grievance meet, enquiry counters, display of posters and pamphlets explaining various products are some of the ways to win and retain the customers.

Annual Statement

The company's shareholders, financiers, bankers, depositors, etc., would like to know the financial status of a company. Therefore, releasing financial statement with explanatory notes may clarify the doubts and help them have an insight into the various aspects of functioning of the company.

Corporate Social Obligation

Company has to also focus on the future customers, besides retaining the existing ones. Engaging in social service, organizing health camps, helping during national disasters and outbreak of diseases, contributing to the infrastructure development projects undertaken in the neighbourhood, presenting awards to academic toppers, etc., are some of the initiatives creating good corporate image in the minds of not only the existing customers but also the prospective customers.

Ethical Conduct as a Responsible Corporate

Prompt payment of various dues to public utility, institutions, tax authorities, putting in place pollution control devices, strict observance of various regulatory laws, etc., have potential to project a positive image about the company. In other words, clean administration and observance of standards in its corporate behaviour help to win new customers and retain the existing ones.

TOOLS OF PR

The following are the tools of PR:

Television

Programmes sponsored by the company, the announcer's voice helping in registering the company slogan in people's mind, impressive presentation of advertisements on television, etc., contribute a great deal in taking the message to the targeted audience.

Print Media

Good scholarly articles written by authorities in those subjects published in magazines, journals on themes of current importance, participation in panel discussions and giving press interviews, all heighten the image of the company.

Films

Motion films on the working of the company shown to company visitors, at exhibitions, press meets and in-house get-togethers communicate positively about the company.

Literature

Brochures, booklets, pamphlets and leaflets can be used for image-building. They can be supplied with key-chains, paper weights, calendars, useful telephone numbers, etc.

Direct Mail

Some companies send birthday greetings to their customers. Season's greetings, sympathy cards, invitations, etc., can be used as a medium to reach out to the company's established customers.

Internet

It is a very effective medium for reaching special interest groups.

Radio

It is a medium of mass communication. Radio talks, sponsored radio programmes, advertisement in FM and other radios help in reaching a vast audience spread across the globe.

Manners and Etiquette

The way the employees dress, speak, deal with the clients, respond to queries, etc., speak volumes about the company to the external public.

CONFERENCE

Conference is a gathering of a particular set of individuals who are invited for discussion and are required to present factual analysis on a particular subject or set of topics in a related field.

Conference and meeting serve the same purpose. It facilitates cross-fertilisation of ideas. Meeting is more in-house oriented, while conference includes outsiders also.

Planning the Conference

Planning the conference includes these:

Definition of purpose: First define the purpose of the conference. It may be to co-ordinate activities, build morale, brief the staff, solve problems, exchange information, initiate a policy, launch a product, etc.

Deciding on the theme: The theme and objectives of the conference need to be decided.

Selection of date, time and duration: Selection of date, time and duration of the conference should be decided next. The organizer has to allow sufficient time for the attendees to come prepared for the conference.

Selection of venue: Venue of the conference needs to be selected and visited before the conference to assess the capacity of hall and the facilities available there.

Arranging accommodation: Accommodation for the attendees needs to be decided.

Promoting the conference: Organizers have to promote the conference through websites, posters, notice boards, etc.

Other work: The host has to make arrangements for printing of invitations ensuring confirmation from participants, notes, seating arrangements, name badges, catering, conference kits, deciding on guest speakers, etc.

Conducting Effective Video Conferences

Conducting effective video conferences has to look into:

Proper placement of camera: Where the presenter is making a presentation from the front of the room, the camera should be placed at the eye level of the seated participants so that the presenter is able to maintain an eye contact with the latter.

Familiarity with the operation: The presenter has to be familiar with the placement and operation of cameras, microphones and remote controls.

Intonation: The presenter has to vary the tone and pitch of his voice to add emphasis and meaning. He has to use appropriate facial expressions and gestures.

Choice of appropriate dress: The presenter has to choose a dress suited to his age, colour and occasion.

Font size: When the presenter is using a slide show, it is better to use 36–40 point font size. It is advisable to use graphics to illustrate his ideas.

Face-to-face contacts: If he uses other sources of visual information like power point slide show, a white board or a video tape, he has to alternate between the visual and his face as often as possible to maintain a face-to-face contact.

Lighting: The space used for video conferencing should be well lit with indirect light sources.

Break: Video conferencing should provide for 10 minutes break for every 50 minutes of business interaction.

Proper temperature: Temperature needs to be set at an appropriate level and the chairs should be ergonomically correct.

SUMMARY

The objectives of public relations are awareness creation, sustaining the awareness, to be accepted by the public, creating a bond of trust, winning co-operation from diverse stakeholders and earning recognition.

Means of communication with the internal public are counselling, suggestion scheme, publications, entertainment, felicitation, inviting family members of employees to company functions.

Means of communicating with the external public are organizing mechanisms, annual statements, corporate social obligations and ethical conduct.

The tools of public relations are television, print media, films, literature, direct mail, internet, radio, manners and etiquette.

Planning a conference is done by defining the purpose of the conference, selection of date and time, deciding on the theme, selection of venue, arranging accommodation, promoting the conference and other related work.

Video conference can be conducted effectively by proper placement of camera, familiarity with the operation, intonation, choice of dress, font size of the presentation, face-to-face contact with the audience, lighting arrangement, break and proper temperature.

REVIEW QUESTIONS

Part A: Short Questions

1. What is public relations?
2. Who comes under the internal public?
3. Who comes under the external public?

4. What is a conference?
5. What is a video conference?

Part B: Paragraph Questions

1. Mention the objectives of public relations.
2. How would you plan a conference?

Part C: Essay Questions

1. Discuss the various means of communicating with the internal public and the external public.
2. What are the various tools used for public relations?
3. How would you conduct a video conference?

Part D: Objective Type Questions

Choose the correct answer

1. Who is the external public in the following?

   a. Director b. CEO c. Tax authorities

   (Ans: c)

2. Who is the internal public in the following?

   a. Employee b. Government institutions c. Media

   (Ans: a)

3. Forum or platform to discuss and deliberate the issues confronting a particular field is

   a. Meeting b. Conference c. Press meet

   (Ans: b)

Fill in the blanks

1. An organized effort to link internal and external public is ____________. (Public relations)
2. A forum providing a platform for a particular set of people in a given field to deliberate on various issues affecting them is ______________. (Conference)

PART 10

EMPLOYMENT COMMUNICATION

34

CHAPTER

APPLICATION LETTER AND RÉSUMÉ

APPLICATION FOR APPOINTMENTS

The application for appointment requires the utmost attention of the applicant. It should convince the employer and stimulate action. Otherwise, it has the risk of being rejected. It is a sort of sales letter wherein the applicant tries to sell his services by displaying his merit.

An effective letter of application should contain the following points:

Applicant's Address: The writer's address is generally at the top of the letter, in the right-hand corner. Date is written below the address.

If, however, the address is given at the left-hand top corner, the word *From* should be written first and the address should be given from the next line. In such a case, the word *To* should be written before writing the inside address.

Inside Address: The name and address of the employer is written above the salutation.

If the application is in response to an advertisement, the inside address may start with the designation of the advertiser. For example,

The Human Resource Manager,
The Chennai Refineries Limited,
Chennai – 600 086

If the advertiser has not disclosed his identity, and has given his address as a certain post box number or a newspaper box number, the inside address can be written as follows:

The Advertiser,
G.P.O. Box No. 1741,
Chennai – 600 001

The Advertiser,
The Indian Express,
Box No. 1978,
Chennai – 600 002

The Salutation: If an application is addressed to the government officials, *Sir* is generally used. In all other applications addressed to commercial houses, *Dear Sir* is used.

Source of Information: If the application is in answer to an advertisement in a newspaper, it should refer to the advertisement appearing in the particular newspaper. For example,

With reference to your advertisement in The Hindu of 22nd February 1985, I offer myself as a candidate for the post of ...

If the source of information is a friend or an important official, his name should be mentioned. For example,

I was given to understand by your friend Mr. X, chief accountant that there is a vacancy for the post of credit manager in your office and I would like to apply for it..."

If it is an unsolicited application, the applicant can straightaway explain his experience and interest in the work. For example,

My three years experience in doing advertising work, I am sure, will be useful in your advertising department.

The Name of the Post: The applicant should state the name of the post for which he is applying.

Qualifications: While stating the academic qualification, the applicant should state the name of the university from which he has graduated. Any distinction or prizes won can be added.

If the applicant has acquired any special qualification for the particular post advertised, it can be stressed. For example, if the post is for a stenographer, his skill and experience as a computer analyst can be stated.

Experience: In case the applicant has previous experience, the period of service, positions held, etc., should be stated. Reason for leaving the present post can be stated; criticism of the present employer should be avoided.

Age: Both the age and the date of birth should be furnished in the application.

References: The names and address of references can be furnished. The applicant's suitability for the post can be ascertained from such references.

Testimonials: Mention about the copies of testimonials attached in the application.

Body of the Letter: The body of the letter should be divided into paragraphs, each dealing with a separate item. The application should be drafted in a tone which reveals the applicants' competence to do the job. The family problems or the financial hardships which the applicant faces should never be mentioned. If it is an unsolicited application, the applicant can request for an interview to prove his mettle. For example,

I shall be grateful if you grant me an interview during which I can show samples of my work.

Concluding Paragraph: It is customary to close the letter with an assurance that he will try to satisfy the requirements of the post, should he be selected for it.

Complimentary Close: *Yours faithfully* is an appropriate complimentary close.

Signature: After the signature, the name of the applicant should be typed or written clearly.

If the applicant is a lady, she should indicate whether she is married or unmarried by putting 'Miss' or 'Mrs' in brackets before her signature.

SAMPLE APPLICATION LETTERS AND RÉSUMÉS

Sample 1. A letter of application in reply to the following advertisement.

Wanted an experienced accounts officer. Apply stating previous experience, age and minimum salarly expected to Box No. 999, The Indian Express, Anna salai, Chennai – 2.

14/66, Rodier Mill Street,
Mudaliarpet,
Pondicherry – 605 004

22nd February 2011

The Advertiser,
Box No. 999,
The Indian Express,
Anna Salai,
Chennai – 600 002

Dear Sir,

I believe that my qualification and experience will meet your consideration for the post of accounts officer advertised by you in the *Indian Express* on 20th February 2011.

I graduated from Tagore Arts College, Pondicherry, having passed the B.Com Degree Examination in April, conducted by the University of Madras. I have also obtained a diploma in Office Management. I am 28 years of age, my date of birth being 30th July 1982.

I have been working for Messrs Selvam & Co as senior accountant for the past six years. I am in complete charge of the accounts section and have sufficient experience in closing accounts and drawing balance sheet independently. I can also handle details related to sales tax and income tax.

Due to limited activities in my present concern which does not foster my full development, I seek employment in a large company like yours.

My present employer can be referred to, with regards to my experience and efficiency. You may also refer to Dr. K. Sundar, the director of AB Limited, Chennai – 75.

I am presently drawing a monthly salary of ₹ 25,000. The minimum salary expected can be discussed at the interview, during which you will have a better opportunity to judge my ability.

I assure you that should I be selected for the post, I shall try my best to give you full satisfaction.

May I have an interview at your convenience. I shall give you any further details you may need to know about me.

Yours faithfully,
S. Balasubramanian

Sample 2. Draft an application in response to the followings advertisement: Vijai Nicole software company, Velacherry requires a System analyst with knowledge of Oracle. Salary ₹ 50,000 per month. Apply giving age, education, experience and references.

11, Subbaraya Nagar,
Cuddalore – 607 001

1st February 2011

Vijai Nicole
Velacherry,
Chennai – 600 109

Dear Sir,

I like to apply for the post of system analyst advertised in your website.

The enclosed personal record sheet will reveal my experience and attainments.

I assure you that should I be fortunate in being selected for the post, I will discharge my duties devotedly and I will soon gain your confidence.

Yours faithfully,
Dillip

Encl: Personal Record Sheet.

Professional Summary

1. Total 12 + yrs in Oracle.
2. Experience in project management, interfacing with customers, design & development of highly technical software applications.
3. Worked in all phases of SDLC: Understand requirements, convert them into documents, technical specifications preparation, coding, testing & implementing the developed programs in production.
4. Worked as project manager, technical consultant, project leader, team member and software maintenance support.
5. Worked in banking, networking, transport, insurance-based projects.

Oracle Spectrum

- Involved in the development of forms, reports and UNIX-based shell scripts which will invoke ORACLE scripts.
- Designed, developed and implemented client/server & web-based Applications.
- Many conversion projects to migrate data using PL/SQL, SQL Loader and UNIX utilities such as Awk & Grep to load data from one system into another.
- Tuned SQL Queries using Explain Plan, tkprof as part of DBA work.

Project Profiles

06/2003 - 09/2004 Hartford Life Insurance (US)

Role: Project manager for offshore team of 25 members.

Oracle Client/Server Application (7.3.4, 8i), Data Warehousing & Database Migration –

Offshore infrastructure setup, team building, project status, SLA monitoring, performance management & issue resolution.

10/2002 – 05/2003 Workflow management system (GE Power Systems)

Role: Senior consultant

Oracle 8i, PL/SQL Scripts, Developer 2000, ERWIN design tool

Responsible for workflow, technical design, study, analyze the business processes, co-ordinate offshore and onsite team.

08/2001 – 06/2002 US Department of Agriculture (USDA)

Role: Senior consultant

Oracle 8i, PL/SQL Scripts, Developer 2000, ERWIN design tool, ORACLE 9i AS

Involved in requirements capturing, data modeling to find out the entity, attributes, unique identifiers, relations and entity relationship. Developed procedures to send e-mail from web forms using Oracle & Java built-in packages. Also developed lot of back-end related packages (using PL/SQL) to group all the business logic in one place.

07/2000 – 07/2001 Real time Accurate demand-planning, Analysis & reporting (CISCO Inc, USA)

Role: Senior consultant

Oracle 8i (Forms 6.0, Forms 6i, PL/SQL Scripts, Forms development and deployment on Web), Sun Solaris, Unix, Korn shell

Involved in data modeling for system enhancement and prepared technical specifications for the given business requirements. Provided technical guidance to the team.

02/2000 – 06/2000 Traffic Management System (Traffic Station Inc, USA)

Role: Consultant

Oracle 8i (Forms 6.0, Forms 6i, PL/SQL Scripts, Forms development and deployment on Web), Windows NT, Jinitiator 1.1.7.2.7

Developed front-end applications in Forms 6.0 for daily transaction processing and maintenance purpose. Also developed lots of PL/SQL scripts to capture the data feed from traffic reports.

05/1997 – 01/2000 Timeplex Network Tracking Systems (Timeplex Group Inc, USA)

Role: Senior developer

PL/SQL Scripts, Pro*COBOL, BAAN IV, HP-UX UNIX, Korn shell, SQL*NET, Oracle 7x/8.0, Forms, Report Writer

Wrote migration scripts to move the data from Oracle-based legacy system into BAAN ERP.

Academic:

–1991, Master of Computer Applications (M.C.A)

–1987, Master in Mathematics (M.Sc)

Technical Skills:

- Standard MS Office
- Win 2000, Win XP, Unix
- Unix Shell Scripts, SQL, PL/SQL
- Forms (2.3 till 6i)
- Reports (2.5 till 6i)
- Oracle Utilities such as SQL Loader
- Export & Import, Query Tuning
- ERWIN, Designer 2000 design tools
- ORACLE Application Servers
- Worked on Oracle 6.0, 7+, 8i
- 9i Concepts

Contact Details

E-Mail ID:

Maran-Kumararaj@satyam.com

Ph: +91-098490 67841

Sample 3. Draft an application in response to the following advertisement:

Wanted a sales representative, willing to travel extensively in South India to distribute cosmetic powder. Salary will be commensurate with qualification & experience. Apply within five days to Box No. 9876, The Times of India, Mumbai.

The Advertiser,
Box No. 9876
The Times of India,
Mumbai – 400 038
25th June 2011

Dear Sir,

With reference to your advertisement in today's *Times of India*, for the post of sales representative, I give below my qualifications and experience for your consideration:

Name	: K. Ramu
Address	: 10, Vinayagar Koil street, Karamanikuppam. Varakalpattu – 607 109.
Age	: 22 years

Marital Status	: Unmarried
Physique	: Height 5' 7"; Weight 62 kg. Health in excellent condition.
Education	: M.Com First class with Salesmanship and Advertising as my special subjects from Sarfoji College, Thanjavur. Diploma in Advertising & Marketing with special reference to cosmetics.
Experience	: Computer literate. Worked as sales representative in Navjeevan Cosmetics for the period from 1992 to 2010. My duties involved wide and frequent travelling all over South India.
Languages Known	: Besides English and Tamil, I can converse fluently in Telugu, Kannada, Malayalam and Hindi.
Special Traits	My experience as a sales representative has given me an opportunity to interact with a variety of dealers. My sociability and amiability have helped me to build contacts with a wide range of dealers. Perseverance, patience, tact and pleasant personality are some traits suited for salesmanship, which I am happy to possess.
Reasons for leaving	: For better prospects.
References	: eferences may be made to my present employer.

Should I be selected, I will do my best to win your confidence through hard work, diligence and devotion to my job.

Yours faithfully,
K. Ramu

Sample 4. Draft an application for the post of Assistant Professor of Commerce to the Management Committee, Jawahar Science College, Chennai.

134, East Car Street,
Chidambaram – 608 001

2nd May 2011

The Secretary,
Management Committee,
Jawahar Science College,
Chennai – 600 030
Sir,

This is to request your consideration of my qualification for the post of Assistant Professor of Commerce in your college, advertised in today's *Indian Express*.

I have worked for four years at K.K. Arts College, Villupuram which has given me a thorough foundation in subjects like Advanced Accountancy, Cost Accounting and Marketing.

Since I wanted to improve my academic attainments, I left my previous job to do Ph.D and this research study has no doubt fortified my theoretical knowledge.

My enclosed personal record sheet will show that I have been interested in various extracurricular activities which have also given me useful experience.

I shall come for an interview at your convenience.

Yours faithfully,
K. Sundar

Personal Record Sheet:

PROFILE

Name	: Dr. K. Sundar
Permanent Address	: S-5 Ganesh Apartments, Block-2, 45 Thomas Street, Kadapperi, Tambaram, Chennai - 600 045. Mobile: 94862 83473
Educational Qualification	: M.Com., M.Phil., Ph.D
Designation	: Associate Prof of Commerce
Official Address	: Commerce Wing, Directorate of Distance Education, Annamalai University.
Experience Profile	:
U.G. Experience	: 10 years (B.Com., B.B.M.)
P.G. Experience	: 10 years (M.B.A., M.Com.)
M.Phil	: 5 years
Examiner	: Madras university, Pondicherry University and Bharathidasan University.
Paper Setting	: Manomaniam Sundaranar University, Madurai Kamaraj University, Madras university, Pondicherry University, Periyar University, Mother Theresa University, Kerala University, Calicut University and Autonomous Colleges and Directorate of Technical Education.
Other Assignments	: Member, Board of Studies, Alagappa University.

Membership in Professional Bodies	:	Member in Chennai Management Association (Membership No. 1032) and Life Member, United Writers' Association, Chennai (Membership No.876/99).
Papers published	:	40 Papers (HRD Times, Yojana, Kissan World, University News, Industrial Herald, Tamil Nadu, Journal of Co-operation, Office Digest, Global Business, Third Concept, Indian Journal of Marketing, Eight Ms, Rural India, Productivity Journal, Edu Track, Journal of Academia, Journal of Training and Development, Southern Economist Management Matter, Maharashtra Cooperative Journal, Economic Panorama, Journal of Syndicate, Journal of Productivity, Journal of Banking & Finance, Indian Journal of Accounting, Infinity Journal of Management.
National & State Level organized seminars	:	35 years of participation at conferences by different institutions i.e., Pondicherry University, Gandhigram Rural University, Annamalai University, Periyar Arts College, Pachiyappas College, M.O.P. Vaishnav College, Political Science Dept. of Madras university, Karpagam Arts & Science College, Kadir Mohideen College, MGM Pollachi Muthammal College, UDC College and other institutions.
Workshop and Seminar Participation	:	Attended four workshops organized by Anna Adarsh College, Chennai; School of Management, Annamalai University; Political Science Dept., Annamalai University. Attended five Conferences conducted by Dept. of Commerce, Annamalai University.
Book Publication	:	Income Tax Law and Practice by A. Kumararaj and K. Sundar, Banking Law and Practice by Kumararaj and K. Sundar. Currently authored twelfth standard Commerce book for Tamilnadu Text Book Society. Prepared Course Materials for the books 'Investment and Portfolio Management' and 'Project Management & Entrepreneurship'.

Research Activities	: Produced 5 M.Phils; guiding 15 M.Phils; guiding 5 Ph.D. scholars.
Training Undergone	: Personality Development training organised by Nehru Yuvakendra, Cuddalore; In-service training for faculty members organized by Annamalai University; attended Orientation course at Academic Staff College, Madras university; Refresher course by Department of Economics, Annamalai University; Refresher course conducted by Commerce Department, University of Madras.
Subjects Familiar	: Corporate Accounting, Financial Accounting, Tax Accounting, Marketing, Banking, Business Law, Company Law, HRD, Co-operative Management, Entrepreneurship, Foreign Trade Management.

I hereby certify that all the information furnished is correct to the best of my knowledge.

Signature

K. Sundar

SUMMARY

Application for a situation should contain applicant's address, inside address, name of the post, qualification, experience, age, reference, testimonials, body of the letter, concluding paragraph, complimentary close and signature.

REVIEW QUESTIONS

Part A: Short Questions

1. What is inside address?
2. What is salutation?
3. What is complimentary close?
4. What is testimonial?
5. What is reference?

Part B: Paragraph Questions

1. What points are to be covered in an application for a situation?

Part C: Essay Questions

1. Wanted an experienced accounts officer. Apply stating previous experience, age and minimum salary expected to Box No. 999, The Indian Express, Anna Salai, Chennai – 2.
2. Ashok Software Company, Velacherry requires a system analyst with knowledge of Oracle. Salary ₹ 50,000 per month. Apply giving age, education, experience and references.
3. Draft an application in response to the following advertisement: Wanted a sales representative willing to travel extensively in South India to distribute cosmetic powder. Salary will be commensurate with qualification & experience. Apply within five days to Box No. 9876, The Times of India, Mumbai.
4. Draft an application for the post of Assistant Professor of Commerce to the Management Committee, Kovalan Science College, Chennai.

Part D: Objective Type Questions

Choose the correct answer

1. The name and address of the employer is written above the

   a. Salutation   b. Inside address   c. Complimentary close

   (Ans: a)

2. In applications addressed to the government officials, the salutation is

   a. Dear sir   b. Respected sir   c. Most respected sir

   (Ans: b)

3. Appropriate complimentary close in an application for a job is

   a. Yours sincerely   b. Yours faithfully   c. Sincerely yours

   (Ans: b)

Fill in the blanks

1. The name and address of the employer is written above the _______. (Salutation)
2. In applications addressed to the government officials ________ is generally used. (Sir)
3. In all other applications addressed to commercial houses ________ is used. (Dear Sir)
4. _________ is an appropriate complimentary close in applications for jobs. (Yours faithfully)

35

CHAPTER

EMPLOYMENT DOCUMENTATION

INTRODUCTION

When an employer is looking out for new employees, he advertises in different media to get new recruits. This is an advertisement copy. On selection of a candidate, an appointment letter is sent to him.

DRAFTING AN ADVERTISEMENT COPY

The employer tries to select the best possible candidates so as to ensure greater productivity and efficient performance. The advertisement inviting applications should contain as much relevant information as possible so that only the right persons will apply for the post. Selection process will thereby become easier.

Contents of an Advertisement Copy

The information to be given in the advertisement copy depends upon the nature of the job, skills required, technical or academic qualification to be possessed, responsibilities to be borne, etc.

The usual contents are:

- Age limit
- Educational qualification
- Whether the candidates have to attend interview, tests at their own expense
- Emoluments
- It may end with calling for a complete biodata, especially with reference to the details of nature of work performed in different positions, salaries drawn and salary expected along with copies of certificates and testimonials

For jobs involving usual skills: If the job to be performed is of a routine nature involving manual work or routine clerical work, it will suffice if the advertisement mentions the name of the job, the number of vacancies, scale of pay, etc. Applicants understand the skills required for performing this type of job.

However, if minimum educational qualification is desired, it must be mentioned.

Sometimes clerks may also be required to do computing work. In such a case, the desirability of computer knowledge must be specifically stated.

For jobs involving special physical skills: With regard to posts involving constant and extensive travel and close personal touch with a number of people like those of sales representatives, nature of duties involved such as frequent tour to be undertaken, languages required to be known must be mentioned.

For jobs requiring special educational qualification: Certain jobs require a pass in certain examinations conducted by certain professional bodies. In such a case, this fact must be clearly stated. For example, posts calling for company secretaries should specifically state that applicants should be associate members of the Institute of Company Secretaries of India.

For jobs involving technical expertise: In the case of engineering or technical work, the advertisement must specify the particular discipline such as chemical engineering, textile technology, mechanical engineering, etc.

With regard to posts of certain specialists/scientists, etc., the advertisement must mention the special qualification required. For example, the post of agronomist may require more than a M.Sc. degree in agriculture, probably a post graduate degree with specialisation in agronomy.

For top level or middle level management posts: Besides stressing on educational qualifications, the advertisement copy should specify certain minimum years of experience in management positions. The advertisement should also contain the following additional points:

- To whom the incumbent will be reporting. For example, to the managing director, general manager, etc.
- Job specification. For example, an advertisement for the post of materials manager must say that the incumbent will be responsible for material requirement planning, procurement, inventory control, etc. Further, it may also specify certain abilities required such as good negotiating ability, knowledge of sourcing and vendor evaluation.

Emoluments

In the case of low level jobs like clerks and stenographers, remuneration can be clearly mentioned in the advertisement copy itself. But in the case of middle or top level management, it is customary to state that remuneration will be commensurate with merit and experience. Merit and experience matter more for top level management position, so remuneration should not drive the best brains away; very attractive pay and perks together with privileges should not only lure them to the organization but also help retain them for a long period. Hence, the advertisement copy can state that salary and other perks will not be a constraint for the right candidates.

The advertisement copy may also state where the applicants may have to work. It may also seek to know when they will be able to join duty, if selected.

Sample 1: An advertisement copy calling applications for the post of marketing manager. The advertisement copy need not disclose the name of the company.

Wanted

Marketing Manager

A well-known progressive group with annual turnover of ₹ 1000 crores wishes to recruit a marketing manager for one of its divisions with a projected turnover of ₹ 10 crores.

The candidate should be an engineering graduate with MBA from a well-known institution. He should have a minimum of 10 years experience in marketing industrial products, preferably chemicals. Holding, position at a senior level for five years is very desirable. The preferred age is between 35 and 45 years.

The incumbent has to report to the Chief Executive of the Division. He will be responsible for the formulation of marketing strategies and achieving targeted sales turnover.

Since it is a senior position, salary and prequisites have been structured to attract the best candidate.

Applications giving full details of age, qualification, experience, achievements and salary drawn should be sent within 10 days to
Box No. 1189
c/o Indian Express,
Chennai – 600 002

Sample 2: Draft an advertisement copy for certain key posts such as (i) secretary and finance manager (ii) personnel officer and (iii) materials manager for a motor manufacturing company shortly opening an automative ancillary project. This company is setting up an industrial unit jointly with Tamil Nadu Industrial Development Corporation.

(Note: The advertisement copy in such a case should contain the location of the factory, details of skills required, functions to be performed, responsibilities to be borne, etc.)

Wanted Executives for an Automative Ancillary Project

Pallavan Motors Limited and Tamil Nadu Industrial Development Corporation are jointly setting up a modern factory to manufacture truck bodies and bus bodies using latest technology. The factory is being located in the SIPCOT Industrial Complex at Kudikadu, 5 km from Cuddalore.

The following key executives are required:

i. Secretary and Finance Manager

The selected candidates will report to the managing director and will be responsible for financial planning and control, maintenance and finalisation of accounts, mobilisation of funds and for developing and implementing management information system.

He will be responsible for company's secretarial and taxation matters, and should be capable of independent liaison with banks, financial institutions and legal matters.

Qualifications:

Applicants should be chartered accountants/cost accountants and an associate member of the Instituteof Company Secretaries of India.

Age and experience:

They should be in the age group of 30–40 years with an experience of 7–10 years in responsible positions in reputed industrial organizations.

ii. Personnel Officer

The incumbent will be responsible for all aspects of personnel management including manpower planning, recruitment, establishment, training and development, appraisals, industrial relations, labour welfare as well as administration.

Qualifications:

Applicants should have a graduate degree and an MBA.

Age and experience:

They should be in the age group of 30–40 years with around five years of experience in managerial capacity in the field of personnel management and industrial relations with good functional knowledge and human relations skills in reputed industrial organizations. They should have a working knowledge of Tamil. Placement will be at the factory.

iii. Materials Manager

The incumbent will be responsible for material requirements planning and procurement including imports and store-keeping, inventory control of all items required for the manufacture of automative cars, bus and truck bodies.

He will also be responsible for purchasing plant machinery, contracting and all related commercial matters. The materials manager will report to the managing director.

Qualifications, age and experience:

Applicants should be graduates, preferably engineers in the agegroup of 30–40 years with around 7 years of experience in purchasing/materials management in reputed industrial organizations.

He should have a good negotiating ability and a sound knowledge of sourcing and vendor evaluation, selection and development.

He should be familiar with import policies and procedures, customs and excise formalities, etc. The materials manager will report to the managing director.

Emoluments:

Salary and other perks will not be a constraint for the right candidates and will be competitive with the best companies in the field.

How to apply?

Please apply in strict confidence within 10 days, giving complete profile including details of experience, nature of work performed in different positions, salaries drawn and salaries expected. Also send copies of certificates and testimonials together with two copies of recent passport size photograph to

Managing Director,
Pallavan Motors Ltd,
99, Anna Salai,
Chennai–600 002

Sample 3: Draft an advertisement copy inviting applications for the post of (a) accounts clerks (b) stenographers (c) electrical supervisors for a large manufacturing company.

Vanavil Electronics Ltd.

77, Madura Road,
Trichi - 620 008

Applications are invited for the following posts:

Category	No. of posts
i) Accounts clerks	: 50
ii) Stenographers	: 10
iii) Electrical supervisors	: 5

Educational Qualifications :

For post (a): Applicants should possess B.Com degree preferably with accounts and sosting as optional subjects.

For post (b): Applicants should have passed higher secondary examination and should have passed both typewriting and shorthand (English) higher.

For post (c): Applicants should hold the Supervisor's Competency Certificate issued by Electrical Licensing Board. They should have experience in maintenance of high and medium voltage installations including lighting and running and maintenance of diesel generator sets, besides working knowledge of maintenance and repair of electrical equipment.

Terms:

i. Age limit: 20 to 26 years. Relaxable in the case of experienced candidates.
ii. Remuneration will be commensurate with merit and experience.
iii. Probation period will be one year.
iv. The candidates will have to attend the interview at their own expenses.
v. Separate applications should be made for each post.
vi. The post applied for should be mentioned on the envelope.
vii. Candidates should apply to the Chief Executive Officer, Vanavil Electronics Ltd., Trichy along with biodata and expected salary, two xerox copies of certificates and testimonials should be enclosed with the application.

Sd. B. Kasthurirangan,
Chief Executive Officer,
Vanavil Chemicals Ltd.
Trichi – 210 486

Sample 4: Draft suitable advertisement copies for the following:

a. A textile processing unit requires sales representatives
b. Vellore Commercial Corporation wants a stenographer for their office.
c. Chidambaram Chemical Industries Ltd., Chidambaram wants a cashier (Identity of the advertiser not to be disclosed).
d. An export-import company requires two junior assistants for their shops.
e. Anna Arts College, Villupuram wants a suitable candidate for the post of Assistant Professor of Commerce.

a) Pondicherry Textile Processing Ltd.

We are a progressive textile processing unit with modern machinery looking out for the following result oriented-personnel:

Sales Representatives: They must be capable of touring extensively to procure targeted job processing orders for bleaching, dyeing, printing and other textile processing.

Salary will be commensurate with qualifications and experience of selected candidates. Please apply giving full details within 10 days to

No. 112, 2nd Cross,

Elango Nagar,

Pondicherry – 605 011

b) Experienced Stenographer

Wanted an experienced stenographer with good speed in shorthand and typewriting. Filing experience will be an advantage. Liberal salary. Apply with copies of testimonials to Box No. 555, The Hindu, Chennai – 2.

c) Experienced Cashier

Wanted a cashier for a large industrial and commercial concern in Mysore. Candidates must be able to handle accounts independently.

Candidates with previous experience in reputed commercial concerns will be given special preference.

Apply stating qualification, experience, salary expected etc, to Box No. 326, The Indian Express, Anna Salai, Chennai – 2.

d) Junior Assistant

Wanted by M/S Dhanaraj & Co, Importers and Exporters, 77, New Thandavaray Gramani Street, Old Washermenpet, Chennai – 21, two well-educated young men as junior assistants.

Scale: 15000–500–2500 with usual allowances. Experience in this line will be an added advantage. Knowledge of stenography is essential.

Apply stating age, references, education and experience within ten days.

e) Assistant Professor of Commerce

Anna Arts College, 89, Periar Road, Villupuram, requires an Assistant Professor of Commerce.

Scale of pay:nAs per U.G.C. scale of pay.

Allowances as applicable to Govt. colleges in Tamil Nadu. Higher start depends on experience.

Qualifications: (a) M.Com. or B.Com. Hons. with accounts as optional subject. Pass in SLET or NET examination preferred.

Experience: Not less than three years teaching experience at UG level.

Age: Below 30 years.

Applications with biodata and attested copies of certificates should reach the Secretary, Management Committee, Anna Arts College, Villupuram before 18th June, 2011.

Secretary

Letter verifying the reference cited

Sample 5: A letter to the person (referred to by an applicant for a post) seeking opinion on the suitability of the candidate for the post.

Madura Metals Corporation

Private & Confidential

178, North Masi Street,
Madurai – 625004

2nd June 2011

Thiru R.K. Udayar,
Secretary,
Modern Breweries,
187, Big Street,
Chennai – 600 005

Dear Mr. Udayar,

Mr. K. Paari of Chennai, an applicant for the post of sales manager, has given your name as a reference.

I would be grateful if you could give me your opinion as to his intellectual ability, reliability and character.

Any information you may give or opinion you may express will be treated as strictly confidential.

Yours sincerely,
M. Maran
Personnel Manager

Sample 6: A reply to a letter of enquiry as regards the fitness of an applicant for the post of sales manager. The reply should be in the nature of recommending the person for the post.

R.K. Murthy, M.Com., A.C.A.
Secretary,
Modern Breweries,
187, Big Street,
Triplicane,
Chennai – 600 005

Residence: 102, First Cross St,
Kilpauk Gardens,
Chennai – 600 008

10 June 2011

Strictly Confidential
Mr. M. Maran,
General Manager,
Madura Metals Corporation,
178, North Masi Street,

Madura – 625 004

Dear Mr. Maran,

I have your letter dated 2nd June 2011.

I know Mr. Paari, about whom you have enquired, since 1995 when he joined our company as sales officer.

I have always found him a man of active habits. His pleasing personality and suave manners have won many contracts for the company. His capacity for target achievements and his altertness for action have never been in doubt.

We would be sorry to lose his services but we do not want to stand in the way of his career improvement since we ourselves cannot offer him promotion right now.

I have no doubt that his experience and intellectual ability would stand him in good stead and that he will do justice to the job.

Yours sincerely,
K. Udayar
Secretary

DRAFTING APPOINTMENT LETTERS

Since a letter of appointment constitutes a contract of service between the employer and the employee, care and caution must be exercised while drafting it.

Points to be Incorporated in a Letter of Appointment

The following points must generally be incorporated in a letter of appointment:

1. The post to which the person is appointed must be specified.
2. The nature of appointment whether it is a temporary or permanent one.
3. The length of probationary period, if any, on the satisfactory completion of which the appointment is to be confirmed.
4. The scale of pay for the post and the stage at which the selected candidate is appointed. (Starting salary)

The various allowances to which the appointee is eligible must also be mentioned. For example, it may be stated as ₹ 16000–1000, 1800–2000–2400–4000–4500. It means that the annual increment is ₹ 1000 till the basic pay reaches ₹ 16000 and the increment will be ₹ 2000 afterwards and so on.

5. If the post carries a consolidated pay, the fact that no dearness or other allowance is payable must be made clear.
6. Other benefits such as provident fund, gratuity, pension, applicable for the post should also be stated.
7. Leave facilities available to the appointee i.e. casual leave, medical leave, privilege leave etc., should be mentioned.
8. The date on or before which the candidate is to report for duty.
9. Period of notice required for either side in case of termination of service or resignation.

Drafting a Letter of Appointment

The first paragraph starts with a reference to the application and the interview. It also contains an expression of pleasure on the appointment of the candidate.

The last paragraph concludes with good wishes for the candidate.

The letter also seeks a letter of acceptance of appointment from the selected candidate.

The terms of appointment are given either in the body of the letter itself or on a separate enclosed sheet.

Important points that must be covered in a letter of employment are mentioned under the heading 'points to be incorporated in a letter of appointment'.

Though *Dear Sir/Madam* is used generally, some firms prefer '*Dear Mr/Miss* If the saluation is by name, then the complimentary close shall be *Yours sincerely*. Otherwise, it shall be *Yours faithfully*.

Sample 7: A letter of appointment to a selected candidate incorporating important terms of service.

Narumanam Cosmetics Ltd.

144, Imperial Road,
Cuddalore-607 002

July 30, 2011

Thiru K. Balasubramaniam,
166, Rodier Mill Street,
Pondicherry - 605 004

Dear Sir,

With reference to your application for the post of sales representative, we are glad to inform you that the Recruitment Committee of the Board of Directors of our company has decided to appoint you to the post.

Please note that the appointment will initially be on a temporary basis for one year and will be confirmed on your satisfactory completion of the probation. Other terms and conditions:

i) During the period of probation you will be given a consolidated salary of ₹ 10,000.

On your being made permanent, you will be fixed in the scale of ₹ 20,000–100–2000–3000–30,000. You are eligible to draw D.A. and other usual allowances as modified from time to time.

ii) During the period of probation you have to guarantee a minimum business of ₹ 5,00,000 and thereafter ₹ 10,00,000.

iii) You are eligible for the usual T.A., D.A. and out-of-pocket expenses as admissible to your cadre and as modified from time to time.

vi) The appointment is subject to termination after a month's notice on either side.

You are required to report for duty on or before 16th August 2011.

Yours faithfully,
for Narumanam Cosmetics Limited,
Pugazhenthi
Secretary

Sample 8: An employment letter intimating the selection of a candidate for the post of senior clerk.

Progressive Corporation Ltd.

1, Jones Road,
Cuddalore - 607001

4th June 2011

Mr. V. Seran, B.Com
Thirukandeeswaram,
Nellikuppam - 607 108

Dear Mr. Seran,

With reference to your interview on 18th June 2011, for the post of senior clerk, I am happy to inform you that you have been selected for appointment. The post carries a salary in the scale of ₹ 16,000–2500–22,000 and D.A. at State government rates.

You will be on probation for one year, and will be confirmed if your services are found satisfactory.

Please intimate your acceptance of the appointment by return of post and report for duty before 21st July 2011.

Yours sincerely,
R. Annamalai
General Manager

LETTER OF RECOMMENDATION

A letter of recommendation is a letter addressed to a person known personally to the writer with the intent to help the bearer of the letter. The help sought may be to get a job or some business favour.

Letter of Introduction

A letter of introduction is a letter introducing the bearer of the letter to someone known personally to the writer. If it is written by a businessman to another, it may be with a view to enabling the bearer to have business relations with the person addressed.

Characteristics of a Letter of Recommendation

It has the following characteristics:

1. It should contain no exaggerated statements.
2. If it is a recommendation for a job, it should plainly state the candidate's ability and skill, his aptitude and sincerity.
3. If it is a letter recommending credit facilities, it should point to his capacity for repayment, his sense of commitment to repay and to his honesty and integrity.
4. A letter of recommendation should not be vague nor should it be too general. It should help to form a definite opinion as to the reliability of the person recommended.

Contents of a Letter of Recommendation

It includes:

a. Name and details of the person recommended.

b. The purpose for which he is recommended.

c. A definite opinion as to the conduct, character, financial standing and uprightness or as to the aptitude, efficiency, reliability, talents, etc.

d. A request to assist him.

e. The letter ending with a thanks for the help that may be rendered in pursuance of this letter of recommendation.

TESTIMONIALS

A *testimonial* is a kind of certificate with respect to the experience, efficiency, capacity for hard work and general conduct of a person. This is not addressed to anybody in particular. It is, in short, an open letter of recommendation *to whomsoever it may concern* type.

The writer certifies that the bearer of the testimonial is known to him personally for a certain length of time, having perhaps worked under him and mentions in the testimonial, qualities that he has observed in him during the period.

It usually concludes with a recommendation that the bearer is fit to hold a similar post with benefit to any organization which may absorb him. The testimonial is handed over to the person recommended. This may be given by any superior officer in his personal capacity on his personal letter-head or by the company itself officially.

Sample 9: A general letter of recommendation needed by an employee on his leaving the office.

To whomsoever it may concern

This is to certify that Thiru. M. Mathew was in our employment as a junior accounts officer for the past five years. He has impressed us by the dint of his hard work and dedicated service. Never a shirker, he discharged his duties to our entire satisfaction and has won our confidence. He bears a good moral character.

We have no doubt that he will prove to be an asset to any concern which has him in its employ.

For ABC & Co,
V. Karikalan
Managing Partner

Sample 10: A testimonial to a company's computer programmer who has to leave the organization because of the necessity of moving his family to another place.

Coimbatore Electrical Limited

111, Avinasi Road,
Coimbatore – 641 038

30th July 2011

To whomsoever it may concern

This is to certify that Mr. K. Saravanan, B. Com, is known to me for the last four years, during which period he was working in our company as a computer programmer.

He was always punctual and regular in attendance. His cheerful disposition, willingness to do any work assigned to him with utmost sincerity and his pleasing manners were greatly liked both by his colleagues and superiors.

He leaves his present employment solely because he has to shift his family to Chennai owing to his father's failing health.

Mr. Saravanan, a young and energetic man, will show his merit in a better way should any chance be given to him in a large firm.

Good Spheperd
Secretary

Sample 11: Your friend wants to find a new market for his goods in Ahmedabad. Write a letter of recommendation to M/s. Kurinji & Co., cloth merchants in Ahmedabad.

Abdul Razak and Co.

71, East Street,
Chidambaram - 608001

17th September 2011

Messrs A. Morarji & Co.,
Cloth Merchants,
512, South Road,
Ahmedabad - 380 002

Dear Sir,

It gives me great pleasure to introduce to you, Mr.Thomas, the bearer of this letter. He is the managing partner of thomas & Co., situated at 99, Rajaraja Sozhan St., Thanjavur. They are dealers in cloth.

Mr. Thomas is a close business friend of mine. In the course of my dealings with him for the past 10 years, he has proved himself to be a business man of good reputation.

With a view to expand his business and to develop new business connections in Ahmedabad and Mumbai, he has started on a tour and he will be visiting Ahmedabad shortly in this connection.

I shall be grateful, if you will kindly help him with your valuable advice in business matters and assist him in contacting local merchants of repute.

Any service you may render Mr. Thomas will be viewed as a personal favourextended to me and I assure you of my service to you in similar matters. Please accept my sincere thanks.

Yours faithfully,
A. Abdul Razak
Proprietor

LETTER OF CREDIT

A letter of credit is a letter of recommendation, requesting the recepient to advance a certain sum of money within a specified limit to the person introduced with a proof of identity and signature.

The person introduced or recommended is generally a traveller on business or pleasure.

Contents of a Letter of Credit:

a. The name and address of the firm to which the letter is addressed.
b. Name, address and occupation of the person in whose favour the letter of credit is issued.
c. The total amount to be paid.
d. Instructions regarding payment.
e. The period during which the letter of credit will be valued.
f. Specimen signature of the person introduced. The specimen signature may be given in a separate letter of advice too.

Circular Letter of Credit

When a letter of credit is addressed to a number of parties in different places each being requested to advance amounts within specified limits when contacted by the person recommended, it is called a circular letter of credit.

Endorsement of each payment is to be made on the back of the circular letter of credit.

SUMMARY

Contents of an advertisement copy includes age limit, educational qualification, need to attend interview, emoluments and calls for biodata.

Drafting an appointment letter includes specifying the post for which appointment is made, nature of appointment, length of probationary period, scale of pay, other benefits, leave facilities, date of joining and notice period for termination of service.

Letter of recommendation includes name and details of the person recommended, the purpose for recommending, a definite opinion of the bearer, a request to help him and thanking him in advance for the help rendered.

Letter of credit contains the name and address of the addressed firm, name and details of the favoured person, total amount paid, mode of payment, value period of the letter of credit and specimen signature of the introduced person.

REVIEW QUESTIONS

Part A: Short Questions

1. What is an appointment letter?
2. What is a letter of recommendation?
3. What is a letter of credit?
4. What is a circular letter of credit?
5. What are testimonials?

Part B: Paragraph Questions

1. What points are to be covered while drafting an advertisement copy?
2. Invite applications for various categories of jobs.
3. What points are to be incorporated in a letter of appointment?

Part C: Essay Questions

1. Draft an advertisement copy for certain key posts such as (i) secretary and finance manager (ii) personnel officer (iii) materials manager for a motor manufacturing company shortly opening an automative ancillary project. This company is setting up an industrial unit jointly with Tamil Nadu Industrial Development Corporation.
2. Draft an advertisement copy inviting applications for the post of (a) accounts clerks (b) stenographers (c) electrical supervisors for a large manufacturing company.
3. Write a letter of appointment to a selected candidate, incorporating important terms of service.

Part D: Objective Type Questions

Choose the Correct Answer

1. Letter recommending a certain person to the receipient requesting the latter to advance a certain sum within a specified limit to the former is

   a. Letter of credit b. Testimonial c. Creditcard

   (Ans: a)

2. Letter addressed to a large number of receipient spread over a wide geography requesting each to advance a certain sum within the specified limit to the person recommended in

   a. Letter of Credit b. Testimonial c. Circular Letter of Credit

   (Ans: c)

3. The certificate with reference to one's age, experience, capacity for hardwork and conduct is

   a. Letter of Credit b. Testimonial c. Circular letter of Credit

   (Ans: b)

Fill in the Blanks

1. ____________ is a king of certificate in the respect to experience efficiency and capacity for hardwork an general conduct of a candidate. (Testimonial)
2. ____________ is a letters of recommendation requesting the recipient to advance a certain sum to money with in a specified limit to the person intoduced. (Letter of Credit)

36

CHAPTER

INTERVIEWS

INTRODUCTION

An Interview is a two way communication. There are two parties involved in the interview: One is the interviewer and the other is the interviewer. The former provides information about the organization, its goals, objectives, policies, etc., while the latter gives information about his academic and non-academic profile and impresses the former on how he can help in the goal-attainment by accepting a role in the organization. The interview can also be used for imparting instructions, issuing orders, warnings, giving reprimands to the existing employees or for appraising and recording their work.

STEPS IN INTERVIEW PROCESS

The interviews are conducted only after the completion of the following steps:

Preparation for Conducting the Interview (Pre-interview process)

Since the interview is only for a short period, it is better to decide in advance how the interview should be held. Under this, objectives of interview, methods of interview, number of interviewers, preparing a brief profile about the candidates and working out administrative details would facilitate smooth conduct of an interview.

Determining the objectives of an interview

The objective of an interview is to gather as much information about the candidate as possible in order to decide the suitability of the candidate for the post. Therefore, it is better to collect information about the following:

- Personal characteristics of a candidate
- Technical competence relavant for the job
- Initiative, common sense, approach towards work
- Ability and urge to learn
- Capacity to adjust and work in a team
- Potential for growth

Determining the methods of interview

Among the different methods, decision is to be taken on the choice of method and need to inform the candidate accordingly.

Determining the number of interviewers

The number of interviewers is dependent on the type of interview. For example, single interviewer will do for one-to-one interview, but a number of interviewers are required for a panel interview. Similarly, the type of post plays a role in deciding the size of interviewers. For example, the lower the cadre, the lesser the number of interviewers and vice versa. After deciding the size, the next step is to decide on the persons who will be the interviewers. For example, subject experts, psychologists, HR manager, etc.

Preparing a summary of profile of the interviewees

Since each interviewer needs to have a basic idea about each and every candidate so as to direct appropriate questions to the candidate, summary of profile of the candidates has to be prepared.

Administrative details

It includes deciding the venue, duration of the interview, physical facilities in the interview hall, seating of candidates, providing them with relevant information about the modality of interview, calling them for the interview, travelling allowance and daily allowance for the interviewers, etc.

Conducting the Interview

It involves the following processes:

Establishing rapport

Interviewer has to make the interviewee feel at ease. Unless the interviewee is mentally stress-free, the interviewer cannot get the appropriate answers. Therefore, the chairman or head of the interview has to ask the candidate to share information about himself.

Soliciting information

Serious questions may be put at this stage to test the subject knowledge, general awareness, non-intellectual traits, aspirations, goals, etc.

Recording information

It is better to videotape, audiotape or hand-record the interview so as to accurately evaluate the candidate for the given post. This arrangement will make the candidate answer responsibly in the interview.

Closing the Interview

Just as the beginning creates an initial impression, closing also should create a final impression of the candidate about the whole interview process. Therefore, asking the candidate about his opinion about the company and thanking the candidate for attending the interview would keep the interviewee in good humour.

Finalising the Evaluation

After the interview is over, the panel members can discuss the suitability of the candidate in terms of vital parameters established by the company. They can give grades or points for different credentials of the candidate and for his performance at the interview. Then, they have to recommend the appropriate number of candidates for the posts.

INTERVIEW AS A SELECTION TOOL

The interview is undoubtedly a selection tool of major importance for nearly all types of jobs. In many companies, interview is the only tool used in recruiting employees. Interview is a face-to-face, observational method adopted to assess the suitability of a candidate for a particular job.

Merits of the Method

There are many merits of interview as a selection tool:

- It helps in finding out the physical appearance of the candidate.
- It provides a sample of the applicant's behaviour, which enables the interviewer to judge the candidates.
- It proves a clue to the candidate's motivation, attitude and ambitions.
- It gives some indication about the candidate's mental alertness and presence of mind while dealing with a problem.
- It provides an opportunity to know the candidate's ability to express himself clearly. The power of expression and ability to converse freely, fluently and convincingly, is an essential trait required especially for the post of sales executives.
- In the case of non-directive interview, the candidate is expected to show a good deal of initiative by raising issues of contesting view points of others. This brings to light his mental make-up and his ability to analyze issues.

Limitations of Interview as a Selection Tool

Though there are many merits, there are also a few demerits:

- If the candidate does not feel free to talk about his achievements, hopes and aspirations, he will be misjudged.
- The candidate may be possessing vast knowledge and good practical experience, yet his lack of capacity to express himself may not bring to the surface his innate talents. Such a candidate is likely to be ignored.
- Similarly, a very fine conversationalist may create a favourable impression on the interviewers, but he may not be good at work.
- If the interviewer is emotional or argumentative, this selection tool will fail to realise the objective.
- If questions unconnected with the requirements of job are asked at the interview, then the interview as a selection tool will not be a good method.

Points to be looked into at the time of interview

There are certain factors which must be remembered by the interviewer during an interview:

- The work the candidate is expected to do after appointment must be clearly borne in mind.
- The job requirements i.e. the types of abilities required for performing a job must be kept in view.
- The candidate's applications form will give a clue as to his abilities and talents. They must be studied before the candidate is interviewed.
- The candidate should be made to feel at ease. Questions which will reveal his knowledge, character must be put across to him. In short, he should be enabled to reveal himself at the interview.
- Irrelevant and irritating questions must be totally avoided.
- If the interviewers do not give a good picture of their own ability and sincerity, and the firm's policies and programmes, the candidate may receive a poor impression. In short, only if the interview is conducted so as to find out people possessing talents required for a job, the interview as a selection tool will be a success.
- Any prejudice or predetermination to select a particular candidate should be avoided. The interview, in such a case, becomes a formality observed rather than a method of finding out real talents.

DIFFERENT KINDS OF INTERVIEWS CONDUCTED IN THE SELECTION PROCESS

An interview, which is face-to-face and an observational method to evaluate a candidate with regard to his suitability for a job, is of many kinds:

Direct Interview

This is a face-to-face, question-answer type interview. The interviewer poses questions to the interviewee with a view to assess the candidate's general ability, attitude, etc. If the candidate does not express himself, his innate talents may not be judged correctly.

Non-Directive Interview or Indirect Interview

In this method, no questions and answers are involved. The interviewee is encouraged to express himself on topics of his choice or to contest others' view points. The interviewer is a patient listener without expressing any opinion on what the candidate says. In short, the candidate is given complete freedom to *sell himself without the encumbrances of the interviewer's questions*.

Patterned Interview

In this kind of interview a pattern of standard questions and answers are prepared in advance. The answers given by the candidate are compared with the prepared ones; thus, his suitability for the job is assessed.

In-Depth Interview

This kind of interview is also planned in advance and the detailed questions to be asked on a particular subject are framed. The candidate's attitude and attainment are sought to be assessed by examining the candidate intensively.

Stress Interview

Here the candidate is put under conditions of stress and strain. The purpose is to know how he reacts to such a situation. For example, while conducting an interview for a salesman, the interviewer may assume the role of an irritating customer posing inconvenient questions. If the interviewee remains calm and composed and replies convincingly, he may be selected.

Panel Interview

Here a committee of interviewers question the candidate. Each interviewer may be a specialist in his field and try to put questions concerning his area. For example, one may ask questions to know the candidate's general knowledge, another to know his in-depth knowledge of his special subject, yet another to assess his attitude and so on. Thus, a candidate is assessed from different angles.

Group Interview

In this method, a number of candidates are brought together and interviewed simultaneously. Each interviewee is asked to participate in the discussion on a situation posed before them.

QUALITIES OF AN INTERVIEWER

The following ought to be the qualities of an interviewer:

1. He should be a mature person.
2. He should have a positive outlook.
3. Should be able to control his ego.
4. Able to show warmth and affection so that he develops rapport with the interviewee.
5. Should have enough knowledge of technical aspects of the job so as to evaluate the technical competence of the interviewee.
6. Should have a knowledge of recent developments in the field of his specialization.
7. Should be a good listener and conversationalist.
8. Should have knowledge of the behaviour pattern of interviewees.

INEFFECTIVE INTERVIEW

An interview can be ineffective due to many reasons. Some of them are as follows:

1. Interview starting without developing rapport with the interviewee.
2. Interviewer having prejudice or bias.
3. Poor communication skill of the interviewer.
4. More number of questions disproportionate to the time available.
5. Irrelevant questions.
6. Interviewer's lack of interviewing skills and aptitude for conducting interviews.
7. Interviewer expecting his own qualities in the interviewee.
8. Interviewers judging the candidate on the basis of the characteristics of the group he belongs to. For example, students of a particular school, college, family background, communal background, religious background, etc. Such judgement mars fair selection.
9. Interviewer judging all the traits of interviewee on the basis of a few positive or negative traits. This is called a halo effect.

All the aforesaid things mar the effectiveness and consequent fair selection of the candidate.

MEASURES FOR MAKING AN INTERVIEW EFFECTIVE

Since a lot of time, effort and money are invested in conducting an interview, the following measures must be followed to make it effective:

- There should be a proper planning before the interview. A clear plan should be devised as to who is to conduct the interview, who is to be interviewed, what are to be tested, how many points for various aspects, etc., to avoid ambiguity in interviewing.
- Physical setting should be conducive. The place of interview should be free from noise, dust, sound, etc.
- Maximum time should be allowed for the interviewee to talk on a variety of subjects so that the interviewer can judge his taste, hobbies, preference, attitude, aptitude, outlook, subject knowledge, goals, aspirations, etc.
- Interview should be closed with pleasant remarks.
- Evaluation of the candidate should be done after the interview is over. The selection of the candidate should be based on a consensus of all the interviewers, after deliberating the various aspects of the performance in the interview.

PREPARATION FOR INTERVIEW

An interview is the most dynamic and intense communication situation a person may encounter in his life. Hence, he has to prepare adequately for its success.

Pre-interview Initiatives

- One should self-analyze. In other words, a candidate should assess his strength and weakness and work to minimize his weaknesses. He should know the knowledge and skills he possesses.
- A candidate should find out the relevance of his competence to the job he is seeking and how he can use it in performing the required duties.
- He should gather relevant information about the organization in areas like historical profile of the organization, the product portfolio, branch network, ownership pattern, financial performance, goals, visions, developmental plan, organizational culture, etc. The candidate should visualize the role he can play in its growth and development.
- If possible, he may discuss with the employees of the organization about the work culture, professional ethics, etc.
- Anticipate the possible questions likely to be asked and the probable answers to be given.

Smart Interviewee Behaviour

At the time of interview, the candidate should sound positive to the interviewer. Some of the qualities appreciated by an interviewer include punctuality, immaculate physical appearance, cheerful dispostion, pleasing mannerism, presence of mind, optimistic attitude, clear tone and confident voice. These features send a positive signal to the interviewer about the candidate. As a result, he is likely to be called for an interview; his ideas and perspectives would be listened to with interest and attention. Practical hints on the desirable conduct of the interviewee:

Punctuality: Reach the venue well in advance for the interview and wait patiently for one's turn.

Waiting for turn: Before your turn comes, you can initiate conversation with other interviewees to know their backgrounds.

Greeting: When a person is called inside, it is a good manner to knock the door and greet all the panel members depending on the time of the day. Sit, only when you are asked to sit. Sit in a national way

Cheerful disposition: Maintain a cheerful disposition and present the relevant information about your academic profile in an organized way.

Attention to questions: Pay attention to the questions asked and respond to them naturally but consciously.

Honest response and answer: Be honest in responding to questions. Admit politely, if you do not know the answer for any question asked.

Brief answers: Answers should be brief and to the point.

Validating views: Support various views with mature and proper arguments. Cite statistical evidence, if you have them and only use authentic source to validate your views and arguments.

Use of humour: Use humour in your answer, if possible.

Honesty in referring: Be honest while referring to events, situations and experiences.

Consciousness of body language: Be perceptive to the body language of the interviewer.

Conversational style: Speak in a conversational style and avoid pedantic verbosity.

Avoiding bad mannerisms: Ensure that your body language does not show any oddity like rapid blinking of the eye, eyebrow raising, playing with keys or pen, putting a finger in one's mouth, scratching the head, biting the nail, adjusting tie knots, etc.

Courtesy: Control ones negative emotions and impulses. Always be courteous.

Thank the interviewer: Thank the interviewer at the end, and exit in a confident manner.

KINDS OF INTERVIEW

There are different types of interviews that employers conduct. It depends on how and what the employer wishes to obtain about a person.

Employment Interview

The main purpose of employment interviews is to assess the suitability of a candidate for the job. The applicant may be an outsider or an insider seeking a new position in the same organization. The interviewer assesses the candidates' aptitude, attitude, communication skill, mental maturity, emotional intelligence, general knowledge, passion for a challenging job, etc. Similarly, the applicants also evaluate the position of an organization and its potential as a satisfying place to work. Though it is not a full-fledged tool to assess the entire personality of a candidate, it is still a vital tool to measure the majority of traits of the candidate.

Orientation Interview

The purpose of orientation interviews is to acquaint the new employee with the job and his role. He must be furnished information about the job, reporting relationship, returns to be submitted, if any, various employee benefits, performance evaluation, company policies, equipment to be handled in the work process, organization culture, dress code, probation, confirmation, precautions to be observed, etc. It is usually conducted by the superior at the helm of the department concerned. In short, newly selected candidates are introduced to the job, colleagues and superiors in various layers of the department concerned.

Counselling Interview

The employees encountering problems seek this type of interview voluntarily. In other words, an employee who faces problems in the work climate or in a family environment which adversely affect the quantity and quality of work, seek conselling from officers' designated for this purpose. The problem is discussed and factors leading to the problem are unearthed during the deliberation. The counselling officer puts the employee in the correct mental attitude and repack him with renewed confidence and courage. This type of interview is helpful in the growth and development of an employee who is emotionaly disturbed.

Performance Review Interview

This interview is conducted to ascertain the achievements and pitfalls in a performance. Even before the interview is conducted, evaluation report is submitted by superiors in various departments to their seniors designated for this purpose. The candidates are called for the review interview. This interview gives a clear picture about the quality of performance of the reviewer concerned. Appreciation of positive aspects builds up the morale of the candidate, while discussion of negative remarks enable not only the employee to rectify his weakness but also the employer to arrange a suitable remedial training to correct the negative performance. Thus, this interview plays a vital role in the performance development of an employee.

Grievance Interview

The employee who complains about the constraints he is facing in the work environment is given an opportunity to vent out his pent-up feeling. Normally, a grievant may feel shy of expressing his grievance because of the exalted status of his superiors. Therefore, a forum is created in many organizations to give an opportunity to the employees to open up their grievances. It is an opportunity for an organization to know the weak spots in its functioning. The approach of an organization should be clinical or healing rather than legalistic and authoritative.

Correctional Interview

This type of interview is conducted when the employees seriously break the personal code of conduct, deliberately violate organizational norms or fail to meet the requirements of the job. The employee's representative or mediator is allowed to be a party in the interview. The employee charged with an offence is given an opportunity to explain his stance. The members in the interview panel suggest remedies to correct the dysfunctional behaviour of the employee.

Exit Interview

Such an interview is viewed as a mirror reflecting the image of the employer in the minds of the employee. The exiting employees are well poised to disclose the hindrances, constraints and barriers obstructing the smooth performance and career growth of the employees. It helps the employer to eliminate such barriers and take positive initiatives to build up the employer's brand name.

Information Gathering Interviews

The progressive organizations, which intend to improve their performance on various dimensions, constantly take feedback from different stakeholders like suppliers, customers, consumers, employees, regulators, etc. Based on the information gathered, organizations take steps to improve upon the weakness perceived by the party concerned.

Table 36.1 The communication behaviour of successful interviewees

Behaviour	Unsuccessful Interviewees	Successful interviewees
Statements about the position	Had only vague ideas of what they wanted to do; changed 'ideal job' up to six times during an interview.	Specific and consistent about the position they wanted; were able to tell why they wanted the position.
Use of company name	Rarely used the company name.	Referred to the company by name four times as often as the unsuccessful interviewees.
Knowledge about the company and the position	Made it clear that they were using the interview to learn about the company and what it offered.	Made it clear that they had researched the company, referred to specific brochures, journals or people who had given them information.
Level of interest, enthusiasm	Responded neutrally to the interviewer's statements; 'OK', 'I see' indicated reservations about the company or location.	Expressed approval of information provided by the interviewer non-verbally and verbally; 'That's great' explicitly indicated desire to work for this particular company.
Non-verbal behaviour	Made little eye contact; smiled infrequently.	Made eye contact and smiled.
Picking up on the interviewer's cues	Gave vague or negative answers even when a positive answer was clearly desired ('How are your math skills?').	Answered positively and confidently and backed up the claim with a specific example of 'problem solving' or 'toughness'.
Response to topic shift by interviewer	Resisted topic shift.	Accepted topic shift.

Behaviour	Unsuccessful Interviewees	Successful interviewees
Use of specifics in answers	Gave short answers, 10 words or less, sometimes only one word; did not elaborate. Gave general responses: 'fairly well'.	Supported claims with specific personal experience, comparisons, statistics, statements of teachers and employers.
Questions asked by interviewer	Asked a fewer number of general questions.	Asked specific questions based on knowledge of the industry and the company. Personalized questions: 'What would my duties be?'.
Control of time and topics	Interviewee talked 37% of the interview time; initiated 36% of the comments.	Interviewee talked 55% of the total time, initiated subjects 56% of the time.

Source: Based on research reported by Lois Einhorn, 'An Inner View of the job Interview: An investigation of successful Communicative Behaviours', Communication Education (30 July, 1981), 217-218; and Robert W. Elder and Michael M. Harris, eds., The Employment Interview Handbook (Thousand Oaks, CA: Sage, 1999).

SUMMARY

Steps in interview process are preparation for the interview, determining the objective, methods of interview, number of interviewers, preparing the profile of interviewees, administrative details, conducting the interview, establishing rapport, soliciting information, recording the information, closing the interview and finalizing evaluation.

Qualities of an interviewer are bening a mature person, positive outlook, control over one's ego, kind towards the interviewee, enough knowledge of technical aspects, Knowledge about recent developments, good listening skill, knowledge of behavioural aspects of the interviewee.

Ineffective interviews are due to no rapport with the interviewee, interviewer's bias, poor communication skill of the interviewer, more questions, irrelevant questions, lack of interviewing skill of the interviewer.

Measures to make an interview effective are prior planning of the interview, conducive physical setting, allowing maximum time to the task, judging taste, preference, hobbies, closing the interview and consensus-based selection.

Kinds of interview includes employment interview, orientation interview, counselling interview, performance review interview, grievance interview, correctional interview, exit interview, information gathering interview.

Smart interviewee behaviour includes punctuality, waiting for turn, greeting, posture of sitting, cheerful disposition, attention to questions, honest response, brief answers, validating views, use of humour, honesty in referring, consciousness of body language, conversation style, avoiding bad mannerisms, courtesy, controlling negative emotions, not criticizing previous employer and thanking the interviewer.

REVIEW QUESTIONS

Part A: Short Questions

1. What is an interview?
2. What is a panel interview?
3. What is a stress interview?
4. What is a one-to-one interview?
5. What is a group interview?
6. What is an in-depth interview?
7. What is a patterned interview?
8. What is a direct interview?
9. What is an orientation interview?
10. What is a counselling interview?
11. What is a performance review interview?
12. What is a grievance interview?
13. What is a correctional interview?
14. What is an exit interview?
15. What is an information gathering interview?

Part B: Paragraph Questions

1. Specify the qualities of an interview.
2. What factors make the interview ineffective?
3. What are the various types of interviews?
4. What points should be looked into at the time of an interview?
5. Suggest measures to make an interview effective.
6. What are the steps an interviewer has to take in pre-interview stage?

Part C: Essay Questions

1. List out the various stages involved in an interview.
2. Analyze the merits and demerits of interview as a selection tool.
3. Explain the different types of interviews?
4. Write how an interviewee has to conduct himself at the interview?

Part D: Objective Type Questions

Choose the correct answer

1. Face-to-face question-answer type of interview is

a. Patterned interview b. Direct interview c. In-depth interview

(Ans: b)

2. Placing the candidate under mental pressure comes under

a. Group interview b. Panel interview c. Stress interview

(Ans: c)

3. A committee of experts interviewing the candidate comes under

a. Group interview b. Panel interview c. Stress interview

(Ans: b)

4. A candidate answering pre-prepared questions is classified under

a. Patterned interview b. Panel interview c. Group interview

(Ans: a)

5. An interviewee free to speak on any subject comes under

a. Panel interview b. Non-directive interview c. Direct interview

(Ans: b)

Fill in the blanks

1. A number of candidates are simultaneously interviewed in _______interview. (Group)
2. A candidate is thoroughly probed in _______ interview. (In-depth)
3. Direct face-to-face observation method to evaluate a candidate is __________. (Interview)
4. Standardized questions are asked in _________interview. (Patterned)
5. The Candidate is put under deliberate stress in _________ interview. (Stress)

Status enquiries — Letters written to business houses to ascertain the advisability of granting credit to specified parties when fresh applicants for credit approach them are called letters of status enquiries.

Tender — Offer for the supply of specified goods or the performance of a specified work at prices and under conditions set out in the tender notice.

Testimonal — Kind of certificate given to one as to one's efficiency, experience, capacity for hard work, general conduct.

Trade reference — Names and addresses of individual firms which can be contacted to get information about the credit standing of the applicant.

Upward communication — Communication transmitted upwards from lower level employees to superiors and top echelons of the management.

Verbal communication — Communication made through words.

Video conference — It is a technology-enabled facility, whereby people and individuals in different locations hold interactive meetings.

INDEX